NORTHEASTERN ILLINOIS UNIVERSITY

3 1224 00397 6692

HyperCard:
The Complete Reference

WITHDRAWN
NORTHEASTERN ILLINOIS
UNIVERSITY LIBRARY

HyperCard®:
The Complete Reference

Stephen L. Michel

Osborne **McGraw-Hill**
Berkeley, California

Ronald Williams Library
Northeastern Illinois University

QA
76.8
M3
M53
1989

Osborne **McGraw-Hill**
2600 Tenth Street
Berkeley, California 94710
U.S.A.

For information on translations and book distributors outside of the
U.S.A., write to Osborne **McGraw-Hill** at the above address.

A complete list of trademarks appears on page 711.

HyperCard®: The Complete Reference

Copyright © 1989 by Stephen L. Michel. All rights reserved.
Printed in the United States of America. Except as permitted
under the Copyright Act of 1976, no part of this publication may be
reproduced or distributed in any form or by any means, or stored in
a database or retrieval system, without the prior written permission of the publisher, with the exception that the program listings
may be entered, stored, and executed in a computer system, but
they may not be reproduced for publication.

1234567890 DODO 898   *Bl QM 3/15/89*

ISBN 0-07-881430-8

Information has been obtained by Osborne **McGraw-Hill** from sources believed to be reliable. However, because of the possibility of human or mechanical error by our sources,
Osborne **McGraw-Hill**, or others, Osborne **McGraw-Hill** does not guarantee the accuracy,
adequacy, or completeness of any information and is not responsible for any errors or omis-
sions or the results obtained from use of such information.

Ronald Williams Library
Northeastern Illinois University

To Margaret, Lyal, and Richard Michel

CONTENTS

At Osborne/McGraw-Hill, I want to thank Jeff Pepper, Madhu Prasher, and Dusty Bernard for their help in keeping this book on track. My technical editors, Michael Fischer and John and Patricia Hedtke, had to work hard to make sure that scripts worked and that text made sense. Picky, picky, picky. While the technical editors had a great deal to do with the accuracy of the book, any inaccuracies that might have survived are my own.

The participants in CompuServe's APPHYPER forum were an invaluable resource for good ideas during the writing of this book, as were the many disks kindly lent me by the Berkeley Macintosh Users' Group. The entire community of HyperCard users, which has produced an excellent, varied body of stackware, has been a constant source of inspiration.

Additionally, I want to thank the usual suspects, in no particular order: Eric Alderman, Dale Coleman, Bob Kermish, Tay Vaughan, Roger Strukhoff, Arthur Naiman, Brian Molyneaux, Dan Ruby, and Clair Whitmer. If I've left anyone out, my apologies.

Of course, I must offer deep gratitude to the members of the HyperCard team. Bill Atkinson and Dan Winkler have created a singular program, and it is easy to see how it could have gone astray during its long development. The HyperCard we have today is not a perfect program, but it is on its way to being one. It is the forerunner of a new type of software that has the potential to drastically affect everyday life in the next decade and beyond.

But the biggest acknowledgment of all goes to my family, who suffered through a summer of my writing and working with HyperCard, and thus being largely unavailable for large blocks of time. Their patience and help have made it possible for me to write this book, and their presence has given me reason to do so.

ACKNOWLEDGMENTS

xv

The word "complete" in the title of this book has weighed heavily on my shoulders these last few months: HyperCard can handle such a multitude of tasks that attempting to document them all is an exercise in futility. Nevertheless, the boundaries inherent in covering all the commands, functions, and other elements of the program do provide a good guideline. Instead of attempting to follow an alphabetical or encyclopedic approach to HyperCard, I have grouped the elements of the program and the language into categories that that are governed by functionality. As a reader, not just a writer, of computer books, this approach has served me best in the past.

Since the scope of the book is so large, it should be useful to HyperCard users and programmers at just about any level. Those new to HyperCard will benefit from approaching the book in a linear manner. The first eight chapters discuss such things as installing HyperCard on your hard disk, working with the stacks supplied with the program, using HyperCard with other programs, printing stacks, and painting with HyperCard's graphics tools.

If you are familiar with HyperCard in general and have used the stacks that came with it or have acquired stacks from other sources, you might be ready to design your own stacks. Chapters Nine through Eleven introduce you to designing HyperCard applications and present the Hyper-Talk programming language.

The remainder of the book presents HyperTalk. If you have already used this excellent programming language, you will find in these chapters numerous scripts that perform a wide variety of functions. These scripts are written in as generic a manner as possible, so that you can adapt them easily for use in your own stacks.

This book was written using a wide variety of software, most especially HyperCard itself and Microsoft Word 3.02, on a Macintosh SE with a SuperMac Dataframe XP40. Apple's MultiFinder, which allowed both HyperCard and Word to be in RAM at the same time, made it easy to switch quickly between the two programs and greatly eased the amount of work to be done. Other programs used include

INTRODUCTION

MacPaint, FullPaint, TOPS (for transferring files to DOS format), Dave McWherter's McSink desk accessory (which also helped in transferring files), Keith Esau's Camera Desk Accessory (for screen shots of dialog boxes and menus), and SuperMac's DiskFit (an excellent disk backup utility).

Disk Offer

If you want to avoid typing in the scripts in this book, you can order a disk that contains them. All the scripts in the book are easily accessible in the form of a HyperCard stack, organized according to the chapters in which they appear. Also on the disk is my HyperCard stack, Port Authority, which automates the process of importing text into Hyper-Card from files in a tab-delimited format and exporting text from HyperCard to that and other formats.

To order the disk, send the order form that follows, with a check (drawn on a U.S. bank) or a U.S. postal money order for $20 (plus 6.5% sales tax for California residents), along with your name and address, to:

Stephen Michel
1563 Solano Avenue, Suite 224
Berkeley, CA 94707

Order Form

Please send _____ copies, at $20 each, of the scripts from *HyperCard: The Complete Reference*. California residents add 6.5% sales tax. (When placing foreign orders, please add $5.00 for shipping and handling.)

Name: _____

Address: _____

City: _____
               State   ZIP

Send to:

Stephen Michel
1563 Solano Avenue, Suite 224
Berkeley, CA 94707

This is solely the offering of the author. Osborne/McGraw-Hill takes no responsibility for the fulfillment of this offer.

Approaching HyperCard

What Is HyperCard?
Ways to Look at HyperCard
HyperCard and You
The Future

Few developments in the personal computer world have caused as much of a stir as the introduction of HyperCard in August 1987. The question that seemed to be on many people's minds was "What is it?" HyperCard had features that were similar to those of a database, it had a rich set of painting tools, and it featured an easy-to-use programming language called HyperTalk that allowed you, without much programming background, to create your own applications. What was this thing?

Apple called it system software and included it free with every Macintosh sold. Apple's promotional material accented HyperCard's ability to form links between documents—links that could connect virtually any HyperCard file or stack to any other.

HyperCard's creator, Bill Atkinson, called HyperCard a software erector set and seemed to stress its flexibility, which allows you to develop a set of tools for creating your own applications or tailoring existing applications to your own needs.

Some other software manufacturers called HyperCard unfair competition and withdrew, or threatened to withdraw, their products from the Macintosh market. A group of entrepreneurs, who called HyperCard an opportunity, started publishing "stackware" (HyperCard applications), as it became known, and have done well indeed.

Macintosh users—a lot of them—called HyperCard the most exciting thing they'd ever seen and started to work with it. Taking the erector-set approach, they produced a wide range of programs for doing such disparate things as simulating the Battle of Britain and estimating the weight of objects that people could lift without damaging their backs. Definitions aren't important, they seemed to say, and started to do things with this new beast.

HyperCard, then, can be seen as a kind of computer Rorschach test—people look at it and see different things depending on what they are looking for. That seems to be a natural part of HyperCard and one of its strengths—you can make of it what you will.

What Is HyperCard?

What is it about HyperCard that made it cause such a stir? HyperCard is a program of many elements, and many of those elements exist in other programs. However, it is the manner in which the elements are integrated and integral to one another that makes HyperCard unique. The elements together make a program that is greater than the sum of its parts.

The basic unit in HyperCard is the card, and cards are organized into stacks, which is what HyperCard documents are called. To understand how HyperCard works, think of the stack as similar to a drawer full of library cards. Each card contains the details of one book—its author, title, subject, cataloging information, and so on. With HyperCard, you can move in sequence from one card to another, just as you can with a physical collection of cards.

HyperCard, however, extends the power of physical cards. You can form links with HyperCard that take you directly to cards in different parts of the stack, or even to cards in different stacks. You can use HyperCard's sophisticated Find command to search for cards that contain particular words. Cards can also be sorted quickly to put them in different orders.

HyperCard may look as if it is a database or filing program; to an extent it is. HyperCard stores its text in fields on cards, as do filing programs. Each card is a separate record in the file. Stacks are analogous to database files.

HyperCard cards, unlike physical cards, can contain *buttons*, which are active parts of a card that cause things to happen when you click the mouse on them. Buttons can perform a number of functions. They can take you to different cards or stacks, they can sort a stack, and they can perform complex activities.

HyperCard also features another way to organize cards within a stack. How a particular card looks is governed, in part, by a kind of template design, called the *background*, that affects many cards. Each stack of cards contains at least one background that defines how the cards appear and what fields will be contained on them. Unlike the physical card catalog, though, in which all cards are essentially the same, a HyperCard stack can contain many different backgrounds, or card designs. This allows you to create different types of cards that coexist in the same stack, perhaps containing very different kinds of information.

Another feature of HyperCard is its rich set of painting tools. That HyperCard has sophisticated painting tools is no surprise. Its creator, Bill Atkinson, also created the pioneering Macintosh program, MacPaint, which has been copied by many other programs on the Macintosh and other computers. Atkinson also wrote much of the QuickDraw programming that is responsible for everything shown on the Macintosh screen.

In HyperCard, graphics can be part of the background or part of the card. Background graphics appear on all cards that share that background; card graphics appear only on a particular card. One of the many purposes of graphics in HyperCard is to create cards that look just like real cards. The Address stack included with HyperCard, for example, uses a background graphic that makes the card appear to be a standard Rolodex card.

Graphics can also be stored with HyperCard. The Clip Art stack included with HyperCard uses card graphics to contain pictures of different types. A field on the card allows you to search for specific pictures, or specific types of pictures, with the Find command.

Perhaps the key element of HyperCard is its powerful programming language, HyperTalk, which allows you to control virtually all aspects of HyperCard activities. It is probably the easiest programming language to learn and use that has been devised to date. HyperTalk's ease of use derives from its flexible, English-like syntax, from its object-oriented nature, and from its integrated association with HyperCard.

Unlike other programming languages, HyperCard and HyperTalk take care of much of the "dirty work" of writing programs for you. Such things as screen design, activation of buttons, and control of events are handled for you. It makes few demands about such things as declaring variables and defining data structures, freeing you to do what you want to do: make things work. And since HyperTalk can control all elements of HyperCard, you can control the painting tools with HyperTalk programs for purposes ranging from animation to graphing.

Ease of learning and use were made part of HyperTalk's design to open up Macintosh programming to a new level of users. Before HyperCard, those who wanted to program had few options other than learning a sophisticated language such as C or Pascal. To learn to program the Macintosh itself required in-depth knowledge of a set of books known as *Inside Macintosh* (Reading, Mass.: Addison-Wesley, 1985, 1986, 1988)—well over 1000 pages documenting the internal programming that performs such functions as creating menus and dialog boxes, drawing pictures, and displaying text on the screen. It is a daunting set of books, requiring much study to master. With HyperTalk, much of the Macintosh user interface is handled for you, obviating the need for a complete understanding of *Inside Macintosh*. It frees you from having to learn the internals of the machine in order to present a simple program.

To make it even easier to learn and use, HyperCard implements a set of *user levels*. These levels allow new users to work with the program in a more limited manner than experienced users. You can start using the program at the Browsing level, which lets you look at stacks created by others, and graduate at your own pace to levels that allow you to add text, graphics, and buttons to HyperCard. Some will never graduate to the highest level, Scripting, and will be content to browse through stacks created by others; that is part of what HyperCard lets you do. Others will graduate quickly to the Scripting level and begin creating their own stacks almost immediately; that, too, is part of what Hyper-Card lets you do. The choice is yours.

Finally, HyperCard was designed to be an *information publisher*—a program you can use to organize information, including text, graphics, and sound, and make it available to other Macintosh owners. And since users are able to modify stacks, HyperCard allows readers of information to change that information. You can delete material that is not relevant to your needs, you can add material, or you can just change things for the sake of changing things—whatever you need to do to make a stack work the way you want it to work.

Ways to Look at HyperCard

The previous section examined some of the key elements of HyperCard. This section will examine different ways to look at the program. HyperCard can be used in a number of ways, and as time goes on you will probably find yourself using the program in all of the ways discussed in the following pages.

As a Personal Toolkit

If you have used a personal computer for a long time, you have probably experienced situations in which you wanted to accomplish something, but the program or programs you had just couldn't quite do the job. For example, you might be curious about the actual, measurable effects of time dilation as a person in a spaceship approaches the speed of light. Or you might want to put together some information and be able to add to it for future reference, as you do when taking notes for a research project. But the applications you have are *hardwired*—you cannot go into the programs and change the way they operate by adding functions or making changes to the way existing functions work.

Solving these problems is part of the reason HyperCard was developed. You can, with some practice, write the calculations for figuring out time dilation. If you use applications designed by others, you can change the way the buttons in those stacks work, or even add new buttons. You can build your own applications from scratch—perhaps creating something you can sell to others or even creating a program that is of no use to anybody but yourself.

HyperCard is, therefore, a toolkit, which includes parts and tools that you can use to assemble materials in different ways. Figure 1-1 shows a card from the Button Ideas stack that is included with HyperCard. Each of the buttons on this card can be used in your stack.

As a Database Program

Many features of HyperCard are similar to those of database programs. HyperCard uses fields to contain data. The cards in HyperCard are equivalent to the records in databases. You can sort the cards, find data on them, and perform arithmetic operations on values contained in the fields on those cards.

For many users of low-end databases or filing programs, HyperCard can work just as well. Indeed, one of the prime applications of those low-end programs—the name and address file—is found in HyperCard's Address stack. Hyper-Card stacks created to manage such information sets as checkbooks, project scheduling, library management, and

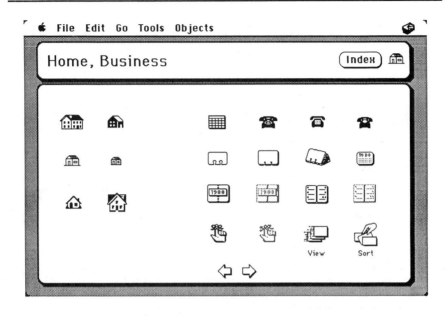

Figure 1-1.   A card from the Button Ideas stack that is included
with HyperCard

more have appeared on the bulletin boards and in the libraries of user groups.

Given HyperCard's ease of use and versatility in the
Macintosh system and its unique ability to link different
items to one another, it is hard to see the value of using other
filing programs when HyperCard can be used.

Figure 1-2 shows a database used to catalog books,
including date read, author, title, subject, and some comments.

HyperCard falls down somewhat, however, when compared with the more powerful database programs. Although
it does work with large files, it does not function as efficiently as the full-fledged databases. You cannot easily build
indexes that allow complicated queries to be made of the

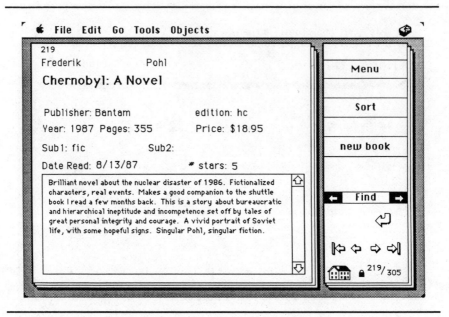

Figure 1-2.   A "books read" database in HyperCard

data. Data can be linked together, but it is relatively slow at relational look-ups of information from other files. Also, although HyperTalk's printing resources are unique and powerful, they do not constitute as sophisticated a report-writing capability as that found in the more powerful dedicated packages.

As an Information-Publishing Medium

Before HyperCard, a person wanting to publish information or data and make it available to others in machine form faced a quandary: how can it be done?

If the data was a textual report or manuscript, a word processor was used. The text was entered into Microsoft

Word, for example, and that file saved to disk for another user. However, if that other user had a different word processor, the text had to be saved in a text-only mode, and all its formatting and graphics were lost.

If the data was structured—as in a database or filing program or a spreadsheet—then the information browser still needed to have the same program. Files could be saved in interchange formats with these programs, but they might lose some of their functionality in the process. And since these programs can only rarely make use of graphics (and almost never sound), there were limits as to what could be shared.

The same is true of several other applications. Programs such as Glue allow users to share images from different programs with one another. However, when this program is used, what is shared is not the data itself, but an image of the data. You cannot change the data or annotate it.

HyperCard has definitely changed all this. Because HyperCard is included free with every Macintosh (and at a reasonable price for those who bought their Macs before HyperCard), its use is widespread. This makes HyperCard a new medium. To publish with HyperCard, you don't need a run-time license from the manufacturer, and you don't need to hire a programmer. Instead, you just place your data into HyperCard and design the buttons that allow you to navigate through it.

HyperCard can also work with several different types of data. It can handle structured data, as in a spreadsheet or database. It can include free-form information, of the type that might be entered in a word processor, as well as graphics and sound. And all these different types of data can be put together in a way that allows them to trigger one another and be linked together.

The heart of HyperCard is its interactivity. When you publish data with HyperCard, you give it to someone who is able to add new cards to your stack or create new buttons that link to other cards. In short, the data can be changed to suit someone else's purposes.

Note: HyperCard does allow you to lock your stacks, preventing anyone else from modifying them. (Locking your stacks is discussed in Chapters 9 and 34.)

Figure 1-3 shows a card from the Grolier U.S. History Demonstration stack, included on Apple's Learning Disk CD-ROM sampler. This stack includes animation, text, sound, and some new concepts to provide an interactive tool for education.

As a HyperText Program

HyperText and HyperMedia are concepts invented by Theodor Holm Nelson in the 1960s to indicate a new type of reading or information exploration that could take unique advantage of the capabilities of the computer. Realizing that the body of human knowledge is in principle, if not in practice, a linkage of individual knowledge, Nelson hypothesized an information network based on computer access to this linkage. If you were reading about a particular topic in one document, you could have instant access to all other documents that related to that topic. For example, if you were reading this book in a HyperText environment, you could point to the word "HyperText" and see a definition of it. You could also look up Nelson's original work on the HyperText concept, as well as additional work done by others. If you were reading a HyperText version of Joyce's *Ulysses*, all the footnotes created by all the scholars who have explored this work in the last 60 years would be immediately accessible. While some progress is being made towards fulfillment of a Nelson's dream, it seems obvious that the linkage of all (or even fraction) of human knowledge will occur only well into the future.

HyperCard has many HyperText-like features. One card can be "linked" to another, even if that card is in a different file or stack. With help from the programming language, you can even create scripts that allow browsers to go from one word to a linked card with a click of the mouse button. And buttons don't have to be text—they can include or be composed of graphics. Clicking on the hat in the Clip Art stack takes you to another card that has a hat on it.

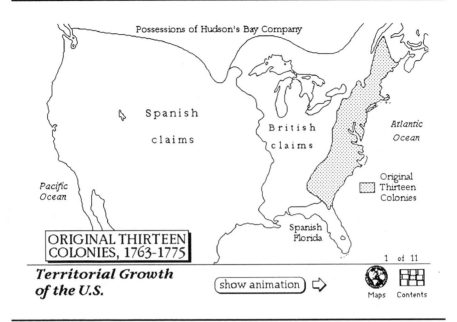

Possessions of Hudson's Bay Company

Spanish

claims

British

claims

Atlantic
Ocean

Pacific
Ocean

Original
Thirteen
Colonies

ORIGINAL THIRTEEN
COLONIES, 1763-1775

Spanish
Florida

1   of 11

*Territorial Growth
of the U.S.*

show animation

Maps   Contents

Figure 1-3.   The growth of the United States is illustrated in an
animated sequence from the Grolier U.S. History
Demonstration stack

On the other hand, HyperCard has limitations as a
HyperText program. Words embedded in text cannot be
made the triggers for HyperText operations without some
difficult programming. Only one card and document can be
on the screen at one time. Text fields are limited to 30,000
characters, so long documents need to be subdivided into
chunks this size or smaller.

As a Programming Language

Built into HyperCard is a friendly, flexible programming language, HyperTalk. HyperTalk allows you to build your own
programs and create your own scripts that cause significant
things to happen. Because HyperTalk borrows many con-

cepts from SmallTalk and other object-oriented programming languages, it is very readable, flexible, and expandable. Since it runs in the HyperCard environment, HyperTalk does many chores for you: you don't need to painstakingly create every menu and dialog box on the screen. Moving buttons and instructing them to respond to user clicks is very easy, and the data structures you need are partly built for you in the form of fields, cards, and stacks. HyperTalk is easy for beginners to learn.

On the other hand, HyperTalk is a verbose language, requiring more lines of code for certain operations than other languages. HyperTalk is an interpreted language, meaning that each line has to be interpreted anew every time the script is run, which slows down processing. HyperTalk does not give you access to the inner workings of the computer; you must use another language.

The balance of the arguments for and against Hyper-Talk tips toward the side of HyperTalk. While it is certainly not a perfect language, it is useful for creating a wide variety of tools for a wide variety of functions. While you might not create a spreadsheet with it, you can easily imagine using it to perform many functions that spreadsheets also perform.

As a Replacement for the Finder

The most ubiquitous of the first stacks that were available were the Finder or Home replacement. HyperCard can be used to perform many of the standard functions that are done with the Finder: locate documents on disk, report on their size, record information about who created them and when, and open or print them with the programs that created them.

As a Finder replacement, however, HyperCard is weak. While icons can be created with HyperCard, you cannot close folders and put them away. There are few automatic tools for entering icons into cards. You cannot copy files from disk to disk or drag them into the trash with HyperCard.

Given these limitations, however, HyperCard can act as a front end to the computer. Its programmability allows expert users to set up menus in the computer for novice users. As HyperCard grows, it will be able to handle communications with other computers—including distant mainframes—and it will be able to handle complex communications through networks.

As a Painting Program

A major component of HyperCard is its graphics tools. These tools include some features that make duplicating images much easier. It can work with a large number of pictures in the same file. It has a set of painting tools that compares well with any painting program on the market. For many users, it will be one of their prime tools for managing and creating paintings.

On the other hand, HyperCard has some graphics limitations. It doesn't work with color or gray-shaded images. It cannot create or manage object-oriented graphics of the type that MacDraw creates, or PostScript files created with Adobe Illustrator or Aldus' FreeHand. You cannot make pictures that are larger than a HyperCard card—the size of the original Macintosh screen.

Graphics are a big part of HyperCard. They define the look and feel of HyperCard stacks. They can include scanned images, and they can be created under control of a script, producing precision angles, automated shapes, or animation. And by storing images on cards, HyperCard can serve as a database or storage area for frequently used graphics.

As a Help and Demonstration
System for Software

Several software publishers have created their help features in HyperCard. Virtually all Macintosh users have Hyper-

Card, and since HyperCard programming is relatively easy, it might not be a bad way to go.

On the other hand, HyperCard Help runs in a different application than the original. And since HyperCard is a fairly memory-hungry program, users might have to upgrade their machines to allow HyperCard and the application to run together. Otherwise, the user must quit the application to start HyperCard, just for a little help. Because HyperCard is a separate application, it also cannot include context-sensitive help.

Note: The HyperCard system is constantly changing, and new tools such as HyperDA from Symmetry Software are allowing software authors to incorporate HyperCard help into their applications.

On the other hand, using HyperCard as a demonstration system makes some sense. HyperCard stacks can be created easily and can be made to mimic the user interface of some other programs. Demonstration systems can thus be created inexpensively and given away.

The preceding catalog of potential HyperCard applications does not come near to exhausting the possibilities. It is only meant to suggest a few uses of the program to you. Chances are there will eventually be almost as many uses for HyperCard as there are users of HyperCard. That's one of the beauties of the program: it allows you to make of it what you will.

HyperCard and You

How will you use HyperCard? That depends, in part, on how you use your computer. You might be a *browser*—using others' stacks but not creating your own. HyperCard stacks full of information including text, images, and sounds, will be available for your use.

However, if you are the type of person who creates complex macros with a program like Excel or applications with databases like Double Helix, Omnis, or 4th Dimension, you might take a different approach to HyperCard. Because its programming language, HyperTalk, is flexible and easy to learn, you will probably find yourself creating applications for yourself and possibly for others.

How to Learn HyperCard

With a program as complex and powerful as HyperCard, it is simply not possible to give you a short recipe for learning it. Learning a new program depends on the functions the program performs. HyperCard presents new opportunities for learning. It comes with several stacks that you can work with while learning. You can also learn a lot by working with stacks created by others; you don't have to design your own stack.

To start with, the stacks delivered with HyperCard present a lot of places to explore. Set your user level to Browsing (user levels are discussed in Chapter 4) and take a look at the Clip Art stack or other stacks included with HyperCard. If you want to start using the Datebook and Address stacks, set your user level to Typing and start experimenting. Later, you might want to use the Painting level to copy pictures from the Clip Art stack or to add your own pictures to that stack.

Learning to create new stacks is a little more complicated. When your user level is set to Authoring, you can create new buttons to link cards or stacks together. Setting the user level to Scripting allows you to experiment with HyperTalk.

Many of the scripts in this book are devoted to helping you learn HyperTalk. You can use these scripts in their present form, or when you become more experienced, you can modify them to suit your purposes. Studying scripts is a good way to learn what they can be made to do, but creating your own scripts is the best way.

To get started, create a new stack called something like Test, and use it as a testing ground for your experiments. In this stack, you can make new backgrounds, cards, buttons, fields, and pictures to your heart's content, without having to worry about damaging your Home stack. You can also make copies of any of the stacks included with HyperCard as a starting point for exploration.

Examining stacks created by others is a very good way to experiment. Stacks are becoming ubiquitous in the Macintosh world. CompuServe is a good source of stacks, as are other electronic services. If you belong to a user group, the chances are they have a large library of stacks written by others. If you don't belong to a user group, join one. The Berkeley Macintosh User's Group in Berkeley, California (415-549-2684), is a good one; they publish a fat newsletter twice a year and have a HyperCard library of over 50 disks. They encourage mail-order members, and the $40 yearly membership is a bargain for the newsletters alone.

The Future

Whither HyperCard? While it is not possible to make absolute predictions, there are some directions in which Apple could take HyperCard. It is clear that Apple sees HyperCard as a key to increasing the sophistication of their product line and plans to continue improving the program.

In the short term, it is likely that some of the limitations of HyperCard will be corrected. New developments could offer the ability to work with larger screens and to format characters in fields, the use of animation tools, and more.

It is harder to see what will come in the long term. Perhaps portions of HyperCard will be merged into the Macintosh operating system, permitting such things as links between documents created by different programs. True multitasking on the Macintosh—beyond the limited abilities of MultiFinder—could allow HyperCard and other programs to work together in new ways.

Whatever specific features Apple adds to HyperCard, one thing is clear: the program will be around for some time and we can expect its continued development.

Installing HyperCard

The HyperCard Distribution Disks
Installing HyperCard on a Hard-Disk System
Installing HyperCard on a Floppy-Disk System

The first thing you need to do with any new program is set it up so you can use it. As it is with most Macintosh applications, this is a fairly straightforward process with Hyper-Card. In relation to this process, you will see references to the Home stack. For further information on the Home stack, see Chapters 1 and 4.

One of the advantages of the Macintosh Finder and HyperCard is their fluidity. If you decide to install Hyper-Card in one way (for example, in a particular folder on your hard disk) and need to change it later, it is as simple as dragging your HyperCard icon to that different folder. There is no "hard-wired" information in HyperCard that prevents you from changing the way you have your hard disk set up. The best thing to do is to experiment until you find a manner of working that feels right to you.

The HyperCard Distribution Disks

HyperCard—including its help files, idea stacks, and sample stacks—is shipped by Apple on four disks. These disks are made for slightly different purposes, and you do not need to install and use them all. Here are the contents of the distribution disks:

Disk	Contents
HyperCard and Stacks	HyperCard
	HyperCard Stacks folder
	More Stacks folder
HyperCard Help	Help Stacks folder
HyperCard Ideas	Idea Stacks folder
HyperCard Startup	HyperCard
	System
	General
	ImageWriter
	HyperCard Stacks folder

Some versions of HyperCard may include additional files, such as a ReadMe stack, which describes later versions. The last disk listed in the table is for use on floppy-based systems.

Note: You should *never* copy System and Finder files from a floppy disk into any folder on your hard disk except the System folder (and even this should be done only when you are sure of what you are doing). The Macintosh can become very confused if there are multiple copies of these files on your hard disk, and they waste space. (This rule applies to all software, not just to HyperCard.)

Installing HyperCard on a Hard-Disk System

HyperCard works so well with a hard disk that it seems as if it were designed especially for that environment. Many of its features—its ability to backtrack through multiple cards and stacks that you have looked at before, its fast "find" capability, and its seemingly unquenchable thirst for disk storage—make running it with a hard disk almost essential.

HyperCard is not very picky about where on a hard disk—in what folders—you put it. Virtually the only requirement is that the Home stack be located where Hyper-Card can find it. Otherwise, you can install HyperCard in any manner that is consistent with the way that you manage your hard disk.

It is usually a good idea to create a new folder for Hyper-Card. Choose the New Folder command from the Finder's File menu. Make sure that the new Empty Folder icon is selected and type **HyperCard**, or whatever name you want to give the folder. You can then copy HyperCard and the other stacks into this folder by dragging the icons from the floppy disk into that folder. (If you are unsure about the techniques for copying files, consult your Macintosh user's manual.)

Probably the best procedure is to put the Home stack into the same folder as HyperCard itself. When you double-click on the HyperCard icon (or a stack icon), if the Home stack is in a different folder, you will be presented with the dialog box shown in Figure 2-1. If you get this dialog box, use standard Macintosh folder navigation techniques to show HyperCard where Home is located. (Again, if you are unsure of these techniques, consult your Macintosh user's manual.)

You should copy all the sample stacks that were on the HyperCard distribution disk to your hard disk. They contain a lot of stacks that can be useful when you are exploring HyperCard, and if you later run short of disk space or find that you are not using certain stacks, you can delete them. These folders include HyperCard Stacks, More Stacks, Idea Stacks, and, of course, Help Stacks. Simply drag these folders into the HyperCard folder on your hard disk. If you want to move them to different locations on the disk, you can do that later.

Another way to install HyperCard is to put HyperCard and its related stacks into the HyperCard folder and put the Home stack at the top level—in the window that is shown when you double-click on your hard-disk icon. This allows

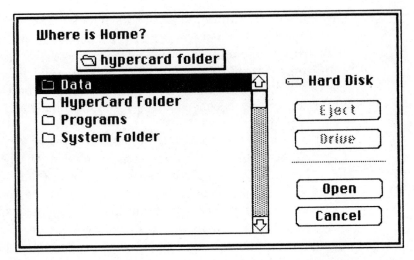

Figure 2-1.   If you start HyperCard, and the Home stack is not in the same folder as HyperCard, you get this dialog box

you to start HyperCard simply by double-clicking on that icon. You will not have to open one or more folders to get to it, thus leaving open a simpler desktop on the screen. One of the disadvantages of this method is that when you are at the Home stack, the Open Stack dialog box will show the top level of your hard disk, but will not necessarily show the folders in which your HyperCard stacks are located.

The most common way to install HyperCard is to put both HyperCard and the Home stack in a folder called HyperCard. The remainder of the HyperCard stacks are put in other folders that are located either in that folder or in other folders at the top level of the disk. As you will see in Chapter 4, HyperCard's Home stack can keep track of the names of folders in which you have installed stacks, making it easy to manage them.

It is also possible to put the Home stack into the System folder of the hard disk. Since the Macintosh automatically searches this folder for all files, HyperCard will not have any trouble finding it there. On the other hand, System folders can become quite large, with hundreds of files in them. If yours is large, you will notice a considerable delay when opening it from the Finder.

Installing HyperCard on a Floppy-Disk System

As mentioned earlier in this chapter, HyperCard is designed to work on a hard-disk system. A program as powerful as HyperCard is of necessity large (both in the room it takes on disk and in its RAM requirements). However, if you do not have a hard disk, or if, for example, you are preparing Hyper-Card for demonstration purposes, you might need to install it for floppies.

Essentially all you need to do to install HyperCard for use on a floppy system is make a copy of the HyperCard Startup disk. Remember this disk is set up with the bare essentials to run HyperCard.

Note that there is no copy of the Macintosh Finder on this HyperCard Startup disk. Because of the space require-ments of the System file, a printer driver, HyperCard itself, and the Home stack, there is not enough room for the Finder. HyperCard is installed as the startup application; when the system is started from this disk, the first thing you see is HyperCard, not the Macintosh Finder. The version of the System file that is on this disk is a special version that runs HyperCard as the startup application, not the Finder. When you quit HyperCard, the disk will eject itself, as if you had chosen Shut Down from the Finder's Special menu.

The HyperCard Startup disk contains some stacks that you may not need when running HyperCard. With the excep-tion of the Home stack, the stacks located in the HyperCard Stacks folder are not essential.

After making a copy of the HyperCard Startup disk, the

next step in making a HyperCard floppy disk is ensuring that the disk will work with your printer. If you are using a standard ImageWriter, you can go right to work; this disk contains the ImageWriter file that allows the Macintosh to talk with that printer. If you are using a LaserWriter or ImageWriter LQ, you should drag the ImageWriter file into the trash and copy (from one of the disks that came with your Macintosh or printer) the correct printer driver. Remember, if you are using a LaserWriter, you need to copy both the Laser Prep and LaserWriter files. If you will not be printing, you can recover some disk space by deleting the ImageWriter file.

The General file on the HyperCard Startup disk is for use by the Control Panel desk accessory. If this file is not present, you will not be able to use this desk accessory. The General file uses only 14K of disk space, and the convenience of using the Control Panel makes it worth this amount of space.

If you are going to be using the Address stack, or any other stack that dials the phone, you should keep the Phone stack on the disk. There are many other stacks that use the Phone stack to do their dialing for them. It takes up only 12K on the disk.

The files that are essential to have on a floppy disk for HyperCard are

- The System file
- HyperCard
- The Home stack
- A printer driver (if you need one)
- The General file

If you are using a one-drive Macintosh Plus, this system will not be very usable, and you should buy a hard disk or at least a second floppy drive. If you have a two-drive system (either a Mac SE or Mac II with two floppies, or a Mac Plus with both internal and external drives), you can keep HyperCard on the disk in one drive and use the other for storage of the stacks you are using.

Another point that should be mentioned about using HyperCard on a floppy system is the use of fonts. Macintosh fonts, like everything else, take up disk space. The System file on the HyperCard Startup disk contains a minimal set of fonts and desk accessories (DAs). If you need other fonts or DAs, you can install them with the Font/DA Mover program, but you will pay a price in the amount of room they take up on a disk.

Meeting HyperCard

Now that you have installed HyperCard on your system
(either on a hard disk or on floppies) you can examine the
program itself. In this chapter, you will take a look at some of
the documents—called *stacks* in HyperCard—that come
with the program. You will use these stacks to learn some of
the key concepts that are used in HyperCard.

THREE

It is assumed that you are familiar with the Macintosh. You should know how to do such things as point and click with the mouse, use menus, select text, and locate files on your hard disk using standard Macintosh techniques. Because these kinds of operations are standardized on the Macintosh, this book will not belabor them. Any differences between HyperCard and other Macintosh applications will be discussed.

Metaphors

The best of software often employs metaphors to make its functions clearer. These metaphors are often real-world activities that are familiar to users, enhanced with the assistance of a computer. The Macintosh Finder uses the metaphor of a standard office desktop. HyperCard uses a metaphor of a stack of cards. HyperCard is unique, however, in that it can also be used to create software that has its own metaphors.

Consistency of Design

Good software not only uses a clear metaphor, but also features consistent design. A program that works the same way in all its functions is inherently better than one that forces you to learn different ways of performing similar functions. Consistency helps the learning process and makes it easier to remember how to do things if you've been away from the program for a while.

As you become more familiar with HyperCard, you will find it is a consistent program. Similar principles apply throughout its various levels, making it easier for you to learn. HyperCard's consistency also makes it a lot easier for you to graduate from being a casual user of the program to creating your own stacks.

Consistency is not only important within a program, it is also important across several programs. The chief strength of the Macintosh user interface is that users who are new to a program already know how to use many of the functions of that program, because those functions work in a way very similar to those in other programs. This has made the Macintosh and its programs easier to use than other computers.

Starting HyperCard

The best way to learn a program is to use it. The material presented in the remainder of this chapter is best used with HyperCard running on your machine.

To start HyperCard, start the Macintosh either from your hard disk or from a copy of the HyperCard Startup disk. You can open either the HyperCard application itself or the Home stack. The icons for both HyperCard and the Home stack are shown here:

HyperCard   Home

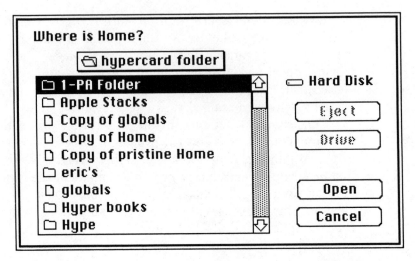

Figure 3-1. If HyperCard is unable to locate the Home stack, it presents you with this dialog box when it starts

If you open HyperCard, and it is unable to find the Home stack on your disk (perhaps because it is not in the same folder as HyperCard itself), then you will be greeted by the dialog box shown in Figure 3-1. Use standard Macintosh disk and folder navigation techniques for locating Home. When you find Home, click on it, and then click the Open button.

When HyperCard finds Home and finishes loading, you will get a display much like the one in Figure 3-2. This is the *Home card*, the first card in the Home stack. No matter where in HyperCard you are, you can always return to Home by choosing Home from the Go menu or by pressing its keyboard equivalent, COMMAND-H. You might get confused with

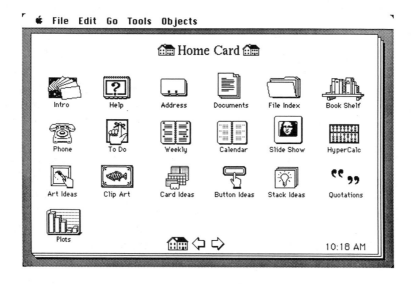

File Edit Go Tools Objects

🏠 Home Card 🏠

Intro	Help	Address	Documents	File Index	Book Shelf
Phone	To Do	Weekly	Calendar	Slide Show	HyperCalc
Art Ideas	Clip Art	Card Ideas	Button Ideas	Stack Ideas	Quotations
Plots					

10:18 AM

Figure 3-2.   The Home stack, as shipped by Apple, is the first thing you see when you start HyperCard for the first time

HyperCard, and you might find that you seem to be lost, but all roads lead Home, and it's just a keystroke away.

Welcome Home

The Home stack is a special HyperCard document. Its various components will be detailed in Chapter 4.

As you saw when installing HyperCard, Apple has included with it a number of documents or stacks for you to use when learning and using HyperCard. The Home card contains buttons that will open each of those stacks, making it easy for you to find them. You will take a look at some of these stacks later in this chapter.

Saving in HyperCard

If you have used the Macintosh (or any other computer, for that matter), you are aware of the need to frequently save your information to disk. Programs such as word processors and spreadsheets hold in the computer's RAM all the data with which you are working. If you turn off the computer without saving your data, it is gone for good; therefore, you must save your file to disk frequently.

HyperCard, however, does not make you do this. While HyperCard is running, it is constantly saving your data to disk. It does this in the idle moments when you are not actually typing at the keyboard or when the program is not busy doing some work for you. This has the obvious benefit of eliminating your worries about lost data. Because there are many idle moments when any program is running (your word processor actually spends most of its time waiting for your next keystroke or command), Hypercard saves data quickly and efficiently. You don't need to worry, therefore, about the fact that there is no Save command in HyperCard.

There is a Save a Copy menu item under HyperCard's File menu. This allows you to make a *backup* copy of your stack at any time. This is a useful tool that should be used frequently. Since HyperCard saves any changes you make to your stack, if you want to preserve the condition of a stack before you make any changes you might later regret (for example, deleting cards), make a backup copy. This becomes especially important when you start creating your own stacks.

Cards and Stacks

The fundamental object in HyperCard is the *card*. A card is always the size of the original Macintosh screen—512 pixels or dots wide and 342 pixels long. You can see only one card at a time in HyperCard (even if you have a larger monitor).

In keeping with its name and guiding metaphor, you can think of HyperCard cards as being analogous to 3×5 cards in a card file or individual cards in a Rolodex-type file. Those familiar with database products can consider cards analogous to records.

You can do many of the same things with HyperCard cards that you can do with physical cards. You can flip through them one at a time, from front to back. You can sort them to be in a specific order. You can type information into them or draw pictures on them. You can also make copies of them.

HyperCard cards, however, add some functionality to paper cards. With HyperCard you can search through all cards to find some particular information—for example, a person's phone number. You can jump quickly from one particular card at one place in the stack to another card somewhere else.

Cards are organized into *stacks*, which are HyperCard documents. Think of a stack as a file full of index cards or a stack of photographs or phonograph records. HyperCard stacks are displayed with the same icon as is used for the Home stack. Stacks can consist of any number of cards from one to thousands. Because you can only look at one card at a time, you can also only look at one stack at a time. Frequently, (although not always), stacks are organized to contain cards of the same type. All your cards that contain names and addresses, for example, will be in one stack, as will the cards you use to record the books in your library.

Backgrounds

Stacks *can* have different types of cards in them, and those cards can have very different appearances from other cards in the stack. This is handled with *backgrounds*. A background is a template that features items—graphics, buttons, fields—that are common to cards that share that background. The Datebook stack, for example, has four distinct backgrounds that give different appearances and functions to different cards in the stack. Cards in HyperCard actually have two layers: the background layer, which is the same for all the cards sharing that background, and the card layer, which is unique for each card. You will be working with backgrounds in Chapter 7.

The Help Stack

Also included with HyperCard is a help facility that is really a separate HyperCard stack. You can summon Help in several ways: by choosing Help from the Go menu or by typing its keyboard equivalent, COMMAND-?. Some stacks, such as the Home stack, include Help buttons that take you directly to the Help stack. (Other stacks might include Help buttons that summon help specific to that stack.) Help also contains some excellent introductory matter about HyperCard, and if you are just beginning to use the program, you might take a few moments to browse through that stack.

Tools

If you have used a painting program such as MacPaint, you are familiar with the concept of *tools*. Tools are the devices you use to do your work. HyperCard features several tools that are used for specific tasks.

• **The Browse tool** The act of viewing a stack — moving through it, finding information, and so on — is called *browsing*, and the Browse tool is what you use to do it. When the browse tool is in effect, the mouse pointer takes on the shape shown here:

(At certain times when you are browsing, the mouse pointer will change to a different shape. This is explained later in this chapter.)

With the Browse tool, you can do such things as click buttons and enter text in fields.

• **The Field tool**   The field tool is used to create new fields, which are discussed later in this chapter.

• **The Button tool**   The button tool is used to create new buttons.

The Painting Tools

Along with the Browse, Button, and Field tools, HyperCard has a number of tools that are used for painting. Each of these tools is discussed in detail in Chapter 8.

Menus

If you are at all familiar with the Macintosh, you know something about menus. HyperCard menus work in the same way menus in other programs work. And, like some other Macintosh programs, HyperCard's menus can change, depending on several things. If you are using HyperCard at one of the lower user levels of HyperCard (as explained in Chapter 4), certain choices will be unavailable to you. The HyperCard menus also change to reflect the capabilities of the various tools the program uses. (Note that the HyperCard menu bar itself may not always be visible to you; HyperTalk scripts can hide it to get more information on the screen. If it is hidden, you can usually show it by pressing COMMAND-SPACEBAR.)

Buttons

To initiate events in HyperCard, you click a button. On the Home card, each of the icons that represents a unique stack is a separate button, as are the two arrows at the bottom of the screen.

If you have used the Macintosh a little, you might find some things that are different about buttons. First, although buttons often have icons associated with them, these icons are not the same as the icons in the Finder that represent files. You do not need to double-click these buttons to activate them; a single click suffices. (HyperCard usually discards the second click anyway.) This is actually the way most Macintosh buttons work (as opposed to icons in the Finder).

You can always find the locations of the buttons on a card by pressing the COMMAND and OPTION keys on the keyboard. In the Home stack, notice that shaded rectangles appear around all the different pictures or icons on the card, as well as around the Previous and Next buttons at its bottom. (If you are using a version of HyperCard greater than 1.1, clicking a button when these two keys are down takes you to a special window for editing HyperCard scripts. If this happens to you, click the Cancel button at the bottom right of this window.)

Fields

Text, the information that you store in HyperCard, is held in *fields*. If you have worked with a database or filing program before, you are familiar with the concepts of fields.

Just as you can see all the buttons on a card with the COMMAND and OPTION keys, you can see all the fields on a card with the COMMAND, OPTION, and SHIFT keys (the buttons are still visible). You can also see some of the fields by moving your mouse over the text that is in them. If the mouse pointer turns into a text-editing I-Beam, as shown here, then it is over a field:

$$\mathcal{I}$$

Text in fields can be selected, cut, copied, and pasted, just as it can in most Macintosh programs. You can also set the font, size, and style for text fields; however, all text settings for a field affect *all* the text in the field, not just selected characters.

Fields are discussed in greater detail later in this chapter and in later chapters.

The Message Box

While fields, buttons, and menus may be familiar to most Macintosh users, HyperCard adds a new element to the Macintosh interface: the *Message box*. The Message box is a small window into which you can type short commands to HyperCard. These commands can be as simple as typing **Go next card** or they can call up complicated actions.

The Message box is also sometimes used for HyperCard programs to communicate with you.

There are two ways to summon the Message box: you can choose Message from the Go menu or you can press its keyboard equivalent, COMMAND-M.

At first the Message box might seem alien to you, especially if you are an experienced Mac user without much experience with other computers. The Mac's interface is of the "point and click" sort, not the "remember and type" sort: you communicate with it with the mouse, menus, and buttons. The operating system of the PC-DOS-type machines is very similar to the Message box: you almost always have to type commands to get anything to happen. At first glance, HyperCard's Message box seems to be a throwback to that old style of computers. However, the power you have with the Message box will grow on you. Experienced HyperCard users have been known to press COMMAND-M in numerous other programs and have been disappointed when the Message box did not show up.

Now that you have learned a few concepts and terms, you can put them to use by taking a look at a couple of the stacks that Apple ships with HyperCard.

The Datebook

The Datebook is a sample HyperCard stack that helps you to automate one of the biggest headaches of modern life: managing appointments, jobs to do, and reminders. While this is not a full-blown application and probably won't meet all your needs, it is a useful stack.

The Datebook is represented on your Home card by three buttons: Calendar, Weekly, and To Do. The Calendar button summons up the screen shown in Figure 3-3. Take a quick look at this card and its buttons, and you will see one of HyperCard's strengths. Using HyperCard's graphic tools, the authors of this program have created a visual analog of a paper datebook. Three months are displayed on each "page" of this datebook, and the "spiral" along the middle of the card reinforces this metaphor.

At the bottom-left corner of this card you will see the small icon with the question mark in it, which calls up a Help screen for this stack. This Help screen shows how to make a copy of the stack and tells you a little about how it works. Clicking anywhere on this Help screen returns you to the Calendar card.

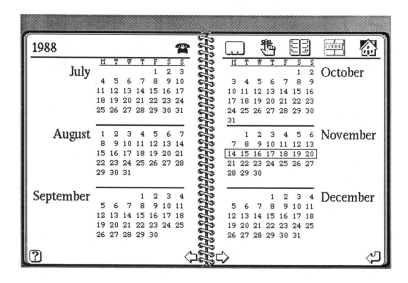

Figure 3-3. The Calendar button takes you to this card in the Datebook stack

Moving across the bottom of the screen, the next two buttons are used to take you to the previous card (the arrow pointing to the left), and the next card (the arrow pointing to the right). Clicking these buttons "turns the pages" of the calendar. The button at the lower-right corner of the screen is used to return you to your starting point.

At the top of the card is another row of buttons. The one that looks like a telephone is used to take you to the Phone stack. This stack will be discussed later in this chapter. The other buttons are for the Address, To Do, Datebook, and Calendar cards. Because you are on the Calendar card, the latter button is grayed out. Use the final button to take you Home.

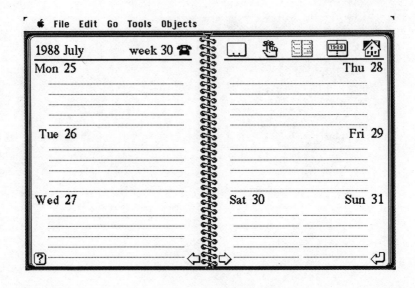

Figure 3-4.   A Weekly card from the Datebook stack

Note that the current week is highlighted, with a box around it. If you want to go to the Weekly card for any week shown on this card, simply click your mouse on the row representing that week. You will get a screen like the one in Figure 3-4. Note that this card is very similar to the one you just left: the buttons are the same. However, this card shows a detailed view of the week, and has places for you to type in your appointments for each day. These are fields. Notice that when you move the mouse pointer over one of the dotted lines, it changes into the text-editing I-Beam. If you click on one of these fields, a blinking cursor appears.

Later in this chapter, you will see how the Datebook and Address stacks interact in a way that is unique to HyperCard.

The Address Stack

There are two ways you can get to the Address stack. If you are still in the Datebook stack, you can click on the unnamed Address icon (which looks like a small Rolodex card) at the top of that stack. If you are Home, click the Address button that also has this icon. The Address stack will open, and you will see the card shown in Figure 3-5.

Just as the Datebook stack used the metaphor of a daily calendar to help you understand its functions, so the Address stack uses the familiar metaphor of a name and address Rolodex to make you feel right at home with the application. The central part of the Address card design is a white card

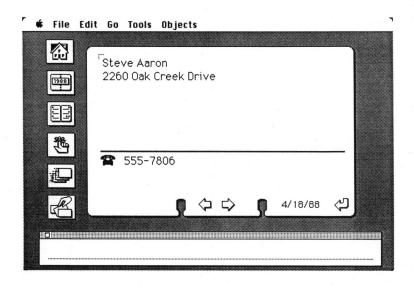

Figure 3-5.   The Address stack

that looks like a Rolodex card—it even features the tabs for fitting it into the Rolodex holder.

The Address card consists of three fields. The main field can display up to seven lines of information and is used for the name and address. You can click on the top line of the field, type a name, press RETURN, type the address, and so on, until you've entered all the information about the person that you need. Notice that the Address stack imposes no structure on how you type this information. You can type just a first name, just a last name, just a name and no address— whatever you need. If you want sorting to work correctly, however, you should type the first name, followed by a space, and then the last name. When you have entered all this information, press the TAB key, and the insertion point moves to the "Phone Number" field, which is next to the small picture of a telephone (more about this in a moment). Notice that when you press the TAB key, the final field on the card, which contains the date, is automatically filled in for you with today's date.

You will recognize some of the buttons on this card from the Datebook and Home stacks. They include Next and Previous buttons at the bottom of the card and a Return button in its lower-right corner. In a column to the left of the Rolodex card portion of the card are some more buttons. The first four buttons take you to different stacks: the Home stack and different parts of the Datebook stack that correspond to the different types of calendars the Datebook can show you.

The fifth and sixth buttons in the column are new to the Address stack. On the fifth button is a picture of three cards with "motion" lines to show the cards whizzing by. This illustrates what the button does: it shows you all the cards in the stack. If you click this button and then see a card you want, click the mouse button to halt the process. This is a faster way to navigate through these cards than flipping through each card individually with the Next button.

Figure 3-6.   The dialog box that appears when sorting the Address
stack

The sixth button sorts the stack of cards. Clicking it
summons the dialog box shown in Figure 3-6, which allows
you to choose to sort the stack according to first or last name
or to cancel the sort. HyperCard doesn't know the difference
between first and last names, of course. When you sort by
last name, it uses the last word on the first line of the "Name
and Address" field. When you sort by first name, it sorts on
the first word of that field. As mentioned earlier, this stack
imposes no structure on how you enter information. If you
put "Uncle Martin" on the first line of this field and then sort
by last name, this card will fall after "John Martin" and
before the card with "John and Mary" on it. While this is no
major disaster, you should be consistent in how you enter
names and addresses.

You can also search for specific text in the Address
stack, although there is no button that does that. You must
use the Message box (which appears automatically whenever
you enter this stack) to find information. To do this, make
sure that your insertion point is in the Message box (as
opposed to one of the fields on the card), type **Find "Bill"**,
and press RETURN. You will see a spinning beach ball for a
moment while HyperCard searches for the word "Bill". If it

finds Bill, but not the Bill you had in mind (for example, if it found "Bill Diamond" when you wanted "Bill Carat"), then just press RETURN again. HyperCard executes the statement in the Message box as if you had just typed it.

If you are using HyperCard version 1.2 or greater, there are more things you can do with the Find command. Suppose, for example, you were looking for "Mary" in your Address stack. The standard Find command will find any text that begins with those characters, whether or not they are a word to themselves. A search for "Mary" would also turn up someone living in Marysville. If instead you type the command **Find whole "Mary"** into the Message box, HyperCard will find only the whole word "Mary". If there are multiple Marys in your Address book, you can specify the Mary you want by typing **Find whole "Mary Smith"**.

There is also a shortcut to entering this information into the Message box. Whether or not the box is visible, selecting Find from the Go menu will put

find ""

into the Message box, with the insertion point between the two quotes. All you need to do is type the characters you want to find. You can also use the keyboard shortcut COMMAND-F. If you want to insert "Find whole" into the Message box, press SHIFT while choosing Find from the Go menu, or press SHIFT-COMMAND-F.

Deleting names or cards is simple. If you want to delete some text on a card, select the text you want to delete and press the BACKSPACE key (or use the Cut or Clear commands on the Edit menu, as with any Macintosh program). If you want to delete all the contents of a card, choose Delete Card from the Edit menu. This removes the card from the stack as if you had pulled a card from your address file and tossed it in the trash.

It is also easy to add your own names to this stack. As with any Macintosh application, you can replace existing text by selecting it and typing over it. This is fine for making small changes to the stack, such as replacing names that are already there. If you want to add new cards to the stack (and you will if you are going to be using this stack as an address file), choose New Card from the Edit menu. A new, blank card will be created and inserted *after* the card you are seeing when you choose this command. You can also save some mousing with the COMMAND-N keyboard equivalent of the New Card option.

Integrating the Datebook and the Address Stacks

The Datebook and the Address stacks are integrated in a manner that allows you to perform some operations with fewer keystrokes or mouse clicks. To illustrate this, return to the Datebook stack, either by clicking the Weekly button in the Address stack or by clicking the same button in the Home stack. You should be at a card similar to the one in Figure 3-4. Move the cursor to one of the date fields and click. Type **Call Bill** into one of these fields, as if it were something that you needed to do on a certain day.

Suppose you don't remember Bill's phone number. You can use the Find command to find Bill's number. Select the word "Bill" by double-clicking on it. Without clicking anywhere else, click on the Address icon at the top of the card. You will see the beach ball cursor, indicating that Hyper-Card is busy, in a few moments the Address stack will appear, and HyperCard will automatically find the first "Bill" in the stack. If this is not the Bill you want, you can then use the Find command to find the next Bill, as discussed earlier in this chapter.

Integration between two or more stacks is one of HyperCard's most useful features, and it even goes a step further, in the stacks that Apple supplies, with the ability to dial phone numbers.

The Phone Stack

The Phone stack, shown in Figure 3-7, dials the phone for you. It is integrated with the Address stack and can also be integrated with a number of other stacks. Before looking at how it works when integrated, take a look at the stack itself. Use a Home button or the Go Home command to return Home. Click the Phone button to go to the Phone stack.

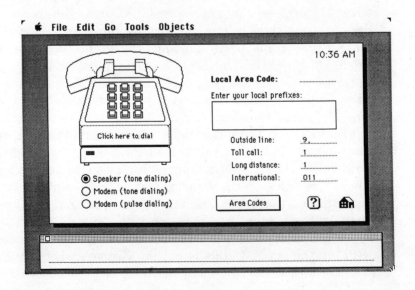

Figure 3-7.   The Phone stack

Below the picture of the phone (which is seated on a modem) are three radio buttons that allow you to tell the stack how you wish to dial: one for speaker dialing and two for modem dialing.

Speaker dialing causes the Macintosh to generate telephone tones through the Macintosh speaker. These tones can be sent to the telephone in two ways. First, if the speaker on your Macintosh is set loud enough, you can simply pick up the phone and hold it next to your Mac's speaker (located on the front of a Mac SE or Mac II and on the left side of a Mac Plus). The telephone will pick up the tones and dial the number just as if they had been dialed from the phone itself. It might take a little experimentation to get this to work. Second, there are several devices available that connect the Macintosh sound jack (located on its back) directly to a phone. If you are going to be dialing a lot of numbers with this stack, you might look into one of these devices.

Modem dialing is more flexible. If you have a modem connected to the phone connector at the back of the Macintosh, the Phone stack will use the modem to dial the phone. (There are two buttons for modem dialing; use the bottom one if your phone system does not support tone dialing.) You can then switch to voice when the modem has finished dialing. (You don't need to do anything special to switch to voice unless you are using a version of HyperCard earlier than 1.2. If so, you will need to modify the scripts in this stack. These modifications are shown in Chapter 26.) Modem dialing is your only choice if your phone system does not support tone dialing.

To the right of the picture of the telephone are the following fields in which you can enter some information about how your phone system works:

• **Local Area Code** Type your local area code here, and the Phone stack will not dial this number if it appears as part of any number you are dialing. This can be useful if you travel with your machine. Simply enter the area code for your location, and you don't need to worry about the Phone stack dialing that area code.

• **Local Prefixes** These are prefixes that are local calls to you. For any prefixes entered here, the Phone stack will not generate numbers needed for long distance calls.

• **Outside Line** If your phone system requires that you dial a special number to get an outside line (that is, outside your building or place of business), then enter that number here. The Phone stack will automatically dial this number before dialing the phone number itself.

• **Toll Call** Toll calls are calls to numbers inside your area code, but they require a prefix. If your phone system requires this, put a 1 (or whatever number is needed) into this field.

• **Long Distance** In some areas you may need to dial a 1 before dialing a long distance number. If so, type **1** into this field, and the Phone stack will automatically dial this number before dialing any numbers that are not in the local area code.

• **International** To generate international calls, an 011 prefix is usually used.

An Area Codes button below these fields allows you to search for area codes. This button is especially useful if you have a message to call someone in an area code you don't recognize. When you press this button you get the screen shown in Figure 3-8. You can search for an area code, or you can type the name of a city if you need to find the area code for a specific city. (There were some bugs in the first version of this stack. If you are using the Area Code stack that was shipped with HyperCard version 1.0.1, you should upgrade this stack to the version shipped with 1.1 or later; the earlier version would not find certain cities.)

You can return to the Phone stack using the Back command from the Go menu or by pressing its keyboard equivalent, the TILDE (~) key.

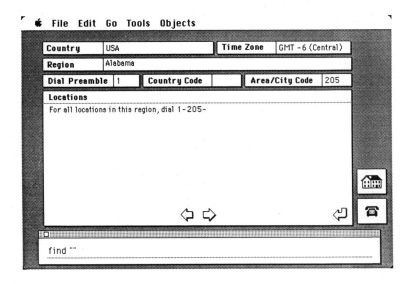

Figure 3-8.   The Area Code stack

To illustrate how the Phone stack is integrated with the Address stack, first click the Speaker radio button under the phone in the Phone stack (even if you are going to be using modem dialing, you probably don't want to actually dial now). Now return to the Address stack. As you may recall, the Address stack contains phone numbers as well as a button showing the icon of a telephone. Find a number (it doesn't matter which one), and click the telephone button next to it. HyperCard will switch to the Phone stack. If the prefix (first three digits) of the phone number are not in the "Enter your local prefixes" field, the Phone stack will ask you if it is a local, nontoll call. If you answer yes, that prefix will be saved in this field. If you answer no, the number will be dialed using the digit you entered into the "Toll Call" field. When the Phone stack has finished dialing, you will return to the Address stack.

Integration of this sort is not unusual in HyperCard, and not only in the stacks supplied by Apple. Indeed, this sort of integration is one of the most significant features of Hyper-Card. While it lacks the power of full-fledged relational data-bases, HyperCard can do such things as look up information in different stacks. Commercial applications developed in HyperCard often feature multiple stacks that are tied togeth-er to increase functionality and power. When done correctly, this is transparent to you. The Phone stack, in particular, is often used by other stacks that dial. This trend will continue.

Clip Art

HyperCard can also be used as a graphics database and Apple supplies a stack that illustrates that function. The Clip Art stack also illustrates how different items can be linked together. To get to the Clip Art stack, return Home, and click the Clip Art button with the mouse. You will be taken to the card shown in Figure 3-9. This stack features a consistent background design of a frame for the pictures that are on the cards.

At the top of each card is a field that contains keywords relating to that picture. When you opened the Clip Art stack, the Message box became visible (if it wasn't already). Type into the message box **Find "eyes"**, and the next card that contains this word in the "Keywords" field will be shown. You can press RETURN or ENTER to repeat the command as many times as you need to.

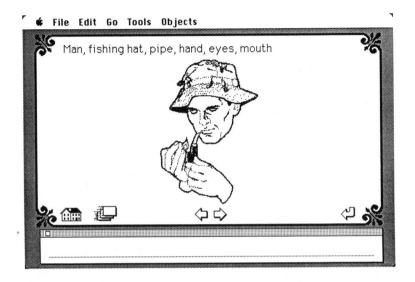

Figure 3-9.   The Clip Art stack

At the bottom of the card are Previous and Next buttons, which should be familiar to you now. Click them a couple of times to see different pictures. To the left of these buttons is a Show All Cards button. Click this to see all the cards in the Clip Art stack.

Besides these standard buttons, there are also a number of buttons that link different pictures together. To see these buttons, press COMMAND-OPTION. Figure 3-10 shows the first card in the stack, which appears when these keys are held down. (If you inadvertently click one of these buttons with these two keys held down, you might enter the Edit window of the script of that button. If so, just click the Cancel button on that window, and you will return to the card.)

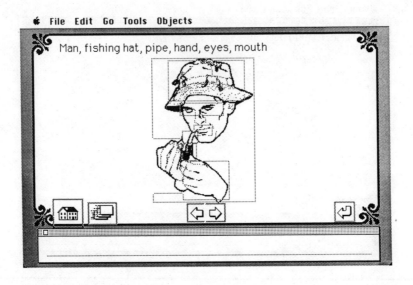

Figure 3-10.   Holding down the COMMAND and OPTION keys shows all of the buttons on the card

Clicking any of these buttons takes you to another card that contains a similar item. Clicking on the man's eye, for example, takes you to another card that has an eye on it. In Chapter 7 you will learn how to make your own links in this stack.

The Ideas Stacks

Two other stacks that are included with HyperCard are the Stack Ideas and Card Ideas stacks. These contain partially functional templates that you can use when creating your own stacks. You might want to take a look at these stacks now, but you will learn how to use them when creating your own new stacks in Chapters 6 and 9.

The Button Ideas stack is similar to the Card Ideas and Stack Ideas stacks, but it contains buttons that can be copied and pasted into your own stacks. You will take a closer look at these buttons in Chapter 6.

Other Sample Stacks

In addition to the stacks mentioned in this chapter, a number of other useful stacks are included with HyperCard. Taking a look at them will give you a better feel for how HyperCard works. The function of most of them is straightforward, and the best way to understand them is to explore them.

A Closer Look at the Menus

Now that you've had a chance to take a look at some Hyper-Card stacks, let's go through and recapitulate the functions of each of the HyperCard menus. Many of their elements have already been discussed, but another look should fill in the blanks.

The menus in HyperCard can change based on several things. The user level, which is discussed in Chapter 4, is one thing that controls the appearance of some of the menus. If you don't see certain items on a menu, it could be because your user level is set too low for some of them. Other menu items can change depending on the HyperCard tool you are using, or what you have selected.

Many of the items on the HyperCard menus have COMMAND-key equivalents. These equivalents, of course, allow you to use the command from the keyboard, exactly as if you had done so using the mouse.

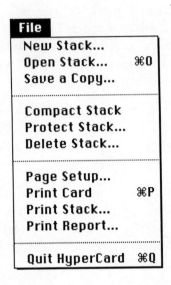

Figure 3-11. HyperCard's File menu

The File Menu

The File menu, shown in Figure 3-11, performs many of the same functions that it performs in most Macintosh programs, allowing you to open, save, and print stacks. It also has some other features specific to HyperCard.

New Stack

This option allows you to create a new stack. Since Hyper-Card requires that all its stacks be named, it brings up a standard Save File dialog box. Creating new stacks is discussed in Chapter 6.

Open Stack (COMMAND-O)

Just as it does in most applications, this menu item opens an existing stack. One difference in HyperCard is that you do not use this as often as you do in other programs because buttons can be used to take you to other stacks.

Save a Copy

This option makes a copy of the current stack. It asks you to name the new stack, and it proposes the name of the current stack with "Copy of" in front of it. HyperCard automatically saves all the changes you make to a stack; therefore, you don't need a normal Save command. Use this command when you are about to make major changes to a stack and want to preserve the original before doing so.

Compact Stack

If the stack you are using is locked, or if your user level is set to a level lower than Painting (user levels are discussed in Chapter 4), then this menu item is not available to you. As a stack is changed, a certain amount of free space will be generated in the stack—space that the file is using on disk, but is not really used by the stack. Use this command to compress the free space from the stack.

Protect Stack

Like Compact Stack, this option is not available with lower user levels. It allows you to assign a password to the stack to prevent others from using or modifying it.

Delete Stack

Also not available at the lower user levels, this menu item deletes the current stack from disk. You cannot undo this action.

Print Commands

These commands print cards and reports. They are discussed
in detail in Chapter 5.

Quit HyperCard (COMMAND-Q)

This option does what it says it will do.

The Edit Menu

Again, many functions of the Edit menu, shown in Figure
3-12, will be familiar to experienced Macintosh users.

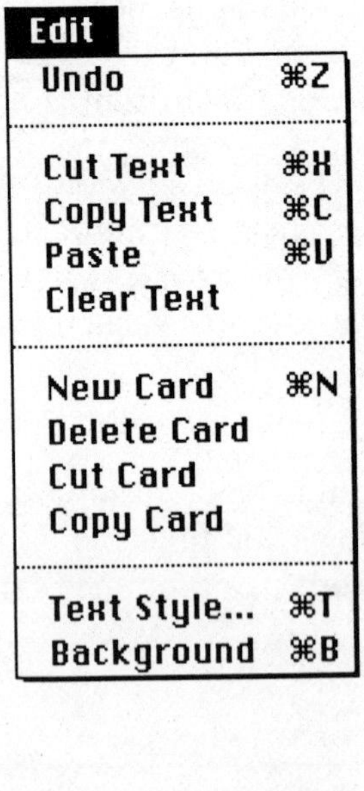

Edit

Undo	⌘Z
Cut Text	⌘H
Copy Text	⌘C
Paste	⌘U
Clear Text	
New Card	⌘N
Delete Card	
Cut Card	
Copy Card	
Text Style...	⌘T
Background	⌘B

Figure 3-12.   HyperCard's Edit menu

Undo (COMMAND-Z)

The Undo command in HyperCard works much the same way it does in other applications: it allows you to reverse your last action. Note that there are many commands that HyperCard does *not* allow you to undo. As mentioned earlier, Delete Stack is one of them, because that command actually deletes the file from the disk. Undo does work, however, with the Delete Card command. It works with many of the same types of commands that it does in other programs: deleting text, deleting pictures, and so on.

Cut, Copy, Paste, Clear

Again, these commands work in much the same way they do in most Mac programs. In HyperCard, these menu items change: Cut, Copy, and Clear will tell you what is selected (such as Cut Text, Cut Picture, Cut Button). Paste will change to show you what is on the Clipboard. If the last thing you cut or copied was text, the menu item will be Paste Text. If the last thing you cut or copied was a picture, it will be Paste Picture. Clear, of course, deletes what you have selected without placing it on the Clipboard.

If you are pasting text, it will be pasted at the current insertion point. If text is selected, the pasted text will replace the selected text. If you are pasting a card, the new card will be placed after the current card. Chapter 8 discusses pasting graphics.

These commands use standard Macintosh keyboard equivalents: COMMAND-X for Cut, COMMAND-C for Copy, and COMMAND-V for Paste.

New Card (COMMAND-N)

This command creates a new card and places it after the current card in the stack. If your user level is not set to at least Typing, this command will be dimmed. User levels are discussed in Chapter 4.

Delete Card

This command deletes the current card. If your user level is not set to at least Typing, this command will be dimmed and not available.

Cut Card and Copy Card

There is no way in HyperCard to select a card for use with the standard Cut and Copy commands. Therefore, these two commands allow you to cut and copy cards. After you have cut or copied a card, you can use the standard Paste command to paste the card; the option will be Paste Card. For these commands to work, your user level must be set to at least Painting.

Text Style (COMMAND-T)

This command is only available if the user level is set to Painting or higher. When using the paint Text tool, it allows you to change the font and style of "paint text" as discussed in Chapter 8. When using the Browse tool, it allows you to change the text in the field. Remember that all the text in the field is set with this command; you cannot change the font or style of individual characters within the field.

Background

When working with the Button, Field, or any of the paint tools, this controls what "layer" of HyperCard your changes affect. This will be discussed in more detail in Chapter 6. This command is only available if your user level is set to Painting or higher.

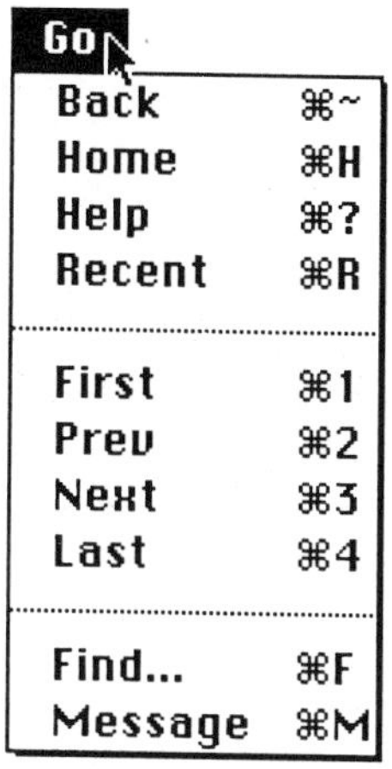

```
 ┌──────────────┐
 │ Go▶          │
 ├──────────────┤
 │ Back      ⌘~ │
 │ Home      ⌘H │
 │ Help      ⌘? │
 │ Recent    ⌘R │
 │ ············ │
 │ First     ⌘1 │
 │ Preu      ⌘2 │
 │ Next      ⌘3 │
 │ Last      ⌘4 │
 │ ············ │
 │ Find...   ⌘F │
 │ Message   ⌘M │
 └──────────────┘
```

Figure 3-13.   HyperCard's Go menu

The Go Menu

The items on this menu, shown in Figure 3-13, are used for
navigation in HyperCard. Aside from the standard complement of COMMAND-key equivalents, some of these commands
can be executed from the Message box; the equivalent message for these commands is shown in parentheses.

Back (Go Back)

This command steps you back through the list of cards that you have visited.

You can invoke this command in several ways. You can choose it from the menu or type its COMMAND-key equivalent, COMMAND-TILDE (~). (In this case, the COMMAND key is not really necessary, although it shows on the menu.) The tilde key works by itself to execute the Back command. On the Mac SE or the Mac II with the newer keyboards, the ESC or ESCAPE key at the upper left of the keyboard does the same thing. You can also enter **Go back** into the Message box.

Home (Go Home)

This command takes you to the first card in the Home stack. COMMAND-H does the same thing.

Help (Go Help, or Help)

This command takes you to the first card in the Help stack. Its keyboard equivalent is COMMAND-? or COMMAND-/ (the SHIFT key is not necessary). You can enter **Go help** or just **Help** into the Message box.

Recent (Go Recent)

This is one of HyperCard's most useful commands. When you choose it, you get a display such as the one in Figure 3-14. This display shows miniature versions of the last 42 cards you have visited. Clicking on any of those cards takes you directly to that card.

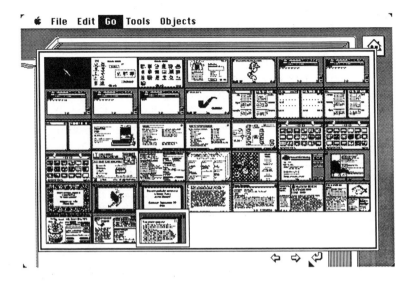

Figure 3-14.   The Go Recent command display

First, Previous, Next, Last
(Go First, Go Previous,
Go Next, Go Last)

These commands take you to the specified cards. First takes you to the first card in the stack, Last to the last card. Any of these commands can be entered directly into the Message box (for example, type **Go first** to invoke the First command).

Find

If the Message box is not visible, this command shows the Message box and types the Find command into it, with the insertion point between two quotes. Type any text you want between the quotes, and HyperCard will find the text in the current stack, if the text is there to be found. You can also type **Find** and the text you want to find, set apart with quotes, directly into the Message box.

Using the keyboard shortcut COMMAND-F is the same as selecting the Find command with the mouse.

If you are using HyperCard version 1.2 or greater, you can use COMMAND-SHIFT-F to display the Message box showing the Find Whole command. This version of the Find command ensures that only complete words are found. With the regular Find command, searching for "man" will find "manuscript" and "mankind". With the Find Whole command, only the whole word "man" is found.

Message

This command displays the Message box if it is hidden, and hides it otherwise. Get to know the COMMAND-M shortcut for this, as it's a command you'll probably use often.

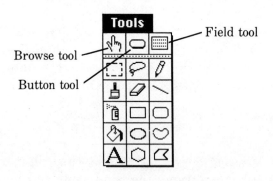

Figure 3-15.   The Tools menu

Tools

If your user level is set lower than Painting, this menu is not available; you will always use the Browse tool. The Tools menu is shown in Figure 3-15.

HyperCard uses different tools to present you with different functions. For looking at stacks, you always use the Browse tool—the one that looks like a small hand. For creating and working with buttons, use the Button tool, and use the Field tool when working with fields. When painting, there are several tools, similar to those in a program such as MacPaint, that perform a number of functions (see Chapter 8).

Objects

The Objects menu, shown in Figure 3-16, is used for manipulating HyperCard objects—buttons, fields, cards, back-

Figure 3-16.   The Objects menu

grounds, and stacks. Since you use it when you are creating new objects or working with existing ones, it only becomes available when your user level is set to at least Authoring. Since the Authoring level of HyperCard is discussed in Chapter 6, details of this menu will be discussed there, too.

Paint Menus

If your user level is set to Painting or higher, and you choose one of the paint tools, three new menus become available — Paint, Options, and Patterns. These menus are discussed in detail in Chapter 8.

The Home Stack

A Card-by-Card Look at the Home Stack
Changing the Home Stack

This chapter introduces you to the Home stack of Hyper-Card. You will probably see the Home stack more than you see any other stack, and since it acts as the hub for all Hyper-Card operations, it is here that you will create your first HyperCard buttons. With these buttons you can form a link between the Home stack and another stack on disk.

The Home stack is your base of operations for Hyper-Card. It acts something like a "hub airport." A hub airport, such as Chicago's O'Hare or those in Denver or Atlanta, is one from which all airlines can fly to any other airport. You might not be able to go directly from Seattle to Omaha, for example, but you can almost certainly fly from Seattle to Denver and then from Denver to Omaha. So it is with Hyper-Card. A particular stack may not have a button that takes you directly to another stack, but if the Home stack does have a button for that stack, you can always return to the Home stack and then click the button to take you to that stack.

Returning to the Home stack is easy. Almost every stack has a Home button. You can recognize this button by the distinctive standard icons that are used for it. The icons used may vary, but they are all, appropriately, images of houses, so their function is perfectly clear. The various standard Home icons are shown in Figure 4-1.

Not all stacks that you use will have Home buttons, and they are not strictly necessary. You can almost always choose "Home" from the Go menu. (If the menu bar is not visible, pressing COMMAND-SPACEBAR will display it.) Or, you can usually press COMMAND-H to go directly to the Home stack.

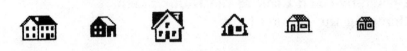

Figure 4-1.   Representative Home icons return you to the Home stack

A Card-by-Card Look at the Home Stack

There are a number of cards in the Home stack, each of which serves a specific purpose. To move through these cards, you can click on the arrows at the bottom of the cards. The arrow pointing to the right takes you to the next card; the one pointing to the left takes you to the previous card.

The Home Card

The Home card, shown in Figure 4-2, contains buttons for all the stacks that are included with HyperCard when Apple ships it. Using the mouse to click any of the buttons takes you directly to the stack or card represented by the icon on the button.

The Stacks Card

The heading on the Stacks card, shown in Figure 4-3, is "Look for Stacks in." This card is used to tell HyperCard in what folders you are storing stacks. Each line in the field constitutes a pathname that ends with the name of a folder in which stacks are stored. Since folders can be placed inside folders, the list of these folders can be long. Folder names are

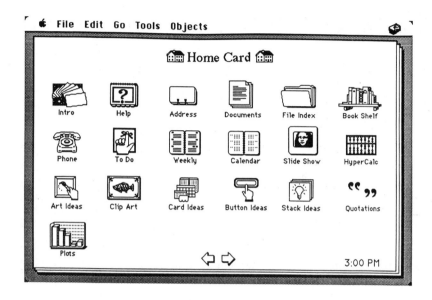

Figure 4-2.   The Home card, as shipped by Apple, contains buttons that take you to all the stacks included with HyperCard

separated from one another with a colon. For example, if you have placed HyperCard's Help stacks into a folder called Help folder, which is in turn inside your HyperCard folder, the pathname for the Help stack would be "Hard disk:Hyper-Card Folder:Help Folder". Note that stack names are not included. When you type pathnames into this field, do not include spaces as part of the folder name unless there are actually spaces in that name. A folder named " help" is a different folder from one named "help".

If you think it might be difficult for you to remember the names of all the folders you are using to store HyperCard stacks, you are right. But HyperCard does something to help you out. Whenever you click a button for a stack that Hyper-

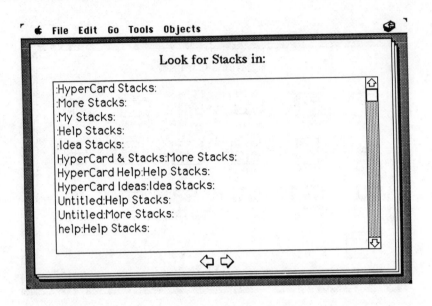

Figure 4-3. The Stacks card tells HyperCard in what folders you have stored HyperCard stacks

Card cannot find, it presents you with a dialog box that asks for the name of the folder containing that stack. When you click on the name of a folder, HyperCard will then automatically add that folder to the list of folders where stacks are located. If you have just installed HyperCard and have experimented with some of the stacks that are included with it, you have probably already encountered this dialog box and see listed on the Stack card the names of folders you have had to enter.

The longer you use HyperCard, the more folders will probably be listed on this card. This field is not locked, which means that you can click it and change any of it. From time to time you may want to go through and delete folders that you have erased from the disk. Note that it does not really matter if there are nonexistent folders listed on this card;

HyperCard will not try to look into these nonexistent folders, and they will not cause errors.

The Applications Card

The card headed "Look for Applications in:" does for standard Macintosh applications what the Stacks card does for HyperCard stacks. It allows you to tell HyperCard in which folders on disk your applications are stored. This card is shown in Figure 4-4.

As you saw in Chapter 1, HyperCard can act as a "base of operations" for your use of the Macintosh, allowing you to run other programs besides HyperCard and open or print specific documents with those applications. Just as the

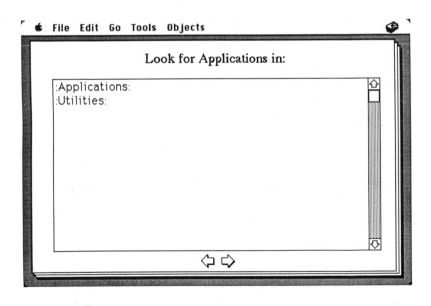

Figure 4-4.   The Applications card tells HyperCard where your other programs are stored

Stacks card tells HyperCard where you are storing its stacks, the Applications card tells HyperCard where you are storing your applications.

The Documents Card

The Documents card, shown in Figure 4-5, works the same way as the Stacks and Applications cards. As you saw in Chapter 1, you can open applications such as MacWrite from within HyperCard and work with specific documents created by those applications. This card tells HyperCard where on disk you are keeping those documents. (Remember, a document is a file created by a program; for example, files saved from MacWrite are MacWrite documents.)

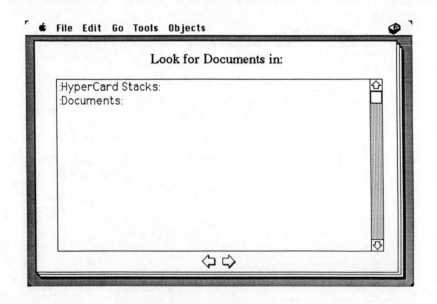

Figure 4-5.   The Documents card

The User Preferences Card

The User Preferences card, shown in Figure 4-6, allows you to set up certain parameters for how HyperCard will work for you. From this card you can set such things as the user level—an item that controls which of HyperCard's tools will be available. The following sections discuss the function of each field in the User Preferences card.

User Name

This field is merely used to store your name. Other HyperCard stacks can get your name from here and use it automatically.

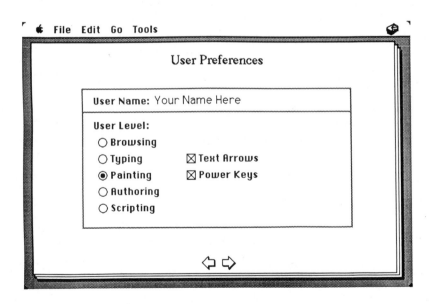

Figure 4-6.   The User Preferences card tells HyperCard at what level you are using the program

User Level

As discussed in Chapter 1, HyperCard allows you to set various levels at which you will use HyperCard. You can set the level to approach HyperCard from a simple point of view and then graduate from that easy level to more powerful and difficult levels. You can set the default level at which you will be using HyperCard by using the User Level button of the User Preferences card. Remember that each user level incorporates all the powers of the level below it. For example, while in the Painting user level, you are also able to do all the things that Typing and Browsing allow you to do.

When HyperCard was created, it was assumed that most users would start their HyperCard exploration at the Browsing level, and as their familiarity with HyperCard grew, they would move up gradually to more sophisticated levels. It hasn't quite worked out that way. A substantial number of HyperCard users start right at the Scripting level, without experiencing any of the previous levels. This is not really surprising. HyperCard is not very hard to learn, especially for those with some programming experience.

The following sections explain what the various Hyper-Card levels allow you to do.

Browsing   At this level you can look at stacks created by others, but you are not permitted to change any information in a stack. You can only click buttons, such as those that take you from one card to another or return you to the Home stack.

Typing   When you are at the Typing level, you can enter data into fields in HyperCard. You can see the effect of this by going to the User Preferences card. Click the Browsing button to set the user level there. Now move the cursor to just after the User Name field. The cursor does not turn into the familiar text-editing I-Beam, and you are not able to change the user name. Change the level to Typing and move again to the User Name field. The cursor turns into an I-Beam and you are able to select and edit text.

When you set the user level to Typing, you will notice that a new button, the Text Arrow check box, becomes visible to the right of the Typing radio button. With this button you can alter the way the arrow keys on the Macintosh keyboard work. (This is true only for keyboards that work on the Mac Plus or later machines. The original Macintosh keyboard did not have arrow keys.) If this box is not checked, the arrow keys are always used to navigate among cards and stacks.

Here is what the arrow keys do in that mode:

Key	Function
LEFT ARROW	Go to previous card
RIGHT ARROW	Go to next card
UP ARROW	Go to next card in the "recent list"
DOWN ARROW	Go to previous card in the "recent" list

The arrow keys will continue to operate this way, unless you are editing text in a field and the Text Arrows box on the User Preferences card is checked. If that box is checked, then the arrows work the way you would expect them to work: they move the insertion point through the text. The UP ARROW takes you to the line above the one you are on, the DOWN ARROW to the line below, and the LEFT and RIGHT ARROWS move you one character to the left or the right of the insertion point. If you are using a version of HyperCard earlier than 1.1, this option is not available; it was added to HyperCard with version 1.1 in response to user requests. (If you are using a version of HyperCard less than 1.2, you should upgrade your copy.)

Note that when you have the user level set below Painting, only three of HyperCard's menus are available: the standard Apple and File menus and the Go menu, with which you can navigate through cards and stacks. At these levels you cannot use any of the options on the other menus, so to avoid confusion they are not shown. Additionally, certain items on these menus are either not enabled (grayed-out) or are not present at all.

Painting   At the Painting level, the Tools menu becomes available, allowing you to use these tools. Since you are now able to paint, it makes sense for HyperCard to show them.

When Painting is enabled, a second check box (in addition to the Text Arrows check box) appears to the right of the Painting button and is labeled Power Keys. Enabling Power Keys enhances the utility of the painting tools by allowing you to type one-character commands to HyperCard while you are painting. These powerful keys will be discussed in Chapter 8.

Authoring   At the Authoring level, you are able to create new buttons and fields and link buttons to other stacks. You are not able, however, to edit the scripts of any buttons or fields, or of any stacks, backgrounds, or cards.

Scripting   Scripting is HyperCards most powerful level. While at the Scripting level, you are able to do everything you can do at all the other levels, and you can also edit the scripts of any HyperCard objects: buttons, fields, stacks, backgrounds, and cards.

When Scripting is enabled, another check box appears called Blind Typing. When you click this button, you can type commands to HyperCard even if the message box is not visible, and they will be executed when you strike the RETURN key. This is a useful feature that saves time when you need to enter a command quickly. Unless you are a very accurate typist, however, you are likely to increase the number of error messages that HyperCard presents to you as it tries to interpret something like "gp czrd !" instead of "go card 1."

Changing the Home Stack

The Home stack is very functional as shipped by Apple. It provides easy access to the stacks that Apple includes with HyperCard, such as Help, the various idea stacks, and the introduction to HyperCard. Soon, however, you will want to change the Home stack to reflect the way you work. You will probably want to add new buttons for new stacks that you have acquired and perhaps remove some of the buttons for stacks that you do not use very often.

The Home Card Versus the Home Stack

There is some confusion about the difference between the Home card and the Home stack. While the Home stack is a special and specific HyperCard entity, the Home card is the first card in the Home stack and the card to which the Go Home command takes you. If you wish to make another Home card, all you need to do is create a new card that goes in front of the first card. The newly created card becomes the new Home card. (This procedure is discussed later in this chapter in the section titled "Adding and Removing Cards.")

Adding Buttons

Suppose you have just received a new stack, and you want to add a button on your Home card to take you directly to that stack. (Many stacks include self-installing buttons that automate this procedure, but in this case assume that your new stack does not include such a button.)

The first thing you will need to do is copy that stack to your hard disk and then put it into your HyperCard folder. Once that is done, follow these steps to create the new button:

1. The user level must be set to at least the Authoring level. Use the left arrow at the bottom of the Home card to take you there. Click on the box marked Authoring if the user level is set below that.

2. Go back to the Home card. You can do this in several ways, from the User Preferences card, but perhaps the easiest way is to click on the arrow that points right— the Next button. You can also Go Home which will take you to the first card in the Home stack.

3. From the Tools menu, choose the Button tool (the middle one in the top row of buttons), as shown in Figure 4-7. Note that the various buttons on the card become outlined, as shown in Figure 4-8.

4. Position the mouse where you want the new button to appear and press the COMMAND key. The mouse pointer changes to a cross, as shown here:

$$+$$

Keeping the Mouse button down, drag to form a rectangle. This rectangle will be your new button. Let go of the Mouse button when you have made the size rectangle you want.

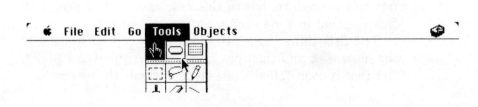

Figure 4-7.   Choosing the Button tool from the Tools menu

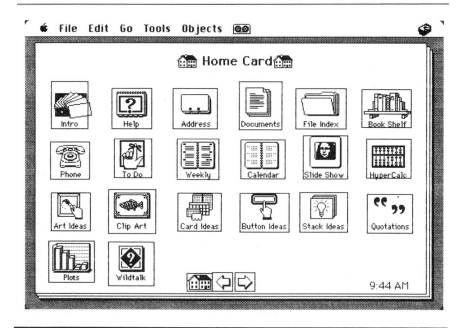

Figure 4-8.   When you choose the Button tool, borders appear around all the buttons on a card

The button is automatically selected: Around its shape slowly march "ants" (similar to those that appear when you use the Marquis or Selection tool in a Paint program) to tell you that it is selected. Figure 4-9 shows the new button at the bottom of the Home card.

You now have a new button, but it does not do anything yet. Here is the procedure for telling the button what to do:

1. Without choosing any other tool, double-click the new button. A dialog box like the one in Figure 4-10 will appear. Type **Test** as the name of the button (you do not need to click there first). In order to make the name visible on the button, click on the check box labeled Show Name.

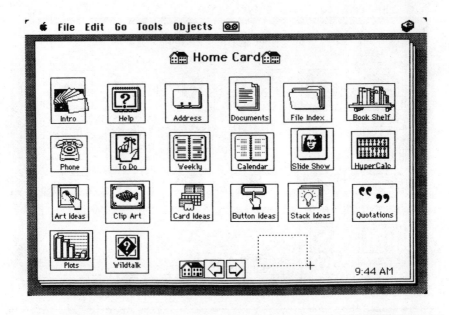

Figure 4-9.   A new button has been created toward the bottom of the card. The "marching ants" tell you the button is selected

Now you need to form the link between this button and the stack. For this example, you will link it to the Address stack.

2. Click the linkTo button on the dialog box. The dialog box dissappears, and you see a window like the one shown in Figure 4-11.

This small window is similar to many Macintosh application windows. You can drag it around the screen so it will not block your view of crucial screen areas. It is a *modal* window, in that you are limited in the things you can do while this window is active—only navigation tools or buttons that go to different cards work.

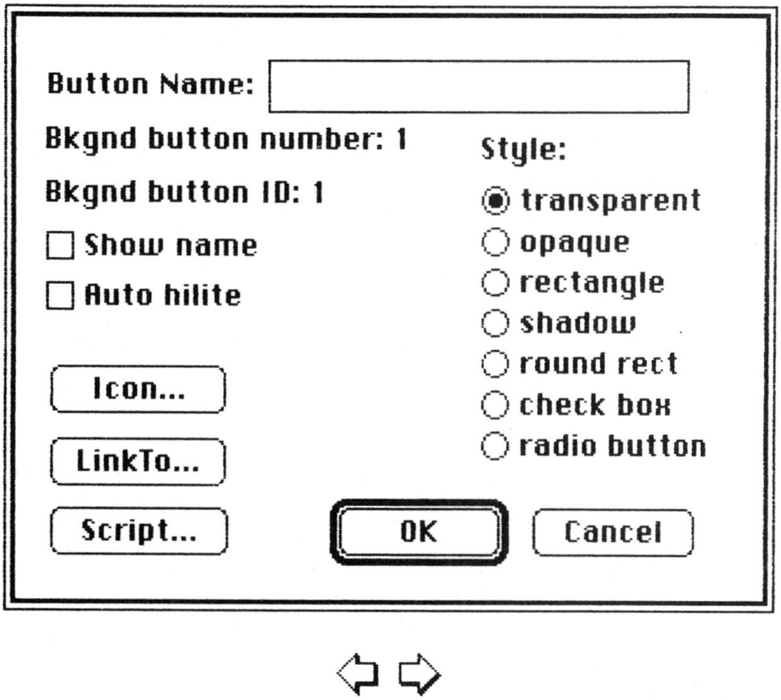

Button Name:

Bkgnd button number: 1   **Style:**

Bkgnd button ID: 1   ⦿ **transparent**

☐ **Show name**   ◯ **opaque**

☐ **Auto hilite**   ◯ **rectangle**

                                    ◯ **shadow**

                                    ◯ **round rect**

[**Icon...**]   ◯ **check box**

                                    ◯ **radio button**

[**LinkTo...**]

[**Script...**]   [**OK**]   [**Cancel**]

⇦ ⇨

Figure 4-10.   The Button Info dialog box allows you to specify a button's name, style, icon, links, and script

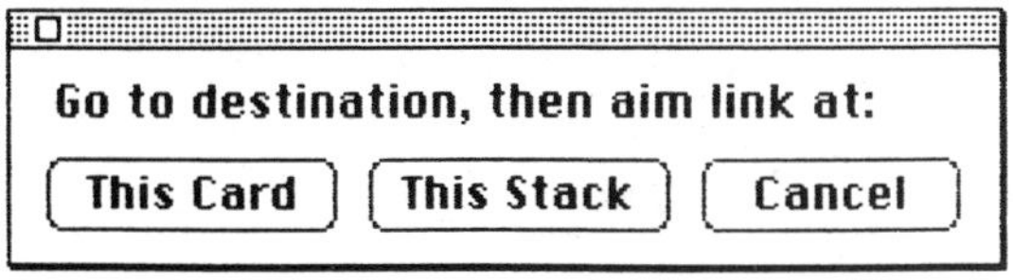

Go to destination, then aim link at:

[**This Card**]   [**This Stack**]   [**Cancel**]

Figure 4-11.   The Link To window allows you to link a button to another stack or card

3. Go to the stack you want to link to—in this case, the Address stack. There are several ways to go to that stack. You can click the existing button for the Address stack on the Home card, for example. In this case, use the Open Stack command under the File menu. Use standard Macintosh folder navigation techniques to get to this stack. Note that when you arrive at the stack, the Link dialog box is still visible.

4. You have two choices for how you want to form the link. If you click the This Stack button in the Link dialog box, you will be linking the new button to the first card in the stack. Alternatively, you can go to a specific card and click the This Card button, which forms a link directly to that card. If you've decided you do not want to link to any card or stack, click the Cancel button or click on the Close box of the Link dialog box.

5. When you have chosen an option, HyperCard returns to the Home stack. The new button you created has a simple appearance—it just shows the name "Test" that you typed earlier. It has no outline or icon associated with it. To satisfy yourself that it works, choose the Browse tool from the Tools menu. Then click on the new button, and it takes you to the card or stack you selected—in this case, the Address stack.

You have now created your first HyperCard button, one that links one card to another. This is one of the most basic of HyperCard techniques, and you can use it over and over again to link two cards together. Entire HyperCard applications can be created that include no more sophisticated programming than that which you have just done—linking cards and stacks together.

Adding and Removing Cards

Although it is possible to remove cards from the Home stack, it is not a good idea to do so until you become familiar with HyperCard and how it works. When you remove any of the existing cards, you need to adjust the scripts inside the Home stack to compensate for their absence. This procedure requires a familiarity with the needs of HyperCard and the Home stack.

One thing you can do without a lot of experience is revise some of the buttons that are included on the standard Home card. There is not much room on that card for adding new buttons, and it is a good idea to keep that card in its original condition so you can refer to it and use it later. What you need to do is add a new card, which becomes the first card in the Home stack, and move the original Home card to the second position in the stack. Here is how you do it. (Make sure that you've set the user level to at least Authoring to do this.)

1. Go to the first card in the Home stack, if you are not already there. The quickest way to do this is with the Go Home command, which you can use even if you are already in the Home stack.

2. While at the first card, select "Copy Card" from the Edit menu to copy the first card.

3. Immediately after doing this, choose "Paste Card," again from the Edit menu. This pastes the card you just copied, so that it is after the current card.

4. Now you have two cards that look just the same. To differentiate the original Home card from the one you are going to modify, select the Browse tool and select the words "Home Card" at the top of the card. Type in a new name—Motel Card or Old Home, for example.

5. Now you can go back to the new Home card by clicking the Previous button at the bottom of the screen.

You can delete buttons by selecting them with the Button tool (making sure the "marching ants" appear on the button to show it is selected), and selecting "Clear Button" from the edit menu. Pressing the DELETE or BACKSPACE key on the keyboard also works.

When you delete some buttons, you will notice that the images that seem to be part of the buttons do not also disappear. That is because these icons are not part of the button but are instead pictures created on the card. Painting with HyperCard will be discussed in Chapter 8, and you will see there how to get rid of these pictures.

The Home stack and the Home card are very important in HyperCard. You will see later in the book that this stack can be used as more than a hub. Indeed, it can include many programs or scripts, icons, and sounds that you can use in all your HyperCard applications. The one thing you should remember is that it is your Home stack, and just like your real home, you are free to make of it what you will. You can continue to use it in the manner in which Apple shipped it, or you can modify it to your heart's content.

Printing

Page Setup
Printing Cards
Print Report
Saving Print Setups

In some respects, printing with HyperCard is beside the point. How can you print a sound or animation? How can you show links with printing? Buttons can't do anything on paper, so why print them? If HyperCard presents a new way of publishing information, then printing is an atavism—a throwback to paper-based information.

Nevertheless, at times you do need to print your information. Not everyone has HyperCard (or a Macintosh), so you might want to disseminate to them some of the data you have gathered. You might need to prepare documents, such as tax information, for individuals or agencies that cannot or will not accept a disk. And sometimes it just feels more secure to have your information down on paper, just as it feels (and is) more secure to have many copies of disks that contain important files.

HyperCard gives you two ways to print the information stored in stacks. It can either print cards exactly the way they appear on the screen, or it can print reports. If you're familiar with printing from other Macintosh applications, printing from HyperCard is not going to be too difficult to pick up.

Printing in HyperCard, however, is a mixed bag. As you will see in this chapter, the various print dialog boxes make it easy to set up pages that look exactly the way you want them to look when printed. Developers of all applications would be well served to take a look at these dialog boxes as a model for printing and page layout. Graphic representations of the page make it easy to create a report that looks just as you want.

On the other hand, there are a couple of irritating aspects to printing in HyperCard. You can't save card or report layouts for repeated use with specific stacks. You can't print parts of stacks or specific pages from a report. Hyper-Talk programming helps correct these deficiencies partially, but not entirely. Several third-party products, such as Media-genics' Reports!, discussed in Chapter 35, help solve these problems.

Page Setup

As do most applications, HyperCard uses the Page Setup dialog box from the File menu to set up certain parameters for how the program is going to deal with the printer. Since these settings vary somewhat depending on the printer you have, each printer will be discussed separately. All printer commands are on the File menu, as they are with most Mac applications.

ImageWriter Page Setup

The Page Setup dialog box is shown in Figure 5-1 as it appears if you have an ImageWriter printer. The various options are fairly self-explanatory. The items toward the top of the dialog box allow you to tell HyperCard what size paper you are using, and the two icons at the left tell you in what orientation you want to print. Because HyperCard does not support the 50% Reduction and Tall Adjusted options for ImageWriter printing, these two items are not available. You can, however, set No Gaps Between Pages to "true." This is useful if you are working with tractor paper and want the program to print continuously.

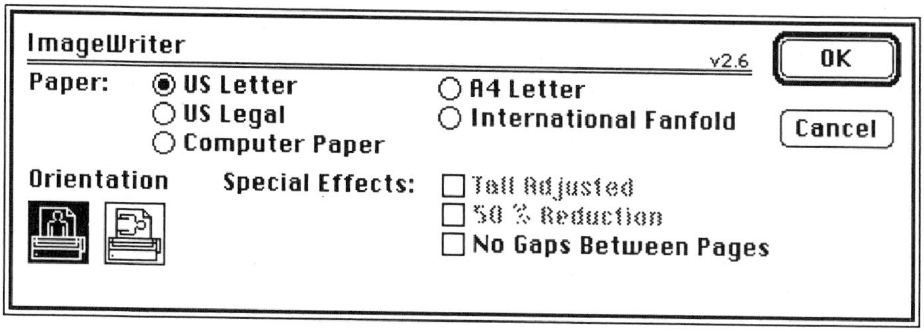

```
┌─────────────────────────────────────────────────────────────────┐
│ ImageWriter                                    v2.6   ┌─────────┐ │
│                                                       │   OK    │ │
│ Paper:     ● US Letter        ○ A4 Letter             └─────────┘ │
│            ○ US Legal         ○ International Fanfold  ┌─────────┐ │
│            ○ Computer Paper                           │ Cancel  │ │
│                                                       └─────────┘ │
│ Orientation     Special Effects:  ☐ Tall Adjusted                 │
│  ┌──┐┌──┐                         ☐ 50 % Reduction                │
│  │  ││  │                         ☐ No Gaps Between Pages          │
│  └──┘└──┘                                                          │
└─────────────────────────────────────────────────────────────────┘
```

Figure 5-1.   The ImageWriter Page Setup dialog box

LaserWriter Page Setup

If you are using an Apple LaserWriter or any other printer
that works with PostScript, your Page Setup dialog box looks
a little different. The paper-size options are about the same
as they were on the ImageWriter, and the icons illustrating
the orientation of the document on the page are about the
same. The LaserWriter dialog box, shown in Figure 5-2, has
the following additional check boxes.

Font Substitution

Font Substitution causes the LaserWriter to replace three
specific Macintosh screen fonts with three built-in LaserWriter fonts. The Macintosh screen fonts usually look better on

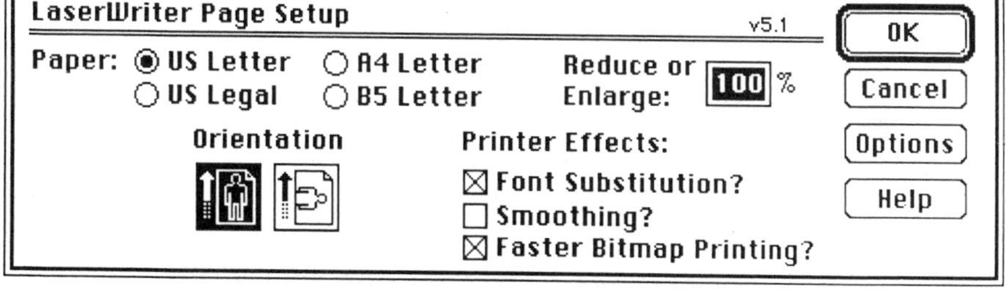

```
┌─────────────────────────────────────────────────────────────────┐
│ LaserWriter Page Setup                         v5.1   ┌─────────┐ │
│                                                       │   OK    │ │
│ Paper: ● US Letter  ○ A4 Letter   Reduce or ┌───┐ %   └─────────┘ │
│        ○ US Legal   ○ B5 Letter   Enlarge:  │100│     ┌─────────┐ │
│                                             └───┘     │ Cancel  │ │
│           Orientation          Printer Effects:       └─────────┘ │
│            ┌──┐┌──┐            ☒ Font Substitution?   ┌─────────┐ │
│            │  ││  │            ☐ Smoothing?           │ Options │ │
│            └──┘└──┘            ☒ Faster Bitmap Printing?└────────┘ │
│                                                       ┌─────────┐ │
│                                                       │  Help   │ │
│                                                       └─────────┘ │
└─────────────────────────────────────────────────────────────────┘
```

Figure 5-2.   The LaserWriter Page Setup dialog box

the screen (and on an ImageWriter), but the built-in Laser-Writer fonts, not surprisingly, look better on the LaserWriter. Here are the Macintosh screen fonts, and the LaserWriter fonts with which they are substituted:

Screen Font	LaserWriter Font
New York	Times
Geneva	Helvetica
Monaco	Courier

Remember that this font substitution affects only the text that appears in HyperCard fields and not the text that is painted onto the screen with the Paint Text tool.

Smoothing

The Smoothing option causes the LaserWriter to smooth the bit-map images that it prints. All HyperCard graphics are bit-map images (as opposed to the object-oriented images created by a program such as MacDraw), which slows down the printing process quite a bit. With Hypercard, therefore, it is best to leave this option unchecked. Stacks that have a lot of graphics in them (as do most stacks) will print *very* slowly with this option checked. On the other hand, leaving this unchecked might cause your graphics to appear chunkier when printed than they do on the screen. Try this option, and decide for yourself if the smoother print is worth the wait.

Faster Bitmap Printing

Because everything in HyperCard is a bit map, except for text in fields, it makes sense to leave this box checked. There are some printers such as high-end typesetting machines, that don't work well with this checked. If you have an Apple LaserWriter or other standard PostScript printer, however, this option works well.

Note: Faster Bitmap Printing must be checked if the orientation of the page is set to Landscape (chosen by clicking on the rightmost of the two orientation icons) instead of Portrait. HyperCard printing is slowed down considerably by the Landscape option.

Reduce or Enlarge

Although you can type any figure in this box, it has no effect on printing with HyperCard.

Other LaserWriter Options

In addition to the standard Page Setup dialog box items, you can set other options for printing to a LaserWriter. They are accessed by clicking the Options button in the Page Setup dialog box. Another dialog box, shown in Figure 5-3, appears, giving you more control over the appearance of your cards on the page.

When you check any of the options listed here, the page to the left of the check boxes (with the picture of the dog on it) changes to indicate which settings are currently in effect and how they will influence your printing.

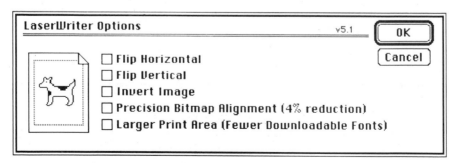

Figure 5-3.   LaserWriter page setup options

• **Flip Horizontal and Flip Vertical**   The Flip Horizontal and Flip Vertical options do precisely what they say they will, and the orientation of the little dog changes to illustrate this. You should choose these options carefully — HyperCard is graphically oriented, so doing this kind of flipping can cause printing to slow down a great deal.

• **Invert Image**   The Invert Image option also should be used cautiously. It causes all black dots on your screen to print white and all white dots to print black.

• **Precision Bitmap Alignment**   Most laser printers have a different resolution from the Mac screen (300 dpi on the printer, 72 dpi on the screen). Sometimes, therefore, text will not be positioned correctly with regard to nearby graphics. If you find that your printed cards do not match their appearance on the screen, try this option.

• **Larger Print Area**   The Larger Print Area option allows the printer to print more of a page, but it also reduces the printer's memory for fonts. You will use this option rarely with HyperCard. It is useful, however, with programs such as MacDraw, when you might want to print to the edge of the page.

If you have a printer other than an Apple printer, you might have some different options than these. The best thing to do is experiment with the different settings, printing one or two cards at a time to see how they work out.

Printing Cards

Which of the two commands you use to print cards depends on whether you want to print one card or several. Both the Print Card command and the Print Stack command are not available if you are using any of the Painting tools. The commands work only while you are using the Browse, Button, or Field tools.

The Print Card Command

This command, also available with the COMMAND-P key combination, prints the current card, using the current Page Setup dialog box specifications. The card is always printed full size, regardless of what enlargement or reduction you have selected.

The Print Stack Command

This command prints all the cards in the stack, in the order in which they appear in the stack. It doesn't matter where you are located in the stack when you choose this command; printing will start at the first card in the stack and proceed to the last card.

Print Stack brings up the dialog box shown in Figure 5-4. (It might look different, depending on how it was last set.) With one exception, this dialog box is the same whether you are using an ImageWriter or a LaserWriter.

The Print Stack dialog box is one of the most useful print dialogs of any Macintosh program. Probably its best feature is its display of the current card on the screen, showing how it will look on the page and reflecting the different choices you make. You don't need to do sample prints to find out how things will look.

On the negative side, this dialog box does not allow you to print a few cards in the stack; you must print all the cards. To print part of a stack requires some HyperTalk programming, discussed in Chapter 26.

The first three items on the dialog box set up the following standard parameters for printing the stack:

• **Manual paper feed** If this box is checked, you will be signaled to feed a new sheet of paper at the beginning of each page.

• **Darker printing** If you have an ImageWriter, this check box will appear below the "Manual paper feed" option. It is similar to the "high quality" or "best" mode that other applications offer with the ImageWriter.

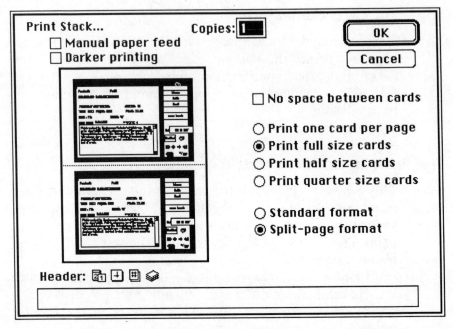

Figure 5-4.   The Print Stack dialog box with "Print full size cards" selected

• **Faster Laser Printing** This checkbox appears instead of the "Darker printing" checkbox if you have a laser printer. It speeds up the printing process with a laser.

• **Copies** You can print multiple copies of each page by typing the desired number in this box. However, using a photocopy machine, if you have one nearby, is probably a quicker and less expensive way to get multiple copies of the printout.

Down the right side of the Print Stack dialog box, there are some check boxes and radio buttons that allow you to specify the number of cards that will appear on the page and their format.

The first check box, "No space between cards," is useful if you are printing many cards on a page. It eliminates the border of white space that surrounds each card, thus allowing you to fit more cards on a page. It also blends the cards together, which gives some interesting effects, but you probably won't want it all the time.

Next is a group of radio buttons that allows you to specify the number of cards you want on the page. As you check the boxes, the graphic display of the page changes to reflect your choices. You can easily try these changes out to see how they work. Remember that as you make the cards smaller, everything on them shrinks, and some text and fine graphics are not going to look good. Figure 5-5 shows how the page looks with one card per page. Figure 5-4 shows how the page looks when printing full-size cards. Both these options print cards that are the same size; the "Print full size cards" option, however, puts two cards on a page. Figure 5-6 shows half-size cards.

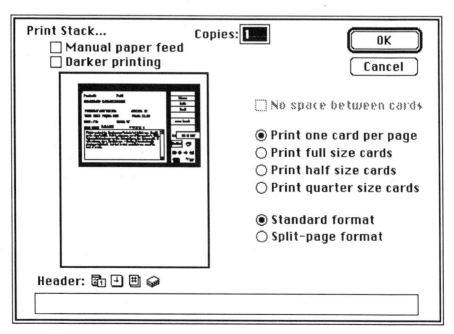

Figure 5-5.   The Print Stack dialog box with "Print one card per page" selected

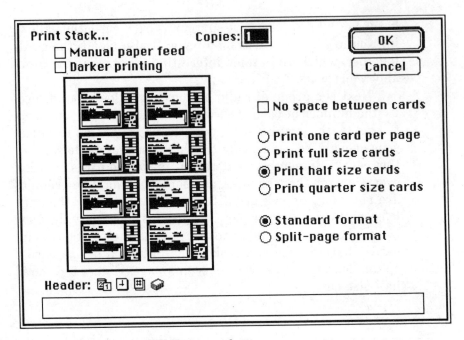

Figure 5-6.   Half-size cards

The last set of radio buttons on this dialog box allows you to choose between two formats for printing. "Standard format" prints the cards evenly spaced on the page, leaving enough room at the left for the pages to be punched and inserted into a binder. "Split-page format" is for sheets that will be kept in a smaller binder; you can fold them over, punch holes at the top and bottom of the page, and put them into a small binder without creasing the image of any card. Figure 5-7 shows the Print Stack dialog box with both "Print full size cards" and "Split-page format" checked.

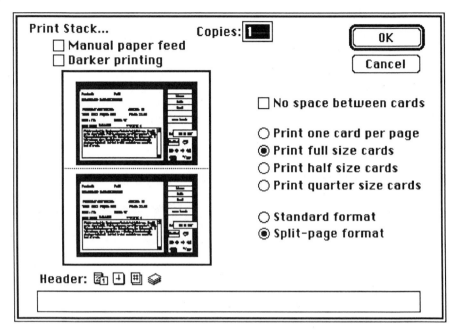

Figure 5-7.   Full-size cards with "Split-page format" selected

Print Report

You don't always need or want to print entire cards. As mentioned earlier, graphics printing can slow down the printing process, and if you just want data from certain fields, you've wasted a lot of time and paper in that printing. That's what Print Report is for.

The Print Report dialog box, shown in Figures 5-8 through 5-10, is similar to the Print Stack dialog box. It is divided into four parts.

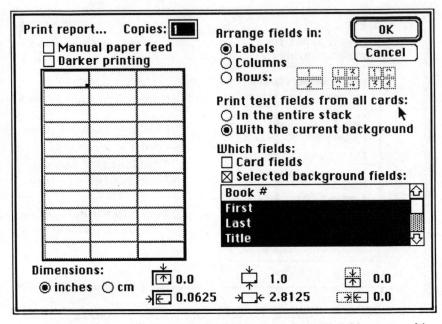

Figure 5-8. The Print Report dialog box with the fields arranged in label format

The top part allows you to specify the number of copies you are printing and whether or not you want to use the "Manual paper feed" option. With this option printing pauses after each page, and you receive a signal to insert a new sheet of paper. If you are using an ImageWriter, "Darker printing" is available. This is similar to the "best" quality printing that is available from other Macintosh applications. If you have a LaserWriter, "Faster laser printing" is available, which speeds up the printing.

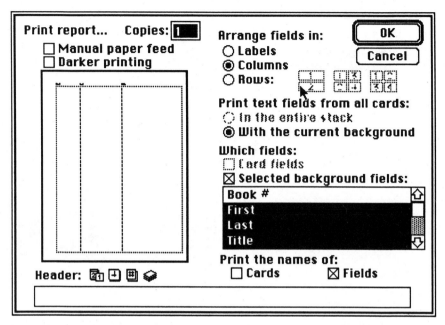

Figure 5-9.   The Print Report dialog box with fields to be printed in column format

Below these options on the dialog box is a graphic representation of how the page will look when you print it. Instead of showing actual cards, however, it illustrates where on the page your fields will appear and how they will be separated from one another.

The most important part of this dialog box though, is along its right side. The first set of radio buttons, headed "Arrange fields in" lets you tell HyperCard whether you want to print your report in labels, columns, or rows.

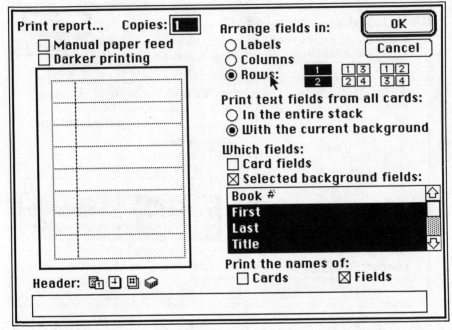

Figure 5-10.   Printing fields in row format from the Print Report dialog box

Printing Labels

Label printing puts selected fields onto areas on the page that are suitable for such things as labels. Although labels are usually printed to be used as mailing labels, you can also print labels for such things as file folders, floppy disks, or cassette or VCR tapes. The difference is mostly in the size of the labels and how they are laid out on the page.

As you can see in Figure 5-8, when you have clicked the Labels radio button, the image of the page to the left shows a number of rectangles on the page. These rectangles indicate how tall and wide the labels will be. The icons displayed at the bottom of the dialog box indicate the size and spacing of the labels. These icons and their meanings are shown in Figure 5-11. The distances shown can be measured in either

⬆⬇ **0.0**	distance from top of page
→⬅ **0.0625**	distance from left margin
⬇⬆ **1.0**	label height
→⬅ **2.8125**	label width
⬇⬆ **0.0**	vertical space between labels
→⬅ **0.0**	horizontal space between labels

Figure 5-11.   When printing labels, these icons indicate how labels will appear on the page

inches or centimeters. If you have a ruler that shows centimeters, it is more convenient to use this measure. Both inches and centimeters are given in decimal form, and it can be time-consuming to convert 3/16 inch to .1875.

Note: When the space between the labels is very small, it can be ignored. Set that space to 0, and measure the height of the label from the top of one label to the top of the next. Unless you are trying to squeeze a lot of text onto one label, the 1/16 inch between the labels has little consequence.

If you have purchased labels before, you know that they come in several formats. There are those that only have one label across the page. Known as *one-up* labels, these are typically a thin page that can be inserted into the tractor sprockets of a dot matrix printer. Labels also come in larger pages, with two or three labels across the page, called *two-up* or *three-up* labels, respectively.

As Figure 5-8 shows, when you first click the Labels radio button, the page is automatically formatted for three-up labels. Notice that the label in the upper-left corner of the page has a solid border and a small sizing handle in its lower-right corner. The the label in the bottom-right corner has a dark border, but no size handle. At the bottom of the dialog box you can see that these standard labels are 1 inch high and 2.8 inches wide. One-up labels, however, are 1 inch high and 3 1/2 inches wide.

Note: Label sheets for dot matrix printers are different than standard paper sizes; usually they are 12 inches high instead of 11 inches high. To fix this, use the Page Setup dialog box, and click the International Fanfold paper size button. Check the "No Gaps between pages" check box to indicate that you don't want margins at the top of the page.

   To illustrate printing one-up labels, take a look at the Address stack supplied with HyperCard. Because this stack stores names and addresses, you might want to use it to print such things as labels to send Christmas cards or new product announcements to the persons on this list. The Address stack contains one field that holds the name and address for the people on the list, so printing it should not be too difficult.
   The first thing you need to do is change the width of the labels. To do that, click on the size handle on the upper left-hand label, and drag it to the right, until the size shown at the bottom is 3.5 inches. As you do this, you'll see that the number of labels across the page changes. You now have two labels across the page. To get rid of the extra row of labels, click on the label in the bottom right of the page and drag it to the left until it disappears from the page. Notice how the measure of the horizontal distance between labels changes. When the label is completely off the page, release the mouse button. What is now the bottom label on the page has a bold border.
   To finish you need to make sure that there is no top or left margin on the labels—one-up labels usually don't have any. To set the top margin to 0, drag the top label to the top

of the page until the top margin indicator at the bottom shows 0. Drag it all the way to the left to get rid of the left margin.

Now check your work. There should be 12 labels down the left side of the page, there should be no space between the pages, and the top and right margins should be set to 0, as should the space between the labels.

In HyperCard report printing there is no way to print just one or two pages; therefore, when testing you should keep your hands near the keyboard so that you can cancel the printing quickly. It's also a good idea to do your test prints with plain sheets of paper and then superimpose those sheets over the labels to see how they work out. When report printing in general, and label printing in particular, several test prints may be necessary to get things to work out.

Two-up and Three-up Labels

To create these labels you follow the same steps as you did for one-up labels except that you must also adjust the space between the labels.

Selecting the Fields to Print

After laying out the labels, you need to select the fields to print. This is easy when printing labels from the Address stack. Because there are only three background fields, and you probably don't want the phone number and date to appear on the labels, click on the Name and Address field. This field will then appear on all labels.

If it is not already checked, you should make sure that the "With the current background" radio button is checked. Although there is only one background in the Address stack as it is shipped by Apple, if you have made changes to the stack, you will want to select the appropriate choice.

Printing a Report in Columns

When printing in columns, selected fields from the current background will be printed side by side in columns across the page. This is a standard report option used by most database and filing programs.

Figure 5-9 shows the Print Report dialog box with the Columns radio button checked. Notice that the graphic representation of the page shows vertical columns. The icons for the space between labels are replaced with a Header field for typing in information. The first icon inserts the date the report is printed. The second inserts the time. The third inserts the page number. The final icon prints the name of the stack.

Printing columns is a straightforward procedure. The first thing you need to do is select which fields you are going to print. The fields that you select will appear on the page in the order in which you select them.

Figure 5-9 shows a Print Report dialog box of a stack that was used to manage a personal library. Different fields were used to store the author's first name, last name, and the book title, and other fields were used for such things as publisher, edition, and year. In this report, however, only the author's name and the title of the book were printed, in alphabetical order by author name. How was this dialog box set up?

First the stack was sorted. Sorting, which is discussed in Chapter 18, requires at least a little knowledge of HyperTalk.

The Print Report dialog box was called up next. Since fields are printed on the report in the order they were clicked, the Last field was clicked first. Next, holding down the SHIFT key, the First field was clicked. SHIFT-clicking, you will remember, is used by most Macintosh applications to extend the selection. Had First been clicked without the SHIFT key, that field would have been selected, and Last would have been canceled. To select the final field you want printed, SHIFT-click on the Title field.

Vertical dotted lines appear on the page representation to show where each column will start. HyperCard will space those columns evenly on the page, based on the number of columns on the page.

To adjust the spacing of the columns on the page, you can drag the lines that appear on the page. In this example, because the authors' first names are usually much shorter than their last names, and the titles are the longest of all, you will want to drag to the left the second dotted line, which shows where the First field will appear, and then do the same with the Title field.

Suppose that a field is too long to fit in the space you have allocated. That may happen in this case because some of the book titles are very long, but don't worry. HyperCard will take care of this. Book titles that are too long will be wrapped to the next line of the report, starting where the Title field starts. This is a feature that is very hard to implement in some Macintosh databases.

To finish the columnar report, you can check the Fields check box below the list of fields, and the names of the fields will appear at the top of every page. If you check the Cards check box, a column containing the name of every card will be printed on the report. In this case, since the cards do not have names, it is not necessary.

Printing Reports in Rows

Row format is similar to label format in that information from each card is printed in a block. However, there are differences between the two formats.

Figure 5-10 shows the screen display of the Print Report dialog box when you have checked Rows at the top of the screen. A new set of icons becomes active, allowing you to specify the order in which your cards will be printed. Here is what each icon does, in order of its appearance on the screen from right to left.

• The first icon tells HyperCard that you want one field to be printed across the page, with each field below the previous one. It might seem that this icon indicates that only two fields will appear per page (as when printing full-size cards in the Print Stack dialog box). This is not the case, however, as you can see from the representation of the page that appears when the Rows button is clicked. One line will be inserted between each field.

• The second icon prints the fields in a manner similar to the newspaper-style or snaking columns that some word processors allow you to print. When formatting the page, HyperCard will print the cards down the entire left column, start again at the top of the right column, and so on to the bottom of the page. Unlike label printing, the width of the fields and cards cannot be changed.

• The third icon changes the order in which the cards are printed. Instead of snaking from top to bottom, the order flows from left to right. A card is printed at the left margin, the next is printed to its right, then the order flows back to the left margin of the line below.

Print Text Fields
from All Cards

The two buttons in this option allow you to specify whether the entire stack or just the current background is used when printing label or row reports. Generally, you will keep the "With the current background" button on to maintain uniformity in the report. Even when printing from the entire stack, you are only allowed to choose fields on the current background. Backgrounds in HyperCard are used to keep data that is similar together.

Which Fields

The two check boxes here allow you to specify whether or not card fields as well as background fields are to be printed. If "Card fields" is selected, then all card fields on all the cards will be printed; there is no way to choose specific card fields. If neither of these check boxes is selected, you will get a report, but it will be blank! This option is not available when printing column reports.

Print the Names of Fields

This option is available if you are printing column or row reports, but not when you are printing labels. When used for column reports, it puts the names of the selected background fields at the tops of the columns for those fields. When used for row reports, field names appear at the left edge of the card printing area and can be sized by dragging a vertical dotted line.

Print the Names of Cards

When this option is selected, the card name is treated exactly as if it were a field. When a column report is being printed, the card name becomes the first column on the page. When a row report is being printed, it becomes the first row. This option is not available when printing labels.

Header

You cannot print a header when printing labels. The header format is exactly the same as when printing stacks. You can type text into this field, and it will be shown on the page representation. Icons are used to insert the date and time of the report, the name of the stack, and the current page number.

Saving Print Setups

HyperCard saves your print setups, but only until they are changed the next time. For example, if you print a report one time with certain settings, the next time you print you will get the same settings even if you have changed stacks. It is not possible to save print settings in any other way, even when using HyperTalk.

One way to avoid losing your print setups is to document your settings, especially for reports. You can do this on paper, of course, or you can use HyperCard to help you by creating a card for each stack that contains print setting details. Another alternative is to use a keyboard macro program such as Apple's Macromaker utility, included with System Software version 6 and greater, or a more sophisticated program such as CE Software's QuicKeys or Affinity's Tempo. When using one of these programs, you can have the Macintosh record certain keystrokes and mouse clicks (which would include all the clicks that create the report), and call them up by name or by keystroke. Another alternative is to use Mediagenics' Reports! program, which adds more sophistication to HyperCard printing.

Stopping Printing

When printing has started, an alert like the one in Figure 5-12 appears. The page number shown will change, of course, depending on the page that is being printed. If you are printing a stack, you will also see the current card that is being

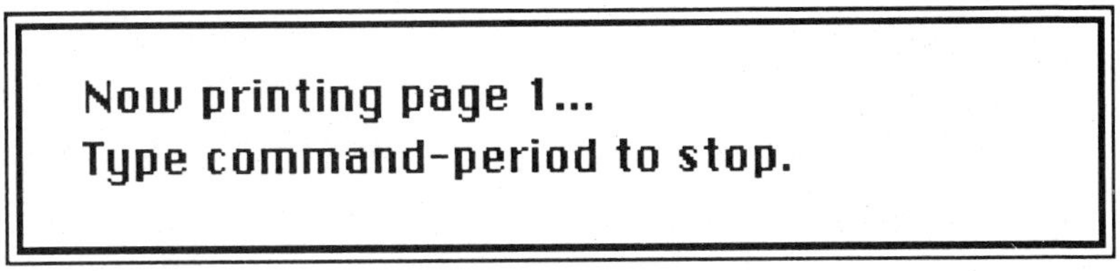

Now printing page 1...
Type command-period to stop.

Figure 5-12.   The dialog box that appears while printing indicates
that pressing COMMAND-PERIOD stops printing

being printed. Reports are handled a little differently: HyperCard scans all the cards in the stack and builds the report
before it starts printing.

Printing can usually be stopped by pressing COMMAND-
PERIOD, as it says in the alert in Figure 5-12. However, you
might not be able to effectively stop printing if you are using
the background print capability of MultiFinder, or if you are
using a print spooler. In these cases, you should use the desk
accessory or spooler application to stop the printing.

Sometimes pressing COMMAND-PERIOD once does not do
the trick. You might need to hold down the keys for a second
or so.

A Closer Look at Stacks and Their Elements

Working with Stacks
Backgrounds
Cards
Fields
Buttons
Scripts
Layers

In Chapter 3 you took a quick tour through some HyperCard stacks, and in the process you learned about some of the elements that make up this program and the stacks it creates. In this chapter, you will take a closer look at the elements of stack building—making new stacks, backgrounds, and cards and creating buttons and fields.

The way to learn any new program is by working with it. Hands-on experience is even more important with Hyper-Card than it is with other programs. In this book, you will not be taught how to build a particular stack; any stack you build by reading a book is of limited use to you. Instead, you will learn to use HyperCard's stack building tools along with many examples of specific scripts that are useful in a wide variety of situations.

Since this chapter deals with stack elements, your user level must be set to at least Authoring for the commands to work.

Working with Stacks

As mentioned in Chapter 3, a stack is a collection of Hyper-Card cards. It is the document created by HyperCard, just as a graphic is created by MacPaint and a letter is created by MacWrite. HyperCard stacks can be very large—sometimes too large to fit on most hard disks. HyperCard can, in fact, create stacks that are the size of a CD-ROM disk—over 500MB.

The process of building a particular stack depends on a number of things, but the primary factor is the use to which you wish to put the stack. If you are making a stack for your personal use, you can proceed in just about any manner that gets the job done and worry about the fine points as they occur to you. On the other hand, if you are creating a stack for others to use, the process becomes more complex. Issues of design, testing, and debugging raise their heads. The purpose of a button may be perfectly clear to you but unclear to others who were not involved in the design process. (Issues of designing stacks for other users are discussed in Chapter 9.)

Creating a New Stack

To create a new stack, use the New Stack command on the File menu. This command summons the New Stack dialog box shown in Figure 6-1. You can use standard Macintosh folder navigation techniques to place the new stack where you want it.

At the bottom of this dialog box is the "Copy current background" check box. If you check this box, the new stack will have a background design that is a duplicate of the one you are now in. This includes all graphics, fields, and buttons that are part of the current background, as well as all the stack and background scripts.

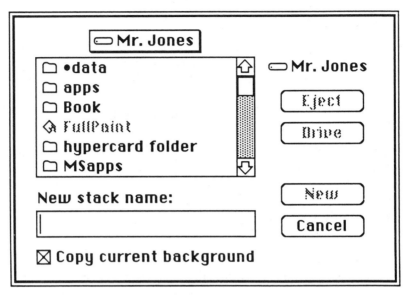

Figure 6-1.   The New Stack dialog box

A number of useful *templates* for stacks are included with HyperCard. These designs, included in such stacks as Card Ideas and Stack Ideas, are available for you to use in your own new stacks. By going to the card you want and using the New Stack command with the "Copy current background" box checked, you can modify the stack thus created to add your own functions. Undoubtedly, as Hyper-Card matures, similar collections of card and stack ideas will become available.

Saving a Copy of a Stack

If you are about to make some drastic changes to a stack, first use the Save Copy command on the File menu to make an exact duplicate of your stack. (This process is discussed in Chapter 3.) Since HyperCard is constantly saving changes you make to cards and stacks, using this command is the only way you can revert to a previous version should you change your mind. Use it often, and chances are you will save yourself some grief.

The Stack Info Command

You can get information about a stack with the Stack Info command, located on the Objects menu. The Stack Info dialog box for the Home stack is shown in Figure 6-2.

Stack Info might seem to be a small dialog box, but it gives you a lot of information about the stack. At the top of the dialog box you see the name of the current stack. You can edit this field: by typing a new name into this field you can rename the current stack. Typing a new name here does the same thing as selecting the file name in the Finder and typing a new name.

Note: You are not permitted to rename the Home stack. If you try to do so, you will get the dialog box shown in Figure 6-3.

The next thing this dialog box tells you is the location of the stack. This includes the stack's full path—the name of the disk it is on, followed by the names of all the folders it is in. The Home stack shown in Figure 6-2 is on the disk named Mr. Jones and is in a folder called Hypercard Folder.

The next two fields indicate the number of cards and backgrounds the stack contains. The standard Home stack contains seven cards, and two backgrounds. This stack contains twelve cards and four backgrounds, which shows that the stack has been heavily modified.

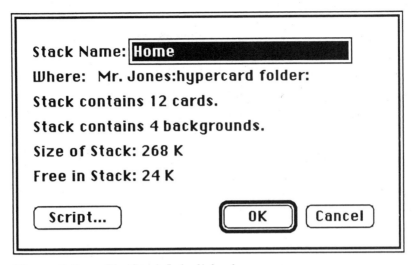

Figure 6-2.   The Stack Info dialog box

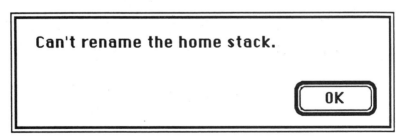

Figure 6-3.   The alert that appears if you try to rename the Home stack

The next field shows the size of the stack, rounded to kilobytes (1024 bytes), just as the Finder's Get Info dialog rounds the size of the file to kilobytes. The stack shown in Figure 6-2 is actually 273,566 bytes. When this number is divided by 1024, the result is 267.15, which is rounded up to 268K.

The "Free in Stack" field tells you how much free space is in the stack. As you make changes to a stack—adding and removing text in fields, changing buttons, drawing new pictures, and so on—the organization of the stack on the disk becomes less efficient. Using the Compact Stack command on the File menu rearranges the stack on disk and makes it work more efficiently. You should compact stacks often to keep them operating as efficiently as possible, as well as to keep as much free space on your hard disk as possible.

Protecting Stacks

To prevent other users from accessing your stacks, you can protect them by choosing Protect Stack from the File menu. This brings up the dialog box shown in Figure 6-4, which shows that there are several ways to protect stacks.

First, you can protect the stack from being modified or deleted by using the check boxes on the left side of the card. If the "Can't modify stack" box is checked, the "Can't delete stack" box also becomes checked (you shouldn't be able to delete a stack you can't modify). You can, however, modify a stack when the "Can't delete stack" box is checked. If the "Can't modify stack" is checked, a lock appears on the menu bar, just as if the stack were locked from the Finder. Both these boxes are checked automatically if the stack *is* locked from the Finder.

You can also make a stack accessible only to yourself by checking the Private Access button.

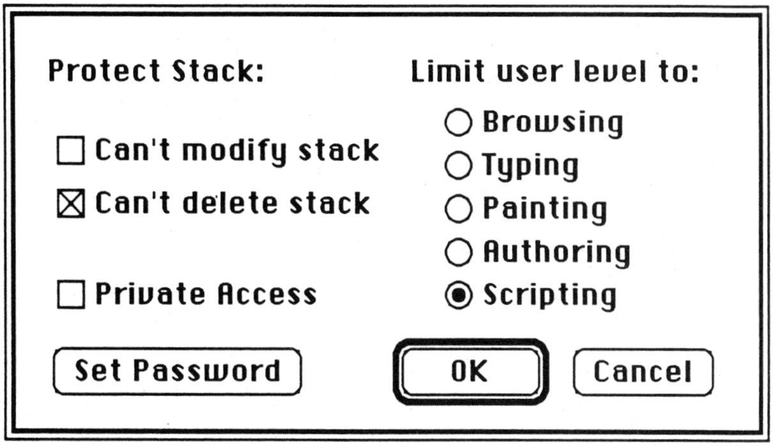

Figure 6-4.   The Protect Stack dialog box

The dialog box shown in Figure 6-5 appears when you use the Set Password button. You are asked to type the password twice so that any errors you may have made in typing it the first time do not become part of the password. Be sure to remember your password. Once a stack has been password protected, it is very difficult to recover it if you have forgotten your password. Although there are some utilities available to remove a stack's password protection, you should not rely on them.

You can also protect a stack so that you are allowed to work only at specific levels in that stack. To do so, choose the appropriate user level among the radio buttons at the right of the dialog box shown in Figure 6-4. If you then attempt to set

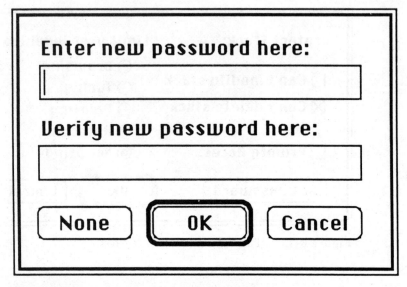

Figure 6-5.   The Set Password dialog box

Figure 6-6.   The dialog box that asks for the password

the user level higher than the protected setting, the dialog box shown in Figure 6-6 appears. You must type the password correctly to be able to change the user level.

If the user level is set below Scripting or if the stack is protected, the Compact Stack, Protect Stack, and Delete Stack menu items will not be visible on the File menu. You can, however, make them temporarily visible by holding down the OPTION key when you pull down this menu. If the user level is set below Typing, Compact Stack and Delete stack will be grayed out, but Protect Stack will work. If you have the correct password, you can then remove the protection from the stack.

Protected stacks can be annoying to those using the stack. One of the advantages of HyperCard is its openness. Experienced users like to explore a stack to find out how it works or make changes to make it work in other ways. You should be restrained about protecting stacks that you are distributing to others. By all means use protection to keep sensitive information from the eyes of others, but don't gratuitously protect stacks to hide your scripts. Since it is possible to remove protection from a stack, it can be nothing more than an annoyance to an experienced user.

Backgrounds

You will remember that backgrounds are templates that determine the appearance and form of all cards that share that background. When the New Card command is used, the card created takes on all the aspects of the current background—its graphics, fields, buttons, and scripts. Every stack has at least one background, and many stacks have several.

A new background is created, therefore, whenever you create a new stack. If you use the "Copy current background" option on the New Stack dialog box, the new background will have all the characteristics of the background you were in when you invoked that command.

There are two other ways to create a new background. First, you can use the New Background command on the Objects menu. This creates a totally blank background—a blank slate for you to make new background pictures, buttons, and fields.

Second, you can create a new background by pasting a card with the background you want into the stack. Go to the stack containing the background you want to copy, choose Copy Card from the File menu, return to the original stack, and choose Paste Card from the File menu. A new background will be created to accommodate the new card.

Cards that are part of a background do not need to be contiguous in a stack, a fact that might take some getting used to. When you create a new card, it is put into the stack after the card you were at when you created the new card, and it takes on all the characteristics of the background that was in effect at that time. However, you can copy the new card and paste it into a different place in the stack where the rest of the cards have a different background. As long as the background is the same as one that is somewhere in the stack, a new background will not be created. New backgrounds are created whenever you paste a card that has a different background design from any other card in the stack. The differences can be major—different fields and buttons—or they can be minor. If even one pixel on the background graphic is different from another background in the stack, a new background will be created.

Three important questions you need to consider early in the process of creating a stack are what elements of the stack will be placed on a background, which background will be used, and what elements will be placed on a card. As a general rule, if a button or graphic is to be used on more than half the cards in the stack, it is more convenient to place it on a background than it is to create multiple elements on cards. Graphics, buttons, and fields can be hidden on specific cards if they do not apply to those cards. (Chapter 9 addresses these questions more directly.)

You can navigate among cards on specific backgrounds with HyperTalk commands typed into the message box. These commands are variations on the "Go next card" and "Go previous card" commands. You can use commands such as "Go next card of this background" and "Go previous card of this background." (Chapter 18 deals with these commands in more detail.)

The Background Info Command

The Background Info dialog box, shown in Figure 6-7, appears when you choose Background Info from the Objects

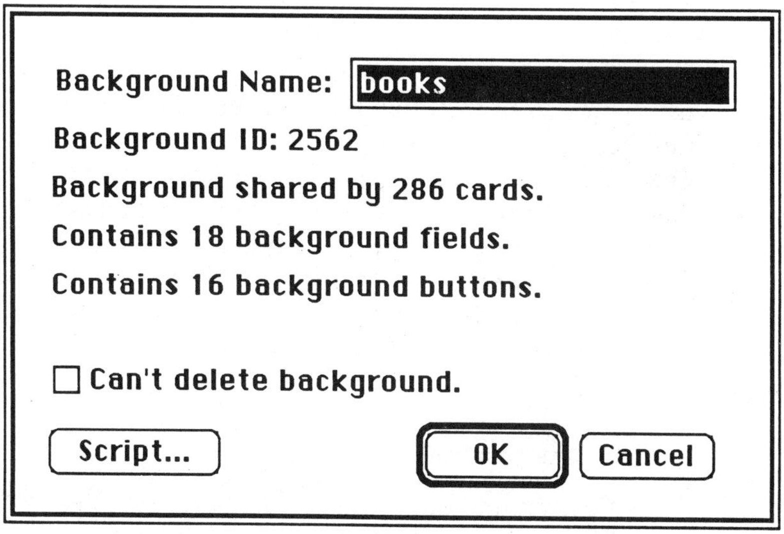

Background Name: books

Background ID: 2562

Background shared by 286 cards.

Contains 18 background fields.

Contains 16 background buttons.

☐ **Can't delete background.**

[Script...]   [[OK]] [Cancel]

Figure 6-7.   The Background Info dialog box

menu. This dialog box allows you to change the name of the current background, and gives you the following information on that background.

Background Name

The name of the current background is displayed in the "Background Name" field. It is not strictly necessary to name backgrounds; you can refer to them by background number or background ID. However, it is usually easier to remember names than numbers, and if you are referring to backgrounds from within scripts, it makes the script easier to debug.

Background ID

ID numbers, whether they are for backgrounds, cards, buttons, or fields, are assigned by HyperCard and not the user. They are four-digit numbers that HyperCard uses internally to work with objects. ID numbers appear to be created almost randomly; the method that HyperCard uses to assign ID numbers is not apparent, nor has it yet been documented by Apple.

Note: There is also a background number, even though it is not visible from this dialog box. A background is assigned a number according to how it appears in the stack. The background associated with the first card in the stack will be background number 1. When there is a new background, it will be number 2, and so on. You can get the number of the current background by typing into the Message box **The number of this background.** You can go to a specific background by typing **Go background 1**, for example.

Shared Backgrounds

The "Background shared by" field tells you the number of cards that are using the current background.

Background Fields and Buttons

The fourth and fifth fields in the Background Info dialog box tell you the number of buttons and fields that are on the current background.

Protecting a Background

When the "Can't delete background" box is checked, the background is protected. You might have noticed that there is no command for deleting backgrounds. You can delete stacks and cards, but not backgrounds. This button actually prevents you from deleting the last or only card that belongs to the background. If you attempt to delete the last card of a protected background, you will get the dialog box shown in Figure 6-8.

Cards

Cards, of course, are the major structuring element of Hyper-Card. Everything you do with the program is built around

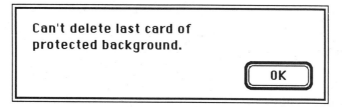

Figure 6-8.   If you attempt to delete the last card in a protected background, you get this alert

the card. You might develop applications in HyperCard in which the card nature of the application is not apparent or is even hidden from the user, but cards are always there. Accordingly, HyperCard gives you a wealth of commands for managing cards.

As you saw in Chapter 3, cards can be cut, copied, and pasted by using the commands on the File menu. These commands work in almost the same way as do their counterparts for working with text. The main difference is that you do not need to first select a card to cut or copy it; the card currently visible on the screen is the card affected by these commands.

The Card Info Command

As do the other Info items on the Objects menu, Card Info gives you information about the current card. In the dialog box in Figure 6-9 you can see the various fields that contain this information.

Card Name

Use this field to set or see the name of the card. In many stacks there are cards without names. In the Address stack, for example, it does not make any sense to have a name assigned to every card—the information on the card tells you what you need to know about the card. However, in a stack where there are cards that perform unique or specific functions, it makes sense to have a name for the card. An example of a card that should be named is a card that constitutes a menu for branching to other cards in the stack.

Card Number

The "Card Number" field shows the card position in the stack. Card 1 is the first card in the stack, for example. The card number is something that is affected by such things as sorting the stack and creating or deleting cards before the current one.

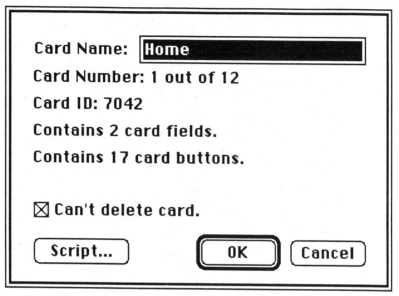

Figure 6-9.   The Card Info dialog box

Card ID

Like other HyperCard ID numbers, this is a number that is assigned by HyperCard. The card ID cannot be changed by the user and is not changed by inserting or deleting cards before the current card in the stack. It is something like the card's social security number, and the card carries it for life. However, when you paste a card into another stack, the ID of the card changes in that stack. If the card carried its ID with it to another stack, there could be a conflict of IDs when pasting into a stack that already has a card with that same ID. From your point of view, card IDs seem to be random numbers.

Whenever possible, access a card by its ID number. This is much faster than using the card name or number in a large stack. (This is discussed in more detail in Chapter 18.)

Card Fields and Buttons

If the card has fields or buttons that are unique to it (that is, they are not background fields or buttons), the number of these fields or buttons will be displayed in the dialog box.

Protecting the Card

When the "Can't delete card" box is checked, you are prevented from deleting the card with the Delete Card or Cut Card command. Most of the cards in the Home stack are protected because they perform specific functions that are necessary for the Home stack to work correctly.

Creating a New Card

To create a new card, use the New Card command from the File menu. The new card will be created and placed right after the current card. It will contain all the graphics, buttons, and fields that are part of the background of the current card.

Deleting Cards

You can delete cards with the Delete Card command from the Edit menu. You can also use the Cut Card command from the Edit menu if you want to later paste the card somewhere else.

There are three conditions under which HyperCard will not allow you to delete cards:

• **If the card is protected**   This was discussed earlier.

• **If the card is the last card in a background that was protected**   Use the Background Info command on the Objects menu and remove protection of the background.

• **If the card is the only card in a stack** You must delete the stack, either with the Delete Stack command under the File menu, or by dragging the stack into the trash from the Finder.

Fields

Fields are the objects that contain text in HyperCard. Text contained in fields can be edited and searched. Fields come in several types, and you use the type of field that suits the purpose of your application or the type of text the field will hold.

When the Browse tool is active, you can always see the outlines of all fields with the COMMAND-OPTION-SHIFT key combination. While these keys are held down, all fields are visible.

The Field Info Command

The Field Info dialog box, shown in Figure 6-10, includes the following fields.

Field Name

The name of the field is very important, but it is not required. Since there are rarely more than a few dozen fields on a card or background, there is no time loss when you refer to a field by its name (with large stacks, however, a small amount of time saved can have a large benefit over the long run). You can type large field names, but it is easier to work with field names that are small enough to fit into the "Field Name" field on the Field Info dialog box.

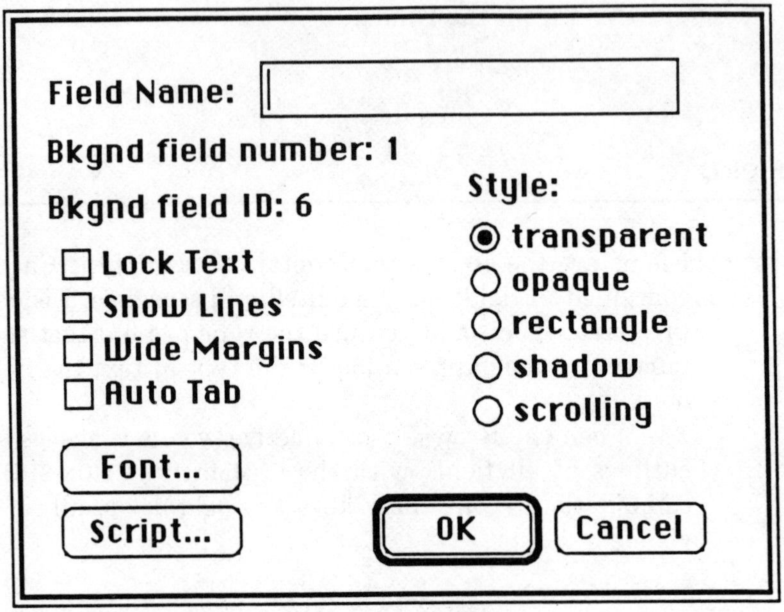

Figure 6-10.   The Field Info dialog box

Field Number

The next field on the dialog box indicates whether the field is a background or a card field. If it is a card field, this will read "Card field number," and if it is a background field, it will read "Bkgnd field number." Remember that a background field and a card field can have the same number— there can be a card field 1 and a background field 1—so it is important to be precise when referring to fields. If you refer to a field by number without specifying whether you are referring to a card or background field, HyperCard will assume that you are referring to a background field.

The "Field Number" field also shows the order in which your field is placed on the card. Remember that you use the TAB key to move from one field to another (except when Auto Tab is checked; see the discussion later in this section). The TAB key always moves you to the next field in order. You use the Bring Closer and Send Farther commands under the Edit menu to change the field's number (these commands are discussed later in the chapter).

Field ID

As with other ID numbers in HyperCard, this number is set by HyperCard and cannot be changed either directly by you or through HyperTalk. Unlike other ID numbers, field ID numbers are set in a straightforward way: the first field you create on a card or background has the ID of 1, the second has the ID of 2, and so on.

Lock Text

If this box is checked, the field is locked, and you cannot change the text in it—the cursor never becomes an I-Beam as it moves over the field. You can still copy text in the field to the Message box, however, by holding down the COMMAND key as you drag the mouse over it.

Show Lines

If this box is checked, dotted lines will show in the field where each line of text will appear. This is useful if you have fields that can hold a lot of text, and you want to enter text. It also works for a small field that is not a rectangle in which you want to enter text; it helps you recognize the field.

Wide Margins

Check this box if you have a field—usually a scrolling field— that must hold many lines of text. It increases the white space between the edge of the field and the text, making it easier to read.

Auto Tab

This function is part of HyperCard version 1.2 or greater. If the box is checked, you can press the RETURN key while on the last line of a field to select the next field, instead of pressing the TAB key. In earlier versions of HyperCard, if you pressed the RETURN key on the last line of a field, a new line was created and the insertion point was moved to the line below. This was disconcerting because if it was not a scrolling field, you could enter text, but you could not see the insertion point. Auto Tab has no effect on scrolling fields.

Field Styles

HyperCard supports a number of field styles that you use to achieve different effects in the text. Figure 6-11 shows the different styles of fields.

Transparent

A transparent field causes the graphics below the field to show through the field and the text to appear to be part of a graphic. Use this type of field if you want the text to appear to be part of the card, but still want to be able to edit the text. Text that appears against a black background, however, will not be visible. (A good way to do reversed text is to put the field over a black background and set the style of the text to "outline." Since outlined text will have white interiors, the text will appear white against a black background.)

Opaque

Opaque fields do not permit graphics to show through them. As shown in Figure 6-11, they will appear as white rectangles over the graphics.

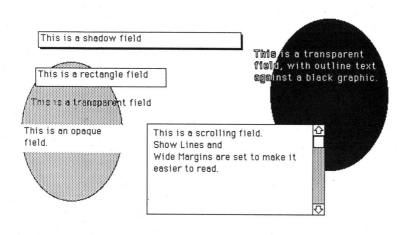

Figure 6-11.   You can use different styles of fields for different effects

Rectangle

With this radio button on, the field becomes an opaque field with a line showing the extent of the field. Rectangle fields better define the field on the card than do opaque fields and are best to use if you expect to enter text into the fields. However, too many rectangle fields on a card can give it a cluttered look.

Shadow

This type of field is similar to the rectangle field, except that it adds a drop shadow to the field to make it float over or stand out from the card. Shadow fields make excellent pop-up fields that contain information and can then be put away. Avoid overusing the shadow field; too many things floating over the card can be disorienting.

Scrolling Field

A scrolling field is similar to a scrolling window in a word processor. The scroll bars to the right of the field allow you to move through the field and read longer text. Auto Tab does not work with scrolling fields, although you can set it anyway. Scrolling fields that contain a great deal of text are also easier to read if Wide Margins is checked.

Fonts

Use the Font button on the Field Info dialog box in Figure 6-10 to set the font of a field. You can also set the font of any unlocked field by clicking on the field and using the Text Styles command on the Edit menu. You get the dialog box shown in Figure 6-12. (The fonts on your system will probably be different from the ones in the illustration.)

Remember that in HyperCard versions 1.2 and earlier, text styles are set for an entire field at once. You cannot simply set a separate style for a specified word or set of characters. This may change in future versions of HyperCard.

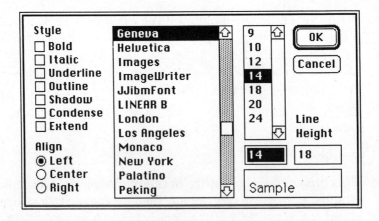

Figure 6-12.   The Text Style dialog box

Style

The check boxes on the left side of the dialog box set the style of the field. A field can have any one of these styles—for example, bold or underline. It can even have all of them, but you should be restrained about setting styles. Too many styles on a card or on the same text only make it more difficult to read. Use bold for items you wish to set off from the others on the card. As mentioned earlier, you can outline text by putting white letters on a black background by using the outline style.

Align

This sets the alignment of the text within the field. A field can only have one alignment, of course, so these are radio buttons. Generally, shorter fields will be center aligned; it is difficult to read fields with several centered lines.

Font

At the middle of the dialog box is a list of the fonts currently available to HyperCard. These will be fonts that are installed in your System file, but fonts can also be installed in the HyperCard application itself or in a particular stack. Click on one of the fonts to select it.

Size

The scrolling field next to the list of fonts shows the available sizes of the selected font. These are the actual sizes of the font that are installed in your system. Click on one of these sizes to select it.

You can also type a font size in the field below the scrolling list of sizes. If you type in a size that is not included in the list above this field, the text will be scaled by the Macintosh to the size you type. This can have varying results and might cause the text to appear jagged. The text will look best if you use a size that is a multiple of one of the sizes listed.

Line Height

This sets the distance in points (a point is 1/72 of an inch) between the lines. When you choose a font size, HyperCard will insert a value here, which you can change. Making it larger increases the distance between the lines; making it smaller decreases the distance.

One thing to remember about fields is that if you are at the Typing user level, you are able to change these fonts on your own. This is convenient because when you get a stack, you might not have a font that was available to the original creator of the stack, or you simply might not like the creator's choice of fonts. When creating stacks for others, do not make assumptions about fonts they might have installed, and do not limit the choice of fonts to the standard set that comes with the system. Alternatively, if you really need to have a particular, non-standard font, you can install it directly into the stack. (This is discussed in Chapter 31.)

Creating and Deleting Fields

To create a new field, select the Field tool and, while holding down the COMMAND key, draw a rectangle with the mouse. Double-click on the field to get the Field Info dialog box.

To delete a field, select the field and use the BACKSPACE or DELETE key, or use the Cut or Clear Field command under the Edit menu. If you attempt to delete a background field you will get this alert:

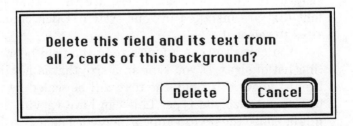

When you delete a field, all the text contained in that field in all the cards will be lost. You cannot undo this command, so be careful.

The Bring Closer and Send Farther Commands

To use the Bring Closer command, first select the field and note its number, then invoke the Bring Closer command. Each time you use this command, it adds one to the field number. Thus, a field 4 becomes field 5, if there are five or more fields on the card (remember that background and card fields are treated separately).

Each time you use the Send Farther command, Hyper-Card subtracts one from the field number.

An example might clarify this process. Suppose you are creating a stack to contain information about your library. You create fields to hold the name of the author, the title of the book, the edition, the number of pages. That's four background fields. After creating those fields, you realize you also want one to hold the name of the publisher of the book. When you create that new field, it becomes field 5. However, it makes sense to type in the name of the publisher after you've typed in the title, so you position the field on the card so that it appears after the title. But since the field number is 5, you are not tabbed to this field until after the field for the number of pages.

Here are the field numbers you have:

1   Author
2   Title
3   Edition
4   Number of pages
5   Publisher

You must change the number of the "Publisher" field to 3 so that you will be tabbed to this field after entering the book's title. Since you know the number you want to use, the simplest way to do this is to type **Set the number of background field "Publisher" to 3** into the Message box. The other fields will be renumbered to make room for the "Publisher" field. "Edition" becomes 4, and "Number of pages" becomes 5.

If you have a large number of fields, however, use the Send Farther and Bring Closer commands to change the field number. Select the "Publisher" field, and invoke the Send Farther command by using the keyboard shortcut COMMAND-MINUS (-). The first time you use it, the number of the "Publisher" field is changed to 4, the second time you use it, the number of the field is changed to 3.

The COMMAND-key equivalents of the Bring Closer is COMMAND-PLUS (+). Each time Bring Closer is used it adds one to the field's number.

These two commands also work to change button numbers, but are rarely used for this purpose because you don't often need to change the numbers of buttons.

Background Versus Card Fields

Use background fields when you want to place the same field on all cards in the stack or background. If you are creating a database or filing application, such as the Address stack, use background fields to ensure that the same fields, and thus the same types of information, are on every card in the stack.

Use card fields for holding text that will be specific to the particular card. A card that acts as a menu for a larger stack, for example, might have fields that explain the particular functions of the card.

Buttons

Buttons are the key to implementing user interfaces in HyperCard. Unlike other programming languages that do not run as part of an applications program, HyperTalk does not provide tools for implementing your own pull-down menus; it provides its own set of menus. Most of your HyperCard development will consist of providing buttons to perform specific actions. Therefore, it makes sense to spend some time discussing them.

The Apple *Human Interface Guidelines* include specifications for three types of buttons: normal (round rectangle) buttons, radio buttons, and check boxes. HyperCard supports these three types of buttons, and adds four more types: transparent, opaque, shadow, and rectangle buttons. Buttons are objects on the screen that the user clicks on to initiate certain actions.

Here are some general guidelines for working with buttons:

• The name of the button should give a clear, concise indication of what it does. You might have noticed in many Macintosh dialog boxes that buttons will often be named with the function they perform, where OK might have worked. In the standard Save As dialog box, for example, the button that actually saves the file is usually named Save instead of OK.

• If a button can be operated by pressing the RETURN or ENTER keys on the keyboard, then the button usually has a heavier outline than do other buttons. It is difficult to implement this on cards in HyperCard, but the dialog boxes produced by the Ask and Answer commands do allow this.

• A button virtually always gives you some sort of feedback that you have clicked on it, either by being highlighted (which can be automatic in HyperCard), by showing a change in the cursor (to a watch or other "busy" indicator), or by an audible beep.

• Buttons are always rectangular. (Although radio buttons appear to be round, they are in fact rectangular, and you are not required to click on the round part; you can click on the name itself.) There are times when buttons of another shape, such as round or irregular shape, would be handy, but they aren't provided for in Hyper-

Card. If you need a screen area of a different shape to act as a button, you can do that with several buttons that perform the same function, and are grouped together to get the approximate shape you need.

In most Macintosh programs, buttons are used primarily in dialog boxes—you rarely find buttons that are not part of dialog boxes or tool palettes. HyperCard buttons, however, work in ways not specified in the *Human Interface Guidelines*. Here are the types of buttons provided in HyperCard, along with some notes about how they are used.

Transparent Buttons

A transparent button is one that allows the graphics part of the card or background to show through it. Use this kind of button when you want it to seem as though you can click on a particular part of the graphic to initiate some action. Transparent buttons, like all buttons, can be located by pressing COMMAND-OPTION, which makes all buttons become outlined with dotted lines. The Apple *Human Interface Guidelines* include no specifications for working with transparent buttons because they are not part of standard applications. However, they are an essential part of HyperCard. Many of the buttons on the standard Home card are transparent buttons.

Opaque Buttons

An Opaque button is just like a transparent button except that it hides the card or background graphics that appear underneath it. Opaque buttons do not have borders.

Rectangle Buttons

If all buttons are rectangular, why have a special type for rectangle buttons? The difference between rectangle buttons and opaque or transparent buttons is that rectangle buttons have borders.

Shadow Buttons

Shadow buttons have drop shadows that make them appear to be set above the card—that is, to float above it.

Rounded Rectangle Buttons

Rounded rectangle buttons are the most common type of button used in Macintosh applications. They are used in virtually all dialog boxes; for example, Figure 6-13 shows the OK and Cancel buttons in the Button Info dialog box. The rounded rectangle button is referred to as a push button in Apple's *Human Interface Guidelines.*

Check Boxes

Check boxes act like toggle switches. Some check boxes are shown in Figure 6-13; both "Show name" and "Auto hilite" are check boxes. These buttons are activated when an "X" appears in them and are not activated when they are empty. Even if check boxes appear together, they are independent of one another—any of them can be on and any of them can be off.

Radio Buttons

Radio buttons appear to be similar to check boxes, but they actually function differently. As with check boxes, when the button is filled it is turned on, and when it is empty it is turned off. However, radio buttons should be in groups that are related to one another, and only one of them should be active at a time. Clicking one of them on turns another one off. You should not create a radio button that you turn off by clicking on it; the best way to turn it off is by clicking a different button in the set.

HyperTalk gives you no automatic help for managing groups of radio buttons; you need to write the handlers for this yourself.

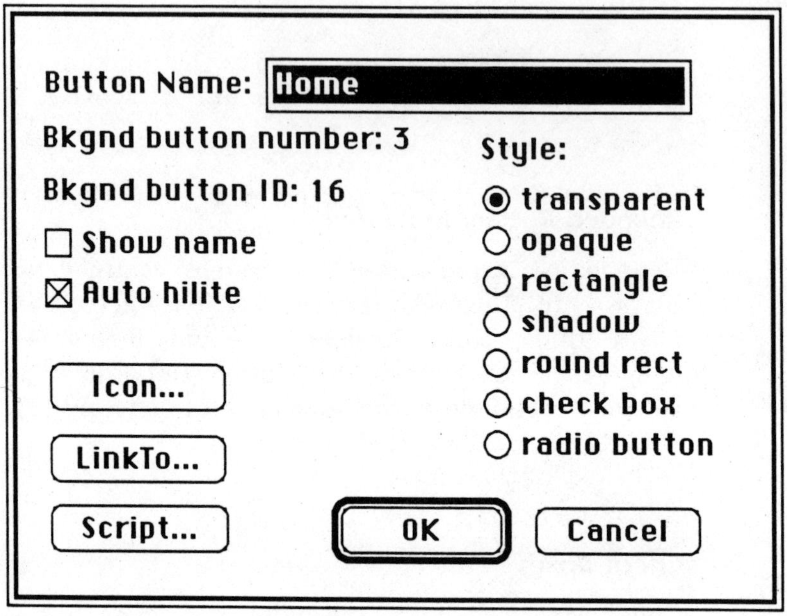

```
┌───────────────────────────────────────────────┐
│ ┌─────────────────────────────────────────────┐ │
│ │                                             │ │
│ │  Button Name: ██Home██████████████████      │ │
│ │                                             │ │
│ │  Bkgnd button number: 3      Style:         │ │
│ │                                             │ │
│ │  Bkgnd button ID: 16        ◉ transparent   │ │
│ │  ☐ Show name               ○ opaque         │ │
│ │  ☒ Auto hilite             ○ rectangle      │ │
│ │                            ○ shadow         │ │
│ │                            ○ round rect     │ │
│ │   ┌──────────┐             ○ check box      │ │
│ │   │ Icon... │              ○ radio button   │ │
│ │   └──────────┘                              │ │
│ │   ┌──────────┐                              │ │
│ │   │ LinkTo...│                              │ │
│ │   └──────────┘  ┌──────────┐ ┌──────────┐   │ │
│ │   ┌──────────┐  │    OK    │ │  Cancel  │   │ │
│ │   │ Script...│  └──────────┘ └──────────┘   │ │
│ │   └──────────┘                              │ │
│ └─────────────────────────────────────────────┘ │
└───────────────────────────────────────────────┘
```

Figure 6-13.   The Button Info dialog box

Button Info

The Button Info dialog box, shown in Figure 6-13, includes several buttons and fields that allow you to set the characteristics of buttons.

Button Name

This field shows the name of the button. You can type a new name in this field if you want to change the name of the button. It is not mandatory that buttons be named; you can refer to them by number instead, although it is probably easier for you to remember a name than an ID or number.

Background or Card Button

The next field shows the number of the button and tells you whether it is a background or a card button. If it is a background button, it will say, as it does in the figure, "Bkgnd button number," followed by the number of the button. "Bkgnd" is one of the many abbreviations you can use for "background." If the button is a card button, this line will read "Card button number."

Note: You cannot directly set the number of the button by using the Bring Closer and Send Farther commands under the Objects menu. These commands are explained earlier in this chapter.

Button ID

Like the field for the button number, this field shows whether the button is a card or a background button. As do cards and backgrounds, buttons have IDs that are set by HyperCard and are internal numbers for HyperCard's use. Unlike card and background ID numbers, however, these numbers are assigned in numerical order. The first button you create on a card or background will have an ID of 1, the second will have an ID of 2, and so on.

Show Name

If this box is checked, the name of the button will appear on it. The font used for the name will be Chicago if the button does not have an icon, and Geneva if it does have an icon (in Chapter 13, you will see that you can change the font of a button with HyperTalk commands). You generally should show the name of the button if it is a rounded rectangle, check box, or radio button. With the other buttons, the choice of whether or not to show the name depends on your stack or card design.

Auto Hilite

If this box is checked, the button will be highlighted automatically when the mouse is clicked on it. Actually, the process is more complex than this: the button turns black whenever you press the mouse button with the pointer inside the button, and the highlight is removed when you release the mouse button or when you move the mouse pointer so that it is no longer inside the button. You can test this by moving the mouse into a button and, while still holding down the mouse button, moving the mouse so it is outside the button. The highlighting disappears.

You won't always want to have "Auto hilite" checked for buttons. For example, large buttons will blacken a significant part of the screen and might be distracting when they are checked. Also, if you have selected any text with the mouse, that text will be deselected when the button is highlighted. This can be a significant problem if the purpose of your button is to work with selected text.

Generally, highlighting is used to give you some feedback that the program has understood and acted on the clicking of the mouse on the button. If the script inside the button is complex, feedback in the form of an action might be slow. Using "Auto hilite" provides you with an immediate sign that something has happened.

Note: "Auto hilite" works differently for radio buttons and check boxes. "Auto hilite" changes the button until it is next clicked, filling the radio button with a dot or the check box with an X to show that it is on. "Auto hilite," therefore, acts as a toggle.

Creating and Deleting Buttons

To create a new button, use the Button tool and, with the COMMAND key held down, draw a rectangle. The button will be selected, and you can then double-click it to get the Button Info dialog box.

To delete a button, click on the button with the Button tool, and then use the DELETE or BACKSPACE key or the Cut or Clear button on the Edit menu. You are not asked for confirmation of the button deletion. You cannot undo this deletion. It is usually wiser to use the Cut command, which places the button on the Clipboard; you can then undo the cut by pasting the button.

Linking

One of the most common uses of buttons is to link cards to other cards or stacks. This procedure is fairly easy and was explained in Chapter 4. Here is a brief review.

Click the Link To button on the Button Info dialog box. The dialog box will disappear, and this windoid will appear:

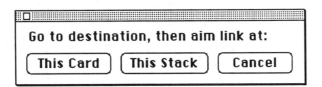

```
Go to destination, then aim link at:
[ This Card ]  [ This Stack ]  [ Cancel ]
```

This windoid is movable on the screen, allowing you to access other buttons or to see more closely what you are doing. You can use all the HyperCard navigation techniques, including buttons and the Find command, to go to the card or stack to which you want to link. Here's a summary of what each of the parts of this windoid does:

• **This Card**   This links the button to the card on the screen. The link will be to the card's ID number. Since not all cards have names, and since the number of a card can change depending on how the stack is sorted, the ID number is the best way to link. It is also faster.

• **This Stack**   This links to the first card of the stack on the screen.

• **Cancel**   This halts the link and returns you to the card containing the button you were linking. You can also cancel the link by clicking in the Close box in the upper-left corner of the windoid.

Once you have made the link or canceled, you are returned to the card containing the button you were linking. You can then click on the button to make sure it works correctly.

Background Versus Field Buttons

In general, it is clear to you whether a button should go on a background or on a card. Background buttons are accessible on every card that is part of the background. Use background buttons, therefore, when you want the button's function to be available on every card. You can hide buttons on specific cards by drawing card pictures on top of the background buttons.

Scripts

This chapter has avoided a discussion of scripting the various elements of HyperCard. You can do a lot with HyperCard using the Link To button on the Button Info dialog box if you simply want to create buttons that take you to different cards. You can also use some of the buttons in the Button Ideas stack to perform functions.

However, discussing HyperCard without talking about HyperTalk scripts is like talking about peanut butter without mentioning bread; there's just no point in it. To get to the real power of the program takes a knowledge of HyperTalk. The discussion of HyperTalk in this book begins in Chapter 10.

Layers

Throughout this chapter we have talked about backgrounds and cards. You can place buttons, fields, and pictures on either the background or the card layer. What you see when you are browsing with HyperCard is a combination of the background and card layers. This includes graphics, buttons, and fields for both the card and background layers.

Figure 6-14 illustrates the layers in HyperCard, with a reproduction of the Who's on Top card from the Help stack. Here are descriptions of each layer and its function:

- **Background picture** This is the foundation for the card appearance. Put onto this layer those graphic elements that you want to be part of every card, including the graphics that form the metaphor that the stack or background is using.

- **Background fields** These are also called shared fields in Figure 6-14. These are fields that appear on every card. Note that since background fields are on top of the background picture layer, opaque fields (such as scrolling fields, shadow fields, and others) will obscure background pictures.

- **Background buttons** These are called shared buttons in Figure 6-14. Background buttons are the next layer and are buttons that appear on every card. Opaque background buttons obscure any background fields and pictures below them; transparent buttons allow pictures and cards to show through them.

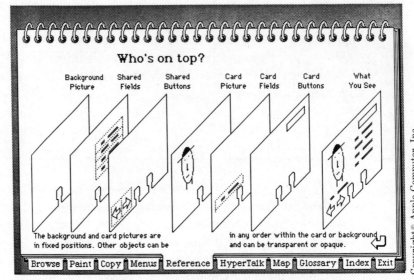

Figure 6-14. What you see on the screen is a combination of the layers that are present in HyperCard

• **Card pictures** Opaque card pictures obscure all background elements. This means that you can hide background fields and buttons by drawing a card picture on top of them. Background buttons will still respond to clicking and will be visible with the COMMAND-OPTION key command. However, you are less likely to click on them because they are hidden by a card picture. Text in a background field can be edited even if it is not visible.

• **Card fields** Opaque card fields obscure everything below them, including card pictures and background buttons. This is a good way to hide a background button. The card field will respond to the mouse click, not the background button below it.

• **Card buttons** These are the top layer in a HyperCard card. Because they are on top of everything else on the card and background layers they can obscure everything. If you have a background button or field that you want to hide, you can always use a card button.

Working with Layers

Sometimes it is hard to remember on which layer you are currently working, and you may find yourself creating buttons or fields on the card layer when you want them on the background instead. You can always see what layer you are on if the menu bar is visible. If background editing is enabled, the menu bar is outlined by bold hash marks, as shown here:

If you do create an object on the card layer that you want to be on the background, it is easy to transfer that object. If it is a button or a field, first choose the correct tool, and then select the object. Press COMMAND-X to cut the object from the card layer, press COMMAND-B to switch to background editing, and then press COMMAND-V to paste the object into the background layer. You can do this fairly quickly, even for several objects. You need to use the selection tool to select pictures before you transfer them.

When you want to select an existing picture, you must be working in the correct layer. With buttons or fields, however, you do not need to be precise. You can select existing background fields or buttons even while you do not have Background Edit active. It is only when creating them that you need to make sure you have Background Edit active; otherwise they will be placed on the card layer.

All elements of HyperCard work together to create an application. Pictures, discussed in Chapter 8, help you create a metaphor for your application. Backgrounds create standard card templates for making a series of similar cards. Fields contain information, and buttons are the tools that do something. What you see on the screen is a result of the combined function of all these elements.

SEVEN

HyperCard in the
Macintosh Environment

Copying and Pasting
Opening Applications
MultiFinder
HyperCard and Desk Accessories
HyperCard and Large Monitors
Networks and Locked Disks

The Macintosh gives you an integrated environment. With HyperCard you have the standard Clipboard to copy text and graphics from one program to another. MultiFinder adds the ability to have two or more programs loaded into memory at one time. Under the current version of Multi-Finder, however, only one of the programs is actually executing. (Communication programs, print spoolers, and network software, however, can be running in the background.) In this chapter you will see how HyperCard works with other programs.

In this chapter you will also do a little HyperCard programming or scripting, just as you did in Chapter 4. There's no reason to worry about this—complete scripts that work are provided. The worst error you can make with a script is typing it incorrectly. If you do make a typing error, Hyper-Card gives you its standard "Can't understand" error message. Just click the Script button to edit the script that caused the error and take a look at the script in the book to make sure it is typed correctly.

Copying and Pasting

As do virtually all Macintosh applications, HyperCard supports the Clipboard. Items that are cut or copied are placed on the Clipboard. When you paste, you take the item from the Clipboard and put it into the document. Consult your Macintosh manual for more details on cutting and pasting.

Graphics

HyperCard is able to accept a graphic from any other program if that graphic is no larger than a card. (Transferring graphics between HyperCard and other programs is discussed further in Chapter 8.) If the graphic on the Clipboard is larger than a card, the center part of the graphic is pasted at the center of the card, and those parts of the graphic that extend beyond the edges of the card are lost. You should remember, too, that HyperCard only deals with bit-map or paint-type pictures. You can paste pictures of other types from programs such as Aldus FreeHand, Adobe Illustrator, or MacDraw, but when the picture is pasted into Hyper-Card, it loses its object nature and turns into a bit map.

HyperCard pictures can also be pasted into other programs that accept graphics from the Clipboard.

Text

Cutting and pasting text is a straightforward procedure with only two unusual aspects you should remember.

First, HyperCard fields cannot hold more than 30,000 characters. If you try to paste more than this into a field, only the first 30,000 characters are pasted, and the rest of the characters are ignored. This shouldn't present much of a problem—30,000 characters is about 16 single-spaced pages, which is a lot to cut or copy.

Second, remember that when copying and pasting between applications, the Clipboard causes text style information to be lost. Again, this isn't much of a problem—HyperCard fields can only have one style for each field. However, information such as the font and style of that field is lost when you paste from HyperCard into another program.

Cards

HyperCard allows you to cut or copy cards to paste into different stacks or into a different place in the same stack. Using the SHIFT key with the Paste command pastes a small picture of the card instead of the card itself. This is also what happens when you paste a card into another application. You can see this for yourself if you have the standard Scrapbook or similar desk accessory installed in your system and you follow these steps:

1. At any card choose Copy Card from the Edit menu.

2. From the Apple or Desk Accessory menu, choose Scrapbook to open the Scrapbook.

3. From the Edit menu, select Paste. A new entry is created in the Scrapbook, and it contains a small picture of the card you copied.

This can be useful if, for example, you are documenting a HyperCard application in a program such as Microsoft Word or PageMaker. You can use these small pictures of the cards to give the user a frame of reference to the stack.

Opening Applications

HyperCard is able to open programs other than itself and, optionally, load documents into those applications.

You can open another program from the Message box by typing **Open**, followed by a space and the name of the program in quotes. Here are two examples:

```
Open "Word 3.0"
Open "MacPaint"
```

If HyperCard does not know in which folder you have put that application, you get the dialog box shown in Figure 7-1. After you choose the folder the program is in, HyperCard adds that folder to the list of folders saved in the Applications card of the Home stack. The next time you open that program (or another program in that same folder), HyperCard looks in that folder automatically.

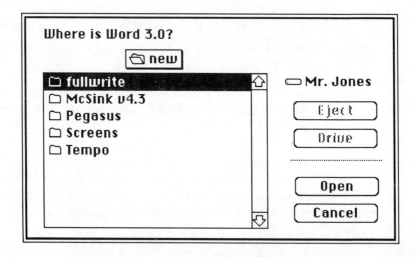

Figure 7-1.   The dialog box that appears when HyperCard cannot find an application that you are opening

Make sure you type the name of the program correctly. You must include unusual characters, such as version numbers and trademarks, that are part of the file name in order for HyperCard to find the program. For example, if you ask HyperCard to open "Word" when the name of the program on the disk is "Microsoft Word 3.02," HyperCard cannot automatically find the program. Capitalization, however, is not important.

When you quit a program that you have opened from HyperCard, you return to HyperCard, not to the Finder. This allows you to create a "front end" to your Macintosh programs with HyperCard. Instead of having to navigate through folders in the Finder to find the program or document you want to open, you can create buttons to open all your frequently used programs. Some of the first stacks that became available for HyperCard were so-called "Finder replacements," and they proliferated at an alarming rate.

For example, here is how you can create a button on your Home card to open MacPaint:

1. Go to the Home stack.

2. Choose the Button tool from the Tools menu. Find an empty spot on the Home card for the new button.

3. Hold down the COMMAND key and draw a new button.

4. Double-click the button, to get the Button Info dialog box shown in Figure 7-2. Type **MacPaint** for the name of the button, and check the "Show name" and "Auto hilite" boxes, as shown in the Figure 7-2.

5. Now you need to assign an icon to the button. Click the Icon button in the lower-left corner of the dialog box. You will get a new dialog box similar to the one shown in Figure 7-3 (the icons shown might differ in your system).

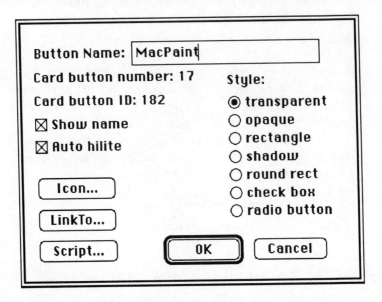

Figure 7-2. The Button Info dialog box

6. Scroll to find the MacPaint icon. When you find it, click on it. At the top of the dialog box, the ID of the icon, and its name, "MacPaint," appears.

7. Click the OK button to return to the Home card. The new MacPaint button has the MacPaint icon, and it is still selected.

8. To put a script into the button, double-click the button again, and then click the Script button in the Button Info dialog box. You are now in the Script editor.

9. Write the short script shown in Script 7-1 to tell this button to open MacPaint when you click it.

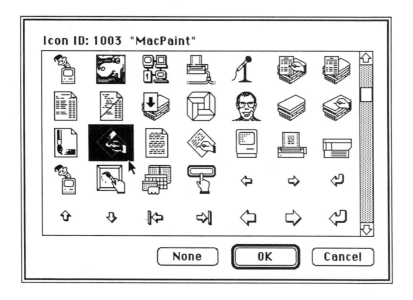

Figure 7-3.   The Icon dialog box allows you to choose an icon for a button

10. When you finish typing the script, make sure you typed it correctly, click the OK button to save the script, and exit the editor.

```
on mouseUp
    open "MacPaint"
end mouseUp
```

Script 7-1.   This simple handler opens MacPaint when you click a button

11. To use your button, choose the Browse tool and click the MacPaint button. If the folder containing MacPaint is not in the list of folders on the Applications card, then HyperCard asks you what folder MacPaint is in. Use standard folder navigation techniques to find MacPaint. That folder must be stored on the Applications card, and you do not need to repeat the process.

You can use similar techniques to create buttons for all the applications you use regularly. Unfortunately, the standard set of icons included with HyperCard does not include icons for programs other than MacPaint and MacWrite.

Opening Documents with Applications

Besides opening a program, the button you created can also open a document, just as you can click on a document in the Finder to open it. The command you use to do this is merely an option of the Open command.

For example, suppose you have a Microsoft Word file on your disk called Letter. To open this file with Microsoft Word, type the following command into the Message box:

```
Open "letter" with "Microsoft Word"
```

You will find yourself looking at the file Letter in Microsoft Word.

If HyperCard cannot find the document you are opening, it presents you with a dialog box asking you to find the folder that contains the document. It then adds that folder to the list of folders maintained in the Documents card in the Home stack. The next time you want to open that document, or any other document in the same folder, HyperCard does not need to ask you.

Printing Documents with Applications

With HyperCard you can select a document and print it using its application, just as you can in the Finder. Type the

Print command:

```
Print "letter" with "Microsoft Word"
```

This works in the same manner as the Open command. When printing is finished, the application quits and you are returned to HyperCard.

An Enhanced Button for Opening Documents

Earlier in this chapter you created a simple button for opening MacPaint. Script 7-2 shows a modified script for this button that allows you to open a document with MacPaint. To make this change to the button, choose the Button tool and double-click the button. Click Script on the Button Info dialog box to enter the editor. Select the line between "on mouse-Up" and "end mouseUp" and type in the new text. (Don't worry if you don't completely understand what is going on here. The Ask and Answer commands are explained in Chapter 25, and the If...Then structures are explained in Chapter 15.)

```
on mouseUp
   answer "Open with a Document or a New file?" with¬
   "Document" or "New" or "Cancel"
   if it is "Cancel" then exit mouseUp
   if it is "New" then
      open "MacPaint"
   end if
   if it is "Document" then
     ask "Type the name of the Document"
     if it is empty then exit mouseUp
     open it with "MacPaint"
   end if
end mouseUp
```

Script 7-2. This handler allows you to work with a new or existing MacPaint document

MultiFinder

HyperCard works well in MultiFinder. In fact, this book was written in Microsoft Word, running in MultiFinder with HyperCard. If you have 1MB of memory, you do not have much room for other applications (the Finder takes 160K of RAM), but if you have 2MB or more, you probably have more than enough room to run HyperCard and one or two other programs.

Memory Requirements

As shipped, HyperCard is set to use 1000K, or just less than 1MB, of RAM. This is a large amount—more than HyperCard actually needs. HyperCard version 1.1 works in 750K of RAM, giving you access to all its tools. HyperCard version 1.2 will run in 700K of RAM.

Here is how you set the amount of RAM taken up by HyperCard (or any other application, for that matter) in MultiFinder:

1. Make sure you are not running HyperCard. If HyperCard is currently executing, you cannot change the memory the Finder allocates to it.

2. From the Finder, find the icon for the HyperCard application. Click on the icon.

3. Choose Get Info from the Finder's File menu, or press COMMAND-I. You will see a dialog box like the one shown in Figure 7-4.

4. The item you want to change is the Application Memory Size, the last item in the Get Info window. Type in the new memory size and close the window. If you set this number to be lower than the number that appears in the Suggested Memory Size field, you will get the dialog box shown in Figure 7-5. Click Yes.

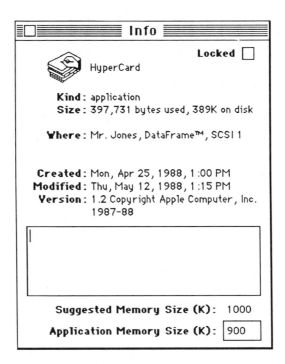

Figure 7-4.   The Finder's Get Info dialog box

If you set HyperCard's memory size lower than 750K for version 1.1 and 700K for version 1.2, your use of tools will be restricted. For example, you will probably not be able to use the Paint tools. If you set the memory size too low, you might not be able to use HyperCard at all. While you are encouraged to experiment, don't go too far or you might risk losing

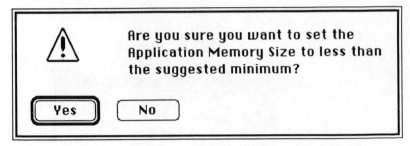

Figure 7-5.   If you set Application Memory Size lower than Suggested Memory Size, the Finder gives you this dialog box

data. Many HyperCard operations perform much better with a lot of memory than they do with only a little memory; the higher you set the memory allocation for HyperCard, the better it will perform.

Opening Programs with HyperCard and MultiFinder

If you are running HyperCard in MultiFinder, you can still open other applications, although things work a little differently. Instead of quitting HyperCard and then starting the other program, the other program is started in a separate "partition" under MultiFinder (see your MultiFinder documentation). You can then switch back and forth between the various programs that are running by choosing them from the Apple menu.

If you tell HyperCard to open a program that is already open, it does not try to open that program again, but instead it quickly switches you to it. If you try to open a program for which there is not enough memory, HyperCard does nothing; you must quit from one of the programs that is currently running.

Working with stacks that are on floppies is different when running MultiFinder than it is otherwise. When you run the standard Finder, you can insert and eject disks from the Open dialog box without worrying about them. When you run MultiFinder, however, every disk you insert is mounted on the Finder desktop. If you are looking through a number of disks for a particular stack, you should do so from the Finder rather than HyperCard's Open dialog box. This allows you to eject the disk by dragging it into the trash, which causes the Finder to forget about it.

HyperCard and MultiFinder should also break you of the habit you may have of not naming disks and keeping the Untitled name that the Finder offers for them. Remember that HyperCard remembers the last 42 cards you have looked at in the Recent list. If you have inserted several disks, all with the name Untitled, both HyperCard and you can become confused about which disk is actually being requested. It only takes a moment to name a disk when it is formatted or to rename it later.

For more details about working with MultiFinder, refer to the MultiFinder manual included with your Macintosh software or with the System Software Update package.

HyperCard and Desk Accessories

If you are not using MultiFinder, you may find that working with desk accessories and HyperCard is different than working with desk accessories and other programs. When you have a desk accessory open, you cannot switch back to HyperCard by clicking on the HyperCard screen and leave the desk accessory running in the background. You must close the desk accessory, using whatever method the desk accessory uses, such as a Close box on the title bar at the top of the window or a Quit command on the desk accessory's menu. Note that this is only the case if you are using a Macintosh with the regular-sized screen. If you are using a larger screen, you can move the desk accessory so that it is not superimposed on the HyperCard window and click on the HyperCard window.

If you are using MultiFinder, of course, desk accessories and HyperCard run in different "layers," and you can switch back and forth between HyperCard and the desk accessory simply by clicking on them.

HyperCard and Large Monitors

HyperCard works well with large monitors. Versions 1.2 and earlier, however, do not take advantage of the larger screen, placing HyperCard in an unsizeable window that is the same size as the original Macintosh screen.

Large screens are an advantage, of course, if you are using MultiFinder. For example, you can place the Microsoft Word and HyperCard windows at different places on the screen and switch back and forth simply by clicking on the windows. While running on a large screen, the title bar at the top of the HyperCard window shows the complete path of the stack in which you are working.

Another thing you can do with larger screens is place the various HyperCard windows—the Message box and the Tools and Patterns palettes—so they are not on the card window. This allows the entire card to be displayed without other windows covering it up. Additionally, the entire card is displayed even when the menu bar is visible.

Networks and Locked Disks

A major drawback of the earlier versions of HyperCard (prior to version 1.2) was their inability to allow several users to share stacks that were on a network server. Since networks are becoming an integral part of the Macintosh environment for office users, this was quite a shortcoming.

HyperCard's inability to work with stacks on a network stemmed from its inability to access stacks that were locked or were on locked disks. *Locked stacks* are stacks that meet any of these conditions:

- The stack is on a locked 3.5-inch disk.

- The stack is locked from the Finder (the Locked box in the Get Info window is checked).

- The stack is on a network server volume to which the user does not have write access. In TOPS, this is a volume mounted in Read-only mode. In AppleShare, this is a volume to which you have only read access.

- The stack is on a read-only device, such as a CD-ROM disk.

In versions 1.01 and 1.1, HyperCard insisted on having write-access to all stacks. Since HyperCard is constantly saving your changes, this was not unreasonable. However, read-only access to certain files is the key to using network servers and CD-ROMs. (HyperCard programming for networks and other locked disks is discussed in Chapter 34.)

HyperCard version 1.2 corrects this shortcoming, allowing you to access locked stacks. When you open a locked stack, it places an icon of a lock to the right of the rightmost menu on the menu bar, as shown in Figure 7-6. When this lock is visible, you can still do most of the things you are used to doing with HyperCard—push buttons, navigate through cards, find text, and select text, buttons, fields, and pictures for copying. However, when you try to change anything in a stack, you get the dialog box shown in Figure 7-7, which tells you that the stack is locked.

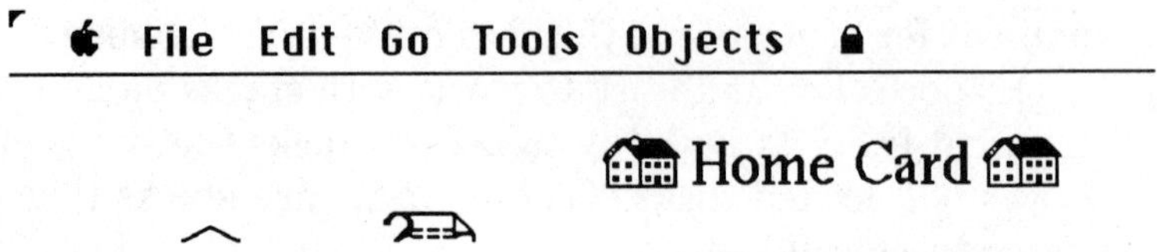

    ⌐ 🍎 **File   Edit   Go   Tools   Objects**   🔒

                        🏠 Home Card 🏠

           ⌒   ⌫

Figure 7-6.   When you open a locked stack, HyperCard puts a small
icon of a lock to the right of the last item on the menu
bar

The rules for accessing stacks on a file server are as
follows:

• If you have read/write access to the volume, you can
access the stack just as if it were on your own hard disk.

• If you have read-only access to the volume, you can
browse the stack and copy cards, buttons, fields, text,
and pictures from the stack.

• If you have read/write access to the volume, but are not
the first user to open the stack, it appears to you as a
locked stack.

Locked Stacks from the Finder

As a hard disk user, you should be backing up your disk frequently. It is too easy to lose data on a hard disk, through
error on your part or that of the hardware, to neglect this.
There are many fine backup programs for the Macintosh
that allow you to back up only those files that have been
changed since the last backup. This is called *incremental
backup*. One of the annoying features of HyperCard, however,
is that it changes every stack you look at, so that those stacks

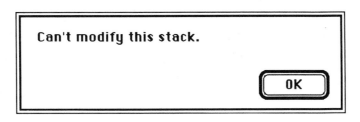

Can't modify this stack.

OK

Figure 7-7.   This dialog box appears if you attempt to change something in a locked stack

also need to be backed up every time you do the incremental
backup. For example, HyperCard changes the modification
date of the Help stack every time you look at that stack. If
you have a lot of stacks, this can mean a lot more backing up
than you are used to.

If you have stacks that you look at or browse frequently
without changing, you should lock them from the Finder.
This ensures that HyperCard does not change them, and they
won't need to be backed up every time you look at them. To
do this, select the stack while in the Finder (if you are using
MultiFinder, make sure that you do not have this stack open
in HyperCard), and choose Get Info from the Finder's File
menu. In the upper-right corner of this window, there is a
check box labeled Locked. Check this check box to lock the
stack.

It is a good idea to do this to the Help stack. It prevents
you from inadvertently altering this stack and will save you
from having to back up that stack each time you browse in it.

Painting
with HyperCard

E
I
G
H
T

Since its inception, the Macintosh has been a graphics computer. One of the first two programs for the machine was MacPaint, which was written by the creator of HyperCard, Bill Atkinson. Graphics tools have increased in sophistication since then to include such things as special curve tools, PostScript output, and more. Painting or drawing tools are now common in many Macintosh programs, from the standard drawing utilities to filing programs, desktop publishing programs, and even word processors.

HyperCard features a rich set of painting tools that work in much the same manner as they do in MacPaint. (MacPaint set the standard for painting programs, so others will work much the same.) If you are experienced with other painting programs, you will have little trouble with HyperCard.

The Purposes of Graphics in HyperCard

Graphics exist in HyperCard for several reasons. At perhaps their most basic level, HyperCard graphics are used to define or reinforce the metaphor of the stack. Examples abound in the sample stacks: a stack such as Address or Datebook uses graphics on the cards to make the purpose of the stack readily apparent from its appearance.

Another use for graphics is when graphics are the subject of the stack. An example is the Clip Art stack distributed by Apple. In this stack, the card graphics are the data being stored. Text fields contain descriptors for each graphic, allowing you to search for a specific graphic item. With standard Macintosh graphics tools—the lasso or the selection rectangle—these graphics can be copied for use in other HyperCard stacks or other Macintosh applications.

Another use for Macintosh graphics, related to the previous example, is similar to the use of graphics in books or references. Stacks are available with such varied topics as maps of the stars and lessons on anatomy. In both these cases and in dozens more, graphics are the *raison d'être* of the stack. This chapter contains only a few tips about the uses of graphics (there are many books that cover the subject in detail). This chapter discusses the rich set of tools that Hyper-Card gives you to create graphics; it is up to you to experiment with them.

The Two Layers of Graphics

Chapter 6 showed that HyperCard divides the elements of a card into two classes: background and card objects. Remember that background buttons and fields appear on all the cards that share that background, while card buttons and fields only appear on a particular card. So it is with graphics. Things drawn on a card while Edit Background is in effect appear on all the cards that share that background. Things drawn on a card when Edit Background is not in effect appear on that card only. This is how the Clip Art stack is composed: the background graphics include the frame around the card graphics, and the Clip Art itself is implemented as card graphics.

Figure 8-1 shows the Clip Art stack, with a drawing of Andy Capp in the card graphics. The Edit menu is pulled down to show that Edit Background is not selected. This

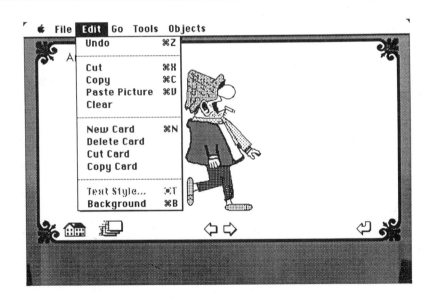

Figure 8-1.   A card from the Clip Art stack, with an added drawing of Andy Capp

figure shows the elements of both card and background layers. Figure 8-2 shows the same screen, but with Edit Background checked. This figure shows which parts of this card belong to the background graphics. The stripes visible on the menu bar are another indication that you are editing the background layer.

You can display and hide the background and card layers in several different ways. When Background on the Edit menu is checked, you are operating on the background picture. Only the background layer is visible, and the hash marks on the menu bar tell you that you are on that layer. When this item is not checked, there are no hash marks on the menu bar, and you are working on the card layer. If you

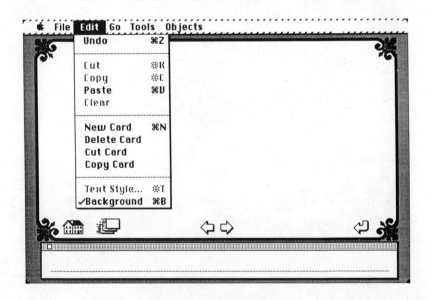

Figure 8-2. The same card with background editing in effect, showing that the drawing of Andy Capp contained on the card layer has disappeared

are using HyperCard 1.2 or greater, however, you can hide either the background or the card layer. Type **Hide background picture** into the message box to hide that picture. This might help you to avoid confusion, but you also must make sure the two images will mesh when the background picture is shown. Type the command **Show background picture** into the Message box to make it visible. If you are working on the background picture, press the OPTION-D key combination to see the card picture quickly.

Whenever you are drawing in HyperCard, therefore, you must decide whether you want the drawing to be present on all the cards in the stack (the background) or only on specific cards. The distinction is important, and deciding how you want your stack to look is an important step in the drawing process.

Setting the User Preference Level

Chapter 4 discussed the Home stack and the User Preferences card that is part of the Home stack. You will remember that the User Preferences card, shown in Figure 8-3, allows you to set the level at which you want to use HyperCard.

To use any of HyperCard's paint tools, the user level must be set to at least the painting level; otherwise none of the drawing tools will be available to you.

The Tools Palette

If you have ever used any Macintosh painting programs, you will see that HyperCard's tools work in much the same way as the tools in other programs. Even if you are familiar with those tools, however, it would be profitable to take a look at this section. HyperCard enhances the operation of standard painting tools in several interesting ways.

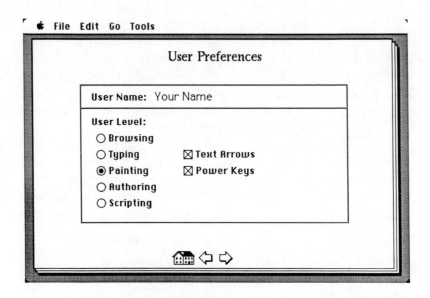

Figure 8-3.   The User Preferences card from the Home stack

First, a note about the Tools palette itself would be helpful. As discussed in Chapter 3, HyperCard includes a new
feature of pull-down menus to the Macintosh: tear-off palettes. When you pull down one of these tear-off palettes, or
windoids, you can keep dragging past the bottom of the
palette. An outline of the palette follows your pointer around
the screen. Release the mouse button, and the palette remains
where you let go. This is a useful feature, especially when you
are using the graphics tools. If you frequently switch back
and forth between the various tools, you can position the
windoid so it is easily accessible to you without having to
move the mouse pointer all the way to the top of the screen.
When any of the painting tools are in effect, you can also tear
off the Patterns palette. Pressing the TAB key with the Patterns palette visible hides it; pressing TAB again shows the

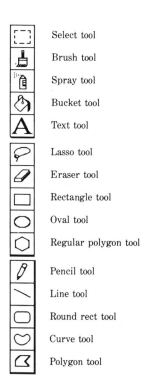

Select tool

Brush tool

Spray tool

Bucket tool

Text tool

Lasso tool

Eraser tool

Rectangle tool

Oval tool

Regular polygon tool

Pencil tool

Line tool

Round rect tool

Curve tool

Polygon tool

Figure 8-4.   The painting tools and their names

palette in the same position you last had it. Figure 8-4 shows all the HyperCard painting tools, along with their names. The top row of the Tools palette contains other tools—for browsing and working with buttons and fields—that are discussed in Chapter 3 and elsewhere in this book.

You can easily switch back to the Browse tool with the COMMAND-TAB key combination. Table 8-1 shows the effect various modifier keys have on the Paint tools.

The following sections discuss each tool individually.

Tool	Double Click*	SHIFT	OPTION	COMMAND
Brush	Chooses brush shape	Constrains to line		Erases
Spray		Constrains to line		Erases
Bucket				
Text	Chooses text style			
Lasso	Lassoes entire picture	Constrains movement of selection	Copies selection	Selects enclosed picture
Eraser	Erases entire picture	Constrains to line		Erases with white paint
Rectangle	Toggles Draw Filled	Constrains to square	Creates patterned border	No border**
Oval	Toggles Draw Filled	Constrains to circle	Creates patterned border	No border**
Regular Polygon	Chooses number of sides	Constrains rotation to 15°	Creates patterned border	No border**

Table 8-1.   Effect of Combining Paint Tools with Various Keys

Tool	Double Click*	SHIFT	OPTION	COMMAND
Pencil	Toggles Fat Bits	Constrains to line		Toggles Fat Bits
Rounded Rectangle	Toggles Draw Filled	Constrains to square	Creates patterned border	No border**
Curve	Toggles Draw Filled		Creates patterned border	No border**
Polygon	Toggles Draw Filled	Constrains angles to 15° increments	Creates patterned border	No border**

*To double-click on a tool, the Tools palette must be torn off
**If Draw Filled is checked, holding down the OPTION key means that there is no black border to the shape

Table 8-1.   Effect of Combining Paint Tools with Various Keys
(*continued*)

The Select Tool

The Select tool

is used to select rectangular areas of a picture. Once it is selected, you can perform many operations on the selection, including copying and cutting, and the various transformations that are shown on the Paint menu. To select an area of a picture, click on one corner of it, drag diagonally, and release the mouse. "Marching ants" will appear on the borders of the rectangle that you created. To select the entire card, double-click on the Select tool on the torn-off Tools palette.

If you press the COMMAND key as you drag, the rectangle will shrink to the smallest possible size that will hold the picture you selected. If you press the OPTION key as you drag, the Select tool will switch to the Lasso tool when you release the mouse, and only black pixels will be selected. You can perform the equivalent action with the S Power key, which is discussed later in this chapter. To select the entire picture, double-click on the Select tool on the torn-off Tools palette. The Select tool operates on only one layer of a HyperCard card at a time—either the background or the card layer.

Once you have selected a portion of a picture, you can move that selection by positioning the mouse on the inside of the rectangle and dragging with the mouse. Pressing the OPTION key while dragging makes a copy of the selection. Pressing the SHIFT key constrains the movement of the drag along a horizontal or vertical line. You can make multiple copies of the selection by pressing the COMMAND-OPTION key combination while dragging. To change the size of the selection, press COMMAND while dragging from a corner. If you press SHIFT while dragging from a corner, the original proportions of the selection will be maintained; otherwise you will distort the image while changing its size. Press COMMAND while dragging from a horizontal edge to change the size of the object on the horizontal axis. From a vertical edge, it changes the vertical size of the object.

The Brush Tool

The Brush tool

works in a very straightforward manner. Select the Brush tool, position the brush icon on the screen where you want to start painting, and drag the mouse around with the button depressed. Where you move the mouse, a trail of paint is left, using the currently selected pattern.

You can choose a different size and shape for the paint

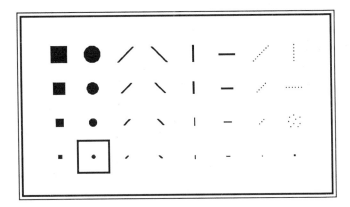

Figure 8-5.   Double-clicking on the brush or selecting Brush Shape
from the Options menu brings up this window

brush by double-clicking on it, or with the Brush Shape item
on the Options menu, which brings up the window shown in
Figure 8-5.

You can paint in a different pattern by selecting one
from the Patterns palette. Note that the Patterns palette is a
tear-off menu, like the Tools palette. Tear it off, and position
it in an out-of-the-way spot on the screen if you are going to
be switching patterns often.

Pressing COMMAND while painting with the brush erases
(turns black pixels to white) whatever the brush passes over.
Pressing the SHIFT key while painting constrains the brush
movements to a straight line.

The Spray Tool

The Spray tool

emulates a can of spray paint, as its icon suggests. It sprays the current pattern onto the screen where you click. Repeatedly spraying at the same location without moving the mouse does nothing. Holding down the mouse button and moving the Spray tool over a small area gradually fills in the area with the sprayed pattern.

Like the Brush tool, the Spray tool erases when the COMMAND key is pressed while spraying. Using the SHIFT key constrains the tools movements to a line.

The Bucket Tool

The Bucket tool

fills solid black and enclosed white areas with the current pattern. Double-clicking on this tool on the torn-off Tools palette makes the Patterns palette appear and disappear.

Figure 8-6 shows an enlarged view of the Bucket tool. This tool's hot spot—the point from which paint is poured— is at the end of the paint that is dripping down out of the bucket. When you click with the Bucket tool, make sure that the hot spot is inside the enclosed area you want to paint; otherwise you can end up with a mess. When using the

Figure 8-6.   An enlarged view of the Bucket Tool

Bucket tool, it is a good idea to keep your left hand poised at the keyboard. You are thus prepared to use the Undo keystrokes—COMMAND-Z or ESC—to quickly reverse any actions that might have resulted from paint spilling into unwanted areas.

Figure 8-7 shows three examples of work done with the Bucket tool. In the first example, the state of Washington has been painted gray by dumping paint into that enclosed area. In the second example, a black oval has been painted gray by clicking inside it. This illustrates that the Bucket tool can be used to paint black as well as enclosed white areas in a different pattern. If the Bucket tool's hot spot is on a black pixel when you click on it, all adjacent black pixels will be replaced by the new pattern. If the hot spot is on a white area, all white pixels enclosed by black pixels will be painted.

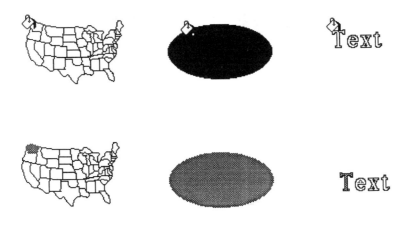

Figure 8-7.   The Bucket tool can fill enclosed white areas and enclosed black areas

The third example in Figure 8-7 shows how you can use the bucket tool with outlined Paint text to achieve unusual effects.

When using the Bucket tool, make sure that the area you are painting is indeed enclosed. Any leaks or gaps in the outline cause the paint to overflow the image and can have disastrous results (remember the Undo key!). Check your figures with Fat Bits to make sure they are enclosed—it is sometimes hard to tell with full-sized pictures. (See the discussion of Fat Bits in the section "Paint Menus" later in this chapter.)

Figure 8-8 illustrates the consequences of not checking for holes in the outline. The "before" figure of the car at the top of this figure shows a hole in the lower-left corner of the

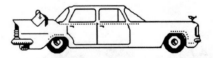

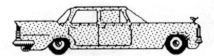

Figure 8-8.   Since there is a gap in the border surrounding the window, paint leaks into it

front door window. The "after" picture shows that that window was indeed painted with the pattern when the bucket was dumped.

The Text Tool

The Text tool

A

is used for typing text into the paint layer of the card. (The differences between Paint text and Field text are discussed later in this chapter.) To use this tool, select it and click where you want the text to appear. As long as you have not clicked at another location with the mouse, you can edit the text using the DELETE or BACKSPACE key at the upper-right portion of the keyboard. Pressing either of these keys deletes a character to the left of the insertion point. The RETURN key moves the cursor to the next line and places it directly under the first character typed. You cannot otherwise select text.

When you are using the Text tool and then click somewhere else on the screen or change tools, the text that you typed becomes frozen—you cannot go back and change that text. The pixels that make up that text blend into the array of bits that form the picture, and you must use other paint tools to change the text.

You can set various text attributes by choosing Text Style from the Edit menu, by using its keyboard shortcut COMMAND-T, or by double-clicking on the Text tool on the torn-off Tools palette. The dialog box shown in Figure 8-9 appears when you set the text styles of either fields or buttons.

Along the left side of this dialog box is a column of check boxes that allow you to set the style of the text. You can check as many styles as you want. If none of these styles are checked, the text style is plain. The radio buttons below these style check boxes allow you to select the alignment of the text. If Align Left is on, the left edge of the text will be aligned with the spot at which you clicked the mouse with

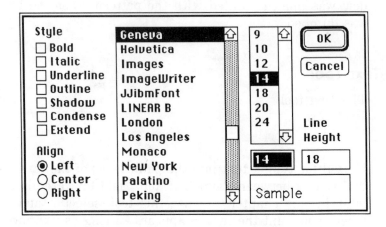

Figure 8-9.   The Text Styles dialog box

the Text tool. If Align Right is on, the right edge of typed text will be so aligned. If Align Center is on, typed text will be centered about this point.

The scrolling list box in the middle of the dialog box shows the names of all the fonts that are currently installed in your system. Clicking on a font name chooses that font. The scrolling list to the right of the list of fonts shows the font sizes (in points) that are currently installed. You can either click on one of these sizes or type the size in the field below this list. While it is possible to type a size that is not shown in the list, the resulting graphic will not look as good as it will when you are using one of the installed sizes. Hyper-Card will have to use one of the installed sizes and scale the text to fit in the specified size.

To the right of the "Size" field is the "Line Height" field. The number in this field represents the number of points between one base line of text and the next. The default value shown in Figure 8-9 is four points more than the size of the text. Typing in a larger figure puts more room between the lines of text; typing in a smaller figure moves the lines of text closer together. If you enter a figure that is smaller than the text size, then the text size is used. (For example, if you are using 14-point type and type in a line height of 10, a line height of 14 is used, and this number is placed in the dialog box.)

Another feature of this dialog box is the sample text shown in a small field below the "Text Size" and "Line Height" fields. The word "Sample" appears here, shown in the currently specified font, style, and size.

Changes to the text style affect text you are currently typing (provided you have not clicked anywhere else with the Text tool). They also remain in effect until you change them again, or until you quit and restart HyperCard.

Note: With the Text tool, you cannot select different parts of text to format. These changes affect all the text currently being typed.

When you type with the Text tool, HyperCard is interpreting the characters you type as text, so the normal paint power keys do not work. If you wish to select all the current text, press COMMAND-S. After selecting the text (remember, it is selected as graphics, not text), other power keys work.

The Lasso Tool

The Lasso tool

is somewhat similar to the Select tool in its purpose. Instead of selecting a rectangular shape, however, it selects an irregular shape. You select a shape by dragging around the object with the lasso. When you release the mouse button, the object is enclosed with a straight path to the starting point. You don't need to go all the way around the object, just far enough so that the straight line will connect the two ends of the circle you drew. A line follows you around as you draw. Figure

Figure 8-10.   Enclosing a picture with the lasso

8-10 shows the Lasso tool used to select the fish graphic. Once the object has been selected, all the black pixels in the object start shimmering to show you which ones are selected.

After selecting the shape, you can do anything with it that you can do with the shapes selected by the Select tool— cut or copy it, or use the commands on the Paint menu. Power keys affect it.

The lasso has the ability to select enclosed shapes automatically. If the shape is enclosed by connected dots, simply click inside the shape while pressing the COMMAND key. The entire enclosed shape is selected, just as if you had lassoed it. Figure 8-11 illustrates this.

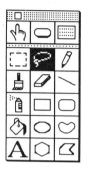

Figure 8-11.   COMMAND-clicking inside an enclosed area with the Lasso tool selects that area

The Eraser Tool

Use the Eraser tool

to erase the part of the screen over which you drag the eraser. Normally, the eraser erases a 16 × 16-pixel square; when in Fat Bits, however, the eraser erases a 4 × 4-pixel square.

If you are working at the card layer on a card that has both background and card pictures, the Eraser tool erases the card layer to display the background layer. You can use this to create "masks" on the card layer that only show particular portions of the background layer, as shown in Figure 8-12.

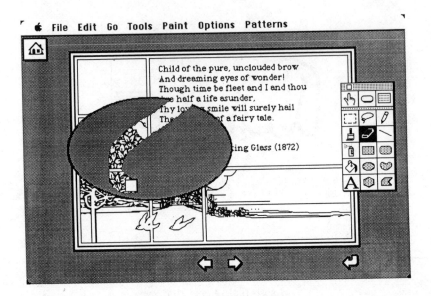

Child of the pure, unclouded brow
And dreaming eyes of wonder!
Though time be fleet and I and thou
~~e half a life asunder,~~
Thy lo~~~~ smile will surely hail
The~~~~ of a fairy tale.

~~~~ing Glass (1872)

Figure 8-12. Using the eraser on the card layer reveals any picture
there might be on the background layer

You can also use the Brush tool as an eraser simply by
painting with the white pattern. This gives you the ability to
choose different-sized erasers, and it gives you a little more
control over what has been erased. Unlike the Eraser tool,
however, the Brush tool will not erase the card to display the
background picture. Instead, opaque white pixels will be
painted with the brush. This is convenient if you want to
remove part of a card picture, but do not want the background picture to show through.

The Rectangle Tool

To draw rectangles with the Rectangle tool

click at one corner of the rectangle, and drag to the other corner. If Draw Centered is checked on the Options menu, the first point you click at becomes the center of the rectangle, and the point where you release the mouse becomes one of the corners.

The border used has the thickness currently set in the Line Size command from the Options menu. A black border is normal; pressing the OPTION key when you start the rectangle causes the line to have the current pattern.

If Draw Filled is checked on the Options menu, the rectangle will be filled with the current pattern. Pressing the COMMAND key when this option is checked causes a rectangle with no borders to be filled with the current pattern.

The SHIFT key constrains the shape of a rectangle to a square.

The Oval Tool

The Oval tool

works in the same way as the Rectangle tool: click at one corner point and drag to another corner point. To constrain the shape of the oval to a circle, press the SHIFT key while you click and drag. If Draw Centered is checked on the Options menu, the oval will be drawn from the center. If Draw Filled is checked on the Options menu, then the oval will be filled with the current pattern.

The Regular Polygon Tool

The Regular Polygon tool

creates polygons with a specific number of sides, all of the same length. In a departure from some of the other drawing tools (such as the Oval or Rectangle tools), the Regular Polygon tool always starts the drawing from the center of the polygon, regardless of whether Draw Centered is checked on the Options menu.

Polygons can also be rotated. Moving the mouse in the direction you dragged after first clicking changes the size of the polygon; moving the mouse in the other direction rotates the polygon. For example, if you click and drag the mouse horizontally, continued horizontal movement changes the size of the polygon, while vertical movement rotates it. Pressing the SHIFT key while rotating constrains the rotation to 15° increments.

You can change the number of polygon sides by double-clicking on the Regular Polygon tool on the torn-off Tools palette or by choosing Polygon Sides from the Options menu. The dialog box shown in Figure 8-13 appears. Clicking on one of these polygons selects that polygon for drawing.

The Regular Polygon Tool uses the line settings from the Line Size item on the Options menu. As with many of the other drawing tools, you can press the OPTION key while dragging to paint borders with the current pattern. If Draw Filled is checked on the Options menu, the polygon will be filled with the current pattern; if the OPTION key is pressed and Draw Filled is checked, the polygon will be filled with the current pattern and will have no border.

The Pencil Tool

At first glance, it might seem that the Pencil tool

works in a manner similar to the Brush tool. However, the pencil has only one shape: a single dot. Only one pixel is changed with each click of the pencil tool. Clicking the mouse button while dragging with the Pencil tool draws lines.

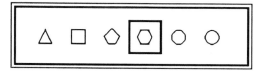

Figure 8-13.   The Polygon Sides dialog box

The pencil does not always place a black pixel on the screen. If the first pixel you click on is already black, then the pencil becomes something of an eraser, drawing in white over the black pixels.

The SHIFT key constrains the movements of the pencil to a line. If your first movement with the pencil is horizontal, it draws horizontal lines; if your first movement is vertical, it draws vertical lines.

The Pencil tool also can toggle you into Fat Bits. COMMAND-clicking with the Pencil tool turns Fat Bits on at the position you click. Double-clicking on the Pencil tool on the torn-off Tools palette turns Fat Bits on and takes you to the screen area you edited most recently. (Fat Bits are discussed in more detail later in this chapter.)

The Line Tool

The Line tool

draws straight lines between two points on the screen. Point to where you want the line to begin, and drag to the point where you want the line to end. If you press SHIFT while you click and drag, the line will be constrained to 15° angles. If you press the OPTION key, the line will be drawn in the current pattern.

You can set the width of the line (and the width of borders of other objects) by double-clicking on the Line tool on the torn-off Tool palette or by choosing Line Size from the Options menu. The dialog box shown in Figure 8-14 appears. Clicking on one of these line sizes chooses that size, and the dialog box goes away. You can also use the number power keys (1 through 8) to select the line size.

The line is not actually created until you release the mouse button (unless Draw Multiple is on); therefore, you can move the mouse anywhere on the screen and release it when you choose.

The Rounded Rectangle Tool

The Rounded Rectangle tool

works the same way as the Rectangle tool. Rectangles are drawn with rounded corners, as shown in Figure 8-15.

The Curve Tool

The Curve tool

draws free-form shapes, drawing a line as long as the mouse button is held down. If Draw Filled is checked, the Curve tool draws a line between the starting point and ending point when the mouse is released, and the resulting figure is filled with the current pattern. As do many other paint tools, it uses the current settings of the Line Size dialog box to

Figure 8-14.   The Line Size dialog box that appears when you double-click on the Line tool on the torn-off Tools palette, or when you choose Line Size from the Options menu

determine how thick a line is used; pressing the OPTION key while drawing causes the line to be in the current pattern.

Figure 8-15.   The Rounded Rectangle tool draws rectangles with their corners slightly rounded

The Polygon Tool

The Polygon tool

draws closed polygons with sides of irregular length. It works very differently from other paint tools. Instead of holding down the mouse button while drawing, you click at the beginning point, release the button, move the mouse to another point, and click again. HyperCard connects the two points with a line. Repeat this action until you have completed your polygon. When you are finished, double-clicking the mouse closes the polygon. Also, if you click the mouse again at the first point you clicked, the polygon is closed.

If Draw Filled is checked on the Options menu, a straight line will be drawn from the first point on the polygon to the point where you double-clicked, and the polygon will be filled with the current pattern.

As with most tools, pressing the OPTION key causes the lines that compose the polygon to be in the current pattern. Pressing SHIFT constrains new lines to angles of 15° increments.

Using the Paint Tools with the Keyboard

You can enhance the work you do with the paint tools by coordinating your left and right hands. Leave your right hand on the mouse and your left hand on the keyboard. Use the SHIFT, OPTION, and COMMAND keys to enhance or alter the way most of the paint tools work. Of course you should keep your fingers ready to press the Undo keys when you make mistakes, especially with the Bucket tool. This is not to say that you need to use the Undo command as soon as you have done something wrong; HyperCard will undo your *last action*, no matter how much time has passed.

The SHIFT Key

The SHIFT key constrains both the angle at which a line is drawn and the shape of an object. With the Line or Polygon tools, it constrains them to producing angles that are multiples of 15. With the Rectangle, Oval, and Rounded Rectangle tool, it constrains them to squares or circles. With the Brush and Pencil tools, it constrains them to a straight line, either horizontal or vertical, in the direction that you first move the mouse while pressing the SHIFT key.

When you have selected an object with the Select or Lasso tool, the SHIFT key constrains the movement of that object to a straight line, in either the horizontal or vertical directions depending on what direction you first moved it.

The OPTION Key

When you draw with most of the tools, the OPTION key causes the line to be drawn in the current pattern instead of the default black. This does not work with the Pencil tool, and since the Brush tool always paints in the current pattern anyway, it also does not affect that tool.

Dragging a selected object while pressing the OPTION key causes a copy of that object to be made. This is a good shortcut to repeatedly copying and pasting pictures, especially when you want to make a number of copies. Simply select the object, press the OPTION key, and drag it to its new location. Release the mouse button and, while still pressing the OPTION key, drag the object to another location.

If the COMMAND key and the OPTION key are pressed, several copies of the selected picture are made. The closeness of these copies to one another is determined by the current line width and the speed at which you drag. Figure 8-16 illustrates this. The face was drawn, selected, and made opaque. Then the COMMAND and OPTION keys were pressed as the shape was dragged around the screen. You can see from the varying distances between the different copies of the face that the mouse was not moved at a constant rate.

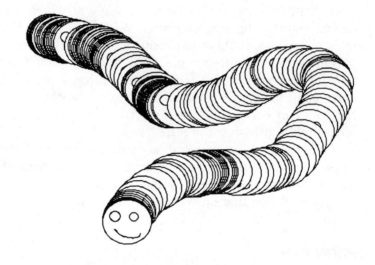

Figure 8-16. Pressing COMMAND-OPTION while dragging a selected picture makes multiple copies of the picture

The COMMAND Key

Since the COMMAND key is used with letters to access keyboard items, its use with the paint tools is limited. It is usually used in conjunction with the SHIFT or OPTION key to enhance the performance of those keys.

With the Brush tool, pressing the COMMAND key causes the brush to erase rather than paint. With the Eraser tool, the COMMAND key causes the eraser to paint opaque white pixels instead of erasing transparently.

The TAB Key

When using the paint tools, the TAB key toggles the visibility of the Patterns window. If that window was not visible, it shows it at the last position it was displayed. With the OPTION key also pressed, the TAB key toggles the visibility of the Tools window.

Double-Clicking and the Paint Tools

Several paint tools feature shortcuts that work by double-clicking on them. You can only double-click on paint tools when the Tools palette has been torn off and is visible on the screen. If you were using the Browse, Button, or Field tool before double-clicking on one of the paint tools, you will have to do it again. HyperCard takes a moment to switch from one of these tools to a paint tool, and it may not notice the second click on the paint tool.

The following table summarizes the function of each paint tool:

Tool	Function
Lasso tool	Lassoes the entire card
Select tool	Selects entire card
Brush tool	Chooses brush shape
Polygon tool	Chooses number of sides in polygon
Text tool	Brings up the Text Style dialog box to allow you to set the properties of the current Paint text (same as choosing Text Styles from the Edit menu or using COMMAND-T)
Eraser tool	Erases the entire picture (on the current layer only)
Pencil tool	Enters or leaves Fat Bits
Line tool	Chooses line size

Tool	Function
Shape tools	Toggle filled or hollow objects (same as choosing Draw Filled from the Options menu)
Bucket tool	Toggles visibility of the Pattern window

Double-clicking on any pattern in the Pattern window allows you to edit that pattern. This has the same effect as choosing a pattern and then selecting Edit Patterns from the Options menu.

Paint Menus

When you are using one of the paint tools, three new menus become available. Since these menus work only with paint tools, it doesn't make any sense for them to be visible otherwise.

Paint

The Paint menu is divided up into four sections. The first section allows you to select recently drawn objects or the entire card. The second and third sections contain commands that work with selected areas of the picture. The final section enhances HyperCard's standard Undo command.

Many of these commands have associated power keys. If so, these keys are shown in parentheses next to the menu item. (Power keys in general are discussed later in this chapter.)

Select (S Power Key or COMMAND-S)

This command chooses the Lasso tool and lassoes the shape you most recently drew. It is the same as double-clicking on the Lasso tool. If you did not just draw a shape, or if you have changed tools since drawing the last shape, it lassoes the entire card. If you have already selected a rectangular area with the Select tool, this power key chooses the Lasso tool and shrinks the selection to contain only black pixels in the enclosed rectangle.

This command is very useful if you have just drawn a shape that is very close to or overlaps other shapes on the screen.

Select All (A Power Key or COMMAND-A)

This is the same as double-clicking on the Select tool. It selects the entire picture.

Fill (F Power Key)

This commands fills the entire selected area with the current pattern. This gives you more flexibility than the Bucket tool does—you don't need to worry about leaks.

Invert (I Power Key)

Invert turns every black pixel in the selection white and every white pixel black.

Pickup (P Power Key)

Pickup allows you to create stencils or masks for pictures. A selected picture can take on the pattern of another part of the screen. The following steps will illustrate how this works:

1. Create a new card or go to a card where you want to experiment.

2. Choose a nonblack pattern, preferably one of the gray patterns or one which is predominantly black. Choose the Rectangle tool, and paint a fairly large rectangle at the bottom of the screen.

3. Choose the Text tool, go to the Text Styles dialog box (either by typing COMMAND-T or double-clicking on the Text tool). Select a sans serif font that is available in a large size, such as Geneva 24. Choose the bold and outline styles.

4. Now click on a white area of the screen, and type your name in all capital letters.

5. Now that you have typed your name, choose the Lasso tool, and lasso your name. (If you use the Select tool, it won't work because the entire rectangle will be picked up.)

6. Move the selection, your name, onto the patterned area of the screen. *Do not click the mouse anywhere else* because this will deselect your name and leave it there. If you do this, press the Undo key to put your name back where you typed it.

7. Press the P Power key.

8. Drag the selected name back to a white area of the screen. All the selected area has taken on the pattern of the area that it was on when you struck the P Power key.

The Pickup command complements the Draw Filled command and the Bucket tool. It gives you a lot of flexibility to create clipped images that are in a certain shape. Note that you don't need to pick up a pattern as in the example; Pickup works with any image.

Darken (D Power Key)

Darken turns randomly selected pixels in the selection black. Each time you choose this command or use the power key, a few more pixels are blackened. Eventually, if you keep pressing the D key, the entire selection will be black.

Lighten (L Power Key)

The opposite of Darken, this command turns a random selection of pixels in the selection white.

Trace Edges (E Power Key)

Trace Edges outlines black areas in the selection in black. Using this command again outlines the outlines in black. Repeated use of it can create moire patterns.

Rotate Left ([Power Key)

This command rotates the selection 90° to the left (see Note following Rotate Right command).

Rotate Right (] Power Key)

The command rotates the selection 90° to the right.

Note: Both of the Rotate commands are among the only HyperCard commands that can cause unrecoverable loss of work. If your rotation takes a part of the picture off the screen, that part is lost and cannot be recovered with the standard Undo command. The Revert command, however, can sometimes recover the picture if you have done nothing since.

Flip Vertical (V Power Key)

This command flips the selection vertically. Text that is part of the selection will be reversed, which can create some good effects. If you do not want the text to be reversed, do not select it, or select it again after you have flipped the selection, and flip it again.

Flip Horizontal (H Power Key)

This command flips the selection horizontally.

Opaque (O Power Key)

The Opaque command makes the selection opaque, so that the background picture cannot be seen through it. If you drag the selection over another part of the card, it will also hide that part of the card picture.

You can use this command to hide parts of the background picture so they don't appear on certain cards.

HyperCard also gives you a tool to find out which areas of the card are opaque. Holding down the OPTION and O keys makes the opaque areas solid black.

Transparent (T Power Key)

The opposite of Opaque, this command makes the white pixels in a selection transparent so that whatever is underneath —either the background picture or another part of the card picture that you move the selection over—shows through.

Keep (COMMAND-K)

Keep tells HyperCard that you want to keep the changes you have made to the picture. Until you use this command, the Revert command will revert the card to the way it looked the last time you opened it. After you use the Keep command, the Revert command will revert to the last version you kept. If you go to another card or click on a tool other than one of the paint tools, the card is automatically kept.

Revert (R Power Key)

This command returns the picture to the way it looked the last time it was saved, either with the Keep command or by changing the card. If a portion of the picture is selected, Revert works only on that portion; otherwise it works on the entire card.

Options

The Options menu includes items that control ways that the various Painting tools work. Some of these commands are available with power keys, and some of them are available by double-clicking on paint tools.

Grid (G Power Key)

This command turns the grid off and on. The grid constrains where you can click or place items with the paint tools. You can only move or draw in increments of 8 pixels apiece. You can see this effect by turning the grid on and drawing with one of the tools. The tool jumps around the screen in 8-pixel increments.

The grid helps you line things up. For example, if you want to put several rectangles on the screen and align their left edges, use the grid. It is difficult to visually line them up without the grid—two rectangles might look like they are aligned, but could be a pixel or two off.

As with other options that are either on or off, a check mark appears next to this menu item when it is on.

Fat Bits

Fat Bits enlarges a section of the screen so that you can easily work on it one pixel at a time. While in Fat Bits, you can use any of the paint tools (which work to scale) just as you normally use them.

There are two ways to get into Fat Bits. The easiest way is to COMMAND-click with the Pencil tool, which takes you into Fat Bits at the location you clicked. You can also use the Fat Bits menu item, chosen by pressing OPTION-F, or double-click on the Pencil tool on the torn-off Tools palette. When you use either of these approaches, you are taken to the area of the screen at which you made the most recent change.

While in Fat Bits, a moveable window appears at the lower-left corner of the screen. This window shows you the same area of the screen in its regular view, allowing you to see exactly how your changes will look on the card.

You can move the picture around in Fat Bits by pressing the OPTION key and dragging. While you press OPTION, the cursor turns into a hand. As you drag, the picture moves to different parts of the card.

To exit Fat Bits you can use any of the commands that you used to get into it, you can click on the small window, or you can choose one of the tools other than paint tools.

Power Keys

If a check mark appears next to this item on the Options menu, power keys are enabled, allowing you to use single-key shortcuts for many of the commands on the Paint and Options menus. Table 8-2 lists all the power keys, along with the commands they represent.

Power keys are disabled when you are using the Paint Text tool. With this tool HyperCard interprets the characters you type as characters to be painted onto the card; therefore, it cannot interpret them as power keys.

Power keys also do not work when the Message box is visible. In this case, keys you type are sent to the Message box and not to the painting part of HyperCard. Hiding the Message box solves this problem. Note, too, that since HyperCard is interpreting your keystrokes as power keys, you cannot blind type HyperCard commands, as you can while you are using the Browse, Button, or Field Tools.

Line Size

This command allows you to set the width of lines drawn by several HyperCard tools. You can also get this command's dialog box by double-clicking on the Line tool.

The Line Size setting controls the lines drawn by the Rectangle, Oval, Line, Rounded Rectangle, Curve, Regular Polygon, and Polygon tools. It also controls the distance separating objects that are repeatedly copied when using COMMAND-OPTION drag, as well as the distance between multiple objects drawn when Draw Multiple is checked.

Key	Function
B	Creates black pattern
D	Darkens selection
C	Toggles Draw Centered
M	Toggles Draw Multiple
F	Fills with current pattern
H	Flips selection horizontally
V	Flips selection vertically
G	Toggles grid
I	Inverts selection
L	Lightens selection
O	Makes selection opaque
P	Chooses Pickup
R	Chooses Revert
S	Chooses Select
A	Chooses Select All
E	Chooses Trace Edges
T	Makes selection transparent
W	Creates white pattern
[	Rotates left
]	Rotates right

Table 8-2.   HyperCard Power Keys and Their Functions

The various power keys that you can use to invoke any of the line widths are shown in Figure 8-17.

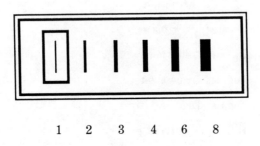

1   2   3   4   6   8

Figure 8-17.   The Line Size dialog box, showing the numerical
power keys for each of the line widths

Brush Shape

This command allows you to choose the shape of the brush
you are using. It can also be accessed by double-clicking on
the Brush tool.

Edit Pattern

This command allows you to modify a pattern. It summons
the dialog box shown in Figure 8-18. If you choose this item
from the menu, you will be editing the current pattern. You
can also edit a pattern directly by double-clicking on that
pattern on the torn-off Patterns palette.

Patterns are squares measuring 8 pixels on a side. When
you are editing a pattern, clicking on a white pixel turns it
black, and clicking on a black pixel turns it white. That's all
there is to it. Keep an eye on how the pixels along the edge
are lined up. The pixels on the top of the pattern window will
be next to those on the bottom, and those on the left next to
those on the right. You can see what the pattern will look like
in the window above the Cancel button, which shows an
enlarged view of the pattern.

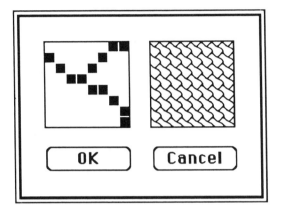 

Figure 8-18.   The Edit Pattern dialog box

If you have put a pattern onto the screen that is not one of the standard patterns (perhaps by mixing two existing patterns), you can pick it up and edit it by clicking on that pattern on the card while the Pattern Edit dialog box is open. An 8 × 8-pixel area of the screen becomes the model of the new pattern.

Patterns are saved with the stack. When you create a new table of patterns especially for use in one stack, the standard set of patterns that is part of HyperCard is not lost. To copy a pattern from one stack to another, copy a selection of a card picture that contains that pattern to another stack, and pick it up into the Pattern window with the method described in the previous paragraph.

Polygon Sides

This command sets the number of sides that will be drawn with the Regular Polygon tool. You can also summon this dialog box by double-clicking on the Regular Polygon tool on the torn-off Tools palette.

Draw Filled

When this item is chosen, the Rectangle, Rounded Rectangle, Oval, Curve, Polygon and Regular Polygon tools draw objects filled with the current pattern. The appearance of these tools on the Tools palette changes to reflect that fact, as shown in Figure 8-19.

Like Draw Centered and Draw Multiple, this item is a toggle—choosing it turns it off if it is on, and on if it is off. Make sure there is a check mark next to the Tools palette on the Options menu, which indicates it is enabled.

Draw Centered (C Power Key)

If this item is enabled, drawing with the Rectangle, Rounded Rectangle, Oval, and Line tools starts from the center instead of one corner. That means that the first place you click before you start drawing becomes the center of the object, not one of the corners.

You can use this option to draw several concentric ovals or other objects with the same center. First mark the center

Figure 8-19.   The appearance of certain items on the Tools palette changes if Draw Filled is enabled

point with the Pencil tool, then start drawing with the other tools from that point.

Note: Regardless of the setting of this item, all drawings with the Regular Polygon tool are drawn from the center.

Draw Multiple (M Power Key)

When this item is checked, HyperCard draws multiple objects as long as you drag with the mouse. It affects these tools: Line, Rectangle, Rounded Rectangle, Oval, and Regular Polygon.

It takes some work to master this tool. The slower you drag, the more objects are drawn, which can cause them to merge to form a black object. If you draw too fast, however, you do not have enough control over the spacing between them.

Figure 8-20 shows how this option affects the different tools.

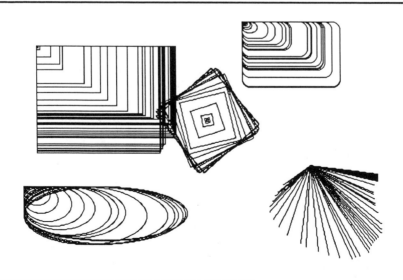

Figure 8-20. Several of the paint tools used with Draw Multiple enabled

Patterns

The final Paint menu is the pattern menu. Like the Tools menu, this is really a palette that can be torn off and positioned anywhere on the screen. This is convenient if you are frequently changing patterns.

Two power keys can be used to select certain patterns. The B Power key selects the black pattern, and the W Power key selects the white pattern. These two keys do not affect selected pictures on the screen; they only choose these patterns for further use with the paint tools.

Importing and Exporting Graphics

HyperCard makes it easy to import and export graphics to and from painting applications, such as MacPaint, FullPaint, or SuperPaint. You can import any images you have created in these applications or save graphics created in HyperCard for use in these programs. The commands to do this are on the File menu and are shown in Figure 8-21. They only become visible (and available) when you are using one of the painting tools.

The HyperCard window is of a fixed size, 512 pixels wide and 342 pixels tall, which is the same size as the screen on the original Macintoshes. HyperCard is unable to deal with graphics larger than this. This is not a problem when exporting HyperCard graphics to other programs, but it can cause some problems when bringing graphics into HyperCard.

Importing Graphics

When you choose Import Paint from the File menu, Hyper-Card displays a standard Open File dialog box. The list of files shown in this dialog box includes only those files that

Figure 8-21.   The Import Paint and Export Paint items become available when you are using one of the draw tools

HyperCard can import. Most programs that create bit maps save those files with the PNTG file type; therefore, only files of that type will be shown.

HyperCard can only deal with graphics that are 512 × 342 pixels, and most paint programs can deal with an entire page of graphics (575 × 718 pixels). You might need to make some adjustments to your picture to get it into HyperCard.

When reading a picture from disk, HyperCard reads in the top-left corner of the image. It reads as much of the picture as it can handle and brings it in. If parts of your picture extend beyond these boundaries, these parts are ignored. There are two ways to deal with this.

First, you can shrink the image down. Most paint programs allow you to scale a picture, either with a menu command or by COMMAND-dragging on a selected portion of the picture. Usually this causes some distortion that you must clean up. If your paint program offers it, use a menu command; it gives you more precise control over how the picture is scaled.

Second, you can move the picture so that it all fits into the top-left portion of the page. This works when the picture you want to import is small enough to fit into a HyperCard card. This is the best method because you don't get any distortion. Most paint programs follow the technique of Mac-Paint. In MacPaint, you can double-click on the Hand tool or choose Show Page from the Edit menu, and a small representation of the page will be shown. A rectangle will show the current window onto the page. By clicking and dragging outside that rectangle, you can move the picture around on the page. Move it to the top-left corner.

HyperCard imports graphics into the layer on which you are currently working. If Edit Background is currently active, then the imported picture will be placed in the background layer. If Edit Background is not active, then the imported picture will be placed into the card layer. Make sure before importing a picture that you are currently editing the correct layer.

Exporting Graphics

Exporting graphics is easier than importing. Choosing Export Paint from the File menu brings up a standard Macintosh Save As dialog box, showing the names of the files in the current folder or on the current disk. Type in the name of the file you want to save, and if a file by that name already exists, you will be asked if you want to replace it.

HyperCard saves these pictures as MacPaint files. They have the PNTG file type and the creator MPNT. When you look at these files from the Macintosh Finder, they will have the MacPaint file icon. Since this format is fairly standard, most other programs that can deal with bit maps will be able to read these files.

HyperCard places the graphics into the upper-left portion of your paint document. The exported picture includes everything that is on the card, such as buttons, fields, and icons. The menu bar, of course, will not be in the exported graphic.

When exporting to a paint file, HyperCard includes the graphics of the layer you are currently in. If you are working on the card layer, all graphics, including background pictures, are exported. If you are working in the background layer, only background graphics are exported. If you have hidden either the background or card pictures with the Hide Background Picture or Hide Card Picture command, these layers will not be included in the exported picture.

Copying and Pasting Graphics

If you are familiar with copying and pasting text or graphics in other Macintosh applications, working with HyperCard graphics will come easily. The main thing you need to keep in mind is the distinction between the two layers. Background and card graphics cannot be selected at the same time.

Graphics can also be pasted into HyperCard from any other application that supports the Clipboard. If Hyper-Card's drawing tools are not sufficient for the task you have in mind, chances are that you will be able to find another program that can do what you want. There is a wide variety of graphics programs on the Macintosh, from MacPaint to professional tools such as Adobe Illustrator, Aldus Freehand, or Cricket Draw. Most scanners and their software can also support the Clipboard or save to a MacPaint file. You should remember, however, that once the picture has been pasted into HyperCard, it becomes a part of the picture on the card. You cannot then paste it back into another program that works in a different way and use that program's editing tools.

The Art Ideas Stack

One of the most useful stacks shipped with HyperCard is the Art Ideas stack. This stack contains 29 cards full of graphics of all sizes that you can use in HyperCard (or, through the Clipboard, with almost any Macintosh application). You should remember to copy, not cut, pictures from this stack because you want to keep them there for later use.

If you are not going to be adding your own pictures to this stack, you should lock it from the Finder by checking the Lock box on the Get Info window of the stack. This prevents you from inadvertently changing it later. This only works, however, if you are using HyperCard version 1.2 or later; previous versions do not work with stacks that are locked.

Paint Text Versus Field Text

HyperCard might seem to be somewhat schizophrenic about how it works with text, and it might take some getting used to.

Paint text—text created by painting it on the screen—works differently than text in fields. Essentially, when you finish typing text with the Text tool and click elsewhere, that text is no longer treated as text. It freezes onto the screen and becomes part of the array of dots that make up a picture. This is very convenient; since the text becomes part of the picture, you can use any of the paint tools and commands to change its appearance. Some commands and tools that work well with text are the Darken, Lighten, Pickup, and Trace Edges commands and the Bucket and Selection tools. After it has been frozen onto your screen, however, you cannot edit Paint text.

You can do few of these things with Field text. You can use none of the paint tools with Field text, so you are limited to changing the font and style. You can, however, edit Field text with standard editing tools.

When to Use Field Text

Use Field text when you will need to edit the text. It is much easier to use the standard Macintosh text editing tools to modify text than it is to repaint it onto the picture.

Field text should also be used when you need to search on the text. If you need the Find command to locate text, you must use Field text.

When to Use Paint Text

Use Paint text when you want special effects. The full range of paint tools is available for modifying Paint text, allowing special effects or designs.

Paint text should be used when you are using an unusual font. For Field text to work, the user must have that font available to him. If he does not have that font in his system (or another location at which HyperCard can get it), then the text will not look good on the screen. Since Paint text is part of the picture, it does not make that requirement.

Also, if you don't need to edit or Find the text, Paint text is best to use.

Paint text also frees you from the need to use LaserWriter fonts. If you have used a LaserWriter or other PostScript printer, you are aware of the need to use special fonts when printing to these printers—either fonts that are resident in the printer or ones that are available for downloading from your computer. When you are using Paint text, however, the font information is not used for printing. All text is treated as a bit map and is printed that way. One of the things you give up, however, is the printer's ability to scale fonts to any size for smooth printing. Since HyperCard is not sending font and character information to the printer, but is only sending an array of pixels, the text will not be scaled on the printer. What you see on the card is indeed what you get on paper. If you want the text to be scaled so that it will be printed well, use Field text.

Final Words About HyperCard Graphics

Bill Atkinson has said that "something like 80% of the bandwidth of information coming into our brains comes in through the eyes." Graphics are an important part of Hyper-Card; they act both as parts of the application that reinforce its metaphors and as the data itself. If you are developing stacks that are to be used by others, keep in mind the rules of graphic art. It is a good idea, in fact, to work with a graphic artist to help you with the look of your stack.

On the other hand, part of the fun of HyperCard is in its encouragement of experimentation and play. Even if you have never considered yourself an artist, you might find after working with HyperCard's tools that you've created several attractive pictures. Create a personal art stack, and start saving your pictures. Children love drawing with the Macintosh. Make stacks for them (kind of the computer equivalent of the refrigerator door) and let them have fun. They may create some pictures that you can use in other situations.

Designing and
Building Stacks

The Human Interface Guidelines
Guidelines for Building Stacks
Design and Testing

So far, this book has focused on using HyperCard—working with stacks you get from others and making small changes to those stacks. The remainder of the book describes the HyperTalk programming language, which is the tool you use to actually make HyperCard do things. First, though, this chapter discusses some points you should remember when building stacks.

Designing stacks to be used by others is an interdisciplinary process. It involves the various skills of the programmer, the writer, and the graphic artist, to name a few. Depending on the type of stack you are producing, you can benefit from the study of such things as television and animation graphics techniques, and expert systems theory. HyperCard, insofar as it is a program for creating interactive multimedia applications, requires that you build a new vocabulary for combining images, animation, sound, and text. While the range of applications that can be created with HyperCard is great, its strength lies in how it gives publishers of information new tools for presenting facts and ideas. This chapter discusses some of the issues involved in designing and testing stacks.

In a way, it is too early to write this chapter. There has not been enough work done with HyperCard—especially as it relates to publishing hundreds of megabytes of integrated text, sound, and graphics on a CD-ROM—for users to know which techniques work best in which situations. When you are reading a book, you can look at the table of contents to find out how it is organized, or you can look in the index to be pointed directly at a particular reference. While reading a particular chapter in a book, you can look ahead to find out how many pages there are in the chapter and decide if you want to read until the end of that chapter or go to bed. Some Hypermedia applications have not given you tools such as indexes and tables of contents. This can cause you to feel lost in the data, or feel that you have not read all the text. For example, one of the problems with early HyperText systems, and one problem that arises with some HyperCard stacks, is that it is easy to get lost. Following links with no clear path back to your starting point can leave you confused and disoriented. Even if you have read the entire document or stack, you want to avoid the feeling that there's something you have missed.

Therefore, while this single chapter cannot be comprehensive—that could take dozens of books—it does discuss some general issues, with more particular notes as they seem appropriate.

Even if you do not plan to create stacks for the use of others, you should still follow these principles (although not as strictly). You may know today what the function of a particular button is, but that does not mean that you will remember what that function is next week or next year. Also, the chances are that if you have a use for a stack, others will too. The stack you build for yourself today might be a marketable product tomorrow. Following the principles of good design can help you, the stack creator, as well as the user.

The Human Interface Guidelines

Apple has done a great deal of work studying the user interface and has published its guidelines in the book *Human Interface Guidelines: The Apple Desktop Interface* (Reading, Massachusetts: Addison-Wesley, 1987). This section is based on material from that book, with notes specific to HyperCard.

Apple has boiled down the essence of a good user interface to ten principles, which are discussed briefly here.

1: Use Metaphors from the Real World

You can better understand programs and stacks that use a metaphor that relates directly to something in the real world. This is illustrated by a few of the stacks that are included with HyperCard: the Address stack has the appearance of the ubiquitous Rolodex-style name-and-address card file; the Datebook stack looks like a common datebook.

HyperCard itself uses the metaphor of a stack of cards, and many of the stacks you build use this metaphor in turn. Library management stacks, for example, can look like cards in a card catalog.

Metaphors are constructed using several tools. The primary tool is graphics. Background graphics make the card look like its real-world analogue. Buttons and fields have names that reinforce the metaphor, as does the vocabulary used in documentation.

Sounds, too, can add to the metaphor. For example, if you are using a metaphor that makes each card look like a page from a book, you can add the sound of a page turning and play it when the Next or Previous button turns the page to another card. (Sounds, however, should be used in moderation, and you should make it easy for users of your stacks to turn off sounds (see Chapter 30). The clever sound effect that is interesting the first time can become irritating after being heard too often.)

Using a metaphor also gives you the burden of restraint. If the metaphor is stretched too far, that too can become irritating. Avoid excessive use of cute jargon; a metaphor is a useful tool but you don't want to take the point too far.

2: Direct Manipulation of Objects

When you are using a computer, you want to be in control and not have the computer controlling your actions. When you do something to an object on the screen, even simply clicking a button, you want quick feedback so that you know the computer has sensed your action.

This feedback might be something as simple as having a button become highlighted when you click it. This lets you know that the button has received the message and is acting on it.

3: See-and-Point

With the Macintosh in general, you see something and point to it; you don't have to remember a command and type it. This is true of copying files from one folder or disk to another, and of selecting text and choosing a Bold command from a Format menu. With HyperCard, you see buttons and click them with the mouse.

This means that you do not have hidden functions in an application that you cannot see directly. It is a burden on you to have to remember that commands need to be typed, or that the SHIFT key must be held down when you click a button. This does not mean necessarily that SHIFT-, COMMAND-, or

OPTION-clicking buttons is bad and should at all times be avoided. These are useful techniques; however, consistency is the key. If OPTION-clicking a particular button does one thing at one time, it should do the same thing at another time, or a similar thing on a different button.

4: Consistency

While the Macintosh user interface is certainly not as consistent as it could be, consistency is certainly one of its strong points. When you buy a new piece of Macintosh software, you can be fairly certain that there will be a Print command under the File menu; you do not need to read the manual just to find out how to print. Consistency across Macintosh applications has made the computer easier not only for the user, but also for the programmer. Software design is easier — programmers do not need to define a new keystroke for printing and then educate their users about its function.

As stated earlier, consistency within an application is important, too. If OPTION-clicking one button modifies the behavior of that button in a certain manner, OPTION-clicking other buttons should affect those buttons in much the same way.

5: WYSIWYG (What You See Is What You Get)

This phrase is most commonly used to refer to the fidelity that a printed document will have to what you see on the screen. HyperCard's printing functions take care of this for you.

However, this principle also suggests that there be no hidden commands or capabilities. Commands should always act immediately, rather than merely promise future results.

6: User Control

You should be in control of the computer, not the other way around. All actions should be directed by you; if you do nothing, the computer should do nothing.

When programming the Macintosh with a language such as C or Pascal, programmers use something called the event loop, which constantly monitors your actions and responds to them. HyperCard takes care of the event loop for the programmer, sending messages to buttons or cards, depending on your actions.

7: Feedback and Dialog

Few things are more disconcerting than having a busy computer and not knowing what it is doing. You can avoid this by having the stack constantly inform you of its actions, especially when performing tasks that can take a while.

The feedback you get should be as close to immediate as possible. When you click a button, the button should be highlighted immediately so that you don't continue clicking the button and wondering what has happened.

8: Forgiveness

Since the earliest days of personal computers, users have neglected to read their manuals. This is as true of the Macintosh as it is of other computers, and perhaps more so, because the Mac's ease and consistency of use have eliminated the need to consult the manual for instructions on such tasks as printing. Instead, with its point-and-click interface and its Undo command, the user can explore the workings of programs by experimenting.

The Undo command—along with dialog boxes and alerts that warn destructive actions and let you back out of them— is partly responsible for this ease of use. With most Macintosh programs, most actions can be reversed immediately after they have been accomplished. Forgiveness on the part of the program allows you to try things out and test the actions of certain commands without worrying that data will be lost.

Of course, when you are writing programs in the Hyper-Card environment, you have no control over how the Undo command works—HyperCard takes care of it for you. However, when you are creating buttons that can perform destructive actions, you should always include a prompt to ask if that destructive action is really desired before the action continues.

9: Perceived Stability

Your program should work, and not only under certain circumstances. It should not change randomly or appear to do things on its own without your direction. If certain conditions are necessary before a button can work correctly, the button must make sure those conditions have been met. If the button does not work, it must tell you why.

10: Artistic Integrity

Finally, the application should look good. Users do not want to interact with applications that are not easy on the eye and visually appealing. All elements in the design should support the metaphor that you are using and should work together to create an appealing whole. Functions that perform similar actions should be grouped together and should have a unified appearance.

Having a consistent, attractive design sometimes means that you must sacrifice some functions simply because they do not fit on the card or into the visual framework. Consider how each element of the stack design adds to the whole of the stack, and eliminate those elements that do not contribute something.

Guidelines for Building Stacks

Beyond the formal Apple *Human Interface Guidelines*, there are a number of commonsense guidelines that can help you make better stacks. While the following guidelines are often presented as hard and fast rules, they are not. They are merely pointers that can help you better organize and present your ideas in HyperCard.

Use Plain Language

When documenting a stack for the use of others, do not assume that they are sophisticated computer users. Many of your users will be new to HyperCard, the Macintosh, or to computers in general. As part of the stack design, keep the language clear, jargon-free, and to the point. If you must use unusual words, make sure that the definitions of those words can easily be found or that they are clear from the context.

Know Your User

Design for your user. If you are publishing information or creating a stack for the use of the members of a specific group, tailor the stack so that it will be useful to those members. Use a vocabulary of both words and images that is understood by your users and means something to them.

Use a Consistent Metaphor

Keep the metaphor consistent. If, for example, you are using a metaphor of a book, do not include functions that are not done with a book (such as sorting the stack).

At the same time, do not go overboard with the metaphor. Maintain the parts of the metaphor that make sense, but keep an eye out for instances where you are stretching things to stay with the metaphor. Outline the properties of the metaphor before you begin. Then pick the properties that serve the needs of your stack.

Use Text, Graphics, and Sound to Present Ideas

HyperCard is a multimedia environment—the first truly flexible environment on a computer for integrating text, images, and sound together. You can combine HyperCard with a video disk to deal with high-quality pictures and images. With CD-ROM, you can create large stacks full of graphics and sounds. Do not restrict your stack to just one of these elements. Use text, pictures, and sound to form a whole, with all the elements reinforcing one another.

Pay Attention to Unity

One of the principles of classical drama, particularly tragedy, is that it should be unified—in character, place, and time. All events in the play should feature the same characters, be set in places in close proximity, and happen over a brief period of time.

Unity in software design is harder to express. Essentially, a good piece of software should try to do one thing and do it well. It is impossible to create a program that is all things to all people; you should decide on one function your program performs, or one type of information you are trying to impart, and stick to it. For example, there is no reason for a Clip Art stack to include Datebook functions, and the stack that includes information on astronomy should leave biology alone.

Allow the User to Set Preferences

Users should be able to control how many parts of the application work. If you use a lot of sounds, for example, include a mechanism that allows the user to turn off the sounds. If you have a fancy title screen, allow the user to make the stack so that the title screen is not shown every time.

Fit into the user's environment. If you are making changes to the HyperCard environment—for example, by changing the user level to a lower value or hiding the menu bar—record the way the user had those settings and restore them to their original state when the user leaves your stack.

Integrate Graphics Early

Start thinking graphically as early in the design process as possible. While it is true that you can incorporate graphics relatively late in the design process, graphic design should be included in your application as early as possible. The graphic look and feel of your application can affect functionality, suggesting new functions you might include and also suggesting which possible functions don't fit into the environment.

Keep Graphics Simple

Despite the Mac's excellent graphics capabilities, simple graphics look better on the Macintosh screen than do complicated, dense graphics. Simple lines, a unified visual appeal, and consistency of content are more effective than complicated graphics that lose meaning because of their complexity.

Avoid Large, Dense Blocks of Text

As nice as the Macintosh screen is to look at, it is still far from ideal. Large, dense blocks of small print are hard to read in any medium, but especially so on the screen. Break up the text and put it into different fields. Allow the user to set the size and font of the text so that it is comfortable to read.

Tailor Your Presentation to the Material

Let the material you are presenting guide how it is presented; do not try to force the material into a mold. A stack that presents information about the planets in the solar system has different requirements than a stack dealing with the history and art of the Renaissance, and so it should have a different style.

Make Sure the User is Given Tools to Navigate

As was mentioned at the beginning of this chapter, one of the horrors of working with large databases of linked text is the "lost" feeling that comes when you have no navigation tools. Make sure you give the user the tools needed to navigate not just through the stack, but also through the data.

HyperCard includes many navigation commands, such as the commands to go to different cards and the Go Recent command. However, the particular structure of your stack might be one for which these simple commands are not enough. Provide tools that allow the user to always get to such items as maps, tables of contents, and indexes. Always allow the user to backtrack directly to the place last visited.

Make Text Entry Areas Obvious

If you expect or need the user to enter text into a card, use a visual style—including graphics and field styles—that make it clear just where you need the user to enter the text. Make it clear, too, just what type of information you need. If you need a number or a date, for example, then say so.

Check Data Entry When It
Is Entered

HyperCard includes tools that allow you to check user input at the time it is entered. By checking it then, you can catch potential errors that might be harder for a script or a user to find later. Warn the user of the error, and request reentry of the information.

Use Graphics to Indicate
Functions of Buttons

HyperCard's icons and button types provide a consistent appearance to the buttons. In addition, you can use graphics —including pictures drawn on the background or card as well as icons—to indicate the function the button performs.

Use Visual Effects

HyperCard features a wealth of visual effects that you can use to enhance the metaphor your stack is using and make it more visually appealing. (See Chapter 20 for a complete discussion of visual effects.) Here are two examples of how to use visual effects.

Use Zoom Open to Look
at Something More Closely

The Zoom Open visual effect works in the same way the Finder works when you open a folder. This effect can be used when the user clicks a button to take a closer look at a particular piece of information; for example, opening items or zooming in to a particular area on a map.

Use Zoom Close to Put
Something Away

The Zoom Close visual effect works the same way as the Finder does when you close a disk or a folder. Use it to back away from detail: for example, when the user is looking at a detail on a map and wishes to view the "big picture."

Provide Maps

Probably the best thing you can do to prevent your users from getting lost when navigating a large stack is to provide a map, allowing easy access to the main parts of the stack. The map should be accessible from any card on the stack. The Help stack provided with HyperCard has an excellent map, and its design should be looked at closely by all Hyper-Card developers.

Provide Help

Including your own on-line help facility is easy. If your stack uses standard HyperCard navigation techniques and all buttons are self-explanatory, then you might not need help. But if you have a complicated stack with many different ways of doing things, include help that documents the different ways the stack can act.

Look at Other Stacks

Stay in touch with what others are doing. This helps you stay up to date with developments in the art of presenting material in HyperCard. You can get new techniques from other stacks, and you can find out how the standard HyperCard vocabulary is developing. Producing any kind of art in a vacuum, separate from what others are doing, leads to an isolation and a lack of awareness that is evident in the end product.

Allow and Facilitate
User Modification

One of the strengths of HyperCard is that you can modify stacks you acquire to make them act the way you want them to. When you are building stacks, make this easier by making the scripts you use modular and transportable. You can also include mechanisms in the stack that allow users to add their own comments to information you present or add customizable help.

Make It Fun to Use

On the one hand, overly cute applications can be grating on the nerves and be more annoying than they are useful. On the other hand, if your application is not enjoyable to use, it won't be used.

Have Fun Creating It

Have you ever listened to a record or watched a movie and thought that it must have been fun to make? When the creators of something enjoy themselves while they are making it, that enjoyment often carries through and becomes part of the product they are creating. Enjoying the product you are making, and enjoying the task of making it, helps ensure that you will carry through on your ideas and present something that others will also enjoy. HyperCard is an enjoyable application to use, and HyperTalk is doubly so. Don't get bogged down on projects that are not fun; you probably won't carry them out to completion, and if you do they might not be as good as they could be if you had enjoyed doing them.

Break the Rules

Finally, feel free to break the rules when you must. Great writers often break the rules of grammar, character, and story structure to accommodate special needs of the material. Developers should feel free to do the same. Sometimes the material you are presenting is new, or standards do not cover the special cases you need. Remember that the rules presented in this chapter are guidelines only. As you saw earlier, the vocabulary and structures for dealing with large amounts of mixed media information are new and are still being developed. Push the edge of the envelope, and perhaps the justification you use to break a rule today will be the standard by which other techniques are measured tomorrow.

Design and Testing

When you are developing any piece of software, whether it is a HyperCard stack or a program written in any other language, you should not work in a vacuum. Make the development process cooperative by using a varied group of testers to see how the program is working, and work with individuals who have expertise in areas with which you might not be familiar.

Again, the remarks that follow are not the last word in how HyperCard development should take place. Instead, they are loose guidelines for the process of developing a stack.

Plan Functions

Planning the stack is first, and you should plan in as much detail as you can. It is tempting to sit down and just start writing HyperTalk code with the hope that eventually you will make all the parts of the stack work. That is fine for small stacks and individual buttons, but it does not work for larger projects.

Outlining the functions involves defining the kinds of data you are going to be working with. Will it be large blocks of text or small pieces of information that use a database metaphor? What means of accessing the data will you use? Will graphics be part of the data? What are the best ways to navigate through the data?

If your stack will be one that publishes information, consult with possible users of the information to find out how they would like things to work. If you research the project before you start working, you can avoid the dead ends that can result from programming functions that are not needed or used.

Graphic Design

As stated earlier, make the graphic look and feel of the stack part of the design process as early as possible. If you are inexperienced at graphic design, use the services of a professional designer to plan the application. It might cost you some money, but in the long run it will be worth it. It has been said that 80% of the appeal of a HyperCard stack comes from the appearance of the stack. While the percentage is open to debate, the essence of the statement is not. Few users will work with an ugly application or one with functions that are confusing because of a chaotic visual interface.

Creating a Prototype to Test the Metaphor

After you have done some design work, create a prototype of the application. This is easy to do in HyperCard. Include as much of the visual design as possible and as much data as necessary to give possible users an idea of how things are going to work. Include all the buttons you have planned, even if they are not working. You can "dummy" the buttons to make them appear as if they are working. A prototype is much more useful for testers than a verbal or written description of the product.

Initial Testing

Once you have created the prototype, you can begin testing. Select a variety of testers, all of whom are potential users of the actual product. (Don't necessarily choose those who are also HyperTalk programmers; they may be watching for how you did something, not necessarily for what you did.)

Watch your testers use the prototype, but don't help them (after all, you will not be around to help the actual users of the product). If possible, videotape the testers and encourage them to verbalize their thoughts as they use the prototype. Watch for things they never use and for things they use incorrectly.

Keep testing. If you fix a problem that your testers had, test the fix to make sure you have done it right.

Throw Out What Is Not Needed or Used

One of the hardest things to do is abandon a function, but it is often necessary. You might have included a function "because it is there"—because it is possible or involves an interesting piece of HyperTalk code. But if people do not use it, if it does not add anything to the function of the product, or if it does not fit well into the user interface, then throw it out. "Featurism" is the downfall of many products. Instead of concentrating on adding new features, make sure the features that are necessary work well.

Script Design

After you have frozen the style and design of the stack, you can start designing the scripts. Always design scripts in advance of writing them. Plan the functions for each button and outline what it will need. This process will be discussed in greater detail in Chapter 11. However, it should be said here that careful script planning can reduce the amount of work that it takes to actually develop the script. Finding common routines that buttons will need allows you to isolate those routines and avoid putting them into every button.

Script Development

You can now implement the scripts. If you have planned the application carefully and have designed the scripts in detail, then actually writing them will be easier than you might think. HyperTalk is close enough to standard English that you can create an English description of a button or script function that comes close to the actual HyperTalk code.

Final Testing

Finally, test the entire product. You should have been testing it throughout the development process, of course, even with partially implemented scripts. But before you ship it, broaden the scope of the testing. Bring in more testers who can help you evaluate the function of the stack as a whole. Don't be afraid to go back to the drawing board if you need to.

TEN

Introduction to HyperTalk

Why Program in HyperTalk?
About Programming
What Can Scripts Do?
Basic Concepts
The HyperTalk Editor
Where's the Program?
Script Openness

So far you have explored how HyperCard works, taking only occasional side trips into scripting. The remainder of this book details scripting: the commands, functions, and other elements that make up HyperCard and its programming language, HyperTalk. The programming language does not exist without the program, and the program is best understood by understanding the language. With this chapter, you begin your exploration of HyperTalk.

Why Program in HyperTalk?

The answer to this question is easy: because HyperTalk allows you to do things with HyperCard that you cannot do otherwise. Programming allows you to better create your own stacks with your own functions and to modify the functions of stacks that you get from others. If you do not do your own programming, you cannot make full use of the program. Even if you see yourself as being mostly a browser in Hyper-Card, an understanding of HyperTalk will help you better use and understand the stacks you receive from others.

About Programming

First, you should abandon the notion that programming is difficult. Though the term "programming" is used often in this book and in other discussions of HyperCard, it is an unfortunate term because it has come to suggest something that only a priesthood or a group of "nerds" does, not normal users. "Programming," you might say to yourself, "that's too hard for me." That is not the case with HyperTalk. A short time spent with the language will show you that it is easy to understand and easy to use.

The more common term used for HyperTalk programming is "scripting." HyperTalk programs are called scripts, and the word gives a better, less threatening, idea of what is going on. A script in HyperTalk is similar to a script in a play: it is a list of instructions that are carried out one at a time, not by actors on a stage, but by HyperCard.

That is not to say that scripting does not require certain skills. Careful planning and logical thinking are necessary. You are, after all, entering commands into a computer. You cannot be vague about what you want the script to do (Hyper-Talk only rarely allows vagueness). Computers require specific instructions.

You might have already used HyperTalk yourself, without necessarily realizing it. When you enter commands into the HyperCard Message box, you are usually entering Hyper-Talk commands, such as **Go card 1**. When you have created buttons that link cards and stacks, HyperCard has written small scripts in buttons for you.

So, if you are having any fears about working in Hyper-Talk, try to rid yourself of them. If you use the Save a Copy command on the File menu before you make changes to scripts, you will always have a backup copy of the stack that you can go to. The best way to learn HyperTalk is to dive in and do it. Think of a task you want to do and try to figure out how to do it. Take a look at some existing scripts and try to understand how they were done. This book includes a number of scripts and explains how they work. Look at these scripts, type them in, and modify them to do the things you want. But don't be afraid; you cannot harm the computer, of course, or the files on disk. You can, however, lose data in a stack, so use the Save a Copy command under the File menu.

What Can Scripts Do?

Scripts can do almost anything. They can be as simple as those that link two cards together or those that instruct a button to go to another card when that button is clicked. They can also be very complicated, performing functions such as exporting all the text in a stack to a file on disk. Scripts can stand on their own in buttons that are easily copied from stack to stack, or they can be part of a complex whole, requiring the presence of other scripts, certain fields, and certain items of information that the user provides. The range is really quite large, and your applications will probably contain a mixture of both long and short scripts.

Virtually anything you can do in HyperCard with the mouse or keyboard can be done in a script. Here are some examples:

- **Link cards to other cards or stacks** You can create simple direct links with the Link To button in the Button Info dialog box, or you can write scripts that find text in other cards to perform the link.

- **Perform calculations** Working with numbers in HyperTalk is intuitive and fast. If you need to perform repetitive calculations, you might as well have HyperTalk do the work for you.

- **Paint pictures** All the HyperCard paint tools can be controlled by scripts. You can use this for special effects or simple animation.

• **Act on information you type into a card**   This can include checking to make sure you typed the right sort of information—a date for example—or creating a complex query-by-example (QBE) card for a large, complex database.

• **Ask you for information**   This can include asking you what you want to do next or how you want a script to sort the stacks. HyperTalk includes two simple commands (Ask and Answer) for displaying dialog boxes and lets scripts do different things depending on which options you include.

Of course these are just a few examples. Just as the English language can form a limitless number of unique sentences, so can the HyperTalk language perform a nearly limitless number of unique functions.

Basic Concepts

HyperTalk uses a number of basic concepts that are common to all programming languages. If you have worked with such diverse languages as BASIC, Pascal, or Logo, then many of these concepts will be familiar to you. These include sequences of commands, control structures, variables, and functions. HyperTalk also includes some fairly special features and concepts that make it unique among programming languages. These concepts—including messages, the hierarchy of message passing, object orientation, and properties—are similar to object-oriented languages such as SmallTalk.

These concepts are introduced in the following discussion. Many of them will be covered in much more detail in later chapters. However, since they all form a whole, it is important to be somewhat familiar with all of them before you concentrate on any one of them.

Messages

Think of what happens when you initiate an action in Hyper-Card or on the Macintosh in general. When you click a button, a message is sent to that button telling it that the mouse has clicked it. But it goes beyond that. You can see this for yourself by following this procedure:

1. In any application, choose Print from the File menu, and you will get a standard Print dialog box.

2. Move your mouse pointer to the OK button. Now, click the mouse on that button, but do not let go. Notice how the button blackens or highlights.

3. Without letting go of the mouse button, move the mouse pointer outside the OK button. Notice that the highlighting of the OK button goes away and nothing else happens. If you move the mouse pointer back inside that button, it highlights again. Release the mouse button while the pointer is inside that button and it begins printing. (If you accidentally release the mouse button while the mouse is positioned on the OK button, press COMMAND-PERIOD to cancel printing.)

Clearly there is more going on when you click a button than that simple action. It is as if certain messages are sent to a button. When you click the button, a message is sent to the button telling it that "the mouse button is down" inside that button. The button highlights in response to that message. When you move the pointer outside the button, that message is no longer being sent, so the highlighting disappears. The OK button actually takes action when the mouse is released on the button, not when you click it. A little experimentation confirms that this happens with all Macintosh buttons.

Similar messages are sent to many Macintosh devices or

objects, as well as programs. Menus work in much the same way: the menu item is selected when you move the mouse over it and is deselected when you move the mouse outside the menu item; and the menu disappears, taking no action, if you release the button outside the menu. When you release the mouse button on a menu item, a message that you chose this item is sent to the program. This is a key to user-driven or event-driven programming. Programming in HyperTalk (and other Macintosh languages) is largely a matter of responding to events and messages generated by the user. HyperTalk scripts are, indeed, composed of handlers that respond to messages (discussed later in this chapter).

The mouse is not the only thing that generates messages, although it is a prime mover. Messages in HyperCard are also automatically generated to say such things as the stack has been opened or a new card or background is on the screen. Programming in HyperTalk also allows you to create your own messages and respond to them.

The Message box is so called because what you do when you enter something into it is send a message, consisting of the text you type, to HyperCard. Using the Message box to send messages is a good way to understand what is going on in HyperTalk, and many of the commands you use in the language can be entered easily into the Message box.

Objects

HyperCard has six types of objects: buttons, fields, cards, backgrounds, stacks, and HyperCard itself. Each of these objects is capable of receiving messages and acting on them.

Programming in HyperTalk is largely a matter of deciding which objects will respond to which messages and what the objects will do when they receive those messages. You then create handlers that respond to the messages.

Hierarchy

What happens if you send a message to an object and the object doesn't know what to do with it? Does the message disappear? No. HyperCard defines a "hierarchy" that determines what happens to each message. If the original object to which the message was sent cannot handle the message, the message is then passed along up the hierarchy until it is received by an object that can handle the message.

HyperTalk's hierarchy of message handling is very important. It makes writing scripts more modular than it might be otherwise. For example, if you have a handler that is used often in your stack, you do not need to place that handler in every button that uses it. You can place it instead into the script of the stack.

Hierarchy is also sometimes referrred to as inheritance, because each button or field has available to it all the capabilities of the card, background, and stack to which it belongs. It inherits those capabilities.

HyperCard's hierarchy of message handling is discussed in detail in Chapter 12.

Properties

An object's *properties* allows you to find out about and control the appearance and functions of HyperCard objects. For example, each button has a property called Style that determines the button's appearance on the screen. If a button is a rounded rectangle, then the Style property of that button is roundRect. Similar properties govern such things as whether a button automatically highlights (the autoHilite property) or if the name of the button is displayed (the showName property). Fields also have properties, as do cards, backgrounds, and stacks. Painting properties determine much of the behavior of the painting tools, and a set of global properties govern the behavior of HyperCard itself.

Properties and their management are detailed in Chapter 13.

Scripts

Each object in HyperCard has a script associated with it. Sometimes the script will be empty, but it is still there. Scripts contain a number of handlers that tell the object how it is to respond to messages it receives.

Handlers

A *handler* is that part of a script that tells the script how to respond to (handle) messages that are sent to that script. A script can have just one handler or none, or it can have many handlers, depending on the messages to which the script must respond. The handler, therefore, is perhaps the most basic element of HyperCard, ranking just above the statement. Think of it as being something like a paragraph of English prose.

There are two types of handlers: normal handlers, which respond to messages, and function handlers. Normal handlers behave as commands do. Function handlers work a little differently in that they send some information back to the statement that called them.

Control Structures

A *control structure* determines in what order HyperTalk interprets statements in a script. Control structures are basic to any programming language, and they perform many functions.

The most basic control structure is the On...End structure, which defines the beginning and end of a handler. Here is an example:

```
on mouseUp
  go card 1
end mouseUp
```

In this example, the "on mouseUp" and "end mouseUp" statements are control structures. They don't tell HyperTalk to *do* anything, rather they define the limits of the handler. When an object receives a message, HyperTalk searches through the script of that object for a line reading "on" followed by the message. It then interprets each of the statements that follow that line until it reaches the End statement. (This is not always true. There are special statements that halt the execution of a handler, but the concept still holds. These are discussed in Chapter 15.)

Another kind of control structure tells HyperCard to repeat a sequence of statements for a number of steps, or until a particular condition has been met.

The final type of control structure is the conditional. Often a script needs to perform one set of tasks if a conditon is true and a different set of tasks if the condition is not true. The If...Then structure provides this sort of control.

HyperTalk's set of control structures are detailed in Chapter 17.

Statements and Commands

As the name indicates, a *command* is something that orders HyperCard to do something. When you enter **Go first card**, it is a statement, as is **Put the date**. In these lines, Go and Put are commands, and the other words are *arguments* or parameters to the commands—they tell the commands exactly what they should do. Scripts are composed of sequences of statements, which are in turn composed of commands and functions followed by their arguments.

Chunk Expressions and
Data Structures

Every programming language needs ways in which it can refer to information. In most programming languages, it is left up to the programmers to define their own data structures—that is, the ways that information is organized so that it can be broken down into its parts and analyzed.

One of the advantages of a language such as HyperTalk, which is part of a larger program, is that it comes with its own built-in set of data structures and statements that access parts of those data structures. In HyperTalk these are called *chunk expressions* because they allow you to access different chunks of data.

HyperTalk's data structures are based on the basic unit of HyperCard data—the field. Fields, however, can also be broken down into smaller structures. These structures are the line, the item, the word, and the character.

A detailed discussion of HyperTalk's chunk expressions can be found in Chapter 17.

Containers and Variables

A *container* is a place where you can store data—text, numbers, dates, and the like—called *values*. Containers include fields, variables, the text selected by the user, the Message box, and a special variable called "It."

In contrast to many programming languages and other programs such as databases, all values stored in HyperCard are text. You do not need to define fields or variables as being able to hold only a specific type of information, such as text, integers, or dates. This gives HyperCard a great deal of flexibility in how it treats data.

Fields

Fields are HyperCard's main data structure for storing and manipulating text stored on cards. If you have data you wish to permanently store in HyperCard and always have available, you store it in fields. Much user input goes into fields.

Variables

A *variable* is a named container that has a value associated with it. Variables are holding places into which you can place values to work with later. You put information into a variable so that you can refer to it later generically instead of having to refer to it directly.

For example, suppose you are a teacher and are using a stack to manage test results for your students. For each student, you have a card that includes that student's name and score on the most recent test. If you want to find the average score for all the students on that particular test, you might use the handler shown in Script 10-1.

In this handler, *totalScore* is a variable to which is added the individual scores of each of the students. When all the scores are added to *totalScore*, it is then divided by the number of students (each student has his own card) to get the average.

When HyperCard is evaluating a line, it attempts to interpret each word on the line. If text is enclosed in quotes, it is a constant, and HyperCard deals with that data directly.

```
on mouseUp
   put 0 into totalScore
   repeat with x = 1 to the number of cards
      go card x
      add value(field "score") to totalScore
   end repeat
   answer "The Average score was" && totalScore / the number
of cards
end mouseUp
```

Script 10-1.   TotalScore is a local variable in this handler

If text is not enclosed in quotes, HyperCard interprets that text as a variable, and HyperCard deals with the data associated with the variable. Here are some commands you can enter into the Message box to illustrate how variables work:

```
put 10 into theNumber -- theNumber is a variable
put theNumber -- puts "10" into the message box
put theNumber / 2 -- divides theNumber by 2, and puts 5 into
the message box
put char 1 of theNumber -- puts the first char of theNumber
into the message box
```

Local Variables

Most variables are *local* to the handler that uses them. In the preceding example, *totalScore* was a local variable; once the handler stopped executing, the value associated with *total-Score* was lost. If *totalScore* were a global variable, it would put the number stored in the variable into the Message box. Local variables are convenient because you don't need to worry if you use the same variable name in different handlers. As long as variables are local, there is no conflict, and the associated values will not be confused between the two variables.

Global Variables

A global variable is a variable that you want to use in several handlers and have the same value. Global variables are distinct from local variables in that they must be *declared* before they are used. To declare a local variable, include the statement **global variableName** at the beginning of every handler that uses that global variable. (Since the variable must be declared to be global before it is actually used by the handler, that statement should be placed near the beginning of every handler.)

Global variables affect every object and every handler that declares them. In the earlier example, if you declare the variable *totalScore* to be global, then the value associated with *totalScore* is available to other handlers in the same script and handlers—including buttons, fields, cards, backgrounds, and stacks—in other scripts. The values of global variables are only changed when they are changed by other scripts that declare those global variables. Those values are lost when you quit HyperCard.

It

"It" is a special container that is used by many commands to store their values temporarily. The command most often used to put a value into "It" is the Get command. Here's an example that you can enter into the Message box:

```
get the date -- nothing happens
put it -- puts the current date
```

When you use the Get command, it gets the value of the expression you used with Get and puts the value of that expression into "It." You can then type **Put It** to display that value.

Here are some other examples:

```
Get the name of field 1
Get the name of this stack
Get field 1 -- gets the text in field 1
```

The commands that automatically put values into "It" are Ask, Answer, Convert, Get, and Read.

"The Selection"

"The Selection" is a container that allows you to manipulate the area of text currently selected with the mouse. With versions of HyperCard earlier than 1.2, there was only one way to refer to "The Selection." With versions 1.2 and greater, there is a larger set of tools that you can use to discover from a script exactly what text was selected. These are discussed in more detail in Chapter 21.

One quirk of all versions of HyperCard is that the selection becomes deselected whenever anything on the screen changes. For example, if you select some text and then click on a button that highlights, the selected text is deselected, and any statements in that button that refer to "the selection" will fail. Typing into the Message box also deselects the selection. If you have buttons that are to work with the selection, make sure they do not highlight automatically.

The Message Box

You are already familiar with using the Message box to send messages to HyperCard, but HyperTalk scripts can also use the Message box to send messages to you. When you use the Put command, you can specify where you are putting the value, but if you do not specify a destination, the default is the Message box. There are two abbreviations for the Message box—msg and Message. These three statements do the same thing:

```
put the date
put the date into the Message box
put the date into msg
```

The HyperTalk Editor

The HyperTalk editor is a mixed bag. On the one hand, it contains some features that make programming in Hyper-Talk easier than it might otherwise be. Chief among these is its automatic indentation, which makes your scripts more readable and also ensures that you have entered commands in proper format. It contains several useful keyboard short-cuts for cutting, copying, pasting, and finding text.

On the other hand, if you have used an editor such as Microsoft Word or QUED/M, you know that there are other things an editor can do. The HyperTalk editor contains no automatic search-and-replace command, making that operation more tedious than it needs to be. Nor does it contain an Undo command, which saves you a lot of grief in other programs. These are areas of HyperCard that definitely need some improvement.

Entering the Editor

There are a number of ways that you can enter the editor to start a script or edit an existing one.

Button Scripts

There are three ways to edit the scripts of buttons:

- Choose the Button tool, double-click on the button whose script you want to edit, and then click the Script button on the Button Info dialog box. (Double-clicking the button with the Button tool is the same as clicking the button once, and then choosing Button Info from the Objects menu.)

- With the Button tool, press the SHIFT key and double-click the mouse button on the button whose script you wish to edit.

- With the Browse tool, press the COMMAND and OPTION keys. All the buttons will be outlined. Click a button, and it will take you to the editor. This only works with Hyper-Card 1.2 or greater.

Field Scripts

Editing the scripts of fields is about the same as editing the scripts of buttons, and there are three ways to do it:

• With the Field tool, double-click on a field and click the Script button on the Field Info dialog box. (Double-clicking on the field with the Field tool is the same as clicking once on the field with that tool, and then choosing Field Info from the Objects menu.)

• With the Field tool, press the SHIFT key, and then double-click on the field.

• With the Browse tool, press the COMMAND, OPTION, and SHIFT keys. All the fields (and buttons) will be outlined. Click on a field, and you will be in the editor, with the script of that field. This only works with HyperCard 1.2 or greater.

Card Scripts

There are two ways to edit the script of a card:

• Choose Card Info from the Objects menu, and then click the Script button on the Card Info dialog box.

• If you are using HyperCard 1.2 or greater, you can press COMMAND-OPTION-C to edit the script of the current card.

Background Scripts

Use the same methods as you used with Card scripts to edit Background scripts:

• Choose Background Info from the Objects menu, and then click the Script button on the Background Info dialog box.

• If you are using HyperCard 1.2 or greater, press COMMAND-OPTION-B to edit the script of the current background.

Stack Scripts

Stack scripts can be edited in two ways:

- Choose Stack Info from the Objects menu, and then click the Script button on the Stack Info dialog box.

- If you are using HyperCard 1.2 or greater, press COMMAND-OPTION-S to edit the script of the current stack.

From the Message Box

If you are a keyboard-oriented person, you can also edit the scripts of many objects by typing commands into the Message window. For example, typing **Edit script of this stack** does just that.

You can also use the Message box to edit scripts of fields and buttons that are currently hidden, as shown here:

```
Edit script of card button 7
Edit script of background field "index"
```

Both these commands will open the Edit window, with the script (if any) of the specified object. You are not limited to editing scripts of objects in the current stack. You can also edit the scripts of other stacks with a command such as:

```
edit script of stack "home"
```

This works even if you are not currently in the Home stack, or any other stack whose script you want to edit. This is convenient if you have a stack that automatically sets the user level to a lower level than Scripting, thus preventing you from editing the script of the stack while you are in the stack. To edit such a stack, go to another stack and type a command similar to the previous one. When you leave the Edit window, either with the OK or Cancel buttons, you will go to the stack whose script you were editing.

Script Peeking

Using the COMMAND-OPTION or COMMAND-OPTION-SHIFT keys with the mouse to open the Edit window is called *script peeking*. If, after opening the Edit window using these keys, you continue to press the keys, you will see that the mouse pointer uses the watch cursor, and it does so for as long as you hold down those keys. If you click again while the mouse cursor is a watch, you exit the Edit window.

Using the Editor

The HyperTalk editor is very straightforward. It features four buttons, and there are less than ten key combinations for cutting, copying, and pasting text.

Cutting, Copying and Pasting Text

The editor supports standard Macintosh cutting, copying, and pasting of text, using standard keyboard shortcuts. Note that since the editor is a modal dialog box, you cannot use the Edit menu to perform these actions. You must use the keyboard shortcuts.

Cut Selection: COMMAND-X   This command cuts (erases or deletes) the selection, and places it on the Clipboard for later pasting.

Copy: COMMAND-C   This command places a copy of the selection on the Clipboard for later pasting. The text that is copied remains in place.

Paste: COMMAND-V   This command places the current contents of the Clipboard into the selection. If the selection is an insertion point, the text to the right of the selection is moved to the right. If the selection is a block of text, the selection is replaced.

Finding Text

While you cannot search and replace text, finding text is fairly easy, and the editor contains some useful extensions to standard search functions.

Find: COMMAND-F   This key combination brings up the dialog box shown in Figure 10-1. Type the text you want to find into the field on this dialog box. Clicking the OK button searches for the text. The search starts from the current insertion point or selection and proceeds to the end of the script. It cannot loop around and start again at the beginning as you can do with the Microsoft Word search function, nor can you search in the reverse direction.

This key combination performs exactly the same function as clicking the Find button at the bottom of the editor.

If the text is not found, the editor beeps once.

Find Next: COMMAND-G   This key combination finds again the current search string (the text you last entered in the Find dialog box). Since you do not need to bring up the Find

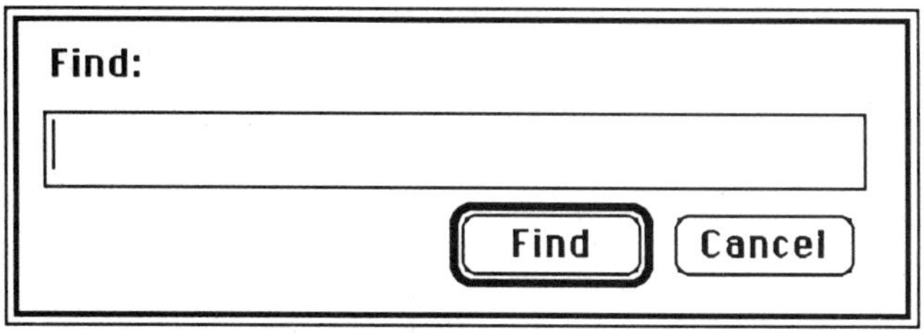

Figure 10-1.   The Find dialog box from the HyperTalk editor

dialog box every time you need to find the same text, this allows you to move quickly through a script where there might be several occurrences of the same text. Press COMMAND-G, and the editor will find the next instance of the search text.

Find Selection: COMMAND-H   This command makes the currently selected text the new search string and goes to the next instance of that text in the script.

Search and Replace

The editor does not have an automatic search-and-replace function, but since simple keystrokes are used, it is not too hard to find and replace text in a script. Here is the process:

1. Click the Find button or press COMMAND-F to get the Find dialog box. Type into this dialog box the text for which you want to search.

2. When the first instance of the text is found, type the new text in its place. Now select the new text—the text with which you want to replace the search text—and press COMMAND-C to copy this text to the Clipboard.

3. Press COMMAND-G to find the next instance of the search text. It will be selected.

4. With the found text still selected, press COMMAND-V to paste the replace text over the search text.

5. Repeat steps 3 and 4 until you have replaced all occurrences of the search text.

Long Lines of Text and OPTION-RETURN

If you have worked in the editor at all, you have probably noticed that it does not include a horizontal scroll bar, nor does it feature word wrap. You can be typing along, and when you reach the right edge of the window (the 72nd character you type), the text keeps going off the edge of the window. It is not surprising that the editor does not feature word wrap. HyperCard interpets code line-by-line, and it would be harder for both you and the editor to parse or understand the code if lines could be arbitrarily wrapped. The smallest unit of programming code is the line, and lines that are short are easier to read and understand than are lines that are long. However, there are times when all your text does not fit on one line. You might be assembling several chunks of text to form one string or be making complicated comparisons. In that case, you can use the OPTION-RETURN key combination to put a soft return at the end of a line. The soft return is represented by this character:

When HyperCard interprets a line that ends with this character, it knows the line does not really end there and considers the next line to be part of the first. Several lines, in fact, can be put together in this manner.

Make sure, however, that you do not put this character into the text of a literal string, which is surrounded by quotes. HyperCard will attempt to interpret the character as part of the string and will find a normal return at the end of the line. You will probably get an error message, or a line will execute incorrectly.

Automatic Indenting: The TAB Key

The TAB key performs one of the most useful functions of the editor—automatic indenting. Indenting in programming languages serves to make the structure of the program or script more intelligible when it is read. Indenting such things as repeat loops and If...Then testing makes the script easier to read and easier for you to navigate through and understand what is going on at each step.

With most programming languages and their editors, however, indentation is not automatic. Different programmers even can disagree on how to indent code, leading to a variety of indenting styles that loses some of the benefits of the indenting itself. Not so with the HyperTalk editor. When you press the RETURN or the TAB key to end a line, the HyperTalk editor does some limited parsing of the code you have typed.

Script 10-2 shows a sample script designed strictly to illustrate HyperCard's indentation (it doesn't actually do anything). Here is how HyperCard indents your scripts:

• At the left margin are the statements that define the handler. In the script, the "on showIndentation" and "end showIndentation" lines define the beginning and end of the handler.

• All other statements that are entered in sequence are indented two spaces from the left margin.

• Statements that are executed as the result of testing with the If statement are indented two spaces in from the line that included the If statement. An "End If" statement is at the same level as the If statement it closes, as is an Else statement.

• Statements that are executed repeatedly in a repeat loop are indented two spaces from the line that contained the Repeat statement. "End Repeat" statements are at the same level as the Repeat statement.

All indentation is relative from the previous statement. For example, if you have several If or Repeat statements, the nested statements will be indented from the previous line.

All this indentation makes debugging much easier. In some languages, it is easy to forget the necessary End If and End Repeat statements. It's not easy to forget them in Hyper-Card. For example, when you type **end handlerName** to end

```
on showIndentation
  --first level commands
  if this is true then
    -- commands executed if the true test is true
    do this stuff
  else -- at the same level as the If test
    do some other stuff
  end if -- back at the same level as the if statement
  repeat forever
    -- all statements inside the repeat loop
    -- are indented two spaces
  end repeat -- back at the same level
  -- now some nested if statements
  if this is true then
    if that is true then
      if theOther is true then
        -- the next statement is only performed if
        -- all the previous "if" tests are true
        do thisTask
        -- the following "end if" statements are at the
        -- same level of indentation as the "if" tests
        -- they are ending
      end if
    end if
  end if
  -- now end the handler
end showIndentation
```

Script 10-2.   This script is designed strictly to illustrate indentation

the handler, if that line is not at the left margin you know right away that something is wrong with the handler as you have entered it.

ENTER

Pressing the ENTER key (remember, the ENTER key is separate from the RETURN key) is the same as clicking the OK button at the bottom of the Edit window. It exits the editor and saves the changes you have made to the script. There is no keyboard shortcut for the Cancel button.

Printing Scripts

At any time, you can print the current script with the Print button at the bottom of the screen. It prints a listing similar to the one shown in Figure 10-2, which shows the date and time the printout was made and the name of the script.

Print Selection: COMMAND-P   If you only want to print a portion of a script, such as a specific handler, you can do so by selecting the text you want to print and pressing COMMAND-P. If no text is selected, the current script is printed, just as if you had clicked the Print button.

searchScript

Included in the standard Home stack is a handler called searchScript. This handler searches through all the scripts in a stack for particular text. When it finds a script that contains that text, it enters the Edit window and presents you with that script. When you exit the editor with the OK or Cancel button, it proceeds through the stack until it has checked every script in the stack.

The syntax for searchScript is

searchScript "text", stackName

If you omit the stack name, searchScript searches the current stack.

When searchScript finds a script that contains the text for which you are searching, the cursor is placed at the beginning of the script. When you are in the first script found, you will need to use the Find button or press COMMAND-F to type in the text you want to find. After you have searched for text once, the Find text is remembered, and you can press COMMAND-G to find it again, even if you are in a different script.

Since searchScript is in the script of the Home stack, it

```
6/30/88  2:06  PM           Script of bkgnd button id 16 = "Home"

on mouseUp
  go home
end mouseUp
```

Figure 10-2.   When you print a script from the editor, it includes
the date and time of printing, along with the name of
the script

is part of the hierarchy, and you can use it no matter what
other stack you are in.

Importing Scripts from Other Editors

Given some of the limitations of the HyperTalk editor, it is
tempting sometimes to use another, more powerful editor for
HyperTalk code. Microsoft Word, for example, provides several features that are convenient, such as a search-and-
replace command and the Again command (COMMAND-A),
which repeats your last action.

However, the HyperTalk editor cannot open disk files, so
you must use copy-and-paste techniques to get scripts you
have edited with other programs into HyperCard. This
works well if you have over 1MB of RAM and are using MultiFinder. If you are not using MultiFinder, it is probably not
worth the effort.

To move the text from an editor into HyperCard, simply
copy or cut the text while in that editor, switch to Hyper-
Card, open the editor with the script of the object into which
you want to paste the new text, and press COMMAND-V to
paste the text.

There is, however, one thing you should not do when using another editor to work with scripts. Since the editor uses the TAB key to perform automatic indentation, the TAB key (or the tab character) is not understood by HyperTalk scripts. Unfortunately, neither is it ignored. If you use your word processor to edit scripts, *do not* use the TAB key to help you with your indentation. Instead, use spaces or do not indent at all. If you use tabs to align lines in your word processors, the tab characters will be pasted along with the text you paste into the HyperTalk editor. If you have a tab character in a line of code, HyperCard will halt execution of the script and present you with the dialog box shown in Figure 10-3. Note that the tab character is invisible. Because the tab cannot be displayed, this kind of error can be hard to track down. The script looks fine, but the invisible tab character prevents the line from being interpreted correctly.

Where's the Program?

One thing that takes some getting used to in HyperCard is the scattered or diffuse nature of HyperTalk programs. With most programming languages, the entire program is created as one piece. There might be modules that exist separately, but in general you can read a program from top to bottom; all its pieces are together.

This is not the case with HyperTalk. Since it is an object-oriented programming language, the script or program for each object is located within that object. However, HyperTalk also features a hierarchy through which commands and messages are passed; therefore, not all the functions that an object performs will be defined within that object.

How to Find the Scripts

With the scripts spread out through the entire stack, how do you find out just where the functionality of a stack lies? How

Figure 10-3.   This alert appears if there are embedded tabs in a
script imported from another source

do you find the program? There are a number of ways to do
this.

A special HyperTalk program can help you. Eric
Alderman's Script Report, from Heizer Software, is probably
the best available tool. Script Report extracts all the scripts
from a stack in a manner that makes their organization
clear. Scripts are grouped hierarchically; the report produced by this program shows the stack script first, followed
by the background script, background button and field
scripts, card scripts, and card button and field scripts.
Script Report can export its report to Outline programs,
such as Acta and More, which help you visualize the structure of the stack in a hierarchical manner. Similar tools are
available from other sources, and scripts for doing this have
appeared in some magazines.

How do you find out what a script is doing without one of
these tools? Probably the best way is to start with the buttons
that initiate the action. Open the script of a button and follow
its logic. You will probably find that the button includes
statements that refer to handlers elsewhere in the stack. To
find those buttons, move up the hierarchy. If the button is a
background button, check the background script; if it is a
card button, check the card script. Next check the stack

script. It might take some work (which is why Script Report was developed), because handlers can be spread throughout a stack. Unless the author has relied extensively on external commands and functions, however, you will always be able to find the code.

Script Openness

One of the most valuable characteristics of HyperCard is the open nature of the scripts in a stack. You can examine the code of virtually any stack you get. This has greatly contributed to the fast learning curve the HyperCard community has experienced with HyperTalk. It is easy for everyone to learn from the successes and failures of others.

Script openness, in short, means that when you make a stack available to others, you are also making available to them the algorithms, logic, and actual code that made your stack work. This is in contrast to other languages, such as C, Pascal, and even many dialects of BASIC, in which programs are delivered to others in a compiled state. The program is not delivered as source code, but rather as instructions that have been compiled or translated into instructions the computer reads directly. It is virtually impossible to translate the application that was delivered to you as, for example, PageMaker, and decipher the logic, let alone modify the program.

Script openness also means that scripters must act more responsibly in two respects than is necessary with other languages.

First, you need to be careful of your borrowing. On the one hand, as we have mentioned, script openness has increased the rate at which people have learned HyperTalk. It also means that development time can be much quicker on new products. Why reinvent the wheel when you can use the algorithm developed by someone else to solve a similar problem? In most HyperCard libraries are several buttons, handlers, and scripts that were copied from various sources. Most scripters do not mind that sort of thing.

There is a line, however, that you should not cross with your borrowing. If you are making extensive use of concepts, scripts, or even buttons that were originally created by someone else, you need to think very carefully about what you have done when you make your stack public. At the very least, you should give credit to the original creator of the concept. If you are using a handler that you have gotten from someone, it would not hurt to ask that person's permission to include the handler in your script. If you are making extensive use of work done by someone else, you could offer to pay them a royalty if your application has the potential to generate royalties.

In short, don't pass off as your own the work of others. Acknowledge the sources of the tools you got from others.

The second responsibility that open code gives you is the flip side of the first. Remember that your code will be open to be seen and used by others, and act accordingly. Write scripts that are easy to read and generic enough to be used in a number of situations. Comment your scripts, especially where their functions might not be clear. Don't be selfish about your code. Just as you have gotten good ideas from others, allow others to share yours.

Some Elements of
HyperTalk Style

Goals of Style
Some Style Tips

Every language—whether it is a spoken or written language, such as English, or a computer programming language, such as HyperTalk—has its own elements that help you create a usable style. For English style you can read Strunk and White's *Elements of Style*. For computer languages, however, there have been few general-interest books published that tell you how to write code with style. That day will come when people have had more experience with languages such as HyperTalk. Nevertheless, there are some general rules you can follow that will make your programs easier to create, read, debug, and modify.

Goals of Style

Do you really need to keep style in mind when creating scripts? Can't you just start coding and let the script's style come from the natural-language nature of HyperTalk to document itself? The answer is yes and no at the same time. HyperTalk is a flexible, natural language that creates scripts that are often easy to write and to read. Understanding simple scripts is often as easy as reading them. On the other hand, when you are working with involved procedures that use many variables or that perform complicated functions, you really do need to keep style in mind and tailor your style of scripting to meet certain needs.

Adopting a consistent style of programming has several goals, which are discussed in the following sections.

Creating Reusable Scripts

With some progamming experience, you will find that once you have solved a certain problem, you can simply adapt existing code to a new situation. Adopting a consistent style makes this easier.

In keeping with the erector-set nature of HyperCard, you can build "button libraries" such as those found in the Button Ideas stack. If the scripts in your buttons are written in a nonspecific manner—that is, if they do not rely on the existence of other buttons, fields, or scripts—assembling a library will be easier.

Creating Scripts That Are Easily Debugged

It is the rare—and simple—script that works the first time. Even if you have carefully planned your script, you usually find that it doesn't work right the first time, and you need to work with it to make it successful. A consistent style facilitates debugging.

Creating Scripts That Can Be Modified

If you need to modify a script a month or a year after you have written it, your job will be easier if you adhere to a consistent style.

Working with a Group

Group stack development is much more difficult than individual stack development. If all members in a group keep to a consistent, agreed-on style of creating scripts and documenting them, the whole process will proceed quickly and easily.

Some Style Tips

The following sections by no means represent a complete set of rules. HyperTalk is a new language—less than a year old as this book is written—and some aspects of the language related to style have not yet been thoroughly explored. Nevertheless, some rules can be put forward, and adopting these rules can do a lot to make your scripts easy to read and maintain.

Use a Flowchart

One of the easiest habits to get into with HyperTalk is to simply create a new button, go right to the script of the button, and start typing in code. This works fine for simple buttons. For longer scripts, however, especially those that require a great deal of decision making, this is not the best way to work.

Flowcharting might seem to be an anachronism, a throwback to the days of COBOL or BASIC programming. When flowcharting is mentioned, you might have thoughts of flowcharting templates, arcane symbols, and the like. Using traditional tools, however, is not as important as developing a personal style that tells you what needs to be done at each step. It's not necessary to rush out and buy special templates or books on programming to chart the flow of a script.

Instead, break the procedure up into discrete steps that can be easily summarized. Come up with a short, one-line description of each step that must be performed. Don't be afraid to scrap the entire design and start over if what you come up with doesn't make sense.

Although it is best to do flowcharting when you begin creating a script, you can also do some flowcharting with existing scripts. This reverse engineering can help you understand what is going on in a particular script and make it easier to modify that script later.

The two goals of flowcharting are to make the logic of a procedure clear in your mind before you start typing the code and to isolate those steps that can be used repeatedly.

When you have made your flowchart correctly, you can use it to help you generate HyperTalk code that seems almost to write itself. As you will see in the next section, which deals with comments, you can easily turn the outline of a long process into the HyperTalk code that actually handles the process.

Figure 11-1 shows a flowchart for a simple button that sorts a stack listing the authors and titles of books. Script 11-1 is the script that was developed as a result of the flowchart. While flowcharting will probably not help you much for such small buttons and handlers, it can certainly help a great deal on longer, more complex projects.

Comment Your Code

Commenting is easily done in HyperTalk. When the Hyper-Talk interpreter encounters two dashes (--), whether they begin a line or are part of the line, it ignores the rest of the characters on the line. Therefore, begin each comment with two dashes.

HyperTalk is pretty much a self-documenting language; it is easy to understand because of its similarity to standard English. However, there will be times when your code becomes less like English, particularly when you are performing many repeat loops, mathematical operations, and the like.

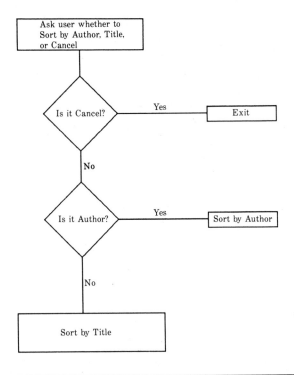

Figure 11-1.   Simple flowcharting need not be elaborate to help you define the logic of a script

```
on mouseUp
  ask "Sort by what?" with "Cancel" or "Author" or "Title"
  if it is "Cancel" then exit mouseUp
  if it is "Author" then
    sort by background field "Last Name"
  else
    sort by background field "Title"
end mouseUp
```

Script 11-1.   This short handler was developed from the flowchart in Figure 11-1

Commenting allows you to insert into your scripts notations that identify the purposes of various parts of the script and document what these parts do. You can comment entire handlers, use one-line comments to describe the purpose of the next line, or insert small comments at the end of a line to remind yourself of what the line does.

Script 11-2 shows a few examples of comments. In this instance, the comments aren't much use because the mouse-Up handler doesn't do anything but put the number 7 into the local variable *daysOfWeek*. The first comment describes what the handler does. You should put a comment like this one in every handler whose purpose is not immediately obvious. The second comment describes the purpose of the variable used.

Commenting can also be used to help you develop scripts. When developing any script, you first plan out the functions of the script—either in your mind or on paper with a flow-chart. If you intend to build a handler to perform a complicated series of functions, put the comments in before you start writing the script. Script 11-3 is an example of commenting to develop a search-and-replace function. The comments isolate all the elements that need to be performed. Each line of comments was transcribed directly from a simple flowchart of the search-and-replace function. (The completed function can be found in Chapter 21.)

```
on mouseUp
  -- this handler does such-and-such
  put 7 into daysOfWeek -- holds number of days in the week
end mouseUp
```

Script 11-2.   This script includes comments

```
on searchReplace findWhat replaceWith whatField confirm
  -- findWhat holds what we are searching for
  -- replaceWith holds what we are replacing findWhat with
  -- whatField defines the field we need to search in
  -- if confirm is true, ask the user at each instance

  -- start at the beginning of the stack

  -- now find the instance of the text

  -- if confirm is true, we need to ask the user

  -- if the user says no, loop back to start over again

  -- if confirm is false or user says yes,
  -- then do the replace

  -- loop back to start the find again

  -- all done!  let the user know

  -- finish the routine

end searchReplace
```

Script 11-3.   This script shows how to use comments as a starting place when developing code

You should be able to see the benefits of this approach. If you start commenting from the beginning, leaving blank lines after the comments, you have isolated each of the specific steps needed to complete the function of the handler. Once you have isolated these steps, proceeding to the actual coding of the script is easy. In fact, sometimes the actual HyperTalk code will be very similar to the comments themselves. Careful planning not only isolates what the handler needs to do, but it also helps to create a compact handler that is already commented —you won't need to go back and insert the comments later.

Write Short Handlers

Writing short handlers is one of the best techniques you can use. When you look at some long handlers, you will often see that they contain repetitive steps that could be more easily modified and understood if they were broken up into smaller chunks. A one-line reference to another handler is much easier to understand than a series of commands or statements.

For example, consider the process of locking certain HyperTalk properties. Often, when going between cards and stacks, scripts set certain properties to false. This is discussed in more detail in Chapters 13 and 18. Normally, to set these various properties to "true," three lines are required:

```
set lockScreen to true
set lockMessages to true
set lockRecent to true
```

At the end of the script, you usually need to set these properties to "false" again, which uses three more lines. The total of six lines of code makes the script long and somewhat hard to read. You can replace each set of three lines with a short handler called doLock:

```
on doLock state
    set lockMessages to state
    set lockRecent to state
    set lockScreen to state
end doLock
```

This handler can then be called with the line "doLock true," which locks these properties, and "doLock false," which unlocks them. If you place this handler into a stack or background script, it will be available to all the scripts that are part of that background or stack. Six lines of code in a handler are replaced with two lines of code (one to lock the properties, one to unlock them). With fewer lines in the script, it is easier to read and debug, and the handler is easier to understand. The doLock handler is a "black box," and each handler that calls it needs to know only which variable to pass to it.

Although doLock is a trivial handler, the same technique can be used with more important handlers that take up many lines of code.

Pass Parameters

As the doLock handler shows, handlers can receive parameters. In the case of doLock, the parameter that handler took could have one of two values: "true" or "false." It received this parameter from the script that called it. Passing parameters to handlers helps you create handlers that are more *portable;* because they receive information they need from the script that called them, they do not need to rely on the existence of other objects in the stacks.

Create Functions

Functions are similar to handlers, but they operate in a slightly different manner. When you call a handler from a script, it performs its tasks and then returns control to the script that called it. When you call a function from a script, the function performs its tasks, but it then returns some data to the line that called it. Also, functions frequently require you to send some information to them.

For example, Offset is a built-in HyperCard function that returns the position of a specific item of text within another item of text. When you type **Offset("C", "Hypercard")**, HyperCard returns 6 because "C" is the sixth letter in HyperCard. You send Offset two items of information — the character you are looking for and the string of text in which you want Offset to find that character. The entire Offset function, including its arguments, can replace the number 6 in a line of HyperCard. For example,

```
put "T" into char offset ("C","HyperCard") of "HyperCard"
```

gives the same result as

```
put "T" into char 6 of "HyperCard"
```

Both commands will cause "HyperCard" to become "Hyper-Tard".

You can write functions that act in a manner similar to the built-in functions. In Chapter 33, there is a function called fileName. This function takes no arguments, but it returns the name of a file to the line that called it. It even checks for errors. All the functions of fileName could have been handled within the script that called it, or they could have been taken care of with a handler instead of a function. However, making fileName a function enables it to send some information back to the handler that called it. In this case, fileName returns the name of the file that you typed.

Take Advantage of the Hierarchy

HyperCard's message hierarchy is the key to writing short, clear scripts. (Hierarchy was discussed in detail in Chapters 10 and 12.) The message hierarchy allows you to put handlers or functions into certain locations—card, background, or stack scripts—and have them accessible to every button that is part of the object. In effect, each object that is part of another object inherits the capabilities of that object. A button inherits the handlers and routines that are part of the card, background, and stack to which that button belongs.

Taking advantage of this is important when you are writing portable scripts. Suppose you have a task that must be performed by many of the buttons in a stack. (The doLock task mentioned earlier in this chapter is an example.) Instead of placing this handler in the script of every button that needs it, you can place it into the script of the stack. That way, doLock is available to every script in the stack, and you need to type it only once. If you want to change the way it functions, you need to change it only once. It becomes a black box that is available to every object.

When you are creating scripts, keep an eye out for routines that you can put into the hierarchy. Flowcharting can be a big help here.

Document Scripts

As already mentioned, it is very important to document your scripts. You should not only comment and describe every handler and many routines in the handler, but also all the scripts, thus clarifying how they work together.

Remember that taking advantage of HyperCard's message hierarchy can save you from using the same lines over and over again in a script, and it can help to make particular scripts and handlers shorter. The problem with reliance on the hierarchy is that it cuts down on the reusability of your scripts. A button that relies on the presence of a function or handler in a stack script will fail if you place it into another stack that does not include that function or handler.

One way around this situation is to document, within a script, all the elements that the script needs in order to work correctly. Especially, this should include elements that are not part of the script itself. You can put this documentation at the top of a script so it is easy to see. Here is a list of standard information you can put at the top of every script:

- **Date written/scripter's name and date modified/ modifier's name**   These two items help you ascertain who did what to the script and when it was done.

- **Handlers and functions in the script**   Simply list the various handlers and functions included in the script. This alone can be a big help in finding out where handlers and functions are located, which can help you in debugging.

• **External handlers and functions that the script uses**   This information is important. When you are moving a script to another stack, you want to make sure that you are also moving all the other elements needed by the script.

• **Global variables used**   For each function and handler in the script, list the global variables that it uses. You should also note separately the global variables *modified* by each of the handlers.

• **A short description of what the script does**   Sometimes the name of a button is not specific enough to tell you everything the script does. Including such a description at the top of a script can help you and others to know just what is going on.

Beginning scripters might think that these steps make it more time-consuming or difficult to create working scripts. It is true that some of them do; however, the time spent creating a complex script might be a small part of the time you actually spend working with that script. Debugging and modification often can take more work than the original job of creation, and that is where the techniques discussed in this chapter help. For small scripts and simple buttons, you don't really need to worry about many of these elements of style. For large, complicated scripts and for portable scripts, however, they can save you time and help produce scripts that work efficiently.

Messages

In Chapter 10 you saw that messages can be sent to a button by moving the mouse pointer over a button and holding down the mouse button. The button highlighted while the mouse button was held down inside the button, it de-highlighted when the mouse pointer was moved outside the button, and the button action was initiated when the mouse button was released while the pointer was inside the button. In fact, a series of messages is sent to the button, telling it that the mouse is within the button, that the mouse button is being held down, and that the mouse button was released on the button.

T
W
E
L
V
E

In this chapter you will see how messages are sent not only to buttons, but also to all the objects in HyperCard. You will learn about the various system messages of HyperTalk. Messages are one of the most fundamental parts of Hyper-Talk. Learning the language depends in large part on developing a mastery of message sending and handling.

What Is a Message?

So what is a message anyway? This chapter documents all the system messages. A *system message* is a message that HyperCard sends in response to events initiated by the user—such as clicking on a button, typing text in a field, and creating a new card.

There is another class of messages, however. These are messages that are not created by HyperCard, but are created and generated by scripts or users.

Here's an example of a message and a way to create a new one. Open the Message box, type **foobar**, and press RETURN. "Foobar" is a word that HyperCard does not understand; it is not in its vocabulary. HyperCard accordingly responds with the alert shown in Figure 12-1.

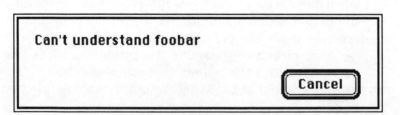

Figure 12-1.   The alert HyperCard gives you if it can't understand a word in a script

However, you can change that by writing a handler for the word "foobar." Follow these steps:

1. Open a card script. It doesn't matter what card you choose to do this with.

2. Into the card script, type the short script shown in Script 12-1.

3. Close the Script editor by clicking the OK button.

4. Now type **foobar** into the Message box again. Hyper-Card responds with the dialog box shown here:

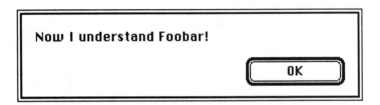

You have just created a handler for a new message—the Foobar message. Of course, this handler is totally trivial, and you should probably get rid of it right now by editing the script of the same card, selecting the Foobar handler, and deleting all its lines. Leave the editor by clicking the OK button.

Although this particular handler is trivial, the technique is not. Programming in HyperCard is a combination of re-sponding to—handling—system messages and generating and handling new messages that you create yourself. The new messages you create behave just as do commands in the HyperTalk language.

```
on foobar
    answer "Now I understand Foobar!"
end foobar
```

Script 12-1.   A handler intercepts a new message

Where Messages Come from

Perhaps the most readily understood source of messages is the mouse, but messages can also come from a number of other sources.

The Menu Bar

When you choose a menu item in HyperCard, a message is sent that you have chosen that menu item. The message that is sent is doMenu *menuItem*, where *menuItem* lists the exact text of the menu item chosen. For example, if you choose the Open Stack command from the File menu, then the message "doMenu Open Stack..." is sent to the current card.

Many HyperCard programmers have used the doMenu message to intercept commands you choose from the keyboard and stop their actions. For example, it is possible to create a stack in which the Go Next command is not appropriate, such as a stack with cards that require specific information to be filled in, but that information has not been filled in correctly. In this case, a handler such as the one in Script 12-2 could be used.

This handler, when placed in the script of a card, reacts to the doMenu message. If the second word of the message, which is held in the variable *what*, is "next" or "previous," then you are warned to fill out the card completely. Otherwise, if the *what* variable contains a different message, that message is passed to the card, and the command is carried out.

The Mouse

The mouse is the most apparent and comprehensible source of messages. In Chapter 10 you saw how the mouse generated messages sent to a button. The mouse also sends messages directly to a field or a card. Mouse messages are detailed later in this chapter.

```
on doMenu what
   if what is "next" or what is "previous" then
     answer "Please fill out the card completely"
   else
     pass doMenu
   end if
end doMenu
```

Script 12-2.   A doMenu handler that stops the user from going to the next or previous card

The Message Box

As its name implies, the Message box is a common generator of messages. When you type something into the Message box and press RETURN, the message you have typed is sent to the current card. As will be explained later in this chapter, you can use the Send command in the Message box to send messages directly to specific objects.

The Keyboard

You can send messages by typing them in the Message box; in addition, certain keystrokes also send messages to the system. Two keyboard messages are sent to active fields, and others are sent directly to the card (see the section "Keyboard Messages" later in this chapter).

Events (System Messages)

You have probably noticed that there is a small field in the corner of the Home card that contains the time, which is constantly updated. The card is responding to a message that is almost constantly being sent to every card—the Idle message—which essentially says that no messages are being sent. Responding to this message, an Idle handler in the script of the Home card puts the time into the "Time" field.

Other system messages are sent in response to certain events: for example, creating new objects or deleting existing ones.

Where Messages Go

When a message gets sent, where does it go? The answer depends in part on where the message was generated.

If the message was generated by the mouse, it is sent first to the object the mouse cursor was over. By clicking on a button, field, or card, you send the message to that button, field, or card. If the script of the object that receives the message has a handler in it for the message, the handler is executed, and the message is sent no further.

If the object to which the message was sent does not have a handler for the message, the message is sent up the hierarchy. The next step is the card script. Again, if the card script has a handler for the message, the handler is executed and the message goes no further.

After the card script, the message is sent to the background script and then to the stack script. If none of these scripts can handle the message, HyperCard checks the resources of the stack to see if the message is handled by an external command (XCMD) or function (XFCN). *External commands* and *external functions* are small programs written in other languages, such as Pascal or C, to add functions to HyperCard. They are discussed in Chapter 32.

After checking the current stack, HyperCard checks the script of the Home stack to see if the message is handled there. This means that you can install handlers or externals into your Home stack and have them available to you no matter what stack you are working in. As long as the message is not intercepted before it reaches Home, it will be executed by the Home stack script.

HyperCard also checks the resources of the Home stack to see if the message is handled by an XCMD or XFCN installed in the Home stack. Again, this means that you can install commonly used externals into your Home stack and use them from anywhere.

Finally, after all this checking, HyperCard itself receives the message. If the message is one of the system messages discussed in this chapter, nothing happens. If the message is one of HyperCard's commands or functions, that command or function is evaluated and executed. If neither of these conditions are met, HyperCard gives you the "Can't Understand" alert, shown in Figure 12-1.

That's a lot of checking for HyperCard to do. Remember, it must do this with every message, command, and function in the language. Fortunately, HyperCard does this message checking so quickly you don't even notice the delay.

Figure 12-2 illustrates how messages pass through the hierarchy. Each level of the hierarchy is described in the following sections.

Buttons and Fields

Mouse messages are sent directly to buttons or fields; for example, when you move the mouse into a button or a field or click it.

Card Script

The next item in the hierarchy is the script of the card. Many messages will be sent directly to a card. Keyboard messages, Message box messages, and system messages are all sent to the current card first. Even messages that are

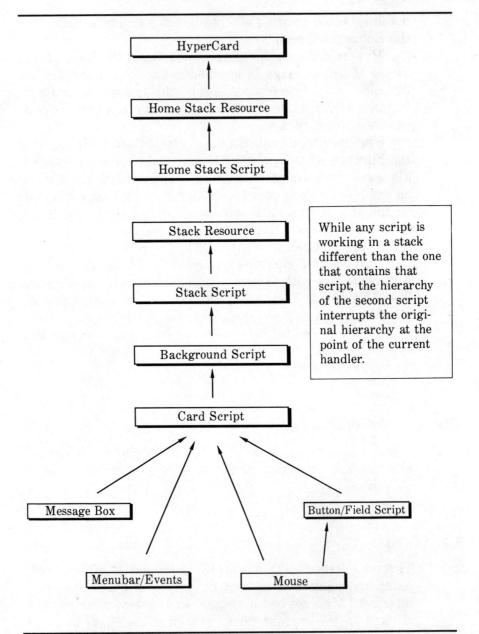

While any script is working in a stack different than the one that contains that script, the hierarchy of the second script interrupts the original hierarchy at the point of the current handler.

Figure 12-2. The hierarchy through which HyperCard's messages are sent

related to backgrounds and stacks (for example, newBackground and newStack) are first sent to the current card.

Background Script

The next item up the hierarchy is the script of the current background. All handlers in the background script are available to all cards (and thus all objects on cards) that share that same background.

Stack Script

The next item in the hierarchy is the stack script. Message handlers in the stack script are available to all the backgrounds, cards, buttons, and fields in the stack.

Stack Resource

Resources are discussed in Chapter 31, but a brief discussion here will help define this level of the hierarchy. HyperCard features two types of resources—XCMD (external command) and XFCN (external function). These are commands and functions that are written in another programming language, such as C or Pascal, and are added to HyperCard. Using these other languages, programmers can add special-purpose commands and functions to HyperTalk that it does not possess in its normal state. There are quite a few of these externals available now, serving such varied purposes as presenting standard Open and Save dialog boxes under control of HyperTalk and adding pop-up menus.

When HyperTalk is searching through the hierarchy of messages, XCMDs and XFCNs are treated in the same way as other commands or handlers. Indeed, it can be helpful to think of an external command or function as an extension of a script.

Home Stack Script

The Home stack script is one of the final steps up the hierarchy. All message handlers in the script of the Home stack are available to all other stacks you have. This is very important and useful for the HyperCard user. You can place into the Home stack handlers that you often use, so you won't need to copy them from stack to stack. As it is shipped, the Home stack includes a number of such handlers—including search-Script which searches through all the scripts in a stack for particular text.

Home Stack Resource

Just as individual stacks can have resources, so can the Home stack. Before its final stop in the hierarchy at HyperCard itself, HyperCard checks the resources of the Home stack to see if the requested handler is there.

HyperCard

Finally, the hierarchy ends at HyperCard itself. When a message reaches the HyperCard level, one of three things occurs:

• If the message is one of those discussed in this chapter, such as newCard or Idle, HyperCard does nothing. It has no built-in handlers for these messages.

• If the message is a HyperCard command or function, the message is executed.

• If the message is not a built-in message, a command, or a function, HyperCard displays an alert telling you it cannot understand the message. If the message was sent as part of a script, execution of the script is halted. In HyperTalk, there is no way to detect this sort of occurrence.

Detours

There are times when the hierarchy is not as simple as the one shown in Figure 12-1. Suppose you have a script in a button in one stack that does some work in another stack; for example, a script that exports text in fields to a text file or a script that searches another stack for specific text. In these examples, the hierarchy of the second stack—the card, background, and stack scripts—is checked *before* the hierarchy of the original stack.

Where to Place Message Handlers

One question you need to decide when creating handlers is where in the hierarchy you are going to place them. Will the new handler be placed in the stack, background, or card script? Will it be placed in the button script itself?

Unfortunately there is no hard-and-fast rule for this. However, it makes sense to put new handlers at the lowest point in the hierarchy where they will do the most good and to avoid duplication of efforts. If you have a handler that is going to be used by the buttons and fields on a particular card only, then put that handler into the card script. If it will be used by buttons and fields on several cards in the same background, then put it into the background script. If it will be used by buttons and fields on all the cards in a stack, then put it into the stack script.

The functions of many of the message handlers you create will dictate where they go. For example, if you are creating a handler for the openStack message, it makes sense to put that handler into the script of the stack.

In the discussion of messages in this chapter, the messages are grouped by the object that generates them or the object to which they are normally directed. This will provide some guidance as to where to place them.

Mouse Messages

Mouse messages are sent in response to mouse activity, and they are sent only when the Browse tool is selected.

Simply clicking a button actually triggers a number of messages. As the mouse pointer is moved into the button, mouseEnter is sent to the button, and mouseWithin is sent as long as the mouse is within the button. When you press the mouse button, mouseDown is sent, and when the mouse button is released, mouseUp is sent to the button. The mouse-Leave message is sent when the mouse leaves the button.

mouseEnter

This message is sent to buttons and fields. It means that the mouse has entered the object.

You can use this message for a number of purposes, such as changing the shape of the mouse cursor when it enters a button. This might be useful when the button is not immediately visible.

The handler in Script 12-3 turns the mouse cursor into a spinning beach ball like that used by HyperCard when it is sorting. Note that this "busy" cursor is only available in HyperCard version 1.2 or greater.

```
on mouseEnter
  repeat while the mouseLoc is within the rect of me
    set cursor to busy
    if the mouse is down then
      click at the loc of me
      exit repeat
    end if
  end repeat
end mouseEnter
```

Script 12-3.   This handler sets the cursor to "busy" as long as the mouse is in its button

This handler works by first reacting to the mouseEnter message. It then constantly keeps track of the mouse location indicated by mouseLoc, and while the mouse is still in the button, it sets the cursor to "busy." If you click the mouse button, the script also clicks the mouse button, sending the mouseDown and mouseUp messages to the button. You could also write this handler as a mouseWithin handler.

mouseWithin

This message is sent to buttons and fields. It means that the mouse is within the boundaries of the target.

You can see the effects of the mouseWithin message when you move the mouse pointer over an unlocked field: the pointer turns into a text-editing I-Beam. This happens, as you have probably noticed, in virtually all Macintosh applications.

mouseLeave

This message is sent to buttons and fields. It means that the mouse has left the boundaries of the target.

mouseDown

This message is sent to buttons, fields, and cards. It means that you have held the mouse button down while the mouse pointer is within the target. If the button is set to autoHilite, then the button will highlight (blacken) while the mouse is down.

mouseStillDown

This message is sent to buttons, fields, and cards. This message is sent as long as you hold down the mouse button. If the button is set to autoHilite, the button will remain black while the mouseStillDown is being sent.

Unlike mouseDown, this message is sent as long as you hold down the mouse button.

mouseUp

This message is sent to buttons, fields, and cards. It means that you have released the mouse button, and the mouse pointer is within the target. This is probably the most used message of all. Handlers for the mouseUp message usually trigger the action that the button will perform. When you create a button and first open its script, HyperCard puts the lines "on mouseUp" and "end mouseUp" into the script and leaves a blank line between those two lines for you to enter the actions the button is to take.

Keyboard Messages

The keyboard can also send messages, aside from the messages that are sent with the keyboard in the Message box. With two exceptions (returnInField and enterInField), keyboard messages are sent to the current card.

returnKey

This message is sent to a card. The returnKey message simply tells the card that you pressed the RETURN key. This message is not sent if the insertion point or selection is in a field; instead, the Return character is typed into the field.

enterKey

This message is sent to a card and indicates that you pressed the ENTER key. This message is not sent if the insertion point or selection is in a field.

tabKey

This message is sent to a card to indicate that you pressed the TAB key.

If this message is not intercepted by a handler, Hyper-Card selects the text of the next field. If no field is currently selected, the text of the first background field is selected.

controlKey

This message is sent to a card.

If you have one of the new Macintosh keyboards (either the kind shipped with the Macintosh SE or II or one of the Extended keyboards), you have a CONTROL key on the left side of the keyboard. When you press the CONTROL key and then press another key, a message is sent to the card signaling the event.

The controlKey message includes the ASCII value of the character that was typed while the CONTROL key was pressed. Typing **w** with the CONTROL key held down sends the message "controlKey 23" to the card.

arrowKey (Left, Right, Up, Down)

The arrow keys also generate messages, in the form of arrowKey *direction*. *Direction* will be replaced by "left," "right," "up," or "down."

If the insertion point or the selection is not in a field and no handler intercepts these messages, HyperCard uses the arrow keys for card navigation (RIGHT ARROW takes you to the next card, LEFT ARROW to the previous card, UP ARROW to the most recent card, and DOWN ARROW to the next card in the Recent list). If the insertion point is in a text field, the arrow keys move the insertion point through the field, and the arrowKey message is not sent.

returnInField

This message, in HyperCard 1.2 or greater only, is sent to the current field (the one the selection point is in).

This message allows a script to take over and determine what to do if you press a RETURN key while in a field. If this message is not trapped by a handler, then one of several things can occur.

First, if the autoTab property of the field is "true" and if the insertion point is on the last line of the field, then Hyper-Card sends the tabKey message to the current field. Second, if the tabKey message is not intercepted by a handler and if the text of the field has been changed, the closeField message is sent to the field, and the text of the next field is selected.

enterInField

This message is sent to a field and signals that you have pressed the ENTER key in a field. It is used for the same reasons as returnInField.

Button-Related Messages

Each class of HyperCard objects has a set of messages that are sent to it. The following messages are commonly sent to buttons.

newButton

The newButton message signals that a new button has been created. If a newButton handler is placed in the script of an existing button, the handler is invoked only when that button is copied and then pasted. If the handler is placed in a card, background, or stack script, newButton is sent whenever a new button is created in that object's domain.

```
on newbutton
   set style of the target to roundRect
   set autohilite of the target to true
   set showname of the target to true
end newbutton
```

Script 12-4.   A newButton handler can make all new buttons look the same

There are a number of uses for this message. For example, suppose you are working on a stack and you want all the buttons in the stack to have the same sort of appearance. Script 12-4 shows a handler that can take care of that for you. You could modify this script to do a number of other things, such as include standard handlers and automatically name the button.

deleteButton

This message is sent to the button when it is deleted. You can delete buttons by selecting them and using the Cut Button or Clear Button command, or by pressing the DELETE or BACKSPACE key.

To prevent a button from being deleted, you can use this message with the handler shown in Script 12-5. This handler simply selects the target (the button to which the message was sent), copies the button, and immediately pastes it again.

Note: There are some problems with this technique. The first button is actually deleted and a new one is created. Therefore, the numbers of the two buttons might be different: the new button will become the last button on the card. Also, as written, this handler will only create card buttons. You could modify it, however, to check if the button is a background button and create a new one.

```
on deleteButton
   select the target
   doMenu "copy button"
   doMenu "paste button"
end deleteButton
```

Script 12-5.   A deleteButton handler that prevents a button from being deleted

Field-Related Messages

A set of messages is sent to fields when you change information in the field or when you copy, delete, or create a field.

returnInField

For HyperCard 1.2 or greater, returnInField is sent to a field when you press the RETURN key while the cursor is in the field.

The purpose of returnInField is to allow a scripter to trap the RETURN key, thus preventing more than one line from being typed into a field. In earlier versions of Hyper-Card, RETURN always generated a new line in the field—a real nuisance if the field displayed only one line on the screen. A script that intercepts this message can do a number of things with the field, including tabbing to the next field and checking the text you typed into the field to make sure it is of the right type or falls into the correct range.

If the message is not intercepted by a handler, if the autoTab property of the field is "true," and if the insertion point is on the last line of the field, then HyperCard sends the tabKey message to the field. If the tabKey message is not intercepted, the cursor moves to the next field on the card. That's a lot of message passing. If the contents of the field have changed since you clicked on it, the closeField message is sent to the field.

enterInField

This message is sent to a field when you press the ENTER key while the cursor is in the field. As with returnInField, it performs a tabKey if the autoTab of a field is "true," if you are on the last line of the field, and the message is not intercepted by a handler in the field.

newField

This message is sent when a new field is created. As with newButton, you can use this message to have HyperCard automatically create new fields for you that have a certain set of parameters, such as type, font, the presence of autoTab, and wide margins.

openField

OpenField is sent to a field when you click on the field or when you enter the field with the TAB key.

closeField

CloseField is sent to a field when you click on the field, type some new text into it, and then use the keyboard to leave the field with the TAB, RETURN, or ENTER key.

It is not sent to a field when you change a field and use the mouse to click in another field, nor if you select a field and type the same text into the field that was already there. It is not sent to a field when a script puts a new value into it.

```
on closeField
  get target
  repeat with i = 1 to length(it)
    if char i of it is not in "0123456789" then
      beep
      select text of the target
      exit closeField
    end if
  end repeat
end closeField
```

Script 12-6.   This closeField button prevents you from entering nonnumeric text into a field

The most common use for closeField is for data validation. For example, if you have a field that asks for a person's age, only numbers will be valid entries. Script 12-6 shows a closeField handler that checks to make sure all the characters typed are numbers.

This handler works in a straightforward manner. First it uses the "get target" line to get the text you entered. (Note that this use of Get works only in version 1.2 or greater.) It then checks each character to see if that character is a number. If it is not a number, it beeps to warn you that an error has occurred and selects the text of the field for retyping. This handler could be revised easily to make sure the numbers fall within a particular range or to include other characters, such as the dollar sign, among the allowable characters.

deleteField

DeleteField is sent when a field is being deleted. As with deleteButton, you can intercept this message to reverse the action of field being deleted. However, it won't do you much good if you want to use it to prevent you from deleting data.

The deleteField message cannot stop a field from being deleted. It only reacts to the deletion of the field, and, of course, when the field is deleted all the text in the field is deleted along with it. When deleting background fields, HyperCard provides its own alert that queries whether you really want to delete the field. With card fields, however, there is nothing you can do to prevent the deletion.

How Mouse Messages Are Sent to a Field

The mouse-related messages sent to a field depend in part on the setting of the lockText property of the field. If lockText is "true," you cannot select text. It can be set in the Field Info dialog box and can be checked with the lockText property, as discussed in Chapter 13.

All the standard mouse messages are sent to a locked field, allowing you to trap for mouse clicks on the field, such as to search for words, and so on.

However, mouseDown and mouseUp are not sent to unlocked fields. HyperCard can, therefore, allow you to click in fields, select text, and so on without interference from mouse handlers in the field's script.

Card-Related Messages

All messages, of course, are sent to cards as the messages move up the hierarchy. The following messages, however, relate specifically to cards.

newCard

This message is sent when a new card is created. A handler for this message is most useful when included in the stack or

```
on newCard
   get the number of cards
   put it into background field "number"
end newCard
```

Script 12-7.   This handler automatically puts the number of the new card into a field

background scripts. One thing you can do with it is to automatically put the number of the card into a field on the card, allowing you to later sort the cards in the order in which they were created. Script 12-7 shows such a handler.

This handler gets the number of cards in the stack and puts that number—held in the "It" variable—into a background field called "Number." Remember, card numbers are changed when the stack is sorted. This handler records the order in which the cards were created in the field, and you can later sort the stack with the statement

```
sort numeric by field "number"
```

deleteCard

The deleteCard message is sent to a card when it is about to be deleted. As with the other delete messages that are sent to buttons and fields, you can use this to prevent the deletion of specific cards. A better way to do this, however, is with the CantDelete property of the card.

openCard

This message is sent to a card when the card is displayed on the screen. This is a commonly used handler. You can use it to set up certain parameters of how the card is displayed.

```
on openCard
  hide background picture
end openCard
```

Script 12-8. With HyperCard version 1.2, you can hide background pictures when a card is opened

For example, when a particular card is shown, you might want to hide the background picture. Script 12-8 shows such a handler.

Script 12-9 shows a more complicated openCard handler. Normally, HyperCard cards act as a circular card file: if you are at the last card and type the command **Go next card**, you will go to the first card; if you are on the first card and type **Go prev card**, you will go to the last card. Sometimes, however, you might want to hide the buttons that take you to the next or previous card if you are at the last or first card in the stack.

```
on openCard
  get the number of cards in this stack
  if the number of this card is it then
    hide background button "Next"
  else
    show background button "Next"
  end if
  if the number of this card is 1 then
    hide background button "Prev"
  else
    show background button "Prev"
  end if
end openCard
```

Script 12-9. This handler hides buttons depending on the card's position in the stack

This script first gets the number of cards in the stack. If the number of the current card is the same as that number, the script hides the Next background button. If the number of the current card is 1, it hides the Prev background button. Otherwise, it shows these buttons.

closeCard

This message is sent to a card when it is closed. There are a number of uses for this message, including undoing the actions of any openCard handlers—such as showing background pictures.

You can also use this message when you are working with a locked stack, on a CD-ROM or on a network. On locked stacks, a script can use the userModify property to allow you to enter text into fields on a card. The text entered will be lost when you go to a different card, so you can use the closeCard handler as a place to save the text you entered into variables for later use.

Background-Related Messages

As with the other messages discussed in this chapter, there is a class of messages that are sent to backgrounds.

newBackground

This message is sent when a new background is created. You can use this message to automatically set up certain ways in which the background operates in the same way that you use the "new" messages sent to other handlers. For example, when used in the handler shown in Script 12-10, it prevents creation of a new background. This handler should be put into the stack script.

```
on newBackground
  answer "You can't create new backgrounds"
  doMenu "Cut card"
end newBackground
```

Script 12-10. A newBackground handler that prevents the user from creating a new background

openBackground

This message is sent when the background is first displayed. This actually happens when you have a card of one background on the screen, and you go to a card with a different background. It is also sent to the first background in the stack when the stack is opened.

closeBackground

This message is sent when you change from a card of one background to a card of another background.

deleteBackground

This message is sent when you delete the *last* or *only* card of a background.

While this message was documented in versions of HyperCard before 1.2, it was never actually *sent* when running those versions. It works in HyperCard 1.2.

Stack-Related Messages

These messages relate to the stack itself. It is not required that you place handlers for these messages in the stack script. They can go in a card or background script as well, to be handled only when the card or background is displayed on the screen.

newStack

The newStack message is sent when a new stack is created. Again, you can use it if you want to set certain parameters of a new stack or to perform certain operations when a new stack is created, such as automatically creating a button on a card in the Home stack to link to the new stack.

openStack

This message is sent when a stack is opened. OpenStack is a commonly used message for a number of purposes, especially to set up parameters that a stack uses to operate. Examples include declaring global variables, changing the user level, and hiding the menu bar or Message box.

One thing you should always do if you change any of the user preferences is record them in a global variable so that you can reset them when the stack is closed. Script 12-11 shows how you can do this. This script declares a set of global

```
on openStack
  global theLevel, thePowerKeys, theArrows
  global theBlind, theMessage
  put the userLevel into theLevel
  put the powerKeys into thePowerKeys
  put the textArrows into theArrows
  put the blindTyping into theBlind
  put the visible of the msg into theMsg
  -- after you've recorded these preferences,
  -- you can then change them
end openStack
```

Script 12-11.   This handler saves user preferences when a stack is going to change them

variables to keep the user preferences in, and then it saves those preferences into the global variables. Unfortunately, you cannot discover from HyperTalk whether the menu bar is visible or not. Of course, you need to record only the settings for properties you are going to change.

closeStack

The closeStack message is sent to the stack when you leave the stack to open or go back to another stack, such as Home.

This is a good time to reset the user preferences, as discussed in the openStack section earlier in this chapter. (You should always remember to reset the user's preferences when you leave the stack. Script 12-12 shows how you can do this.)

deleteStack

This message is sent when a stack is going to be deleted. Using the message to protect a stack from being deleted is not much good; it's better to protect the stack in other ways.

You can use this message when you have a number of stacks that work together. If you delete one of the stacks, it is possible to forget to delete its related stacks, and the entire

```
on closeStack
   global theLevel, thePowerKeys, theArrows
   global theBlind, theMessage
   set the userLevel to theLevel
   set the powerKeys to thePowerKeys
   set the textArrows to theArrows
   set the blindTyping to theBlind
   set the visible of the msg to theMsg
end closeStack
```

Script 12-12.   This handler restores user preferences when the stack is closed

application might not work well without one of the stacks. Use this opportunity to remind yourself to delete those stacks.

Other Messages

A number of system messages are not related to any specific HyperCard objects. As are most messages, they are sent to the current card before moving up the hierarchy.

Idle

As its name implies, Idle is sent to the current card whenever HyperCard appears to be inactive. The Home stack uses an Idle handler to put the current time into a field on the card.

You should be careful with Idle handlers. If the Idle handler changes anything on the screen, the current selection or insertion point will be deselected. Since Idle is sent even while you are typing, this can cause loss of the insertion point, and text typed later will be put into the Message box.

Complex Idle handlers can take some time to execute, which can cause delays in such things as typing in the Message box. You should, therefore, avoid them and find another way to handle complex tasks. The Macintosh is a user-directed computer, and it is disconcerting when the machine seems to do things on its own. Leave complex activities for other objects and messages that you send.

Help

This message can be sent in any of several ways, including all the standard ways of getting help in HyperCard: pressing COMMAND-H, choosing Help from the Go menu, or typing **Help** into the Message box.

You can use this message to intercept calls for help and direct them to cards or stacks that provide help for your own application. You won't need to devise or document your own way of summoning help; you can rely on standard Hyper-Card methods. Focal Point from MediaGenics uses this method of help.

For example, if you have a Help card in your stack, you can direct all requests for help to that card by using the handler shown in Script 12-13.

Suspend

This message is sent to HyperCard when you use the Open command to open another program. This message is sent only when you are running in the Finder, not when you open or switch to a different program under MultiFinder.

When running in the regular Finder, then, you can use this message to do a number of things when HyperCard opens another program. Since all global variables are lost when you open a program with HyperCard, you can, for example, save global variables into fields for use when you quit the second program and return to HyperCard.

Resume

This message is sent to HyperCard after you have used HyperCard's Open command to open a second application, and

```
on help
   go to card "Help"
end help
```

Script 12-13.   You can use the Help message to direct help to a specific card

then quit that application to return to HyperCard. Resume handlers should be placed in the script of your Home stack or other stack from which you open applications. You can use the Resume message to retrieve any global variables that you might have saved into fields in Suspend handlers.

As with Suspend, this message is *not* sent when you return to HyperCard from another application in Multi-Finder.

Quit

This message is sent to the current stack when HyperCard receives a Quit command, either by choosing Quit from the File menu or from a statement in a script (such as doMenu Quit).

Sending and Passing Messages

You are not limited to relying on HyperCard's message hierarchy to direct a message. Instead, you can use two commands, Send and Pass, to give you greater control over how messages are moved through HyperCard.

The Send command

Send *<message>* to *<object>*

The Send command allows you to send particular messages to specific objects, thereby allowing you to change how the hierarchy works.

Here's an example. One of the standard techniques in Macintosh dialog boxes is to have a button with a heavy border on it that is the default button (see Figure 12-3). Instead of having to click this button, you can merely press

Figure 12-3.   The button that has the heavier border is the default

RETURN, and the button acts just as if you had clicked it. You can use a returnKey handler in the card script to take care of this, as shown in Script 12-14.

When the returnKey message is sent to the card, this handler intercepts the message and in turn sends the mouse-Up message to the button. The button reacts just as if you had clicked it.

Another use for the Send command is to direct messages to different stacks. For example, you might design an application that uses several different stacks and has complex handlers that are used by several stacks. You have three choices for where to put each handler:

• **Put the handler in every stack**   This is the best solution for small routines. However, it makes modifications more difficult because you need to go to every stack whenever you change the handler.

```
on returnKey
    send mouseUp to card button "OK"
end returnKey
```

Script 12-14.   A returnKey handler allows you to simulate default buttons

• **Put the handler in the Home stack**   This is fine if you are creating an application for yourself; since the Home stack is part of the hierarchy, you don't need to explicitly send a message to the Home stack to have it executed. However, a maximum of 32,000 characters can be included in the script of the Home stack or in any script, and your Home stack script can become crowded. If you are distributing the stack to others, it is also not a friendly practice to insert a lot of handlers into their Home stack scripts.

• **Install them into a master stack**   This is a better option for long handlers. A master stack that is included with your application, such as a Menu stack, could contain the complex, yet frequently used, handlers that many stacks will use. You can then send messages to this stack from each of your other stacks.

Script 12-15 shows a sendMsg handler that you can put into each of your stacks. This handler simply responds to the message sendMsg, and then sends the message that accompanied it to the master stack, referred to as "Master" in the script. You could then use the following line in any script in any of the stacks that include the sendMsg handler:

```
sendMsg import
```

In the master stack, a handler called Import could then do its work.

This technique has its disadvantages—notably poor performance. HyperCard must load the script of the master stack into memory each time the message is sent, which can take a little time. However, once the script has been loaded and begins, it will execute quickly. Use this method when stacks need to share long, complex handlers, not for the small, quick handlers that are often used.

```
on sendMsg what
   send what to stack "Master"
end sendMsg
```

Script 12-15.   This handler routes special messages to a master stack

The Pass Command

Pass <message>

Sometimes an object may want to handle a message and then pass that message along the hierarchy for use by other handlers. For example, you might have a handler in the Home stack that you always want to handle messages, but you need to put additional handlers in other stacks. Normally, when a handler intercepts a message, the message goes no further when that handler has finished.

Suppose, for example, that you have a handler in your Home stack that deals with the closeStack message. A useful handler such as this is shown in Script 12-16. This handler, when put into the script of your Home stack, intercepts all closeStack messages and compacts stacks for you. However, if the closeStack message is intercepted before it gets to the Home stack, this handler will not do you any good.

It is a useful practice, therefore, to pass many of these messages when you are done with them. If, in a stack that includes a closeStack handler, you type the line **pass closeStack** just before the end of the handler, handlers in the Home stack will receive the message. One message that should always be passed is closeStack. Other messages you should pass include newStack, deleteStack, Suspend, Resume, and Quit.

```
on doMenu what
  if what is "Home" or what is "Recent"¬
  or what is "Back" or what is "Help"¬
  or what is "First" or what is "Last"¬
  or what is "Next" or what is "Prev" then
    beep
  else
    pass domenu
  end if
end doMenu
```

Script 12-16.   This doMenu handler prohibits you from using certain of the commands on the Go menu

Turning Off Messages

A script can instruct HyperCard to stop sending messages with the statement "set lockMessages to true." The lockMessages property governs whether or not HyperCard is sending its messages (as discussed in Chapter 13). Turning off messages can prevent unwanted things from happening and can generally speed up scripts that work with a number of different cards, backgrounds, or stacks. You should, however, be aware of some of the dangers of turning off messages and be careful when you do it. For example, if you have messages turned off when you go to a different stack, then the openStack, openBackground, and openCard messages will not be sent. If the stack used handlers for these messages to set up certain parameters of how it will work—such as declaring globals—it is possible the stack will not function properly.

Commands as Messages

In a very real way, everything that you do in HyperCard, including using HyperTalk commands and functions, generates messages. You don't notice it, but everything that happens passes through the hierarchy. Even a command as simple as Go is sent first to the current card, then to the background, then to the stack, and so on. If nothing happens, it finally reaches HyperCard itself, which then acts on the command. Fortunately, HyperCard handles this movement through the hierarchy very quickly—so quickly that you don't even notice a delay as the message travels.

Intercepting Commands

You can create handlers that will intercept all the HyperTalk commands. One of the things this lets you do is prohibit the use of commands. Simply create a handler for that command and place it in the card, background, or stack script. The handler need not actually do anything, but once a handler has intercepted a command, the command is not sent further up the hierarchy. Remember, however, that such handlers will also intercept commands used in your scripts, so choose the commands you intercept carefully.

Script 12-16 shows a handler that intercepts menu commands and prevents your using the commands Go Home, Help, First, Next, Prev, Last, Back, and Recent. You should only resort to this level of protection if you provide other mechanisms that allow you to navigate, and if you have good reason for restricting use of these alternatives.

The Implications for Programming

HyperCard's message hierarchy has a number of implications for how programs, which are collections of scripts, work in HyperTalk.

Probably the most basic benefit you get from the message hierarchy is the fact that scripts can share handlers. All the handlers in the stack script are available to all the backgrounds, cards, buttons, and fields in that stack. All the handlers in the background script are available to all the cards, buttons, and fields that exist in that background (including card buttons and fields that are not part of the background layer). All handlers in the card script are available to all the buttons and fields that are on that card.

When you are programming, this means that you can write generic handlers that can be used by other scripts and place them at a point in the hierarchy where they will be available to the scripts that need them. This means that individual scripts and handlers do not need to contain all the elements that are necessary to make them work—they can call other handlers located further up the hierarchy.

As a user, you should remember that all the handlers in the Home stack are available to all the stacks you use. This means that you can do a substantial amount of personal customization of HyperCard. If you come up with a handler that you are going to use often, put it in the script of the Home stack, and you can use it whenever you like. HyperCard itself comes with a few useful scripts in the Home stack— including the searchScript handler that searches through all the scripts in a stack for text you type in. Experiment with this handler and use it often.

Properties

T
H
I
R
T
E
E
N

HyperCard's properties govern a number of things about the way HyperCard and its objects behave. Properties should not be too difficult to understand as you work your way through HyperCard.

Properties can probably best be explained by showing how they affect fields. Fields can have a number of properties, governing how the text they contain is displayed. The textFont property of a field, for example, governs the font used for all text in that field. The textSize property governs the size of the text, and the textAlign property governs how the text in the field is aligned.

Buttons, too, have properties. Button properties govern their appearance on the screen and some of their actions.

Many of the properties—especially the global properties —you set in the User Preferences card of the Home stack. Other properties—such as the painting properties or those that relate to stack protection and field or button appearance —you can set in dialog boxes. Still other properties—such as those that contain information about the size of a stack— cannot be set at all, but are *read-only* properties.

Getting the Values of Properties

Probably the most common thing you will do with properties is retrieve their current settings to discover something about the objects themselves or how you want HyperCard to be executing.

The Get Command

get the *property* *<of object>*

The Get command can be used to retrieve the value of any property. You must use "the" with Get when referring to the property or HyperCard will give you an error alert. Get puts the value of the property into "It."

The Put Command

put the *property* *<of object>* *<into container>*

The Put command puts the value of the property into a container. A container can be any valid HyperCard container, such as a field or variable. Used without a container name, Put shows the value in the Message box. It is a more specific form of Get that allows you to put the value of a property into a specific variable, not just "It."

Changing Properties

You can also change the values of properties from within scripts.

The Set Command

set *property* *<of object>* *<to value>*

Set changes the value of a property to a new value. Note that, unlike Get and Put, Set does not require "the" before the property name.

Field Properties

Field properties affect the appearance and behavior of fields.

autoTab

set autoTab of *field* **to true|false**

get the autoTab of *field*

This property performs the same function as the autoTab check box in the Field Info dialog box, as discussed in Chapter 6. It can be retrieved as well as set for any field.

lockText

set lockText of *field* **to true|false**

get the lockText of *field*

This property locks the text of the field, so you cannot select text in the field and change it. If the lockText check box in the Field Info dialog box is checked, this property is "true"; otherwise it is false.

Script 13-1 is a short script for a self-modifying button that unlocks or locks all the fields on a card. Put it into a button named either Lock or Unlock. As you will see from the script, it behaves in accordance with its name.

The first thing this script does is find out the name of the button, with the line "get the short name of target." If the short name of the target—this button—is Unlock, it will unlock all the fields on the card. It does this with two repeat loops. The first repeat loop cycles through all the background fields and sets the lockText property of the field to "false." The second loop does the same for all the card fields. The "set cursor to busy" line, which only works in version 1.2 or later, shows a spinning beach ball for the mouse cursor. This is done simply to let you know something is happening. After unlocking all the fields, the script changes the name of the button it is in to Lock.

```
on mouseUp
  get the short name of target
  put the number of bkgnd fields into numFields
  put the number of card fields into numCdFlds
  if it is "Unlock" then
    set userModify to true
    -- unlock all the background fields
    repeat with x = 1 to numFields
      set lockText of bkgnd field x to false
      set cursor to busy
    end repeat
    -- unlock all the card fields
    repeat with x = 1 to numCdFlds
      set lockText of card field x to false
      set cursor to busy
    end repeat
    set the name of target to "Lock"
  else
    -- lock the background fields
    repeat with x = 1 to numFields
      set lockText of bkgnd field x to true
      set cursor to busy
    end repeat
    -- lock the card fields
    repeat with x = 1 to numCdFlds
      set lockText of card field x to true
      set cursor to busy
    end repeat
    set the name of target to "UnLock"
  end if
end mouseUp
```

Script 13-1.   This handler locks and unlocks card and background fields, depending on the name of the button

If the name of the button is Lock, the script performs the same two loops, this time locking the fields.

At the top of this script is the line "set userModify to true." The userModify property is explained later in this chapter.

scroll

set scroll of *field* **to** *number*

get the scroll of *field*

Number is an integer that determines the number of pixels that are above the top of the field.

showLines

set showLines of *field* to true|false

get the showLines of *field*

This property works in the same way as the showLines check box in the Field Info dialog box. If showLines is "true," then lines will appear in the field to show where text lines will be. If it is "false," no lines will be shown.

style

set style of *field* to

transparent|opaque|rectangle|shadow|scrolling

get the style of *field*

This property allows a script to find or set the style of a field. It can be used with some other properties to find out about a field. A field can have only one of these styles at a time; the buttons for setting these styles in the Field Info dialog box are radio buttons.

wideMargins

set wideMargins of *field* to true|false

get the wideMargins of *field*

This property is the same as the wideMargins check box on the Field Info dialog box. If it is "true," extra space will be inserted between the left and right edges of a field, putting more white space into the field and making it more readable.

Button Properties

Button properties affect the appearance and behavior of buttons.

autoHilite

set autoHilite of *button* to true|false

get the autoHilite of *button*

The autoHilite property either lets a script discover or change whether a button is automatically highlighting or not. In other words, this property governs whether or not the button automatically highlights (blackens) when you click it.

If a button is a radio button or a check box, the autoHilite property puts a black dot or check box into the button instead of highlighting it and then dehighlighting it quickly, as other buttons do; that is, it turns on the option represented by the button.

hilite

set hilite of *button* to true|false

get the hilite of *button*

The property highlights the button. It is not the same as autoHilite, which governs whether or not a button automatically highlights when you click it.

Script 13-2 contains two handlers that work together to simulate autoHilite. Of course, these functions can be replaced by the autoHilite property, but they give you more control over what is going on. For example, when a button automatically highlights, any selected text becomes deselected. If your button deals with selected text, however, you can use the mouseDown handler to get the selected text before it highlights the button. You could put such a line right after the line "on mouseDown."

As was mentioned in the section on the autoHilite property, radio buttons are a different story. When a radio button or check box is highlighted, the button does not quickly blacken and unblacken again. Instead, a black dot is put into a radio button, and an X is put into a check box.

```
on mouseDown
  set the hilite of me to true
  repeat until the mouse is up
    if the mouseLoc is not within the rect of me then
      set the hilite of me to false
    end if
  end repeat
end mouseDown
on mouseUp
  set the hilite of me to false
end mouseUp
```

Script 13-2.   These two handlers simulate the autoHilite property of a button

Standard radio buttons also work in groups, and only one of the buttons should be highlighted at a time. If you click one radio button in a group, it should be highlighted, and the others in the group should be dehighlighted. Radio buttons are used to make selections from a group of choices, and you should be able to choose only one button at a time.

Managing this in a script is easier said than done. Script 13-3 shows a handler that manages all the radio buttons on a card at one time. This handler should be put into the script of the card that contains the radio buttons, and no handlers should be put into the scripts of the individual buttons.

The script might look complex, but its logic is straightforward. The script cycles through each of the buttons on the card, and if the button is a radio button, it sets the highlight of that button to "false." Finally, it sets the highlight of the original button to "true," because it was set to "false" on the first pass through the buttons.

Modifying this script to handle background buttons would not be hard—merely a matter of changing "card" to "background" throughout the script. It is more difficult to

```
on mouseUp
  if the style of the target is "radioButton" then
    get the hilite of the target
    repeat with x = 1 to the number of card buttons
      if the style of card button x is "radiobutton" then
        set the hilite of card button x to false
      end if
    end repeat
    set the hilite of the target to true
  end if
end mouseUp
```

Script 13-3.   This handler manages radio buttons on a card

handle situations in which there might be more than one set of radio buttons on a card. In that case, you need to write specific scripts for your situation.

icon

set icon of *button* **to** *number/name*

get the icon of *button*

All the icons installed in your system, in HyperCard, or in a stack have numbers, and many have names as well. You can see this in the Icon dialog box that you get from the Button Info dialog box. Click on one of the icons, and its number and name are displayed at the top of the scrolling field of icons.

If you set the icon property to a number that is not represented by an icon, the button will have no icons. Icons for buttons can be set by either name or number. When you use the Get command on the icon of a button, however, you will be given the icon's number.

Table 13-1 shows a list of the standard icons that are included with HyperCard, along with their names and numbers.

Table 13-1. The Standard HyperCard Icons, with Their Names and Numbers

Table 13-1. The Standard HyperCard Icons, with Their Names and Numbers (*continued*)

You can set icons for radio buttons and check boxes, but they will not be displayed.

Working with icons, which are resources, is discussed in Chapter 31.

showName

set showName of *button* **to true|false**

get the showName of *button*

If this property is "false," the name of the button will not be shown. This property is the same as the showName check box in the Field Info dialog box.

style

set style of *button* **to**

transparent|opaque|rectangle|roundRect|checkBox| radioButton

get the style of *button*

This property governs the appearance of the button. Its various legal values are the same values as shown in the radio buttons at the right of the Button Info dialog box.

Rectangle Properties

These are properties of any HyperCard objects that are rectangles—namely buttons and fields. The first of the properties discussed here, rect, is available in all versions of HyperCard. The remainder of the properties are present only in version 1.2 or greater.

You can use Set to change the left, top, bottom, top-left, and bottom-right coordinates of any object. When you set any one of these coordinates, HyperCard attempts to leave the remainder of the coordinates as they were. For example, if you change the top-left coordinate of an object, the bottom-right coordinate will remain the same. When you change the width and height of an object, however, it is not as simple— something has got to give. HyperCard then stretches or shrinks the object to give it the new width or height. In so doing, it changes all the other coordinates except the loc property of the object.

rect

set the rect of *button/field* **to newRect**

get the rect of *button/field*

The rect property is a set of four numbers in the form of left,top,right,bottom. You must provide all four numbers if you want to set the rect of an object.

loc

set the loc of *field/button* **to** *x,y*

get the loc of *field/button*

The loc property of a field or a button is a set of two integers that describes its location on the screen. The loc refers to the *center* of the object. The first number is the distance from the left edge of the screen to the center of the object; the second number is the distance from the top of the screen to the center of the object.

left

get the left of *button/field*

set the left of *button/field* **to** *number*

This property is equal to the first number in the rect of an object—its left edge.

top

> **get the top of** *button/field*
>
> **set the top of** *button/field* **to** *number*
>
> This is the same as the second number in the rect of an object — its top.

right

> **get the right of** *button/field*
>
> **set the right of** *button/field* **to** *number*
>
> This equals the third number of the rect of an object — the right.

bottom

> **get the bottom of** *button/field*
>
> **set the bottom of** *button/field* **to** *number*
>
> This equals the fourth number in the rect of an object — the bottom.

topLeft

> **get the topLeft of** *button/field*
>
> **set the topLeft of** *button/field* **to** *x,y*
>
> This is a two-number set. The first number is the same as the left of an object, and the second is the same as the top of an object.

bottomRight

get the bottomRight of *button/field*

set the bottomRight of *button/field* **to** *x,y*

This is a two-number set. The first number is the same as the right of a rectangle, and the second is the same as the bottom.

width

get the width of *button/field*

set the width of *button/field* **to** *number*

This is the same as the value of the right of an object minus the value of the left of the object.

When setting a new width for an object, HyperCard will retain the previous loc of the object.

height

get the height of *button/field*

set the height of *button/field* **to** *number*

The *number* is the same as the value of the bottom of the rectangle minus the value of its top. When setting a new height for an object, HyperCard will change the object's height and leave its loc at its previous value.

Painting Properties

HyperCard's painting properties govern how many of the painting tools work. You set many of these properties when you choose menu items or commands from the paint menus.

All the painting properties can be reset at one time to their default values with the command Reset Paint.

Painting with HyperCard is discussed in Chapter 8; painting under control of HyperTalk scripts is discussed in Chapter 29.

brush

set brush to *number*

get the brush

This painting property sets the brush shape. *Number* should be between 1 and 32. If *number* is less than 1, then brush will be set to 1; if it is more than 32, it will be set to 32. The default value is 8. Figure 13-1 shows the HyperCard brushes and their numbers.

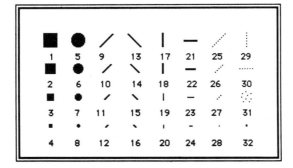

Figure 13-1.   The HyperCard brush shapes and their numbers

centered

set centered to true|false

get the centered

This property sets or gets the value of the Draw Centered command on the Options paint menu. If it is "true," the Rectangle, Oval, Rounded Rectangle, and Line tools will draw from the center. This command is discussed in Chapter 8.

The Reset Paint command resets the centered property to "false."

filled

set filled to true|false

get the filled

Setting this property to "true" is the same as selecting the Draw Filled command from the Options paint menu. The filled property defaults to "false."

grid

set grid to true|false

get the grid

Setting the grid property is the same as choosing the Grid command from the Options paint menu. If the menu has a check on it, the property is "true;" otherwise it is "false." The grid property has a default value of "false."

lineSize

set lineSize to *number*

get the lineSize

Number determines the width of lines drawn in pixels. Valid values are 1, 2, 3, 4, 6, and 8. If you set lineSize to a number greater than 8, it will be set to 8. If you set it to 7, it will be set to 6; if you set it to 5, it will be set to 4. If you set it to 0, it will be set to 1. Attempting to set it to a value less than 0 causes an error alert. The default value is 1.

Setting the lineSize property is equivalent to choosing a line size from the Line Size command on the Options paint menu.

multiple

set multiple to true|false

get the multiple

This property governs whether the Draw Multiple item on the Options paint menu is checked or not. Setting it to "true" checks it; setting it to "false" unchecks it. Its default value is "false."

multiSpace

set multiSpace to *number*

get the multiSpace

Number is a value that determines the number of pixels that separate images drawn when the multiple property is "true." This item can only be set from a script, not from a menu choice or paint command. However, the spacing between objects can be governed by the user by dragging at different speeds.

Number seems to have no upper limit. However, values larger than 513 — the width of the HyperCard window — will not produce multiple images that are too far apart to be viewed on the screen. If you attempt to set multiSpace to a negative number, HyperCard will give you an error alert. If you set it to 0, spacing between the images will be governed strictly by how fast you move the mouse.

pattern

set pattern to *number*

get the pattern

Number is an integer between 1 and 40 that corresponds to the patterns in the Patterns palette, as shown in Figure 13-2. If you attempt to set the pattern to an invalid number (for example, 1.4 or 77), the pattern will not be changed.

polySides

set polySides to *number*

get the polySides

The polySides property determines the number of sides of a polygon drawn with the Regular Polygon tool.

Number can be any number in a range from 3 to 50; if you try to set polySides to a number larger than 50, it will be set to 50. After about 20, they all start to look the same.

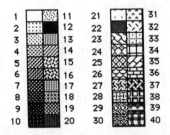

Figure 13-2.   The Patterns palette, showing the numbers of the patterns

textSize

The textSize property of paint text is discussed in the "Other Properties" section of this chapter.

textFont

The textFont property of paint text is discussed later in the "Other Properties" section of this chapter.

textStyle

The textStyle property of paint text is discussed later in the "Other Properties" section of this chapter.

Global Properties

Global properties affect the way HyperCard works in general and then govern the behavior of a number of aspects of HyperCard. You set many of the global properties in the User Preferences card on the Home stack. If your script or stack changes any of these properties, it should save their previous values and reset them when it is finished executing. A closeStack handler is a good place to reset them.

A word of caution about setting properties is due here. HyperCard allows you to set your own preferences for using the program. If you are going to be changing the properties set by another user, it is only good manners to remember how that user set them and to change them back when you leave the stack. If you need to make changes, save the existing preferences in a global variable and reset them by using a closeStack handler.

blindTyping

set blindTyping to true|false

get the blindTyping

The blindTyping property controls your capability to type commands to HyperCard when the Message box is not visible. This property is normally set on the User Preferences card on the Home stack, but scripts can also set this property.

cursor

set cursor to *name/number*

Name can be any one of the following: I-Beam, plus, cross, watch, none, busy, arrow, or hand. *Number* can be any valid cursor number (see Chapter 31). If *number* is not a valid cursor number, it is ignored.

One of the standards on the Macintosh is that the mouse cursor changes its appearance depending on what part of the screen it is moving over or what mode you are currently in. You can see this in HyperCard when you choose a different tool: the mouse cursor changes to show the tool you are using. Other programs use tools in much the same manner. A very common technique, present in virtually all programs, is to use the I-Beam cursor when the cursor is positioned over editable text.

HyperCard allows you to control the appearance of the mouse cursor with the Cursor property. You can refer to cursors in two ways. If you have installed cursor resources into your stack (see Chapter 31 for information about resources), you can refer to those cursors by number. However, Hyper-Card includes seven different cursor designs, which should be sufficient for most uses.

You cannot use the Get command to discover what the cursor is. The cursor is reset to the default of 0 at idle, when your script stops executing.

Figure 13-3 shows the HyperCard cursors and their names.

Hand

This is the cursor used with the Browse tool.

I-Beam

This is the standard I-Beam used when editing text.

Plus

This cursor is used when situating items. It is similar to the cursor used when painting with HyperCard for such tools as Rectangle and Oval. Use it when you are grouping items together or drawing things on the screen.

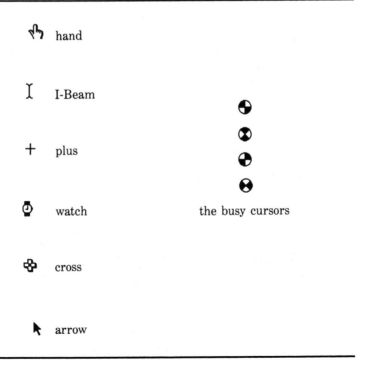

Figure 13-3.   The cursors and their names

Cross

The cross is often used in spreadsheets. In the *Human Interface Guidelines*, Apple recommends that you use the cross
cursor when selecting fields in an array, such as cells in a
spreadsheet. Its appearance suggests that it represents a
mathematical tool, so you can use it when you are performing
math functions.

Watch

This cursor shows that a lengthy operation is in process. As a
Macintosh owner, you have probably already seen the watch
several times—the Mac uses it when it is busy. If your operation is very long, however, you should use the busy cursor.

None

This cursor setting removes the cursor. Use this if you have a
graphics operation in progress or an attractive screen and
you don't want the cursor to detract from the appearance of
the screen.

Busy

This is one of the most useful cursors. Sometimes the watch
cursor does not give you enough indication that something is
happening, and if the operation is very long, you might think
the machine has frozen or stopped working.

Each time "set cursor to busy" is called, the cursor is set
to one of the spinning beach ball cursors shown in Figure
13-3. This shows that the machine is still alive and that something is indeed happening. HyperCard itself uses the busy
cursor when it is doing such things as finding text or sorting
or compacting the stack.

Script 13-4 is a short handler that demonstrates the busy
cursor. Put it into a button and watch it work.

```
on mouseUp
  repeat until the mouse is down
    set cursor to busy
  end repeat
end mouseUp
```

Script 13-4.   This handler demonstrates the function of the busy cursor available in version 1.2

dragSpeed

set dragSpeed to *number*

get the dragSpeed

This property sets the number of pixels per second that the mouse pointer moves during execution of the Drag command (discussed in Chapter 29).

editBkgnd

set editBkgnd to true|false

get editBkgnd

This property lets you discover whether or not background editing is in effect and lets you set the property.

freeSize

get the freeSize of *stack*

This property reports the amount of free space in the stack. As stacks are used—especially when new cards, buttons, fields, text, and graphics are added to the stack—a certain amount of free space is created in the stack, and it becomes larger than it needs to be. The Compact Stack command on the File menu removes this free space. This read-only property gives you the number of bytes free in the stack. You can check for the freeSize of the current stack by typing **Get the freeSize of this stack**, or you can get the freeSize of any other stack by naming it.

Script 13-5 contains a handler that checks the amount of free space in the stack and asks you whether you want to compact it or not.

language

set language to *language*

get the language

HyperCard is able to support different languages through translators that are built in to it for sale in different countries. For example, if you are using a French version of HyperCard, all your scripts will appear in French. The same is true for a growing number of translators. Of course, HyperCard cannot translate your text in a field to French. Your language preference is set in the User Preferences card of the Home stack on international copies of HyperCard.

This property, therefore, allows you to discover what language is being used.

lockMessages

set lockMessages to true|false

get the lockMessages

During execution of a script, if lockMessages is set to "true," then none of the HyperCard messages are sent. The lockMessages property is automatically set to "false" when the script stops executing (that is, when it is idle).

Using lockMessages, like lockRecent or lockScreen, is a good way to speed up execution of scripts that are working with a large number of cards. Since the messages are not being sent, HyperCard doesn't take the time to execute them,

```
on checkSize
  put the freeSize of this stack into theFree
  if theFree > the size of this stack / 10 then
    answer theFree / 1024 & "k free in stack.  Compact?"
    with "No" or "Yes"
    if it is "Yes" then
      domenu "Compact Stack"
    end if
  end if
end checkSize
```

Script 13-5.   The checkSize handler compacts a stack if its free space is greater than 10% of the stack

nor will your script be interrupted by message handlers in the other cards to which it goes.

When lockMessages is "true," you can override it to send specific messages with the Send command.

lockRecent

set lockRecent to true/false

get the lockRecent

If lockRecent is set to "true," when a script goes to another card, the card is not added to the Recent list. The lockRecent property is reset to "false" when HyperCard is idle.

Using lockRecent is a good way to speed up operations on a script that is working with a large number of cards. Since HyperCard is not adding each card to the Recent list, it does not use up any time that would be needed to do so. It also helps you avoid possible confusion when seeing a number of cards in the Recent list that you did not go to by choice. However, once the script has ended, you can use the Go Back command or its key equivalent to go to recent cards.

lockScreen

set lockScreen to true|false

get the lockScreen

If lockScreen is "true," no changes to the screen—including painting on a card, going to other cards, and so on,—are shown when a script is executing. Setting this property to "true" is the same as executing the Lock Screen command, discussed in Chapter 20.

numberFormat

set numberFormat to *formatSpecification*

get the numberFormat

This property determines how numbers are displayed. A format specification is constructed using zeros to specify the number of digits to the left of the decimal point, followed by a period for the decimal point and either zeros or pound signs (#) to show how many digits are to be included to the right of the decimal point.

The numberFormat property affects only how numbers are displayed, not the precision of calculations.

This property is reset to 0.###### at idle.

powerKeys

set powerKeys to true|false

get the powerKeys

The powerKeys property is a global property that determines whether or not the painting power keys work or not. It is normally set by the user on the User Preferences card in the Home stack, but can also be set by a script.

As with all the properties that are set on the User Preferences card, if you change the setting of powerKeys, be sure to reset it to its normal value when you close your stack.

userLevel

set userLevel to *number*

get the userLevel

Number is an integer between 1 and 5. If you use a number larger than 5, userLevel will be set to 5; if you use a number smaller than 1, userLevel will be set to 1.

You can set userLevel in two places. First, it is set as a global property on the User Preferences card in the Home stack. Second, it can be set separately for specific stacks in the Protect Stack dialog box. Setting userLevel in the Protect Stack dialog box only affects the setting of userLevel for the stack; when you go to a different stack, userLevel is set to its global value.

You can use the userLevel property to limit the access that others have to your stack, along with the other items in the Protect Stack dialog. Limiting userLevel to Typing, for example, will prohibit other users from changing items other than text in your stack: they will not be able to change buttons, fields, cards, or backgrounds.

If you change userLevel from a script with the Set command, be sure to reset userLevel to its previous state when your stack is closed. It is very annoying to return Home from a stack and find userLevel set too low.

Version

Version is not a property per se, but rather a function that allows you to find out what version of HyperCard or a stack you are working with. HyperCard 1.2 or greater supports three forms of this function.

the version

This function returns the version of HyperCard you are running. For example, it will return 1.2 if you are running version 1.2 of HyperCard. When you have written a script that will not work in earlier versions of HyperCard, this function acts as a warning that the script will not perform correctly in the earlier version.

the long version <*of HyperCard*>

This function returns an eight-digit number that represents the version of HyperCard you are running. The format used is that specified by *Inside Macintosh* for Macintosh version numbers. For example, HyperCard 1.2 returns 01208000.

the version <*of stack*>

Stack means any HyperCard stack. This function returns a string in the form of five comma-delimited items, which are in the format specified by *Inside Macintosh*. Here is what each item means:

- The version of HyperCard that created the stack.

- The version of HyperCard that last compacted the stack.

- The oldest version of HyperCard that changed the stack since it was last compacted.

- The version of HyperCard that last changed the stack. This will be set to 00000000 if the version of HyperCard is earlier than 1.2.

- The date of the most recent modification to the stack, in seconds, since January 1, 1904. This figure is updated only when the stack is closed, not when the actual modification occurs. Therefore, you need to leave the stack and reopen it for this item to change. (HyperTalk date and time functions are discussed in Chapter 23.)

Apple recommends that, when stacks created with versions earlier than 1.2 are first opened with that version, those stacks should be compacted twice. You can use the version of a stack to see if the stack has been compacted with Hyper-card 1.2.

Other Properties

The properties listed below either affect how HyperCard operates or apply to several different kinds of HyperCard objects.

cantDelete

set the cantDelete of *card|background|stack* **to true|false**

get the cantDelete of *card|background|stack*

If cantDelete is "true" for any valid object, you can not delete that object.

cantModify

set the cantModify of *card|background|stack* **to true|false**

get the cantModify of *card|background|stack*

If this property is "true," you are not allowed to modify the item. Naturally, cantModify is inherited: if cantModify is "true" for a stack, it is also "true" for backgrounds and cards in the stack.

diskSpace

get the diskSpace

This property contains the number of bytes that are available on the current disk—the disk containing the stack that is currently open. You cannot ask for the diskSpace of other volumes. You cannot, of course, set this property.

heapSpace

get the heapSpace

This property contains the amount of free memory available in HyperCard's application heap. The *application heap* is the area of memory in which HyperCard is running. Its size depends on several things: your Macintosh's memory size, whether or not you are running in MultiFinder, and if so, how much memory you have allocated for HyperCard. Hyper-Card itself uses much of the application heap, and so do scripts and variables.

You cannot, of course, set this property.

ID

get the ID of *object*

The ID of any object is a number that is set by HyperCard when that object is created. You cannot set the ID of any object.

IDs of cards and backgrounds are created in a seemingly random manner—the only pattern is that each new background or card gets a higher ID number. IDs of buttons and fields are set sequentially in order of their creation.

If you are working on large stacks, it is always quicker to go to a card or background by referring to its ID number rather than by its number or name. ID numbers are *hard-wired* into the stack—they never change as long as their objects exist. However, using ID numbers in buttons can make the scripts somewhat harder to read than they would be if you used an object's name or number.

When you cut and paste any object, the ID number of that object changes—the paste action creates a new object, so the new object gets a new ID number.

name

set the name of *object* to newName

get the name of *object*

The name of any object is a property that can be discovered with the Get command and set with the Set command. In Script 13-1, the Set command is used to change the name of a button depending on its function.

When getting the name of an object, you can use either its number or its ID, as in these lines:

```
get the name of this card
get the name of card button 17
get the name of background button 1
get the name of this stack
```

You can also use the target with the name. The target is a function that returns the ID of the object to which a message was sent. This allows you to discover the name of an object. In Chapter 30, "Sound and Music," Script 30-1 uses the target to discover the name of the button clicked and plays a musical note based on the name of the target.

Note: In HyperCard, it is not required that objects other than stacks have names. An object that does not have a name is referred to by its ID.

There are three forms of any object's name: the long name, the name, and the short name.

long name

The long name of an object includes information that exactly identifies the object.

The long name of a stack includes the identifier "stack," followed by the complete pathname of the stack in quotes.

```
stack "Hard disk:HyperCard Folder:Home"
```

The pathname includes the name of the disk the stack is on, followed by the names of the folders in which the stack is located, separated by colons.

The long name of a background includes the "bkgnd" identifier, followed by the name of the background in quotes (or "ID" followed by the ID number, if the background does not have a name), followed by "of stack," followed by the complete pathname of the stack that contains the background.

The long name of a button includes the identifier "card" or "bkgnd," depending on whether the button is a card or background button, followed by "button" and the name or ID of the button, followed by the name of the card the button is on. Finally, it includes the complete pathname of the stack. The same is true for fields.

You cannot set the long name of an object, only its name.

name

The name of an object includes an identifier for the object — "stack," "background," "card," "button," or "field" — followed by its name in quotes. If the object is a card button or field, the name is preceded by "card;" if it is a background object, the name is preceded by "bkgnd." If the object does not have a name, the name consists of "ID" followed by its ID number.

short name

The short name of an object consists of its name—the part you see in the "Name" field in an Info dialog box. No quotes surround the name. If an object does not have a name, the name consists of an indicator describing whether it is a card or background object, followed by "ID" and its ID number.

number

get the number of *background/card/button*

The number property is an ordinal that tells you where an object is in relation to other objects of the same name. For example, the first card in a stack is card number 1, and the first background in a stack is background number 1.

You cannot set an object's number directly. For buttons and fields, you must use the Bring Closer and Send Farther commands, which are discussed in Chapter 6.

Cards are numbered are in order of their appearance in the stack. Accordingly, card numbers are changed when the stack is sorted. Background numbers are changed in the same manner. The first background is the one the first card in the stack is on.

script

set the script of *object* to *container*

get the script of *object*

Object can be anything that can contain a script: a stack, background, card, button, or field.

It might take some getting used to, but the script of an object is indeed one of its properties. This allows you to write scripts that examine or modify the contents of other scripts in any stack, and a script can examine or modify itself (though be careful of this). However, you should use this latter capability with care: programs that modify themselves are very difficult to debug, and the possibility exists that a script that goes "out of control" could wreak havoc on itself and perhaps on other scripts, possibly destroying the work that went into developing those scripts.

showPict

set the showPict of *card/background* **to true|false**

get the showPict of *card/background*

The showPict property determines whether a card or background picture is visible. This property is not present in versions of HyperCard prior to 1.2.

Using showPict, you can selectively hide or show background pictures on specific cards. Since the background showPict property affects all the cards on the background, you can use openCard and closeCard handlers in specific cards to hide or show the background pictures when the card is displayed.

You can also set this property with the Hide and Show commands.

size

get the size of *stack*

This read-only property contains an integer value representing the number of bytes the stack takes up on disk. This figure includes the freeSize of the stack. You can ask for the size of the current stack by typing **Get the size of this stack,** or you can ask for the size of any other stack by name.

textAlign

set the textAlign *<of button/card>* **to** *left/center/right*

get the textAlign *<of button/card>*

If you do not specify a button or a card, the textAlign property is set for paint text.

This property governs the alignment of typed text. The textAlign of a button governs the name of the button that appears. It does not affect radio buttons or check boxes.

For fields, textAlign governs how the text will be aligned to the borders of the field. Left-aligned text (which is the default) will be aligned at the left side of the field, centered text will be centered about the vertical center of the field, and right-aligned text will be aligned at the right edge of the field.

With paint text, textAlign governs how the text is aligned with the point at which you click the text tool on the screen. Left-aligned text will have its left edge aligned at the point you click, centered text will be centered about the point you click, and right-aligned text will have its right edge aligned at the point.

textFont

set the textFont *<of button/field>* **to** *fontName*

get the textFont *<of button/field>*

If an object is not specified, textFont sets the font for paint text.

textHeight

set the textHeight *<of button/field>* **to** *number*

get the textHeight *<of button/field>*

Number is an integer representing the number of pixels between one baseline of text and the next.

If you do not specify an object, textHeight will be set for paint text, and the next paint text you type will have that property.

textSize

> set the textSize *<of button/field>* to *number*
>
> get the textSize *<of button/field>*

If you do not specify the name of a button or a field, this sets the textSize property for paint text, and the next paint text you use will be of this size.

Number is an integer representing the point size of the text. You can assign very large numbers to this property; however, the largest text size that will be displayed in a field is 137 points, and about the largest size that can be put on the Macintosh screen is 400 points. When you set this property to very large values—in excess of 1000 points—strange behavior can result, including freezing of HyperCard and system bombs. Since there's no point in doing this anyway, you are better off not trying large values.

textStyle

> set textStyle *<of button/field>* to *style*
>
> get the textStyle *<of button/field>*

Style can be any combination of bold, underline, italic, outline, shadow, plain, condense, or expand. You can specify any number of these styles, separated by commas. The plain style works differently from the other styles: it turns all the other styles off. If you mix plain with any of the other styles, it will not have any affect.

userModify

> set userModify to true|false
>
> get the userModify

This property is only available in version 1.2 or greater. When working with a stack that is locked, you might sometimes need to use a script that allows you to change something on a card. Locked stacks can be on locked floppy disks, on a shared file server, or on a CD-ROM. You might need to enter some text into fields on a locked stack to create a query-by-example screen in which you type in examples of the information you want to find. All changes to the card will be lost when the card is closed. To do this from a script (it does not work from the Message box) type **Set userModify to true**. The userModify property will be reset to "false" when you move to a different card.

visible

set visible of *object* to true|false

get the visible of *object*

Object can be any one of the following: card window, tool window, pattern window, or Message box.

This property determines whether or not the object is visible on the screen. You can also set the visible of any object with the Hide and Show commands.

FOURTEEN

HyperTalk Syntax

Commands
Functions
Expressions
Operators
Precedence: How Statements Are Evaluated
Checking Syntax
Naming

One of the most useful features of HyperTalk, and probably the one thing that makes it so easy to learn, is its flexible *syntax*. The syntax of a language—including both human and computer languages—determines how statements are constructed and interpreted.

There are two ways of expressing most HyperTalk functions: an English-like way that makes a script readable but somewhat verbose, and an algebraic way that saves room in the script. Both methods are discussed in this chapter.

If you look at many HyperTalk scripts—including many of those in this book—one of the first things you notice is that they are readable. Virtually all the words in the language are English words or words derived from English. A line like "on mouseUp," for example, is very understandable once you have grasped the concept of message handlers; it is clear from the line that the handler defined by this line responds to the release of the mouse button. Other lines, such as "add 5 to totalCost" and "put 5 into the message box", are easy to understand once you have learned about variables and the Message box. And a line such as "go to card 5" is self-explanatory.

HyperTalk syntax has fewer limitations than English syntax. A statement such as "Go to card 5 of this stack" is understood in any language, but the line "Go card 5" might be ambiguous in English. Both statements mean the same thing in HyperTalk.

Commands

Commands are instructions that tell HyperCard to do something. Go is a HyperCard command, as are Put and Add. Commands also need *parameters* that tell them what to do. Think of the command as a verb in a sentence. The sentence also needs to have a subject and a predicate. For example, the Go command needs a predicate—it needs to be told where to go—so you would need to enter, for example, **Go card 1**. If you issue the Go command on its own, you will get the alert "Can't understand arguments to command go." The command Put needs to know what to put and where to put it; for example, you can enter **Put the date into card field "date"**. (If you do not tell Put where to put the date, it will put it into the Message box.)

HyperCard commands are entered one to a line. When each command has executed, HyperTalk proceeds to the next line.

Functions

HyperTalk functions work in a slightly different way than the commands. Unlike commands, functions cannot stand by themselves on a line. Instead, they are included as *part* of a line.

A function is an expression that returns a value. Consider this example:

```
put random(10) into card field "number"
```

The Put command puts a value into a field. The first parameter, which is for the Put *command*, is the function Random. When HyperTalk sees this function name, it makes a side trip to the Random function, which performs a bit of magic and then sends back a number between 1 and 10. The Put command then puts this number into the field "number." When you call the Random function, you must also *send* it a number. This is the *function's* parameter.

If, in a script, you put the line

```
random(10)
```

HyperTalk will give you a "Can't understand" alert because a function cannot stand by itself on a line. This is not the case when entering functions into the Message box, however. If you type the same line into the Message box, HyperTalk will put a random number between 1 and 10 into the Message box. In this case, Put is an implicit part of the command entered into the Message box.

Most HyperCard functions have two forms: an algebraic form, such as Random(10), and a verbose form, such as

```
the random of 10
```

This longer form often makes statements easier to read. It does, however, take up more room on a line.

Remember that you can write your own functions in HyperTalk. Just as the handlers you write behave as if they were HyperCard commands, so do your own functions behave as if they were HyperTalk functions. Control is passed to your own function, which then returns a value to the line that called it.

Functions you create behave similarly to HyperTalk's built-in functions. They must be passed parameters or arguments in the form

```
function(parameter1,parameter2)
```

If the function does not take any parameters, you must still pass to the function an empty parameter list by typing (), with nothing between the parentheses. If you are passing several parameters to the function, separate them with commas, enclosing all parameters in the same set of parentheses.

One difference between functions you define and Hyper-Talk's built-in functions is that the functions you define cannot have a long form (such as "The random of 10"). You must use the shorter algebraic form (such as "random(10)") of the function.

Expressions

An *expression* is a phrase that, when evaluated, yields a value for HyperTalk to work with. That value can be text, a number, a date, or a card or stack to go to.

Variables

Variables are a type of expression. When HyperTalk is interpreting a line of code, it needs to decipher what you mean by your line. In the following line HyperCard will search through its list of variables to see if it has one called *totalScore:*

```
put totalScore into field "total score"
```

If *totalScore* exists, HyperCard will put the contents of that variable into the field "Total Score." If HyperCard cannot find a variable by that name, it will do one of several things, based on the statement that contains the reference to the variable. In this example, it will put the word "total-Score" into the field.

If you use a statement such as

```
add 10 to totalScore
```

HyperCard will give you an alert, "Can't understand arguments to add." Before you can use a command such as Add to *change* the contents of a variable, you must first use either the Put command to assign a value to the variable or declare it to be a global variable with the Global command.

If the word that HyperCard does not understand is the first word in the statement or if the word appears on a line by itself, then HyperCard attempts to interpret the word as a message. If there are no handlers in the hierarchy for that message, it will not be able to understand the word and will let you know.

Chunk Expressions

A chunk expression also yields a value. A chunk expression is an expression that isolates a particular portion of text in a container. Here are some examples of chunk expressions:

```
first word of background field "comments"
word 1 to 7 of background field "comments"
item 2 of line 1 of field "comments"
line 1 of field "comments"
put "comments" into thefield
```

Chunk expressions are easy to read in scripts because they express an idea in the same way you would express it in English. Note that in chunk expressions, as in any other statements, variables can substitute for any of the elements, as shown here:

```
put 1 into x
put line x of background field theField
```

Chunk expressions are detailed in Chapter 17.

Operators

Operators work in a way that is very different from Hyper-Talk commands and functions.

First, HyperTalk commands and functions generally precede the data with which they work. For example, the Put command precedes the data you are putting. Operators, however, take two arguments, one on each side of the operator, because operators perform mathematical functions. Here are some examples of operators, along with their English equivalents:

```
4 + 5 -- 4 plus 5
5 - 4 -- 5 minus 4
37 ^ 2 -- 37 to the 2nd power.
```

When HyperTalk is evaluating a line, it treats the three elements that make up the operator expression as one value, after it interpets the operator part of the statement; for example,

```
put line 3 + 5 of card field "comments"
```

is the same as

```
put line 8 of card field "comments"
```

Precedence: How Statements Are Evaluated

When evaluating a group of operators, HyperCard needs to know in what order to interpret them. Ambiguity in a statement could lead to error. For example, the line

```
put 3 * 5 + 15
```

Order	Operator	Type of Operator
1	( )	Grouping
2	not	Negates logical values
3	^	Exponentiation
4	* / div mod	Multiplication and division
5	+ and −	Addition and subtraction sign for numbers
6	& &&	Concatenation of text
7	> < <=> =≤ ≥	Logical for numbers
	is in, contains	Logical for text
8	=, is, < >, ≠	Logical for text and numbers
9	and	Logical
10	or	Logical

Table 14-1.   Order in Which HyperCard Evaluates Operators

could be interpreted two ways. It could mean "multiply 3 by 5 and then add 15," or it could mean "add 5 to 15 and then multiply that by 3." HyperTalk has a built-in order, or precedence, that governs how these statements are evaluated. Table 14-1 shows the order in which the various operations are evaluated.

This built-in order of precedence dictates that the statement "put 3 * 5 + 15" would be evaluated to 30. Since multiplication is evaluated before addition, HyperCard would first multiply 3 by 5 and then add 15 to the result.

The first thing that HyperTalk evaluates is parentheses, so you can control evaluation of statements by grouping things together with parentheses. In the earlier example, if you want the addition in 3 * 5 + 15 to be evaluated first, you can write the statement as

```
put 3 * (5 + 15)
```

It will then be evaluated as 3 * 20, or 60.

Grouping with parentheses can be done in other situations—for example, when evaluating and/or statements, and to make lines easier to read. HyperCard's logical operators are dealt with in Chapter 16, text operators in Chapter 21, and mathematical operators in Chapter 22.

Checking Syntax

HyperCard checks some of your syntax as you type the commands into the editor. You can see the effects of this syntax checking when you press the TAB key to invoke automatic indentation. If HyperTalk does not understand your statements, it will not indent them correctly. Here's an example:

```
on mouseUp
  if the commandKey is down then
    exit mouseDown
    end if
    end mouseUp
```

Notice that the "end mouseUp" line is not flush with the left margin as it should be, nor is the "end if" line at the same level as its "if" line. This is because the fourth line reads "exit mouseDown" instead of "exit mouseUp". The editor checks your syntax to make sure that the "exit" line matches the "on" line. If they do not match and you click a button with such a handler while pressing the COMMAND key, you will get the alert shown in Figure 14-1.

HyperCard provides this sort of syntax checking in the editor for closing handlers and functions. HyperCard's indentation also lets you know whether you have used If and Repeat structures correctly: if they are not indented properly, you have not entered the statements correctly.

Other syntax checking, however, is not done until the script is run. If HyperCard finds an error as it interprets a

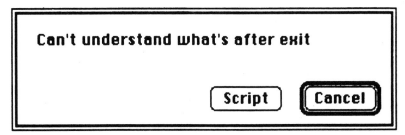

Figure 14-1.   The alert that appears if you do not match your "exit" lines with the name of the handler in which they occur

line of the script, it will give you an alert, such as the one in Figure 14-1, that attempts to isolate the problem as much as possible. When you receive one of these alerts, you can click the Script button to edit the script. When you click the button, HyperCard puts the insertion point on the line that caused the trouble, usually next to the troublesome word.

Naming

HyperCard's rules for variable names are flexible. If you have used early versions of BASIC, you can attest to the nuisance of its two-letter limit on variable names—there just aren't enough characters in the alphabet to come up with enough meaningful variable names. If you have used other languages, you are aware of the limitation of having to include special symbols as part of a variable name to indicate what kind of data it stores. Because HyperCard stores all variables as text, you are freed from this constraint.

When you are naming in HyperCard, be aware that it does not consider case when matching names. To HyperCard, mouseUp is the same as Mouseup or MOUSEUP.

HyperCard uses spaces to separate items on a line from one another, so you are limited to using variable names that have no spaces in them. For example, *mouseHandler* works, but *mouse Handler* is evaluated as two words.

Abbreviation

HyperCard allows you to abbreviate many commonly used words, such as "background," in several different ways. Table 14-2 shows common HyperCard abbreviations.

Word	Abbreviation or Synonym
abbreviated	abbrev, abbr
background	bkgnd, bg
backgrounds	bkgnds, bgs
button	btn
buttons	btns
card	cd
cards	cds
character	chars
field	fld
fields	flds
gray	grey
location	loc
middle	mid
message box	msg, message
picture	pict
polygon	poly
previous	prev
rectangle	rect
regular	reg

Table 14-2.   Common HyperCard Abbreviations

Conventions

Some conventions have arisen for naming such things as values and fields in HyperCard. The standard convention is to use two-word names, with no space between the words and with the second word starting with a capital letter. These constructions are called *interCaps*. HyperCard itself sets this standard with messages such as mouseUp and newCard. This technique is useful when creating variables. HyperCard does not allow you to use a reserved word—one of its commands or keywords—as a variable name. For example, you cannot put a value into a variable named *Card* because HyperCard will not let you use the word "Card" as a variable. If you want to include "Card" in a variable—for instance, a variable to hold card numbers or card names—the interCap convention allows you to use *theCard*. The internal capital letter makes the variable easier to read than, for example, *thecard*.

HyperTalk's syntax in general is designed to serve two purposes: it allows HyperCard to understand your scripts, and it allows you to create scripts that you can read and understand. When programming, use handler and variable names that help you (and others) to understand more easily what purposes are served by various handlers and variables.

Control Structures

On...End
Function...End
Repeat Loops
If Structures
The Wait Command

You have seen that the script is the general structure of the HyperTalk program. Scripts contain handlers that respond to messages and execute commands, and there can be several handlers in any one script. Handlers, too, have structure. One purpose of structuring in a handler is to help define the handler itself. Structuring also helps the handler do different things in different conditions and perform repetitive operations.

On...End

The basic structure of a handler is the On...End structure that defines the handler. The first line of the handler names the handler and optionally lists any arguments or parameters the handler can take. For example, the line

```
on handlerName parameter1,parameter2
```

signals to HyperTalk that this is the beginning of the handler called handlerName and that this handler takes two parameters: *parameter1* and *parameter2*. The line

```
end handlerName
```

signals the end of the handler. Between these two lines are the lines that are executed by the script when it receives the handlerName message.

When you are typing lines into the HyperTalk editor, all "on" and "end" lines should appear flush with the left margin of the editor. If they are not flush with the margin, something is wrong with your script: for example, you might not have enough "End if" or "End repeat" lines to end your If testing or repeat loops, or you might have used an If statement incorrectly. All lines between the On and End statements should be indented at least two spaces from the margin.

Note that you cannot have embedded On and End statements; that is, you cannot define a handler inside the definition of another handler. HyperTalk will not understand this.

You can also pass parameters to HyperCard handlers, just as you can to standard HyperCard commands. For example, in Chapter 33, Script 33-4 includes a handler called readFile that takes two arguments: *fileName* and *numFields*. The readFile handler writes text in a stack to a file on disk. The *fileName* variable contains the name of the file to which readFile is to write, and *numFields* contains the number of background fields it is to write. That readFile takes these two arguments is signaled by its "on readFile" line:

```
on readFile fileName,numFields
```

The two variables are separated on the line by commas, and when you call the handler, you again separate the two variables by commas:

```
readFile "test",7
```

In this example, the name of the file to write is Test and the number of fields is seven.

Variables that are declared in the "on handlerName" line of a handler cannot later be declared global variables inside the handler. Instead, they are local variables inside that handler.

Function . . . End

The "Function...End" structure indicates that the handler is a function and not a regular handler. In many ways, functions work in the same manner as standard handlers, but there are some crucial differences.

When HyperTalk executes a script, it works its way through the lines in the script and executes them one by one. Most lines will use built-in HyperCard commands such as **Go next card**, **Put card field "pages" into numPages**, and so on. These commands can be new messages that are received by handlers in scripts (see Chapter 12). When HyperCard finishes executing a command, it proceeds to the next command.

The purpose of a function, however, is not only to perform an action, but also to *send back*, or *return*, some information to the line that called it. A function may perform a number of actions, but they are in a sense peripheral to its purpose, which is to get or create some value and return it to the line that called it.

Consider the following line:

```
put random(10) into theNumber
```

In this example, the word "random" is a function. As explained in Chapter 14, functions are expressions that HyperTalk treats as values when the line is evaluated. In this case, HyperCard executes the Random function before it executes the rest of the line. The line, after Random is evaluated, might read like this to HyperCard:

```
put 7 into theNumber
```

Random is one of HyperCard's built-in functions. When evaluating a function that you have written, HyperCard works in the same way as it does when it is working with a built-in function. It takes a side trip to execute the function, and then it uses the value returned by the function as it is evaluating the line.

When you call a function in a line, you must *always* pass some arguments to the function, even if it does not require them. For example, suppose you have a function called file-Name. This function returns the name of a file to the line that called it, and it takes no arguments. If you use the line

```
put fileName into theFile
```

to place the name of the file into the variable *theFile*, Hyper-Card will not understand the line. Instead, you need to use the form

```
put fileName() into theFile
```

Normally, parameters passed to a function are placed inside parentheses. In this example, even though the function does not require any parameters, you must include the parentheses. In effect, you are sending an empty parameter to the function. Parameters to a function are defined in the same way as they are with On handlers, as described earlier in this chapter.

As with standard handlers that use the "On...End" pairing, the Function and End statements should be at the left margin of the editor window; all lines between these two statements are indented at least two spaces.

The Return Command

Return *value*

The Return command is used to send a value back to the line

that called the function. When HyperCard encounters the Return command, execution of the function is completed, and control is returned to the line that called the function.

Repeat Loops

Normally HyperTalk executes a handler one line at a time. First, *statement1* is executed, followed by *statement2*, and so on, as shown in Figure 15-1.

Frequently, however, this serial execution of statements is not enough. You want a way to tell HyperTalk to repeatedly execute a definite set of statements. That's what the Repeat structure is for.

Repeat loops give you more power by allowing you to execute a group of statements over and over again until a condition is encountered that stops the loop. Figure 15-2 illustrates this. First *statement1* is executed. HyperTalk then encounters the repeat loop (in this example, the line "repeat 10"), and it remembers how many times it is to execute the lines between that line and the "end repeat" line. It then executes *statement2* and *statement3*. When *statement3* is executed, it starts again at the top of the loop, executing *statement2* again. It repeats this process the number of times specified in the Repeat statement.

```
on illustrate
      ▽
  statement1
      ▽
  statement2
      ▽
  statement3
      ▽
end illustrate
```

Figure 15-1.   Normally scripts execute their statements in order

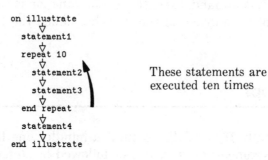

```
on illustrate
    ↓
  statement1
    ↓
  repeat 10
    ↓
    statement2
    ↓
    statement3
    ↓
  end repeat
    ↓
  statement4
    ↓
end illustrate
```

These statements are
executed ten times

Figure 15-2.   Using the repeat loop, the statements between the
Repeat and End Repeat statements are executed
repeatedly

Repeat loops begin with a Repeat statement and end
with an "End repeat" statement. All lines between these two
statements are executed repeatedly and are indented two
spaces from the Repeat and "End repeat" statements.

Repeat [for] *number* [times]

Number is a source that yields the number of times the
statements in the repeat loop will be executed. "For" and
"times" are optional words that can help to make the line
more readable.

Script 15-1 shows a handler that performs the same
function as HyperCard's **Show all cards** command. The
handler is simple. First it sets lockMessages and lockRecent
to "true." As explained in Chapter 13, when lockMessages is
"true," messages such as openCard are not sent to each of the
cards, thus speeding the display of the cards. When lockRecent is set to "true," the cards are not added to the Recent
list. This also speeds things up a little.

Next, the script puts the number of cards in the stack
into a variable called *numCards*. The "repeat" line is next. It

```
on showAllCards
   set lockMessages to true
   set lockRecent to true
   put the number of cards into numCards
   repeat for numCards times
      if the mouseClick then exit repeat
      go next card
   end repeat
end showAllCards
```

Script 15-1.   This handler uses the "Repeat for" structure to emulate HyperCard's **Show all cards** command

simply signals that the next lines, those inside the repeat loop, will be executed *numCards*—the number of cards—times.

Once inside the repeat loop, the mouse is checked. If you have clicked the mouse button the repeat loop is exited, thus stopping the display of cards at the current card. Otherwise, the script simply goes to the next card. The "end repeat" line signals the end of the loop, and the "end showAllCards" line signals the end of the handler.

Repeat until *condition*

This structure repeats the statements inside the loop until *condition* is met. *Condition* is an expression that evaluates to either "true" or "false," and the statements inside the loop are executed until the condition is "true."

Script 15-2 shows a variation on the showAllCards handler. This time, the "Repeat until" structure is used to monitor the status of the mouse, and the loop executes until the mouse is clicked.

Repeat while *condition*

This structure is similar to "Repeat until"; however, it executes while the condition is "true," not while it is "false." The

```
on showAllCards
   set lockMessages to true
   set lockRecent to true
   repeat until the mouseClick
      go next card
   end repeat
end showAllCards
```

Script 15-2.   This handler uses the "Repeat until" construction

handler shown in Script 15-3 again performs the function of showing all the cards until the mouse button is pressed. This time the "Repeat while" structure is used, and the statement constantly monitors the state of the mouse. When the mouse is up, the loop executes; when the mouse is down, that condition is no longer met and the loop halts execution.

Repeat [forever]

This structure causes the statements inside the loop to execute until an "exit repeat" statement is encountered. The word "forever" is optional.

```
on showAllCards
   set lockMessages to true
   set lockRecent to true
   repeat while the mouse is up
      go next card
   end repeat
end showAllCards
```

Script 15-3.   This handler uses the "Repeat while" construction

Use this form of the Repeat statement when you either want a process to continue indefinitely or when there is no obvious way for a script to know beforehand how many times it should execute.

Repeat with *variable* = *start* to *finish*

There are times when a repeat loop will need to do different things depending, perhaps, on how many times it has executed.

If you are using the "Repeat number" structure, the script does not know what iteration of the loop it is on. The "Repeat with" structure allows you to keep track of how many times it has executed or to work with numbers only in a certain range.

For example, suppose you want to perform an operation 100 times. You could use the "repeat 100" structure, but there is no way to discover, inside the loop, at what iteration of the loop you currently are. Instead, you could use this structure:

```
repeat with x = 1 to 100
   put x
end repeat
```

This simple script fragment merely puts the integers from 1 to 100 into the Message box. The x in the Repeat statement is a variable that automatically increments every time the loop is executed. That is, 1 is automatically added to x every time the loop starts over again. Without the variable, you would be forced to explicitly add 1 to the variable every time the loop is executed, as shown here:

```
put 1 into x
repeat 100
   add 1 to x
   put x
end repeat
```

Using the variable form of the repeat loop makes programming much easier and gives you more control over what is going on.

Repeat with *variable* = *start* down to *finish*

This structure works in the same manner as the standard "Repeat with" structure. However, instead of adding 1 to the value each time the loop is executed, it subtracts 1.

Next repeat

This statement allows you to not execute certain statements in the loop. Any statements after the "Next repeat" statement are not executed on the iteration of the repeat loop. Control jumps immediately back to the top of the loop.

You will usually use this with an If test to determine in which instances the statements should be executed.

Exit repeat

This statement allows you to exit the repeat loop, and it works no matter what method of repeating you are using. It is used in Script 15-1: if you click the mouse button while the loop is executing, the script stops execution of the repeat loop.

Nesting Repeat Loops

You can nest loops inside one another for more complicated actions. For example, consider this statement seen recently in a book: "As a matter of fact, the 13th of the month is more likely to fall on a Friday than any other day." Script 15-4 shows how likely it really is, at least as far as the last decade is concerned.

The script is fairly simple, even with the nested repeat loop. First it puts 0 into the two variables used to track the Friday the 13ths. The variable *theFridays* holds the number of Friday the 13ths encountered, and the variable *theDates* holds the number of dates encountered.

```
on mouseUp
  put 0 into theFridays
  put 0 into theDates
  repeat with x = 1960 to 1990
    repeat with y = 1 to 12
      add 1 to theDates
      set cursor to busy
      put y &"/"&13&"/" & x into theDate
      convert theDate to long date
      if item 1 of theDate is "Friday" then
        add 1 to theFridays
      end if
    end repeat
  end repeat
  put theFridays /  theDates * 100 into percentFridays
  answer percentFridays && "Percent Fridays the 13ths"
end mouseUp
```

Script 15-4.   This script illustrates nested repeat loops

Next it starts the outer loop—the one that will move through the years. In this case, you are checking the years from 1960 to 1990. It checks every month of each year in the "repeat with y = 1 to 12" line. The internal loop is executed completely for each iteration of the outer loop.

The next line assembles the date in the form *month/ day/year*. This is then converted to the long date, which has the form *dayOfWeek, monthDate, year*—for example, Thursday, July 21, 1989. (HyperTalk's date commands are discussed in Chapter 23). If the first item of this long date is "Friday," then 1 is added to *theFridays*. When the internal loop has executed from 1 to 12—the months of each year—the external loop is executed again. When the loops have finished executing, the handler reports the percentage of Friday the 13ths that have been found.

By the way, the result in this case is 14.247%. Since an even distribution of Friday the 13ths would have produced the value 14.286%, the author of that book was probably wrong. If you're interested, you can check it yourself over a longer range of years.

Tips for Using Repeat Loops

There are several things you should do when executing repeat loops to gain more control over how to break out of the loop and speed execution of the loop.

Allowing an Exit

The COMMAND-PERIOD key combination will, of course, cause any repeat loop to stop executing. But there is no way for a script to know you have pressed these keys. In order for the script to handle a clean exit, you should provide such a means yourself.

One good way to do this is with the mouse button. Simply check during each cycle of the repeat loop to see if you have clicked the mouse button. This can be done with the line "if the mouseClick then exit repeat", as shown in Script 15-1. Another good way to handle this is to write a separate function that queries whether you really want to stop the process. Script 15-5 shows a function that takes care of this.

Script 15-6 shows a fragment of a handler that calls the reallyStop function. If you put these five lines into a repeat loop, several things happen. First, when you click the mouse

```
function reallyStop
  answer "Do you really want to stop?" with "No" or "Yes"
  if it is "Yes" then
    return true
  else
    return false
  end if
end reallyStop
```

Script 15-5.   A function that asks if you really want to stop

button, the first If statement stops execution of the loop and calls the reallyStop function. (If statements are discussed later in this chapter.)

The reallyStop function uses the Answer command to present you with a dialog box asking if you really want to stop execution of the repeat loop. If you click on the Yes button, reallyStop returns the value "true" to the statement that called it. Otherwise, it returns the value "false." Remember, functions cause the values they return to stand in for the lines that called them.

In Script 15-6, the line "if reallyStop() is true then" is evaluated as "if true is true" when you click the Yes button in the dialog box; since this is, of course, the case, the repeat loop is exited. If you do not click the Yes button, the line is evaluated as "if false is true", which is clearly not the case, and the repeat loop continues.

This allows for instances in which you clicked the mouse button by accident or changed your mind after clicking the mouse button. Your script will now know that you have stopped the operation, and you can act accordingly.

Clearly this sort of technique is preferable to pressing COMMAND-PERIOD to stop a process. It gives the script control over what happens when you want to stop a long process.

```
if the mouseClick then
    if reallyStop() is true then
      exit mouseUp
    end if
end if
```

Script 15-6.   This mouseUp handler shows you how to use the really-Stop function shown in Script 15-5

Keeping Informed

Especially in long loops, it is a good idea to keep informed when something is happening. For example, in version 1.2 or greater, you can use the **Set cursor to busy** command to turn the cursor into a spinning beach ball. Each time this command is called, the beach ball is rotated an eighth of a turn.

Beyond this, if the procedure is especially lengthy, you might want to know how far along the process is. For example, you can create a script that gathers information from every card in a stack and uses the Message box to tell you how far the script has progressed. Script 15-7 shows a handler that goes to every card in a stack, gets the value in a field called "price," and adds the value of that field to a variable *total-Price*. As it moves through the stack, it puts into the Message box the percentage of the stack it has completed.

The first line in the handler sets numberFormat to 0, so that the percentage displayed is an integer —you are probably not interested in the exact percentage the script has completed. (The numberFormat property is discussed in Chapters

```
on mouseUp
  set numberFormat to "0"
  put the number of cards into numCards
  put empty into totalPrice
  put "Percent done: 0"
  repeat with x = 1 to numCards
    go next card
    add bg field "price" to totalPrice
    put x / numCards * 100 into last word of message
    set cursor to busy
  end repeat
end mouseUp
```

Script 15-7.   This handler shows several techniques for keeping informed

13 and 22.) Next, it gets the number of cards in the stack, puts that number into a variable, and then puts "empty" into the *totalPrice* variable.

The next statement puts "Percent done: 0" into the Message box. The repeat statement is next, repeating the loop the same number of times as there are cards in the stack. The loop goes to each card in order and adds the value in the field "Price" to the *totalPrice* variable. Next, it computes the percentage it has completed and puts that integer into the last word of the Message box (which started out as 0). It sets the cursor to busy, rotating the beach ball, and then starts the loop over again.

Of course, this handler doesn't really do anything useful—it doesn't save *totalPrice* into a card field or display it. That's left to you. It also doesn't allow you to stop the process.

Speeding Execution of the Loop

The speed of execution of the loop is proportional to the number of statements in the loop. The more statements inside the loop, the longer it is going to take to complete the process. The best way to speed the loop is to remove from it any statements that are not absolutely required.

Another way to speed execution while in a loop is to set lockMessages to "true." This is especially important in a loop that moves through a number of cards (see Scripts 15-1 and 15-2). When lockMessages is set to "true," messages such as openStack, openBackground, openCard, and their "close" counterparts are not sent. Since the messages are not sent, handlers for these messages will not execute, thus saving time. The lockScreen property is a help, too, if the user does not need to see all the cards as they go by; HyperCard can save the time it takes to update the screen. The lockRecent property can save the short amount of time it takes HyperCard to add the card to the Recent list, and it also will not fill up the Recent list, thus avoiding confusion.

If Structures

Often you will need to instruct a script to perform one set of actions in one set of circumstances and another set of actions in a different set of circumstances. Thinking in terms of If testing is not hard to get used to because it is similar to the thinking you do in daily life for example, —"If this is Tuesday, it must be Belgium."

In general, the If statement has this syntax:

```
If condition then statement1 else statement2
```

Condition is a HyperTalk operator that evaluates to either "true" or "false." If it evaluates to "true," then *statement1* is executed; otherwise (else) *statement2* is executed. This is illustrated in several scripts in this chapter. In Script 15-1, the simplest form of the If statement is used to exit the repeat loop if you click the mouse button.

The Else statement allows you to perform a separate set of circumstances if the main condition is not met. It gives you more control over the alternatives.

Some Style Tips for If Statements

There are more ways to use the If statement than you can shake the proverbial stick at. Some, however, are better than others. Even if the statement works, it might not be good style—it might make the script more difficult to read than it needs to be.

Some Good Styles

This is the one line form of the If statement:

```
If condition then statement [else statement]
```

You should use this form only if it can all fit on one line in the editor window. *Statement* can consist of only one command. Generally, this method is easy to read.

You can use the following structure if you are performing only one statement in either case. Again, this structure is easy to read if the statements can fit on the line. Use this style if you have several statements that need to be executed.

```
If condition then
  series of statements
[else
  series of statements]
end if
```

Each of the statements will be indented two spaces from the "If...End if" statements, which makes the structure of the script easy to read. The "End if" statement is required in this case.

Some Poor Styles

The definition of a poor style is one that is hard to read. In few of these cases does HyperTalk exact a performance penalty for using poor style. However, a style that is easy to read is easier to modify later, and it is easier to understand how it works.

Perhaps you only have one statement to execute, as shown here:

```
If condition
then statement
[else statement]
```

If the condition is true, then you might as well use one of the one-line structures for the If statement. Indenting will help you read the line, but it won't have much value:

```
If condition then
  1 statement
end if
```

In the following example, only one command is executed in the Else statement:

```
If condition then
   series of statements
else statement
```

It is better to put that command or statement on a different line, which will make the script easier to read.

The following is easy to read, but it takes up several unnecessary lines in the script and thus makes the script as a whole a little more difficult to read:

```
If condition then
   1 statement
else
   1 statement
end if
```

Use one of the structures previously mentioned instead.

Of course, none of the suggestions mentioned here are hard-and-fast rules. Just keep in mind that a style that makes scripts easier to read is much better than a style that leads to unclear lines.

Nesting If Statements

Just as repeat loops can be nested, so too can If statements. It is common to use these statements when you need to test whether a number of conditions have been met before performing some particular action. Script 15-5 uses nested If statements to first test for the mouseClick. If you click the mouse, the function reallyStop (in Script 15-4) is called. If that function returns "true" then the "exit mouseUp" line is executed, and the mouseUp handler stops.

The Wait Command

Wait [for] <*number of ticks*>
Wait [for] <*number*> **seconds**
Wait until <*true or false expression*>
Wait while <*true or false expression*>

The Wait command pauses execution of a script for a specified amount of time, or until a certain condition is met.

The first form of the Wait command shown here pauses the script for a specified *number of ticks*. A tick is 1/60 of a second. Ticks are discussed in more detail in Chapter 23. The Wait command uses ticks as its default; for example, if you use the command

    Wait 10

HyperCard assumes you mean ten ticks.

The second form of the Wait command specifies the number of seconds the Wait command is to pause the script.

Typically, however, you will use the Wait command to wait until or while some condition is met. You might be waiting for something such as a sound to stop, or the pause may allow you to press the mouse button.

One use of the Wait command is to stop execution of a script while a sound is being played. This is useful if you are playing a long sound, which might sound scratchy if some other process is taking place while the sound is being played. In this case, you can use the statement

    wait until the sound is "done"

The Wait command constantly tests the Sound function. While the sound is being executed, this function returns the name of the sound being played (sounds are discussed in Chapter 30). When no sound is being played, that function returns "done," and the script continues executing.

Another use is to wait until you take some action, such as clicking the mouse button. There are two ways you can check the the status of the mouse button:

```
wait until the mouse is down
wait until the mouseClick
```

The first line above is something like the Sound function described earlier. When you click the mouse button, the Mouse function returns "down" to the statement that called it.

The second line uses the mouseClick function. This function returns "true" when the user clicks the mouse button. Mouse functions are discussed in detail in Chapter 19.

You can also use the Repeat structure to perform a wait, which gives you more control over what is going on. The Wait command only allows you to wait while one expression is being checked—the parameter that is passed to the Wait command. Repeat loops, however, can include a number of conditions and give you more flexibility.

Logical Operators

The < Operator
The > Operator
The ≤ Operator
The ≥ Operator
The = Operator
The ≠ and <> Operators
The is Operator
The not Operator
The and Operator
The or Operator
The contains Operator
The in Operator
The within Operator
Grouping

Chapter 15 discussed control structures—the parts of Hyper-Card that allow you to write scripts that perform one series of operations in one case and another series in a different case. The scripts in that chapter used some operators that decided whether the cases were true or false. You will also remember from Chapter 15 a discussion of expressions, which are statements that, when evaluated, yield a value that HyperCard can use.

Chapter 14 discussed HyperTalk's *operators*, which generally include three components: two arguments—one on each side of the operator—and the operator itself. When HyperTalk evaluates the statement containing the operator expression, it substitutes the value returned by the operator for the three elements.

HyperCard's logical operators always yield one of two values: "true" or "false." If...Then...Else statements, and some others, base their actions on these expressions.

First, a definition of "true" and "false": they are special constants defined by HyperTalk. In essence, they are nothing more than their text representatives; you don't need to worry about 0 or 1 as you did in some earlier programming languages.

Here are some true expressions:

```
5 = 5
"HyperCard" contains "a"
"a" is in "HyperCard"
5 > 3
```

Here are some false expressions:

```
3 > 5
"HyperCard" contains "z"
"x" is in "HyperCard"
```

You can also explicitly place "true" and "false" into containers with the Put command and then test to see if the variable is true or false. Functions also commonly return "true" or "false," and many HyperCard properties have "true" or "false" values.

The general syntax for logical operators is

<expression1> operator <expression2>

Expression1 and *expression2* can be any expressions that evaluate to a value. A value can be a number or text.

The < Operator

This operator evaluates to "true" if the expression to the left is *less than* the expression to the right.

If you are comparing numbers, the < operator performs a mathematical comparison:

```
1 < 2 -- is true
5 > 6 -- is false
```

However, if one of the values is a character, such as the letter "s," then that character is first evaluated to its ASCII value. (In ASCII, each character is assigned a number: the character "1" has an ASCII value of 49; the character "s" has a value of 115. ASCII values are discussed, along with the numToChar and charToNum functions, in Chapter 21.) Here is an example:

```
"a" < "s" -- is true
1 < "s" -- also true
```

The > Operator

This operator evaluates to "true" if the expression to the left is *greater than* the expression to the right:

```
3 > 5 -- false
5 > 3 -- true
"t" > "s" -- true
```

The ≤ Operator

This operator evaluates to "true" if the expression to the left is *less than or equal to* the expression to the right. You can type this character by holding down the OPTION key and pressing the COMMA or < (less-than) key. Here is an example:

```
3 ≤ 5 -- true
5 ≤ 5 -- also true
```

The ≥ Operator

This operator evaluates to "true" if the expression to the left is *greater than or equal to* the expression to the right. (Press OPTION-PERIOD to produce this character.) Here are two examples:

```
3 ≥ 5 -- false
7 ≥ 5 -- true
7 ≥ 7 -- true
```

The = Operator

This operator evaluates to "true" if both the expressions evaluate to the same value:

```
6 = 6 -- true
"HyperCard" = "HyperCard" -- true
"HyperTalk" = "HyperCard" -- false
```

If you are testing to find out if a certain value is true, you can use a shorter syntax. You do not need to use an expression like this:

```
if useSounds is true
```

Instead, you can use the following shorthand expression:

```
if useSounds
```

UseSounds will evaluate to "true" if it is a function that returns "true" or if it is a variable that contains the text "true."

The ≠ and <> Operators

These operators evaluate to "true" if the expressions do not evaluate to the same values. The ≠ character can be produced by holding down the OPTION key and pressing the EQUAL key; alternatively, you can use the < (less-than) and > (greater-than) symbols together:

```
4 ≠ 4 -- False
1 ≠ 4 -- true
"s" ≠ "t" -- true
7 <> 5 -- true
```

The is Operator

This operator works in the same manner as the = operator. It returns "true" if the statement on the left is the same as the statement on the right.

The **is** operator can also be used with **not**, **within**, and **in**.

The not Operator

This operator negates the value of the statement to the right. It is used with other operators, most often with **is** and **in**. Here are some examples:

```
"a" is not in "HyperCard" -- false
3 is not 5 -- true
5 is not 5 -- false
```

The and Operator

This operator is used to determine whether two sets of expressions are true. It evaluates to "true" if they are both true; otherwise it returns "false":

```
3 < 5 and 7 < 10 -- true
3 > 5 and 5 < 7 -- false
"HyperCard" contains "a" and 3 < 5 -- true
```

The or Operator

This operator evaluates to "true" if at least one of the expressions is true and "false" if they are both false:

```
3 < 5 or 7 > 10 -- true
"HyperCard" contains "a" or 3 > 5 -- true
```

The contains Operator

This operator evaluates to "true" if the expression to the left contains the expression to the right:

```
"HyperCard" contains "a" -- true
1234 contains 6 -- false
```

The in Operator

This operator is used with **is** to perform essentially the same test performed by **contains**, except that the syntax is reversed. That is, **is in** evaluates to "true" if the expression to the left is contained in the expression to the right:

```
"a" is in "HyperCard" -- true
```

You can insert **not** in this statement to negate it:

```
"a" is not in "HyperCard" -- false
```

The within Operator

This operator, new to version 1.2, needs more specific expressions than some of the other operators. Its precise syntax is

location **is within** *rectangle*

Location is a point. Points have two addresses: the first represents how far the point is from the left edge of the screen, and the second represents how far the point is from the right edge of the screen. Here are some expressions that evaluate to points:

```
"50,75"
the mouseLoc -- the current location of the mouse pointer
the loc of card button 1 -- the center of the button
the clickLoc -- the place the mouse was last clicked
```

As you can see from the first example, "50,75", if you are using actual numbers instead of an expression that evaluates to a point, then you must surround the numbers with quotes.

Rectangle is a set of four integers that describes a rectangle. The four points in the rectangle are left, top, right, and bottom. For example, the rectangle of the standard Macintosh screen is "0,0,512,342". (You can get this value with the screenRect function.) As with points, if you are using absolute numbers in a comparison instead of an expression that evaluates to a rectangle, you need to surround the numbers with quotes. Here are some expressions that evaluate to rectangles:

```
"100,100,200,200"
the screenRect -- the size of the screen
the rect of card window
the rect of message window
the rect of card button 1
the rect of card field 1
```

This feature is useful because prior to version 1.2, if you wanted to test whether or not the mouse was within a certain rectangle, you needed to perform four If tests, which took some time.

Grouping

Just as you can use parentheses to group expressions when working with mathematical operators, as you saw in Chapter 14, you can use parentheses to group logical operators. Using parentheses to group statements makes them easier to read and understand.

For example, if you are testing a number to see if it falls between two ranges, you can use a line like this:

```
if theNumber < lowRange or theNumber > highRange then
```

If you use parentheses to group the expressions, the line is easier to read:

```
if (theNumber < lowRange) or (theNumber > highRange) then
```

SEVENTEEN

Chunk Expressions

Containers
Text Structures
An Example
Counting Chunks
Extracting Chunks
Putting Text into Chunks

Every programming language gives you ways to access text and parts of text. HyperTalk uses chunk expressions to allow you to separate and work with different parts, or chunks, of text.

Chunk expressions are one of the most exciting of HyperTalk's features and are an integral part of its operation. They might seem difficult to understand at first, but after some practice they become easy to use and understand. For the most part, HyperCard structures text in familiar forms—in terms of characters, words, and lines. Only *items*, which are chunks of text separated by commas, take some getting used to. Many of the scripts in this book use chunk expressions in one way or another.

Containers

HyperCard's chunk expressions extract text from any of its containers. Containers—such as variables, the Message box, and fields—are HyperCard objects that can hold text that the program can manipulate. Following are some notes about the various kinds of containers.

Variables

In Chapter 10, you saw that variables are used to hold values. A variable can contain as many characters as free memory will allow and can be either local or global. Remember that variables are for *temporary* storage of text only: text held in variables is lost when you leave HyperCard. Global variables can be used by different handlers in different scripts; local variables are available only to the handler that uses them.

The Message Box

The Message box contains text that you placed there either by typing it in or by using the Put command. Scripts can also manipulate text that is contained in the Message box and can place text into that box to send messages. Many of the scripts in this book use the Message box to keep you up to date on the progress of an operation. Chapter 25 presents a technique for using the Message box as a kind of dialog box.

Fields

Fields are the primary means of storing text in HyperCard. Text stored in fields remains there even when you quit HyperCard or go to a different stack. Fields can contain up to 30,000 characters of text.

Text Structures

HyperCard text is structured in four ways.

Lines

A *line* is a chunk of text that ends with a carriage return. Unless a container is empty, it always has at least one line.

Even if there is no carriage return, one is implied, and the return itself is not part of the line. That is, when you use a line such as

```
get line 1 of card field "test"
```

which puts that line into the variable "It," the return at the end of the line will not be part of "It."

Items

An item is a chunk of text that ends with a comma, but the comma itself is not part of the item unless the container has only one item. In that case it might not include a comma. Unless a container is empty, it always has at least one item. Items can contain multiple lines or words.

Note: Since commas delimit items, you should not include commas in numbers when working in HyperCard. If you have a number such as 30,000 in text, you *will* be able to access this number as a *word*, but if you attempt to get the number as an item, only part of the number will be returned.

Words

Words are chunks of text separated by spaces. The text "Hyper,Card" is one word because it does not contain any spaces, but it is two items. Unless a container is empty, it always contains at least one word.

Characters

A character, the smallest element of a chunk of text, is any single element you can type at the keyboard: "a" is a character, as are "t", "1", a return, and a comma.

An Example

Chunk expressions might be better understood with an example:

> Once upon a time, and a very good time it was, there was this moocow coming down along the road and this moocow that was coming down along the road met a nicens little boy named baby tuckoo...¶
> His father told him that story: his father looked at him through a glass: he had a hairy face. ¶

(This is the opening to Joyce's *A Portrait of the Artist as a Young Man*, slightly modified by the addition of some commas to illustrate items. Each type of text structure appears in this text.)

The text example contains two lines. Although the chunk takes up more than two lines on the page, it actually contains only two returns, which are represented in the sample with the ¶ symbol. (This symbol does not appear in Hyper-Card.) These lines, therefore, are delimited with hard returns, not the soft returns that occur when HyperCard or a word processor wraps a line.

The text contains three items. The first item consists of the text "Once upon a time". The second item consists of the text "and a very good time it was", and the third item consists of the remainder of the text.

The text contains 57 words. There are several interesting words in this chunk. The fourth ("time,") and and eleventh ("was,") contain commas because only spaces and returns delimit words. The final word of the first paragraph, "tuckoo...", contains three periods. In the second paragraph, there are two words, "story:" and "glass:", that contain colons.

The text contains 288 characters. There are few surprises here. You should note that the returns that end the line are characters, as are the spaces between words, punctuation such as commas and periods, and the three periods that end the first paragraph.

Counting Chunks

You can use the Number function to find out how many lines, items, words, and characters are in a text container. The form of the Number function is

the number of *items* in *text*.

Items can be lines, items, words, or characters. *Text* can be any container that contains text, such as a variable, a field, or the Message box. Here are some examples:

```
the number of words in theText
the number of items in bg field "List"
the number of characters in card field "comments"
the number of lines in card field "comments"
```

Extracting Chunks

Sometimes you want to work with specific chunks of text. For example, when you use the Sort button in the Address stack, you are asked if you want to sort the stack by first or last name. If you want to sort the stack by last name, the script actually sorts on the last word of line 1 of the field "Name and Address" in that stack. HyperCard gives you several ways to specify different chunks.

Ordinals

Ordinals allow you to work with specific parts of text without having to know how many parts there are.

First

This ordinal allows you to specify the first character, word, line, or item in text:

```
first word of "name"  --  first word in a container
first word of card field "test" -- first word in a field
```

Last

This ordinal allows you to access the last chunk (word, character, line, or item) in text, without forcing you to count all of them first:

```
last item of card field "list"
last word of "name"
```

Middle

This ordinal accesses the middle chunk (word, character, line, or item) in text, without forcing you to count all of them. If there is an even number in the text, it returns the next larger number. This ordinal is not frequently used. Here are two examples:

```
middle character in "HyperCard" -- this is "r"
middle character in "ab" -- "b"
```

Any

This ordinal accesses a random chunk (word, character, line, or item) in text. One use for this would be in a game in which you need to choose from a list of words or numbers.

Second, Third, Fourth, Fifth, Sixth, Seventh, Eighth, Ninth, Tenth

You can use any of these words to access the respective words, characters, lines, or items of text. If you try to get the eighth word of some text that contains only seven words, you will get an empty string, not an error.

Numbers

You can refer to any chunk of text by number, as shown here:

```
character 5 of "abcdefg"  -- is "e"
word 2 of "a b c d" -- is "b"
character 3 of "a b c d" -- second character is a space
```

If you try to work with text that is outside the possible range—for example, getting the 100th character of a text string that contains only 90 characters—you will get an empty string.

Ranges

You can also ask for a range of words, items, characters, or lines from text using the word "to", as shown here:

```
char 1 to 7 of "abcdefghijklmnop" -- "abcdefg"
char 3 to 5 of "abcdefghijklmnop" -- "cde"
```

The range that you request must consist of the same type of chunk. You cannot, for example, ask for the range of "character 2 to word 4" of a variable.

Being More Specific

Chunk expressions can be grouped together to be more specific. This means that you can use different chunk expressions within one line, as shown in these examples:

```
char 1 of item 7 of card field "list"
word 1 of line 2 of bg field "stuff"
char 1 of item 2 of "abc,def" -- "d"
```

Figure 17-1 shows how HyperCard evaluates the last line, which contains two chunk expressions. First it evaluates the last chunk expression of the line, which is

item 2 of "abc,def".

```
char 1 of item 2 of "abc,def"
```

```
char 1 of          "def"
```

```
            "d"
```

Figure 17-1. HyperCard first interprets the second chunk expression of this line and then interprets the first chunk expression

It then evaluates the first chunk expression of the line and returns the character "d".

Other Cards and Stacks

You are not limited to accessing text in fields on the current card. An expression that evaluates to a container can refer to any card in a stack. Here are some examples:

```
card field "comments" of card "annotation"
bg field "comments" of card id 7654
```

However, a chunk expression cannot access text in a field that is in a different stack. If you use an expression such as

```
bg field "comments" of card 17 of stack "books"
```

HyperCard will give you an error alert stating that it cannot understand the line. If you want to get at text in a different stack, you must use the Go command to go to that stack, get the text, and return to the current stack. This has its advantages and disadvantages: it would be nice to be able to work with text in different stacks, but it is probably quicker to actually go to the stack and return with the text, as long as you lock messages and the screen before doing so.

Putting Text into Chunks

You can also use the Put command to change specific parts of text. This works in different ways depending on the structure you are working with.

Consider the following lines:

```
put "HyperCard" into theVariable -- put into a variable
put "a" into char 1 of theVariable -- makes it "ayperCard"
put "abc" into char 2 of theVariable --   "aabcperCard"
```

As you can see, if you put more than one character into a position previously occupied by a single character, the characters after that position are moved to the right to allow it to fit.

When you try to put a character beyond the extent of the variable, HyperTalk merely adds that character to the end of the text, as shown here:

```
put "z" into char 26 of theVariable --   "aabcperCardz"
put "Talk" into word 2 of theVariable -- "aabcperCardzzTalk"
```

This is true of characters and words, but it is not true of lines and items.

After executing these lines,

```
put "HyperCard" into theVariable
put "HyperTalk" into item 7 of theVariable
```

theVariable contains this text:

```
HyperCard,,,,,,HyperTalk
```

HyperCard has *created* the intervening items for you. This

also occurs when you put a line beyond the container's capacity. This gives you a lot of control over how you can structure data. As long as you break up your data into lines and items, you can put values into specific lines or items without needing to explicitly create the structures beforehand.

Note that, if you execute these commands,

```
put "a,b,c" into theVariable
put "d,e" into item 2 of theVariable
```

theVariable will now contain "a,d,e,c". Because the text put into *theVariable* actually contains two items, "c" will be the fourth item in *theVariable* instead of the third.

Other Text Commands

The procedures described in this chapter are only part of the wealth of methods HyperTalk gives you for manipulating text. Other commands—for putting text into containers and controlling where it goes and for accessing various parts of text using the offSet function—are discussed in Chapter 21. Chapter 21 also discusses some functions new to HyperCard version 1.2 that return chunk expressions when you need to determine exactly which text was found by the Find command or selected by you or a script.

Card and Stack Management

**E
I
G
H
T
E
E
N**

Navigating through cards, backgrounds, and stacks is one of the most common activities in HyperCard. Many stacks do nothing more than move you to different cards with buttons that link one card to another. This linking of cards and stacks is responsible for the "hyper" in HyperCard.

Linking

Perhaps the easiest way to create buttons that link to different cards or stacks is by using the linkTo button on the Button Info dialog box. To do this, create a button, summon the Button Info dialog box by double-clicking the button, and click the linkTo button. You can then use any HyperCard navigation tools—including such things as entering Find commands into the Message box—to go to the card or stack to which you want to link the button. When you get to the card or stack, click the appropriate button on the linkTo windoid.

When you have linked a button to a card, take a look at the script that HyperCard has inserted into the button. If the button had no previous handler in it, a mouseUp handler would have been created that includes the line "Go to card ID" followed by the ID number of the card or the name of the stack. If the script had a mouseUp handler in it before you performed the link, the "Go to" statement would have been inserted into the last line of the mouseUp handler. If the handler already included a "Go to" statement to take it to another card, that statement will have been replaced with the link to the specific card. If there were more than one "Go to" statement in the mouseUp handler, only the first would be replaced.

In this situation, you can write scripts that link cards together and then use the linkTo button to actually create the links. You don't need to remember or write down card names, numbers, or IDs.

The Go Command

Go *destination*

The Go command takes you to different stacks, backgrounds, or cards. It features a very flexible syntax, even by Hyper-Card standards. *Destination* can be any expression that tells HyperCard what stack, background, or card you want to go to; it can be specific card IDs or numbers, or it can be more general, as with the Go Next or Go Previous commands.

Going to Other Cards

Moving between cards is easy, and you have several ways to do it. You can go to a card in a general manner, with the First, Next, Previous, Last, Middle, Any, Back, and Forth arguments to the Go command. Unless you specify otherwise, these arguments take you to cards in the same stack.

First, Next, Previous, and Last

These four arguments for the Go command perform the same functions as their counterparts on the Go menu. You can also add a background identifier to any of these arguments, as shown here:

```
go to next card of this background
```

In cases where a stack contains several backgrounds and consecutive cards may have different backgrounds, this command takes you to the next card of the background, not necessarily the next card in the stack.

Going to a card by identifying a specific background can take longer than merely going to the next card in the stack. HyperCard must search through the cards in the specified background to find the correct card, rather than using HyperCard's cache of cards in memory to go to the next card.

Middle

When this argument is included in the Go command, Hyper-Card goes to the middle card in the stack. If you add a background specifier to the command, as in **Go middle card of this background**, execution may be delayed. HyperCard must find the number of cards in the background and then go to the correct card.

Back

This argument tells HyperCard to go to the last card visited before the current card. One of the unexpected results of Go Back, is that it goes back to cards that you don't think you visited. This can occur when a script has moved through a number of cards and lockScreen and lockRecent are set to "true." You don't realize that you've gone to these cards, but you have, and when you use the Go Back command, you return to those cards.

Forth

This argument is the opposite of Back. This might seem to be an impossibility — how can Go Forth take you to the next card you will visit? Instead of reading your mind, Go Forth takes you to the next card *on the Recent list* after the current card. Remember that the Recent list is a record of the last 42 cards you have visited.

Any

With this argument, Go takes you to a random card in the stack. This is a singularly mysterious function: why would you want to go to a random card in a stack? One application could be in games, when you want to bring an element of randomness to the way the stack is seen.

Using Numbers

You can go to cards by number with the Go command. For example, typing the line **Go card 7** takes you to the seventh card. You can also go to backgrounds by number, with a command such as **Go background 1**, which takes you to the first card that has that background. Or you can combine the two methods with a command such as **Go card 7 of background 2**.

Using Names

You can go to named cards with a line such as this:

```
go to card "order entry"
```

This is probably the slowest way to go to cards in a stack because HyperCard needs to search through its list of named cards to find a particular one.

Using ID numbers

Since HyperCard's ID numbers for cards and backgrounds remain the same no matter what order you sort the stack into, the most reliable way of linking cards is by ID number. Indeed, when you use the linkTo button on the Button Info dialog box, HyperCard inserts into the script the ID number of the card you are linking to.

Using ID numbers is also the fastest way to move from card to card, because HyperCard maintains a table of card IDs in memory. HyperCard does not need to search through the stack to find the correct card or background, as it does when you use card or background numbers.

This is not to say that using ID numbers is the best way to move from card to card. Sometimes you want to go to different cards based on the sort order. When you are moving to a different stack, you usually want to go to the first card in that stack; in this case, going to a card by ID number might not get you where you want to go.

Going to Other Backgrounds

You can move to other backgrounds in a stack and to specific cards in other backgrounds. If you don't specify a card on the background, HyperCard takes you to the first card of that background. Here are some examples of lines you could use to go to different backgrounds:

```
go to next card of this background -- takes you to next card
in the background
go to second card of this background
go to second card of second background
go to background "orders"
go to background ID 3768
```

Going to Stacks

If you don't specify a card or background, **Go to stack** takes you to the first card in the stack, which is also a member of the first background in the stack. The Go command allows great flexibility in how you specify going to different stacks:

```
go to stack "home"
go to home
put "Home" into theStack
go to theStack
```

If HyperCard cannot interpret the *destination* as a card or background, it assumes you mean a stack, and it tries to go to that stack. (If the stack is not in any of the folders listed on the Stacks card in the Home stack, you are presented with a standard Open File dialog box asking you to locate the stack.)

You can also specify a card in the stack with commands such as these:

```
go to background "first" of stack "test" -- takes you to the
first card in the background named "first"
go to card 34 of stack "test"
go to card ID 2375 of stack "test"
go to card "order entry" of stack "orders"
```

A Script That Firms Up Links

As mentioned earlier, using the Go command with an ID number for a specific card is much quicker than using a card number or name. It is also more reliable than going to a card by number, since the card number can change as cards are added or deleted and the stack is sorted. However, sometimes it is more difficult to create scripts that link cards by ID because HyperCard users are not used to thinking of cards in terms of their IDs.

To solve this problem, the button script shown in Script 18-1 takes soft links (a soft link is one that links by name or number) in buttons and makes them hard links, which link buttons by ID number. This script handles only card buttons (presumably, background buttons would include Next and Previous buttons that you want to remain soft).

This script should be put into a button called, for example, firmLinks. The script includes a comment warning that

```
on mouseUp
  -- MAKE A COPY OF YOUR CARD OR STACK BEFORE USING!
  set lockMessages to true
  set lockRecent to true
  repeat with x = 1 to the number of card buttons
    -- let the user cancel gracefully
    if the mouseClick then exit repeat
    put "Now processing" && the short name of card button x
    if the script of card button x contains "Go" then
      put the script of card button x into theScript
      --  find the Go command
      repeat with y = 1 to the number of lines in theScript
        if word 1 of line y of theScript is "Go" then
          put firmIt(line y of theScript) into ¬
          line y of theScript
        end if
      end repeat
      set the script of card button x to theScript
    end if
  end repeat
  put empty
  hide the message box
end mouseUp

function firmIt whatLine
  -- changes links to card names or numbers into
  -- links by card ID numbers
  if whatLine contains "stack" then
    return whatLine
  end if
  -- already linked by ID
  if whatLine contains "ID" then
    return whatLine
  end if
  -- remember where we are, card and stack-wise
  push this card
  put the short name of this stack into thisStack
  -- perform the Go command
  do whatLine
  -- handle cases where a stack slipped through
  if the short name of this stack is not thisStack then
    pop card
    return whatLine
  else
    put the short id of this card into theID
  end if
  -- now go back
  pop card
  return "Go to card ID" && theID
end firmIt
```

Script 18-1.   This script changes all the soft links on a card to hard links by card ID

you should make a copy of any stack you process with the script. Although it has been tested and has worked, it is always best to protect yourself when you have a script that modifies other scripts.

The script locks the messages and Recent to speed its progress. Next it cycles through the card buttons. It tests for the mouseClick to allow you to exit gracefully; a COMMAND-PERIOD in this instance could destroy the script. It reports the number and name of the button it is working on.

If the script contains a Go command, the repeat loop then cycles through each line of the script, searching for the Go statement.

When the script finds the Go statement, the line

```
put firmIt(line y of theScript) into line y of theScript
```

calls the function firmIt, which does the work of turning the soft link into a hard link. The firmIt parameter takes one argument: the line of the script that contains the Go command, which is held in the variable whatLine.

First firmIt checks to see if the link was an explicit one to another stack. Presumably, a link to a different stack does not want to go to a specific card in that stack, but rather to the first card in the stack. If this is the case, the function merely returns the line to the handler that called it and stops executing after the Return statement. The function also checks to see if the Go statement referred to a card by its ID. If so, it returns the unmodified line: there is no need to firm up an already firm link.

The line "push this card" remembers the card the button was on, and the next line remembers the name of the current stack. (The Push command is discussed later in this chapter.) Next the function simply executes the line of the script with the line "do whatLine." (The Do command is discussed in Chapter 28.) This command actually takes the script to the card that was referred to in the Go statement.

Again, the script tests to see if it has gone to a different stack. If it has, since you don't want to link to that stack, the card is popped back to the original card. (See the next section, "Pushing and Popping Cards.") The original line—whatLine—is returned to the mouseUp handler.

Next, a new line for whatLine is built. This line is a concatenation of the line "Go to card ID" and the ID number of the card. (Concatenation is discussed in Chapter 21.) This new line, linking the card by ID number, is returned to the calling handler after the script returns to the original card, and control returns to the calling handler.

This handler then sets the script of the button in question to the new script. Remember that scripts are properties, and you must use the Set command to change them.

When the script is finished, it cleans up after itself, putting "empty" into the Message box and hiding it.

There are many modifications you can make to a script such as this one. You could add another repeat loop that executes this script for every card in the stack. You could have it query you about buttons, or make it sensitive to buttons that have links such as "Go Next Card." These alterations are left to you as an exercise. Remember, however, that you should make a copy of your stack before experimenting with this or any other button that alters scripts; this is your protection against accidental damage.

Going to Cards That Do Not Exist

If you use a Go command in the Message box to go to a card that does not exist, you will get the error alert shown in Figure 18-1. This alert also appears if you attempt, from the Message box, to go to a background that does not exist.

However, if you attempt to go to a card or background that does not exist *from within a script*, no alert will appear. Instead, HyperCard will place "No such card" into the special container called "the result," and you will remain at the current card. This allows your scripts to have more flexibility and makes them less error prone. Script 18-2 illustrates using "the result" to perform the simple task of giving you the same information that the error alert gives you from the Message box.

No such card.

Cancel

Figure 18-1. This alert appears if you try to go to a card that does not exist from the Message box

Pushing and Popping Cards

Sometimes, before you go to a card, you want to remember the exact card you came from so you can go back to it later. You can always use Go Back, of course, but that only takes you to the last card. The Push and Pop commands work together to allow you to go to specific cards; Push remembers a specific card, and Pop takes you back to that card.

```
on mouseUp
  ask "Go to what card?"
  put it into theCard
  go to card theCard
  if the result is "no such card" then
    answer "No such card!"
  end if
end mouseUp
```

Script 18-2. This script illustrates using "the result" to discover if a card exists

One way to understand how these commands work is to think of a stack of dishes being washed and dried. After a dish is washed, it is put on top of the stack of dishes to be dried. This is "pushing" the dish. When the dish is picked up from the stack to be dried, it is being "popped." Only the top dish in the stack can be accessed at any one time.

Push and Pop work in the same way. Think of the stack of cards that has been pushed as the stack of dishes. When you push a card, you are placing a new card on the stack. When you pop a card, you are taking a card off the stack.

The Push Command

Push *card*

Push places the specified card on the stack, to store it for later use.

Card can be any expression that points to a card. Here are some examples:

```
Push this card -- puts current card on top of the stack
Push card -- does the same thing as the previous example
Push recent card -- puts the most recent card visited on top
Push card 187 -- puts that card on top of the stack
Push card 1 of background "titles" of stack "bibliography"
```

The last two examples show how you can refer to cards using the Push command. You don't need to be *at* the card to push it.

The Pop Command

Pop card [*into container*]

Pop is the flip side of Push. In its most common form, Pop Card, this command takes you directly to the most recent card pushed.

You can also Pop a card into a container, such as a variable or field. Doing this puts into the container a complete description of the card on the stack, but it doesn't take you to the stack. For example, if you use the command

```
Pop card into theCard
```

where *theCard* is a variable, and then use the command **Put theCard**, the Message box will display something like this:

> card id 74196 of stack "Hard disk:HyperCard folder: Hyperbooks:books"

You can use this information in several ways. For example, you can use the command **Go to theCard** to go directly to that card, or you can save these card addresses for use elsewhere.

Locking and Unlocking the Screen

When moving through a number of cards, you will often want to lock the screen. Locking the screen means that no changes to the screen are shown until the screen is unlocked, or until the script stops executing. HyperCard version 1.2 or greater gives you three ways to do this; with earlier versions you can only use the lockScreen property.

The Lock Screen Command

Lock screen

This command locks the screen, preventing the display of changes to the screen, including the display of different cards to which the stack has gone.

This command does not affect the Message box. The screen will be locked until one of the following occurs:

- The Unlock Screen command is used.

- The lockScreen property is set to "false."

- The script stops executing and HyperCard is idle.

The Unlock Screen Command

Unlock Screen *<with visual effect>*

The Unlock Screen command reverses the action of the Lock Screen command and updates the screen to show the current card. You can optionally use one visual effect with this command. Visual effects are discussed in detail in Chapter 20.

Displaying a Hidden Field

You are not limited to using the Lock Screen and Unlock Screen commands when moving from card to card. For example, they can also be used to display fields that have been hidden.

Suppose you have a field called "popUp," and you don't want it visible at all times. You could create a button to control the visibility of the field and put Script 18-3 into it.

```
on mouseUp
  if the short name of the target is "show" then
    lock screen
    show bg field "PopUp"
    unlock screen with zoom open
    set the name of the target to "hide"
  else
    lock screen
    hide bg field "PopUp"
    unlock screen with zoom close
    set the name of the target to "show"
  end if
end mouseUp
```

Script 18-3.   This script uses the Lock Screen and Unlock Screen commands to show and hide a "Zoom Open" field

This button first checks to find out its name. If the name of the button is Show, the script unlocks the screen with the Zoom Open visual effect. This gives the appearance of the field opening up on the card—the way folders or disks open on the Macintosh desktop. The script then changes the name of the button it is in to Hide.

If the name of the button is Hide, the script locks the screen, hides the field, and then unlocks the screen with the Zoom Close effect. This gives the appearance of the field closing onto the card—the way folders close on the Macintosh desktop. The script then changes the name of its button to Show.

The lockScreen Property

set lockScreen to true|false

Setting lockScreen to "true" is the same as using the Lock Screen command. Setting lockScreen to "false" is the same as using the Unlock Screen command. However, when you are setting lockScreen to "false," you do not have the option of using a visual effect.

Sorting

Sorting stacks with HyperCard is all you could ask it to be— fast, reliable, and stable—and the sorting methods you can use are flexible.

The Sort Command

Sort [*sortOrder*] [*sortStyle*] *expression*

This command sorts the stack according to *expression*, which can be a field, a function, or any HyperCard expression.

Fields

When sorting by fields, HyperCard sorts according to the text stored in those fields. You can also concatenate fields in this manner:

```
Sort by bg field "Last Name" & bg field "First Name"
```

This will sort by the last name followed by the first name and keep all the names together.

Functions

You can also sort by a function—either one that you have written or one of HyperCard's built-in functions. For example, you could sort by the function shown in Script 18-4, using this line:

```
sort by lastFirst()
```

You can also use a function to sort a list of titles. You might not want the titles that start with "A," "An," or "The" to be sorted by first word; rather, you might want to sort by the second word of each title. For example, you might want *A Moon for the Misbegotten* to be sorted next to *Moon Over Miami*, not *A Month in the Country*. Script 18-5 performs this sort.

```
function lastFirst
  return bg field "Last Name" & bg field "First Name"
end lastFirst
```

Script 18-4.   This function combines two background fields for sorting

```
function shortTitle
   get bg field "title"
   if first word of it is "the" or¬
   first word of it is "a" or¬
   first word of it is "an" then
      delete first word of it
   end if
   return it
end shortTitle
```

Script 18-5.   This function allows you to sort a stack on the field "Title," ignoring certain words

The function in this script gets the background field "Title" and checks to see if the first word of that field, held in the variable "It," is one of the words we do not want to sort on. If so, the script deletes that word (from the variable, not from the card field). The function then returns "It" to the line that called it.

Sorting on a function is somewhat slower than sorting on the raw text stored in fields. HyperCard must evaluate the function separately for each card. However, it does give you considerable control over the sorting process.

Other

You can also sort by many of the HyperCard properties and conditions. Here are some examples:

```
Sort by hilite of background field 1
Sort by ID of this card
Sort by length of bg field 1
```

sortOrder

You have two choices, logically enough, of the order in which your stack will be sorted. Specifying an *ascending* sort causes cards with lower values to be placed early in the stack. Specifying a *descending* sort does the opposite. If you do not specify the sort order, HyperCard will sort the stack in ascending order.

sortStyle

Normally HyperCard sorts in a *text* style (alphabetically), but you can sort in other ways as well.

Numeric

This style sorts the stack in numeric order. Suppose you are sorting a stack based on a number in a field. In *text* order, HyperCard sorts in this manner:

   1,100,20,3,35,4

When you specify a *numeric* sort, it sorts the same numbers like this:

   1,3,4,20,35,100

which is probably the way you want to sort.

dateTime

Again, if you are sorting by a *text* order, HyperCard sorts dates in this manner:

   1/1/80,10/1/79,2/2/79,4/4/80

When you specify the dateTime sort order, the sort is done in this manner:

   2/2/79,10/1/79,1/1/80,4/4/80

Again, this is probably the way you want to sort date fields.

International

Normally, when sorting, HyperCard sorts characters as they appear in the ASCII chart. Since certain characters, such as Ä or é, fall at the end of the ASCII list of characters, they will be sorted *after* the standard characters. *International* sorting takes this into account and sorts these international characters into the order in which they belong.

Sort Stability

One useful aspect of HyperCard sorting is its stability. It takes into account the fact that different backgrounds might be in a stack and that not all backgrounds will have the same fields. You can sort on a field in one background without worrying about errors occurring when HyperCard encounters other backgrounds. Those backgrounds will be placed at the beginning of the stack.

HyperCard's sorting stability also means that cards that have the same sort values will remain in the same order in the stack as they were before the sort.

When Not to Sort

Sometimes you will have a stack that you do not want sorted. This could be a stack that has a number of backgrounds and cards in the backgrounds that are not contiguous. Sorting this kind of stack could seriously corrupt its order. Fortunately, you can prevent the stack from being sorted with the handler shown in Script 18-6.

Remember that every command in HyperCard is a message that moves through the hierarchy of messages. When you place this handler in your stack script, the handler will intercept a sort command issued anywhere in the stack, and the sort will not take place.

```
on sort
  beep
  Answer "Sorry, can't sort this stack!"
end sort
```

Script 18-6.   You can intercept the Sort command to prevent a stack from being sorted

Show All Cards

The Show All Cards command is used in the Address stack included with HyperCard. This command displays all the cards in the stack, starting at the card you are currently on. You can interrupt it at any time by clicking the mouse button.

Tips for Constructing Stacks

Stack design is, by HyperCard's nature, very flexible. You have many choices in setting up stacks that allow for easy navigation.

Two Kinds of Stacks

In general, there are two kinds of stacks: those that are homogeneous and those that are not. *Homogeneous* stacks consist of one background, with all the cards in the stack containing that background. The Clip Art stack included with

HyperCard is an example of a homogeneous stack. A *nonhomogeneous* stack contains multiple backgrounds, with various cards that are part of different backgrounds. For example, the Help stack contains 414 cards in 17 backgrounds.

When you create your application, you have two choices. You can construct it so that the entire application is part of one stack, with different backgrounds performing different purposes, or you can create different stacks, each containing only one background.

For example, suppose you have an application that acts as an inventory and order-entry system. You would have one screen form into which new orders are typed. Another screen form would contain information about each of your products: part number, price, and so on. A third would include information about customers. When you type a customer name or part number into the order-entry form, specific information about that customer or part is retrieved from the collection of customer or part information and included in the order-entry form. This procedure is similar to operations that are performed in relational databases.

In databases, this application would be organized as sets of files: one file for customers, another for parts, and a third for orders. You could do the same thing in HyperCard, using three stacks that interrelate; a button on the order entry card would look up the information in the other stacks.

However, HyperCard gives you another way to handle this application. Instead of having the information in different stacks, you could create the three types of screens as different backgrounds in the same stack. Instead of having to manage multiple stacks, HyperCard would look up information in the current stack only, which speeds up the operation. The option method you use is up to you.

Points to Consider
When Constructing a Stack

Deciding how to construct a stack, or series of stacks, depends on a number of points. The importance you place on each of these points depends on what you want your stack to do.

Performance

In this sense, performance refers to how fast your stack operates. In general, searching in one stack—the current one—is much faster than searching in other stacks. Going to different cards in the current stack is much faster than going to different cards in other stacks.

Ease of Use

It's always easier to install a single stack on a hard disk than it is to install multiple stacks. However, navigation through a homogeneous stack is easier than navigation through a stack containing multiple backgrounds.

Size

Generally, holding several stacks on disk takes more disk space than holding only one stack; a certain amount of overhead is required for each stack, no matter how large or small it is. Putting all parts of your application into one stack conserves more disk space than does dividing them into different stacks.

On the other hand, if you expect to add information to the stack, the size of the stack could grow very quickly. This could cause problems—the stack might become too large to fit on a floppy disk. If you think the entire stack will become large, you should break it into several smaller stacks.

Ease of Construction

It's a little more complicated to manage scripting for navigation of nonhomogeneous stacks than it is homogeneous stacks. Creating new cards in a stack where the cards might not be contiguous with their backgrounds can be a tricky proposition. However, programming other elements, such as functions and handlers, can be easier (see the next section).

Conservation of Code

When implementing an application as one stack, you can put commonly used handlers and functions in the stack script so they are available to all the other scripts in the stack. Then, when you change a handler, you need to do it in only one place. If you are working with different stacks, you might need to change scripts in several different stacks. Repeating the same handlers in several places can use up a lot of disk space. The same is true when it comes to other resources, such as external commands and functions, sounds, cursors, icons, and the like.

Plan Ahead

The best way to develop stacks that work is by planning ahead. This is especially important when deciding on the structure of your stack or stacks. It takes a great deal of work to break up a non-homogeneous stack into separate stacks. Combining separate stacks into one is less difficult (although still tricky). Plan ahead, and you'll save yourself a lot of work.

NINETEEN

Working with the Mouse and Keyboard

The Mouse
The Keyboard

HyperCard gives you a number of tools for understanding what is currently happening with the mouse and the keyboard, as well as for controlling both these objects from within HyperCard.

The Mouse

HyperTalk gives you several commands and functions that you can use to discover what is happening with the mouse: whether the button is being held down, the mouse's current location on the screen, and whether the mouse has been clicked and where.

Mouse Commands

You can use two commands when working with the mouse. Both commands allow you to perform some mouse actions from a script, exactly as if you had physically done them with the mouse.

The Click Command

click *at location*

Location is a point on the screen that is described by two integers separated by a comma. The first integer is the distance in pixels from the left edge of the screen, the second is the distance in pixels from the top of the screen. Figure 19-1 shows the coordinates of the four corners and the center of the screen.

Note that when you click at a specific location under script control, the observable location of the mouse cursor does not move. That is, you will not see the mouse move to the point and then click. However, if you use a statement such as

```
click at the loc of card button 1
```

you will see the button highlight, just as if you had moved the mouse to the button and clicked it.

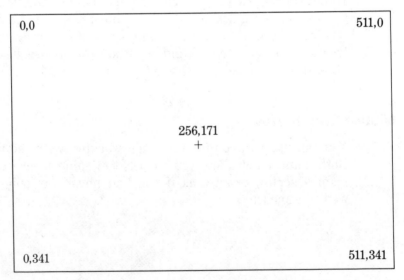

Figure 19-1. The coordinates of the four corners and center of the screen

The Drag Command

drag from *location1* to *location2* <with optionKey| commandKey|shiftKey>

Location1 and *location2* are each sets of two integers, separated by a comma. The first integer is the distance in pixels from the left edge of the screen, and the second is the distance in pixels from the top of the screen.

Additionally, you can specify that certain keys be held down while the mouse is dragged. This works just as if you had held down the keys while dragging the mouse. For example, the following commands will draw a perfect square because shiftKey constrains rectangles to squares while you are manually drawing with the Rectangle tool:

```
choose rectangle tool
drag from 10,10 to 100,150 with shiftKey
```

The Drag command simulates the physical action of clicking and dragging. The mouse button is depressed at *location1*, the mouse is moved to *location2*, and the button is released. This command works with any HyperCard tool. Because the Drag command cannot accept more than two locations, its use with the Polygon tool will cause only straight lines to be drawn.

Mouse Functions

Mouse functions allow you to discover where the mouse currently is on the screen, where it was last clicked, and whether or not the mouse button is being held down.

Mouse

the mouse

mouse( )

The Mouse function returns one of two values: "up" if the mouse button is not being pressed, and "down" if it is.

mouseLoc

the mouseLoc

mouseLoc( )

This function returns two integers that are separated by a comma. The first integer is the distance of the mouse from the left edge of the card window, and the second is the distance from the top of the card window. If you are using a Mac with a screen larger than the original Macintosh screen and the mouse is to the left of the HyperCard window, the first number will be negative. If the mouse is above the card window, the second number will be negative.

mouseH

the mouseH

mouseH( )

The mouseH function returns the horizontal location of the mouse—its distance from the left edge of the card window. The value returned by this function is equivalent to the first integer of the mouseLoc function. If the mouse is to the left of the window on a large screen, this number will be negative.

MouseV

the mouseV

mouseV( )

The mouseV function returns the vertical location of the mouse—its distance from the top of the card window. This value is equivalent to the second integer of the mouseLoc function. If the mouse is above the card window on a large screen, mouseV will return a negative number.

mouseClick

the mouseClick

mouseClick( )

The mouseClick function returns "true" if the mouse is being clicked; otherwise it returns "false."

This function is commonly used in repeat loops, when you want to repeat some actions until the mouse is clicked. Here is an example:

```
on mouseUp
  put 0 into count
  repeat until the mouseClick
    add 1 to count
    put count
  end repeat
  beep
end mouseUp
```

This handler puts increasingly larger numbers into the Message box until you click the mouse, at which time it beeps and stops the repeat loop.

The mouseClick function provides a good means of exiting long routines without requiring the use of COMMAND-PERIOD. This technique is used in the scripts throughout this book.

clickLoc

put the clickLoc

clickLoc( )

The clickLoc function returns a two-integer value that represents the location at which the mouse was last clicked. The first integer is the distance from the left edge of the screen, and the second is the distance from the top of the card window. If you call this function immediately after a mouseUp handler in a script, it will, in effect, return the location of the button containing the script. As with other mouse location functions, if the mouse is positioned above or to the left of the card window on a Macintosh screen, it will return negative numbers.

clickH

the clickH

clickH( )

The clickH function returns the horizontal location of the mouse—its distance from the left edge of the card window. The clickH function is equivalent to the first integer of the clickLoc function.

clickV

the clickV

clickV( )

This function returns the vertical location of the most recent click, measured from the top of the card window. It is equivalent to the second integer of the clickLoc function. If you are using a large screen and click above the screen, the clickV function will return a negative number.

Mouse Properties

The two mouse properties allow you to control the appearance of the mouse cursor and how fast it moves when it is dragged under script control.

The Cursor Property

This property governs the appearance of the mouse cursor. It is discussed in Chapter 13, which also includes a table showing the various cursors that are included with HyperCard.

The dragSpeed Property

This property governs the speed at which the mouse is dragged when executing the Drag command. The dragSpeed property is discussed in detail in Chapter 13.

Mouse Messages

In addition to the mouse commands and functions, you can use the mouse messages to tell you which mouse events are occurring and to handle those events in scripts. These messages are discussed in Chapter 12.

Some Mouse Scripts

Here are several scripts that use mouse commands to create interesting effects on the screen.

Drawing Circles

Script 19-1 draws a black circle on the screen and then erases it with a white circle.

The handler in this script first sets the dragSpeed property to 50, which causes the circle to be drawn slowly. Next it chooses the Oval tool. The Centered property is set to "true" so that the oval is drawn from the center (setting it to "false" also generates some interesting effects). The repeat loop first sets the pattern to 12, which is black. The script then draws from 256,171 (the center of the screen) to 512,342 (the screen's lower-right corner). While the script drags, the SHIFT key is held down, which produces a circle even though the dragging would not otherwise produce a circle. The OPTION key is used to prevent a border from being drawn.

```
on mouseUp
  set dragspeed to 50
  choose oval tool
  set centered to true
  repeat until the mouseClick
    set pattern to 12
    drag from 256,171 to 512,342 with shiftKey,optionKey
    set pattern to 1
    drag from 256,171 to 512,342 with shiftKey,optionKey
  end repeat
end mouseUp
```

Script 19-1.   This script draws two concentric circles with the Oval tool

A Recorder

Sometimes you must automatically create a complex drawing on the screen. Writing down the locations to which you want to drag can take a lot of time. It might be better to have a button that *records* your movements of the mouse and plays them back later. Script 19-2 handles this.

Put this script into a button called Record. The script first declares a global variable called *mouseTracks*. This variable will be used to store the locations to which the mouse was moved. Next, the script checks the name of the button it is in. If the name of the button is Record, it starts the recording sequence.

As it prepares to record, the button alerts you, through the Message box, to click the mouse button when you want to start recording. Move the mouse to the point at which you want to start drawing, and click the button. The Message box then tells you to click again when you are finished. While recording, the script keeps track of the number of movements you have made and adds the number to a counter variable called *mouseMoves*. It then cycles quickly through a loop that adds the current mouse location to the end of the *mouseTracks* variable.

```
on mouseUp
  global mouseTrack
  if the short name of me is "record" then
    put empty into mouseTrack
    put 0 into mouseMoves
    put "Click to start recording"
    wait until the mouseClick
    put "Move the mouse over the path, click when done 0"
    Repeat until the mouseClick
      add 1 to mouseMoves
      put mouseMoves into last word of msg
      put the mouseLoc into line mouseMoves of mouseTrack
    end repeat
    set the name of me to "Play"
  else
    choose brush tool
    put line 1 of mouseTrack into oldLoc
    repeat with x = 1 to the number of lines in mouseTrack
      if the mouseclick then exit repeat
      drag from oldLoc to line x of mouseTrack
      put line x of mouseTrack into oldLoc
    end repeat
    set the name of me to "Record"
  end if
  choose browse tool
end mouseUp
```

Script 19-2.   When placed in a button named Record, this script
records and then plays back mouse movements

The repeat loop executes while you move the mouse, and
it executes fairly quickly. However, you should be careful of
dragging the mouse either too quickly or too slowly while
recording. If you drag quickly, the loop will not have time to
get all the mouse locations between two points, and the result
will be many straight lines. If you drag too slowly, the loop
will gather too many points and take too long to draw.
Experimentation is the key.

When you click the mouse button to signal that you have
finished drawing, the script renames as Play the button that
contains it and then exits.

On playback—when you click the button when it is
named Play—the script chooses the Brush tool. It next puts

the first line of the *mouseTrack* variable into a local variable called *oldLoc*. Since the Drag command needs two locations, the second location is stored in this *oldLoc* variable. Next, a loop starts that proceeds for the number of lines in the *mouseTrack* variable. If you click the mouse button while drawing, the loop is exited, which allows you a safe exit.

The Drag command drags from *oldLoc* to the point specified by the current line of *mouseTrack*. The current line of mouseTrack is then put into the *oldLoc* variable, and the loop starts again. When the loop has finished executing, the name of the button is changed to Record, the Browse tool is chosen, and the script exits.

This button is fun to play with, but it is not very useful as it currently exists. If you quit HyperCard, for example, the contents of the *mouseTrack* variable will be lost. (If you want to save drawings, you can include a line in the record portion of the script that saves the locations into a field. A modified Play button could then retrieve the locations from the field and execute the drawing.) Modifying this script to use different painting tools is also fun.

The Keyboard

Most keyboard input goes to fields or the Message box. You can use keyboard messages, such as returnInField and enterInField, to control input to fields. Messages typed into the Message box are automatically sent first to the current card. Other keyboard commands, such as COMMAND-KEY equivalents for various HyperCard menu functions, are handled automatically by HyperCard.

Generally, keyboard input falls into four categories:

• **Typing text into fields** Text typed into fields is stored in those fields when you leave a stack or quit HyperCard. Managing text stored in fields is covered in Chapters 17, 21, and 24.

• **Using keyboard shortcuts for commands**   A number of HyperCard menu commands feature keyboard shortcuts that allow you to quickly perform those commands without moving your hand from the keyboard. Standard HyperCard shortcuts are covered in Chapters 3 and 6.

• **Modifying actions of the mouse and tools**   Almost all the HyperCard mouse actions perform slightly differently depending on the tool in use at the time and the modifier key or keys held down while the action is performed. For example, when holding down the mouse button and dragging with the Button tool, you create a new button.

• **Messages typed into the Message box**   You use the Message box to send messages to HyperCard. Scripts can also use the Message box to send messages to you. For more information on how messages are handled, see Chapter 12.

HyperCard's commands, functions, and messages allow you to work with text in these four areas. You can also place text on the screen in either fields or graphics.

The Type Command

type *Text* <with *keyModifier*>

The Type command allows a script to type text into fields, the Message box, or the graphics layer of a card, just as if you had typed it from the keyboard. You can use it to create special effects when presenting messages to the user or creating animated graphics. *Text* is any container.

KeyModifier is a modifier key for the text. *KeyModifier* can be the shiftKey, commandKey, or optionKey function. Typing a letter with one of these modifier keys works in the same manner as if you had typed the letter with the modifier from the keyboard.

Before you can type text, you must use the Click command to click at the point you wish to type. If you do not first click at a location, several things can happen. If the blind-Typing property is "false" (which can be set on the User Preferences card in the Home stack) and the Message box is not visible, the Macintosh will beep as the characters are typed and have no place to go. If blindTyping is "true" or if the message box is visible, then the typed characters will be sent to the Message box. If the insertion point was in a field and the button containing the script that used the Type command did not highlight or otherwise change the screen, the text will be typed into the field containing the insertion point.

Typing into the Message Box

As stated earlier, if the blindTyping property is "true" or if the Message box is visible, text will be typed into the Message box, provided the insertion point is not in a field. You can use this command to make sure that text is typed into the Message box:

```
click at the loc of msg
```

You should first use the command

```
put empty into msg
```

to make sure you are not adding to text currently in the Message box.

Typing text into the Message box is not materially different from using the Put command to put text there; however, you can use the Wait command to make text appear slowly, as shown in Script 19-3.

Typing into Fields

You must make sure that the insertion point is at the desired location in a field before you use the Type command to place text there. You can do this in two ways. If the field is empty,

```
on mouseUp
  put "This is an irritating message" into theText
  put empty
  repeat with x = 1 to the number of chars in theText
    beep
    type char x of theText
    wait 2
  end repeat
end mouseUp
```

Script 19-3.   This script uses the Type command to slowly place a message into the Message box

you can use the following command to position the cursor in the field:

```
click at the loc of <field> with shiftKey
```

In version 1.2 or later, using the SHIFT key when clicking in a field causes the insertion point to be placed directly after the last character in the field. If the field is empty, it puts the insertion point at the first character of the field. If the SHIFT key is not used, HyperCard places the insertion point at the leftmost point on the line at which you clicked. Using the SHIFT key has no effect on scrolling fields.

Using the Select command (discussed in Chapter 21) to position the insertion point in a field gives you more control over the insertion point.

Typing Paint Text

If you first choose the Text tool, you can click at a location and type paint text onto the graphics layer of a card or background, which creates some unusual visual effects. To type paint text, you must first issue these two commands:

```
choose text tool
click at <loc>
```

Any text you now type will be placed at the location specified in the second command. You can change the appearance of the text by changing the textStyle and textFont properties.

Typing Commands

You can also use the Type command to perform some keyboard shortcuts. For example, there is no way in HyperTalk to determine whether or not the menu bar is visible, so it might seem difficult to write a script that toggles the visibility of the menu bar. However, simply using this command

```
type space with commandKey
```

does the trick, because COMMAND-SPACE bar is the keyboard shortcut for toggling the menu bar. You can use similar commands to perform any of the HyperCard keyboard shortcuts.

If you have copied a card, you can paste a picture of the card—reduced in size—by holding down the SHIFT key as you use the Paste Card command. (When you hold down the SHIFT key, Paste Card becomes Paste Picture on the Edit menu.) You can perform the same action with the command

```
type "v" with commandkey,shiftKey
```

which types the letter "v" while holding down the COMMAND and SHIFT keys, and places a miniature picture of the card near the center of the screen.

Keyboard-Related Functions

The Macintosh Plus keyboard contains three keys that affect the functions of other keys: COMMAND, OPTION, and SHIFT. HyperCard provides functions for determining whether these keys are held down. The standard keyboard used for the Macintosh SE and II contains an additional CONTROL key.

HyperCard does not provide a function for this key, but when the key is pressed in tandem with another key, the control-Key message is sent. (This will be discussed in more detail later in this chapter.) The extended keyboard available for the Macintosh SE and II also includes a set of function keys, and HyperCard also includes a message that is sent when one of the function keys is pressed.

commandKey

commandKey( )

the commandKey

This function returns the state of the COMMAND key. It will return "down" if you are pressing on the key; otherwise it returns "up."

optionKey

optionKey( )

the optionKey

The optionKey function returns "down" if the OPTION key is being pressed; otherwise it returns "up."

shiftKey

shiftKey( )

the shiftKey

This function returns "down" if the SHIFT key is being pressed, otherwise it returns "up."

Keyboard-Related Messages

These messages are discussed in detail in Chapter 12. It is interesting that controlKey is implemented as a message instead of a function, especially since the other modifier keys are implemented as functions. This is probably because not all Macintosh keyboards include a CONTROL key, and calling that function might produce an error message on a keyboard that does not include it.

controlKey

This message is sent when you hold down the CONTROL key and press another letter. The message sent is

```
controlKey number
```

where *number* represents the ASCII value of the character you pressed when holding down the CONTROL key. The Macintosh ASCII characters are shown in the appendix.

There are some good uses for this message. If you often use HyperCard and a number of other programs with Hyper-Card in MultiFinder, you can create a controlKey handler in the script of your Home stack that allows you to switch easily to one of the other programs. For example, this handler allows you to switch easily to Microsoft Word or to the Finder:

```
on controlkey num
  -- control-w
  if num is 23 then open "word"
  -- control-f
  if num is 6 then domenu "Finder"
end controlkey
```

If the variable *num* is 23, which is CONTROL-W, then Hyper-Card opens Word. If Word is already open under Multi-Finder, then HyperCard merely switches to Word. If you press CONTROL-F (*num* is 6), then HyperCard uses the doMenu command (discussed in Chapter 27) to choose the Finder item from the Apple menu. Since Finder is always present when MultiFinder is running, HyperCard does not need to open it.

arrowKey

The arrowKey message is sent when you press one of the arrow keys on the keyboard. It is discussed in Chapter 12.

enterKey

The enterKey message is sent when you press the ENTER key. It is is discussed in Chapter 12.

functionKey

This message is sent when one of the function keys on the extended keyboard available for the Macintosh SE or II is pressed. As with the controlKey message, you can use it to program the functions these keys perform in HyperCard.

returnKey

This message is sent when the RETURN key is pressed and the insertion point is not in a field. When you press the RETURN key in a field, use the returnInField message discussed later in this chapter and in Chapter 12.

Note: If you have a handler for the returnKey message, it will prevent messages typed into the Message box from being executed when you press the RETURN key. Of course, you might want this to happen to prevent execution of inappropriate commands from the Message box, but be careful; this might have unwanted effects. Using the Pass command in the returnKey handler will not allow messages in the Message box to be sent.

tabKey

This message is sent when you press the TAB key. Normally the TAB key selects the next field on the card. You can use this message to alter this behavior and perform other functions.

returnInField and enterInField

These two field messages are discussed in Chapter 12. They allow you to intercept the RETURN and ENTER keys when the insertion point is in a field.

TWENTY

Visual Effects

The Visual Effect Command
Using Visual Effect with Unlock Screen
The Visual Effects
Added Effects
Speeds

HyperCard's visual effects allow you to control the manner in which new cards are brought to the screen and the manner in which new items are displayed on the current card.

When no visual effects are used, the transformation on the screen from one card to the next is instantaneous—the new card appears suddenly, replacing the previous one. Visual effects help you to reinforce the metaphor your stack is using or to indicate how new levels of information are being presented. Thus, visual effects should not be used in a capricious or haphazard manner; when used incorrectly, they can confuse and irritate.

Visual effects do not, of course, affect the menu bar, the Message box, the Tool palette, or the Patterns palette. To keep them from interfering with your visual effects, hide these items before you use the effects. Visual effects also do not function when any of the paint tools are selected.

The Visual Effect Command

Visual [effect] <*effectName*>
[*speed*] [to <*image*>]

The Visual Effect command works in a very different way from other HyperTalk commands. Unlike other commands, no action is taken immediately when HyperTalk reaches the command. Instead, the visual effects are *cued*, or stored, and executed when HyperTalk encounters the next Go command. However, visual effects are reset when HyperCard is idle, so visual effects entered in the Message box do not work.

Note: The word "effect" is optional in the command. It makes the line a little easier to read but can create a long line.

The *effectName* variable can be any of the following visual effects: Zoom (with either Open or Close), Dissolve, Checkerboard, Venetian Blinds, Iris (with either Open or Close), Wipe (with Up, Down, Left, or Right), Barn Door (with either Open or Close), Plain, and Scroll (Left, Right, Up, or Down). These effects are discussed in more detail later in this chapter.

The *speed* variable controls how fast the visual effect executes. Valid speeds are fast, slow (or slowly), very fast, and very slow (or very slowly).

The *image* variable is not really an image, but rather a pattern that the visual effect turns into before it shows the next card. The various images are discussed later in this chapter.

Combining Visual Effects

When using the Visual Effect command, you can cue several visual effects so that they are executed in order when the next Go command is executed. This can be useful, especially when you are using an effect to dissolve *to* a shade such as black, gray, or white. Combining visual effects is also useful for animation and for enhancing the metaphor of your stack.

Visual Effects on the Mac II

There are a couple of caveats when it comes to using visual effects on the Mac II.

The first caveat, and one that has caused some confusion among new HyperCard (and Mac II) users, is that visual effects are not displayed at all if the monitor is set up to display colors or shades of gray. To allow visual effects to be shown on the Mac II, use the Monitors portion of the Control Panel desk accessory, set the monitor to work with black and white or grays, and set the number of gray levels to 2.

Visual effects will also give you some trouble if you are using two or more monitors. HyperCard must be displayed on the monitor that is currently showing the menu bar for visual effects to work. The menu bar may, of course, be hidden. This is also true of the Mac SE or Plus when connected to more than one monitor.

Using Visual Effect
with Unlock Screen

With HyperCard version 1.2 or greater, you are not limited to using the Visual Effect command with only the Go command. You can also use it with the Unlock Screen command. In this case, Visual Effect does not act as a command, but rather as an argument to the Unlock Screen command.

This means that you cannot cue several visual effects with the Unlock Screen command because it does not execute any saved commands. Instead, cued commands will be used when the next Go command is encountered.

Using visual effects with the Unlock Screen command can be effective for creating such things as pop-up fields. As discussed in Chapter 24, pop-up fields allow you to keep certain fields hidden and then display them with a button. Here is a script that pops up a field and uses the Zoom Open button to make the field appear to open up from the button, just as folders open up in the Finder:

```
on mouseUp
  lock screen
  show background field "popUp"
  unlock screen with zoom open
end mouseUp
```

A field that opens up will probably reinforce the metaphor you are using better than will a field that seems to appear out of nowhere.

The Visual Effects

Unfortunately, it is very difficult to show HyperCard's visual effects on the printed page. By their nature, they are transitory. Therefore, this section examines possible *uses* for each of the visual effects. The best way to get a feel for the ways in which the visual effects work is to experiment with them.

One of the prime purposes of visual effects is to reinforce the metaphor that your stack is using. When designing visual effects, think of how they interact with the stack's metaphor. For example, if your stack uses the metaphor of a book, such as an address book, the Wipe visual effect can reinforce the metaphor by making it appear that the pages are actually turning.

HyperCard's visual effects are very cinematic, working in much the same way that visual effects work in the movies. With no visual effect, HyperCard works in the same way that a "cut" does in a movie: one scene or shot is replaced immediately by another. Dissolves are also used in films, showing the slow replacement of one shot by another, and often used to indicate the passage of time.

You should also be conscious of the pairing of visual effects and how they complement each other. For example, if you use the Zoom Open visual effect to go into more detail about something, use the Zoom Close effect to return to the generalized view. If you use the Wipe Left effect to go to the next card, use the Wipe Right effect to go to the previous card.

Barn Door (Open, Close)

The Barn Door visual effect causes the new card to open to the right and the left from the horizontal center of the current card. Use Barn Door Open to indicate an opening up— perhaps a zooming to more detail on a card or graphic. Use Barn Door Close to indicate putting information away or moving from detail to generality.

Checkerboard

The Checkerboard visual effect causes squares to appear on the screen and grow larger until they fill the screen with a new card. It is somewhat similar to a dissolve.

Dissolve

Dissolve causes one card to gradually dissolve into another card. This effect works well when you are dissolving to a different shade, such as gray, black, or inverse. You can also use two dissolves together, as shown here:

```
visual effect dissolve to inverse
visual effect dissolve
```

The first dissolve inverts the card, and the second dissolves from the inverse of the card to the normal card.

Adding the adverb "slowly" to these lines (after the visual effect, and before any *to* parameters) makes the dissolve take longer and heightens the effect of the dissolve. In films, the dissolve is often used to indicate the passage of time.

Iris (Open, Close)

The Iris visual effect causes the new card to be exposed gradually from the center of the current card. The Iris Open visual effect indicates an opening up of something—perhaps to go into more detail about a topic. The Iris Close visual effect indicates the opposite and is similar to the ending of the Looney Tunes cartoons—after Porky Pig says "That's all folks," the iris closes around him, and the cartoon is over.

Plain

The Plain visual effect is no visual effect at all; it is the same as going to another card without a visual effect. It can be useful when you are combining visual effects.

Scroll (Left, Right, Up, Down)

The Scroll visual effects are similar to what happens when you are using a slide projector—one card slides in to replace the current card.

The Scroll Up visual effect can be used to indicate that you are moving up through a hierarchy, and the Scroll Down effect to indicate that you are moving down through a hierarchy. Tying these visual effects to the action of the arrow keys on the keyboard and to buttons that point up, down, left, or right increases the effectiveness of the metaphor.

Venetian Blinds

The Venetian Blinds effect causes horizontal stripes to appear in the middle of the screen. The stripes gradually become larger until they cover the screen, and the transition to the next card is completed.

Wipe (Left, Right, Up, Down)

The Wipe visual effects cause the current card to be replaced by the next card in a line from the point of origin. For example, if you use the Wipe Left visual effect, the line starts at the right of the screen and moves to the left, replacing one card with the next as it goes.

Just as with the Scroll visual effects, the Wipe Up effect can indicate you are moving up in a hierarchy of cards, to a more generalized view, and the Wipe Down effect can move you to more detail. Wipe Left and Wipe Right effects are used to move through cards that are on the same level as one another.

Zoom (Open, Close)

The Zoom visual effects are similar to what happens when you open a folder or icon in the Macintosh Finder—the item seems to open to show its contents. The purpose of the Zoom visual effect is similar to the Iris visual effect: to indicate an opening from a general topic to a more specific one.

The point of origin for the Zoom visual effect, however, is different from that of the Iris, as is its appearance on the screen. Instead of opening from the center of the card, the Zoom Open visual effect always opens from the point where the mouse was clicked. Rectangles grow from this point until they are the size of the HyperCard window, at which time the new card is displayed. The Zoom Close effect causes the rectangles to gradually become smaller, their destination being the middle of the screen.

Instead of using Zoom Open, you can use Zoom In, and instead of using Zoom Close, you can use Zoom Out.

Added Effects

All the visual effects can be used with the *to image* parameter, where *image* is one of black, white, gray, inverse, or card, as described in this section. If you specify an image, the effect changes the card to that image before displaying the next card.

You can combine these images with other effects. For example, the lines

```
visual effect iris open slowly to black
visual effect iris close slowly
go next card
```

cause the screen to open from the center until it is black; then it closes from the edges, displaying the new card.

In fact, it is best to use combined effects when the first effect opens into a black or white card. This can make the transition much smoother, decreasing the sense of suddenness that occurs when the new card appears from blackness.

Black

As it implies, the black image causes the screen to become black. If there is no second effect, the new card appears suddenly out of the blackness.

White

This image causes the card to become totally white after the visual effect. As with the black image, it is best to use white when you are combining effects to decrease the jump that occurs when the new card is displayed.

Gray (Grey)

With HyperCard 1.2 or greater, this image can be spelled either "gray" or "grey." The gray image can be used with a dissolve. The lines

```
visual effect dissolve to grey
visual effect dissolve
```

create an interesting effect.

Inverse

The inverse image causes the visual effect to change to the inverse of the card you are going to: pixels that are black on that card become white, and pixels that are white on that card become black. Again, this image is most effective when you use it in combination with another effect, as in these lines:

```
visual effect dissolve slowly to inverse
visual effect dissolve slowly to card
```

Card

This causes the effect with which it is combined to make a transition to the card to which you are going. It is not often used, as it is the default for any visual effect. These two lines are the same:

```
visual effect dissolve slowly to card
visual effect dissolve slowly
```

Speeds

The *speed* parameter of the Visual Effect command allows you to control the speed at which the various effects take place. The speed is placed after the visual effect and before any *to* parameters.

Visual effect speeds do not depend on the speed of the machine on which they are running; they take the same amount of time whether you are running on a Mac Plus or a Mac II.

The very slow speed should be used with care. With some of the visual effects, this speed makes the effect appear chunky and fragmented. If several very slow effects are combined, you get restless waiting for the next card.

Managing Text

The Nature of Text
Chunk Expressions
Finding Text
Selecting Text
Changing Text
Other Text Functions
Constants

HyperCard and HyperTalk give you a wealth of tools for handling virtually all aspects of text management. You can find text within a stack, put new text into existing text, store text in fields, select text, determine what text is selected, and more.

The Nature of Text

In a very real sense, everything HyperCard stores that is not graphics is text. Many programs, particularly database programs, require that you specify the type of data that particular fields can contain. In those programs, certain fields can contain only numbers, and typing text into those fields generates errors.

This is not the case with HyperCard. HyperCard treats everything nongraphic as text, no matter what type of information you have actually typed into the field. This leads to a great deal of flexibility with the program, but as discussed in Chapter 22, it makes some demands on the programmer.

Chunk Expressions

Chapter 17 discussed HyperTalk's chunk expressions. A chunk expression, you will remember, is a type of expression that is used to define or work with various parts or chunks of text. Chunk expressions will be used throughout this chapter, so you should be comfortable with them.

You also should keep in mind the fundamental structures that HyperCard gives to text: the character, the word (which is delimited by spaces or returns), the item (which is delimited by commas), and the line (which ends with a return).

Finding Text

HyperTalk includes two features that allow you to locate text. The offSet function allows you to locate a particular string of text within a larger string. The Find command allows you to find text in fields in the stack as a whole.

The offSet Function

offSet(*string1,string2*)

The offSet function returns an integer specifying the location of *string1* in *string2*. If *string1* is not in *string2*, offSet returns 0. The offSet function will report only the *first* occurrence of the string; it can be used only to search for subsequent occurrences if some additional programming is done. The offSet function is fast. Here are some examples:

```
put offSet("a","HyperCard") -- returns 7
put offSet("a","abc") -- returns 1
put offset("d","abc") -- returns 0
```

If *string1* is more than one character long, the number returned by offSet is the number specifying where in *string2* the string begins, as shown here:

```
put offSet("card","HyperCard") -- returns 6
```

The offSet function can use chunk expressions to represent either of its arguments. The statement

```
offSet(word 1 of card field "list",card field "topics")
```

will get the first word of the card field "List" and look for it in the card field "Topics." It will return the number of the first occurrence of that word.

Script 21-1 is a function that returns the number of occurrences of a particular character in some text.

```
function countChar theChar,theText
  if theChar is not in theText then return 0
  put 0 into theCount
  repeat until theChar is not in theText
    add 1 to theCount
    delete char 1 to offset(theChar,theText) of theText
  end repeat
  return theCount
end countChar
```

Script 21-1.   This script uses the Delete command and the offSet function to count the instances of a character in a container

The Find Command

Find [*whole/word/string/chars*] *string*
<*in fieldExpression*>

The Find command searches through fields in a stack for instances of the text contained in *string*. The Find command is generally fast. When text is found, HyperCard goes to the card containing the found text, and a box is placed around the characters for which you were searching. HyperCard will place the box around the entire word found, unless you are using one of the variants of the Find command, such as **Find chars**, which is described later in this chapter. Hyper-Card places the box around an entire word even if you are searching for only one character; if you are searching for multiple words, HyperCard places the box around the first word.

Figure 21-1 shows some found text on a card.

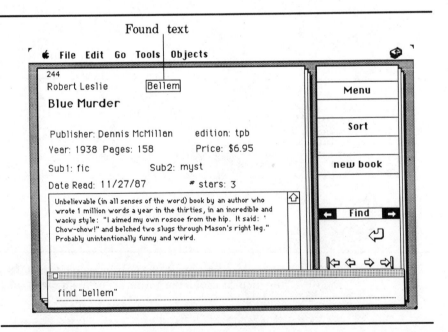

Figure 21-1.   The text outlined with a box was the text found with the Find command

Note: None of the variations of the Find command allow you to search for case-specific text. That is, if you search for the letter "A," words containing "a" will also be found. A script that compares two strings of text to see if they are an exact match (including case) is presented later in this chapter.

The Find command works only on the current stack. To make the Find command work with a different stack, you must first use the Go command to go to that stack.

The Result Function

If the Find command does not locate the text you are looking for, the Result function will return "not found"; if it *does* find the text, the Result Function will return nothing. This allows you to see if the text was found before you proceed.

HyperCard gives you several ways to look for text. The differences in the ways HyperCard finds text might be subtle, but they are important.

Find

Find *string* [in field *fieldDescriptor*]

This version of Find Command is the generic or standard one. You can summon it in the Message box with the COMMAND-F keyboard equivalent. This version finds the first card that contains a word or words beginning with the text specified in *string*. Note that the text found only needs to *begin with* the text specified; Find does not search for whole words only. For example, searching for "man" will find cards that contain words such as "manipulate", "mandate", "manufacturer", and "manuscript". It will *not* find words such as "woman" and "human".

If you use the Find command in this manner

```
Find "man kind"
```

it will find cards that contain words beginning with both these strings. They will not necessarily be together, or even in the same field. This command will find cards that contain words such as "manufacture" and "manuscript," as long as those cards also have words on them beginning with "kind", such as "kindness" and "kindly". The word on the card that begins with the first word of the search string will be highlighted in the box.

If you specify a field for HyperCard to search in, the search will be restricted to that field *unless* the field does not exist on the card you were at when you used the Find command. For example, if you want to restrict the search to a particular background field, and you initiate the search while you are on a card of a different background that does not contain a field by that name, HyperCard will search all fields. If you suspect this might be the case, you should check the text that is found by using the foundField function discussed later in this chapter.

Find Chars

Find chars *string* [in field *fieldDesignator*]

This version of the Find command causes HyperCard to search for words *containing* the search string. Therefore, if you search for "man", it will find cards that contain words such as "woman", "mankind", "human", and "mandate". Only those characters that match will be placed in the box, not the entire word.

Find Whole

Find whole *string* [in field *fieldDesignator*]

This variant of the Find command is new to version 1.2, and you can summon it into the Message box with the keyboard combination SHIFT-COMMAND-F. It searches only for whole words that match *string*. If you include multiple words in *string*, HyperCard will find only cards that contain the *exact* text you type, including spaces and punctuation.

Find Word

Find word *string* **[in** *field fieldDesignator***]**

This variant of the Find command is similar to the **Find whole** command, except that the spaces are included in any found text. For example, if you use the command

```
find word "Robert Heinlein"
```

HyperCard will locate instances of cards that contain both the words "Robert" and "Heinlein", whether or not they are contiguous or in the same field.

Find String

Find string *string* **[in field** *fieldDesignator***]**

This version of the Find command allows you to search for a specific string of characters, including spaces. As in the example of the **Find word** command discussed earlier, if you search for "Robert Heinlein", the **Find string** command will find those words only when they occur next to each other (including the spaces).

Functions for Discovering What Text Was Found

HyperCard versions 1.2 and greater include four functions that allow you to discover the location of text found with the Find command. In earlier versions of HyperCard, only the Result function was provided, and it told you nothing more than whether or not the text was found.

foundChunk

the foundChunk

foundChunk( )

This function returns a chunk expression defining the location of found text. The chunk expression will have a form similar to the following:

```
char 1 to 9 of bkgnd field 14
```

This function allows you to test for several things. For example, you can test to see if the text was found on a background or card field by examining the sixth word of the foundChunk in this manner:

```
if word 6 of the foundChunk is "card"
```

foundField

the foundField

foundField( )

This function returns the field in which the text was found, in the form

```
bkgnd field 14
```

The first word indicates whether the field was a background or card field, and the last word shows the number of the field.

If you want to get the name of the field, you can do so with the statement

```
the name of the foundField
```

which will return something like

```
bkgnd field "comments"
```

You can also use

```
the short name of the foundField
```

which will return

```
comments
```

When you ask for the short name of a field, the name is not enclosed in quotation marks.

foundLine

the foundLine

foundLine( )

This function returns an expression that evaluates to the line and field number in which the text was found in the form

```
line 1 of bkgnd field 14
```

You can see that some of the information this function returns is also delivered by the foundChunk and foundField functions—the number of the field in which the text was found. This gives you flexibility as to which function you use.

It is important to remember that HyperCard defines a line as a string of text that ends with a return. This means that in fields where text automatically wraps to the next line, those word-wrapped lines are not counted as separate lines. It is possible, although difficult, to write a HyperCard function that determines which *visible* line some specific text is on. The difficulty depends on several factors, including the size of the text in the field, whether or not the wideMargins property of the field is set, and how words are automatically wrapped in the field.

foundText

the foundText

foundText( )

This function returns the actual text found. It will always return the entire word containing the string you are looking for.

Optimizing the Find Command

There are a couple of ways to make the Find command work better.

First, include at least the first three characters of the text you wish to find. When new text is entered into Hyper-Card, HyperCard builds, for each card in the stack, a table that contains the first three characters of each word in fields on that card. When you use the Find command and give HyperCard at least three characters to look for, it needs only to consult the table. When it finds those three characters together in the table, it then checks all the words on the card. If you give it fewer than three characters, it must check all the words on each card, which takes much longer.

Second, as mentioned earlier in this chapter, when you confine the search to a particular background or card field, and that particular background or card field is not on the current card, HyperCard will ignore your field restriction and search all fields. You can use the foundField function in this manner to check for such occurrences, as shown in the handler in Script 21-2, to be sure the text is in the found field.

This handler is not as complex as it looks. You can call it from a mouseUp handler and send to it two parameters: the text you want to find and the name of the background field you want to search.

The handler first builds a Find command using the two parameters and concatenating several strings together. This is best illustrated by an example. Suppose you call the findIt

```
on findIt  theText,theField
  put "Find" && quote & theText & quote &¬
  "in bkgnd field" && quote & theField & quote
  type return
  repeat while the short name of the foundField¬
  is not theField
    if the mouse is down then exit repeat
    type return
    if the result is empty then exit repeat
  end repeat
end findIt
```

Script 21-2.   This script builds a Find command and places it in the Message box so you can repeat it easily with the RETURN key

handler with the parameters *good* and *comments*; "good" is the text you are searching for, and "comments" is the name of the field you want to search in. Here is what the Put command on the first two lines of the body of the handler would put into the Message box:

```
Find "good" in bkgnd field "comments"
```

Next, the handler types Return. This executes the command in the Message box. The repeat loop merely executes the Find command (by typing Return) until the short name of the foundField is "Comments." If the result is not found, *theText* is not in the stack, and the repeat loop stops execution.

By building the search expression and putting it into the Message box, you have performed two functions. First, you have made it possible to execute this function by merely typing Return from within the script. Second, once an instance of *theText* has been found in the desired field, you can just press RETURN to go to the next instance of that text.

There is at least one limitation to Script 12-2. It assumes that *theText* does indeed exist in *theField* somewhere in the stack. If *theField* does not contain *theText* anywhere in the stack, and if other fields *do* contain *theText*, then this program will continue to execute over and over, until you stop it by clicking the mouse button.

Some Scripts

The doFinds function shown in Script 21-3 takes one parameter, the variable *theText*, which is the text for which the function is to search. It returns a list of the ID numbers of all the cards in the stack that contain that text. Each line in that list contains a chunk expression in the form

```
char 77 to 80 of bkgnd field 14 of card ID 4405
```

You call this function with a line such as "doFinds(*text*)" where *text* is a variable containing text that you want to find.

This function first puts initial values into two variables. The variable *countCards* will count the number of cards found, and the variable *theCards* will contain the list of the ID numbers of the found cards. The variable *allDone* will be used as a flag to allow the repeat loop to stop executing.

The first thing the repeat loop does is go to the next card. This is done to keep the loop from finding multiple occurrences of the text in the same card and exiting prematurely. Next, the Find command finds *theText*. If the result is "empty," the text has been found.

When the text has been found, the script gets the short ID of the card containing the text, and this ID number is compared with the list of card IDs held in the *theCards* variable. If that ID—held in the container "It"—is not on the list, then a line is constructed that consists of the chunk expression identifying the found text, including the ID number of the card containing the text. This line is added to the end of the variable *theCards*.

```
function doFinds theText
   -- countCards contains the number of hits we've made
   -- theCards contains the short IDs of the found cards
   put 0 into countCards
   put empty into theCards
   put false into allDone
   set lockScreen to true
   set lockRecent to true
   set lockMessages to true
   go card 1
   put "Hits: 0"
   repeat until allDone is true
      -- to keep from finding the text again on the same card
      set cursor to busy
      find whole theText
      if the result is empty then
         get the short ID of this card
         if it is not in theCards then
            -- tell the user how many we've found
            add 1 to countCards
            put countCards into last word of msg
            --char 1 to 5 of bkgnd field 2
            put the foundChunk && "of card ID" && it into¬
            line countCards of theCards
            go next card
         else
            put true into allDone
         end if
      else
         -- none found!
         exit repeat
      end if
   end repeat
   put empty
   return theCards
end doFinds
```

Script 21-3.   This script builds a list of all the cards in a stack that contain specific text

If the ID number of the current card is in *theCards*, then the Find command has looped through the stack and found the same card again. If this is the case, the value "true" is put into the *allDone* variable and the repeat loop stops executing. The list of cards containing *theText* is then returned to the script that called this function.

The doFinds function has several uses. For example, you could use this function with a button to print all the cards in the stack that contain certain text. Script 21-4 shows how this can be done.

Another use for this function might be to create a special Find button. Instead of repeating the Find command every time it is pressed, the Find button would go directly to the next card that contains the desired information by referring to the list of cards returned by this function.

There are some useful modifications that you could make to this script. For example, you could use it with one of the variants of the Find command, such as **Find whole** or **Find string**, to get more control over the Find command, or you could use the Ask or Answer command to cause this function to prompt you as to what kind of Find command you want to use.

Selecting Text

Selecting text is a standard Macintosh procedure. Generally in Macintosh applications, before you can work with text—change its font, style, or size, delete it, type over it, or perform some other operation—you must select it.

```
put doFinds(text) into theCards
open printing with dialog
repeat with x = 1 to the number of lines in theCards
  go card ID last word of line x of theCards
  print this card
end repeat
close printing
```

Script 21-4.   This script fragment could be used to print all the cards found by the doFinds function shown in Script 21-3

Some Macintosh user-interface procedures—for example, selecting an item from a scrolling list as you do in the Font/DA Mover—require working with selected text.

HyperCard gives you commands and functions to select text. You can, from script control, select specific chunks of text, or you can determine what text has been selected.

The Select Command

Select <*chunkExpression*>

The Select command selects the text specified in *chunkExpression*. The chunk expression must refer to a field or to the Message box. If you attempt to select text in a variable, HyperCard will return an alert indicating it cannot understand the arguments to the Select command.

Later in this chapter the Select command is used to select text as part of a search-and-replace command. You can also use it to select text in the Message box.

For example, the COMMAND-F key combination summons the Message box and places the Find command in the Message box and the insertion point between the two quotation marks. COMMAND-SHIFT-F does the same for the **Find whole** command. You could use a controlKey handler to do the same with the CONTROL-F key sequence, perhaps to summon the **Find string** command, as shown here.

```
on controlKey num
   if num is 6 then
     put "Find String" && quote & quote
     select before last char of msg
   end if
end controlKey
```

(The controlKey message is discussed in Chapter 19.) If you press CONTROL-F, this handler puts the text "Find string" followed by two quotation marks into the Message box. It then uses the Select command to place the blinking cursor before the last character of the message box.

If a handler is in the script of a field, it can select text in that field with the line "Select the text of me".

Functions for Determining What Text Is Selected

In addition to allowing you to select text, HyperCard (especially version 1.2 or greater) gives you several functions that allow you to determine what text is currently selected. These functions are basically the same as those that allow you to discover what text was found with the Find command.

Note: It is important to remember when using these functions that anything that changes the Macintosh screen, including buttons that highlight, will deselect the selected text. This means that if you call any of these functions with a button that autohighlights, they will return "empty." The highlighting of the button will deselect the text.

The Selection

get the selection

put *text* **into the selection**

"The selection" is a container that contains the text currently selected. You can get the text selected with the statement

```
get the selection
```

This works in much the same way as the selectedText function described later in this chapter. However, "the selection" is a container, which means you can also put text into it, as shown here:

```
put "HyperCard" into the selection
```

If any text is selected, this statement will replace that text with the word "HyperCard."

selectedChunk

the selectedChunk

selectedChunk( )

This function returns a chunk expression, specifying exactly what text was selected, in the form

```
char 40 to 40 of bkgnd field 14
```

This example indicates that only one character was selected, because the second and fourth words of the expression are the same. If the selection is an insertion point in the field rather than text, the selectedChunk function will return an expression such as

```
char 40 to 39 of bkgnd field 14
```

The fourth word of this expression represents a smaller value than the second word, indicating that the insertion point is between these two characters.

selectedField

the selectedField

selectedField( )

This function returns an expression that indicates the field containing the selection.

selectedLine

the selectedLine

selectedLine( )

This function returns an expression defining the line and field containing the selected text.

Remember, just as with the foundLine function discussed earlier in this chapter, this function refers to lines as strings of text that end with a return, and not to lines created in a field by the automatic word wrapping of text.

selectedText

the selectedText

selectedText( )

This function returns the actual selected text. It is similar to the container "the selection"—the commands **Get the selection** and **Get the selectedText** both give you the same characters. However, "the selection" is a container into which you can put text, whereas the selectedText function only returns text; you cannot put text into it.

Changing Text

Throughout this book you have seen many ways to use the Put command. For example, you can put text into the Message box with commands such as

```
put "HyperCard"
put "HyperCard" into msg
```

The Put command is ubiquitous in HyperCard. Besides displaying text in the Message box, it is also used to assign values to variables, as in the line

```
put 10 into theNumber
```

where *theNumber* is a variable.

One of the ways the Put command is most often used, however, is to change the values of text. When you are using the Put command to replace existing text with new text, you use the syntax

```
Put textExpression preposition destination
```

where *textExpression* is an expression that evaluates to some text and *preposition* is a word that denotes the relationship the text contained in textExpression will have to *destination,* which is an expression that yields text.

For example, the following statement assigns the value "HyperCard" to the variable *theProgram:*

```
put "HyperCard" into theProgram
```

Following is a discussion of the prepositions you can use with HyperCard.

Into

Use this preposition to replace the contents of *destination* with the new contents. It is most commonly used to assign a value to a variable or other container, as in these lines:

```
put 10 into theNumber
put "HyperCard" into theProgram
put the long date into background field "date"
```

However, you do not need to replace the *entire* contents of a container. You can also put text into different chunks of containers, as shown in these two examples:

```
put "abcd" into word 1 of card field "test"
put "abcd" into character 1 of theText
```

The second example replaces the first character of the variable *theText* with the four characters "abcd". In the first example, you could replace one word with several, as shown here:

```
put "one two three" into word 2 of theText
```

You can perform the same operation with lines, as shown here:

```
put "this is a test" into line 1 of theText
```

If you are working with either items or lines, HyperCard will create the structures for you. For example, consider these commands:

```
put "a" into theText -- theText now contains "a"
put "b" into item 7 of theText
```

After execution of the second command, *theText* will contain "a,,,,,,b". HyperCard has inserted enough intervening commas to allow for the new item 7, even if there was only one item in the container initially.

The same thing happens with lines. HyperCard places enough returns in the container to allow for the line you have specified.

Note: If you execute the line

```
put "b" into character 7 of containerName
```

and the container "containerName" does not have at least six characters, HyperCard will *not* insert intervening characters. Instead, the character "b" will be appended to the end of the container, with no spaces separating it. The same thing happens with words: placing new text into word 7 of a container does not add six spaces to the beginning of the container.

After

The After preposition appends new text to the existing text or to portions of existing text. Here are some examples:

```
put "abc" into theText -- thetext now holds "abc"
put "def" after theText -- now holds "abcdef"
put "xxx" after char 1 of theText -- now holds "axxxbcdef"
put "xyz" after word 2 of theText -- now holds "axxxbcdefxyz"
```

In the last statement, since there is only one word in *theText*, and since HyperCard does not add spaces to make multiple words, "xyz" is merely appended to *theText*.

In the following example, since item 2 of *theText* does not exist and is therefore empty, HyperCard adds an item to *theText*, and places "def" after that item. The same operation works with lines.

```
put "abc" into theText -- now holds "abc" again
put "def" after item 2 of theText -- now holds "abc,def"
```

Before

The Before preposition works in much the same manner as the After preposition. Here are some examples:

```
put "def" into theText -- theText now contains "def"
put "abc" before theText -- now contains "abcdef"
put "xyz" before item 2 of theText -- now contains "abc,xyz"
```

Again, since there was previously only one item in *theText*, the Put command adds an item and places "xyz" before the text of that item. Since that item is empty, "xyz" becomes item 2 of *theText*.

The Delete Command

Delete *expression* of *container*

The Delete command removes characters from text in containers. Here are some examples of the Delete command in action:

```
delete word 1 of card field "test"
delete char 2 to 73 of card field "test"
delete item 2 of theText
delete second word of theText
```

In all cases, text *after* the text deleted is moved to the left. For example, if you delete the first character of a container, the second character then becomes the first. The same is true, of course, with words, items, and lines.

Concatenating Text with the & and && Operators

You often need to combine strings of text to form new strings. HyperCard gives you two text operators that allow you to *concatenate* or combine text—**&** and **&&**—and their functions are straightforward.

put *text1* & *text2*

The **&** operator concatenates the text strings on either side of it and adds no spaces between the two strings:

```
put "Hyper" & "Card" -- puts "HyperCard"
```

put *text1* && *text2*

The **&&** operator concatenates the text strings on either side of it and adds a space between the two strings:

```
put "Hyper" && "Card" -- puts "Hyper Card"
```

These operators are used quite often, and examples of their use appear in several scripts in this and other chapters. For example, there are certain characters, discussed later in this chapter, that for various reasons cannot be entered directly into text from the keyboard. HyperCard uses special constants to represent these characters.

You might, for example, want to present a message such as this:

There is no card field "comments"

You cannot do this directly, however, because the quotation marks you want to put around the word "comments" are used by HyperTalk to define the text you want to put. To put a message such as this, you need to construct the statement in this manner:

```
put "There is no card field" && quote & "comments" & quote
```

The **&&** operator indicates you want to include a space between the word "field" and the first quote surrounding "comments." The use of the **&** operator indicates a space is not desired.

A Search-and-Replace Button

As Chapter 11 promised, Script 21-5 is part of a button that performs a search-and-replace function. This button uses the doFinds function discussed earlier in the chapter to form a complete implementation.

Note: While this script does work and has been tested, you should use it with care until you make sure you have typed it in correctly. As always when creating scripts that have the potential for destroying data, it is a very good idea to save a copy of your stack before you use it.

The mouseUp handler in this script performs the dirty work of asking you what text you want to find, what text you want to replace that text with, the name of the background field you want to check, and whether or not you want the script to prompt you before performing each replacement. By declaring global variables in the first line of the script, it is able to remember the last items you entered and present you with them again.

The searchReplace handler uses the list of expressions contained in the global variable *theCards*. Since this variable contains the IDs of the cards containing the text you were searching for, it does not need to use the Find command again. It uses the variable *theCount* to count the number of replacements it has made.

The repeat loop cycles through each of the cards in *theCards*, peforming the operation once for each line of *theCards*. It goes to the card with the ID contained in the last word of the current line of *theCards*. If the *whatField* variable is not "all"—a value that indicates the search-and-replace is to take place in all background fields—then it

```
on mouseUp
   global findWhat,replaceWith,whatField,confirm, theCards
   ask "Find what?" with findWhat
   if it is empty then exit mouseUp
   put it into findWhat
   ask "Replace it with?" with replaceWith
   if it is empty then exit mouseUp
   put it into replaceWith
   ask "In what field? ('all' for all)" with whatField
   if it is empty then exit mouseUp
   put it into whatField
   answer "Confirm each Find?" with "No" or "Yes"
   if it is "yes" then put true into confirm
   else put false into confirm
   Put "Searching for all instances of the text..."
   put doFinds(findWhat) into theCards
   if the number of lines in theCards is 0 then
      answer "None Found!"
      exit mouseUp
   end if
   searchReplace findWhat,replacewith,whatField,confirm
end mouseUp


on searchReplace findWhat,replaceWith,whatField,confirm
   global theCards
   put empty into theCount
   -- findWhat holds what we are searching for
   -- replaceWith holds what we are replacing findWhat with
   -- whatField defines the field we need to search in
   -- if confirm is true, ask the user at each instance
   -- start the count of instances
   repeat with x = 1 to the number of lines in theCards
      -- start at the first card found
      go card ID last word of line x of theCards
      if whatField is not "all" then
         if the short name of word 6 to 8 of line x¬
         of theCards is not whatField then next repeat
      end if
      -- now find the instance of the text
      Select word 1 to 8 of line x of theCards
      -- if confirm is true, we need to ask the user
      if confirm  is true then
         Answer "Replace this one?" with "No" or "Yes"
         -- if the user says no, loop back to start over again
         if it is "no" then next repeat
      end if
      -- if confirm is false or user says yes,
      -- then do the replace
      put replaceWith into the selection
      add 1 to theCount
      -- loop back to start the find again
   end repeat
   -- all done!  let the user know
   answer theCount && "instances replaced."
end searchReplace
```

Script 21-5.   These two long scripts, along with the doFinds function, constitute a Search-and-Replace button for
HyperCard

checks the field containing the text on the current card to make sure it is in the specified field. If it is not, the repeat loop starts over.

The next step is to select the text that was found. This is performed with the line "Select word 1 to 8 of line x of the-Text". This chunk contains a phrase something like "char 1 to 17 of bkgnd field 14" and that is the text that is selected.

If the *confirm* variable is "true," then the handler stops and asks you if you want to replace this instance or not.

Replacing the text is simple. The Put command is used to put the text held in the *replaceWith* variable into "the selection" container, which contains text selected earlier and represents the characters in the field containing the text for which you were searching. The loop adds 1 to the variable *theCount* to keep track of how many replacements were made.

When the loop has gone through all the cards in *the-Cards*, the handler reports the number of replacements made and exits.

To use this routine, place the mouseUp and searchReplace handlers, along with the doFinds function, into a button. It works fairly quickly. There are a couple of things that could be changed, however, and some problems that cannot be avoided. First, you could change it to make sure that the name of the field typed into the *whatField* variable actually exists. You could also use the sameText function presented later in this chapter to provide a case-sensitive search-and-replace.

One problem can occur when text found is underneath the standard location of the Answer dialog box that is presented when you are confirming the replacements of text — you won't be able to see the selected text. Unfortunately there is no way to control the location of the Answer dialog box. The script currently finds and replaces only the *first* instance of the text on any particular card. It is easy to modify the doFinds function so that it lists all instances of found text.

Other Text Functions

HyperCard includes two other functions that are useful for working with text. All text in any computer is stored as a number. Computer manufacturers have agreed on a standard method of mapping characters to these numbers. This is called the American Standard Code for Information Interchange or, more commonly, ASCII. If it were not for the ASCII code, no two computers from different manufacturers would be able to exchange text. A table of the ASCII characters is contained in the appendix.

numToChar

numToChar(*number*)

The numToChar function returns the character that has the ASCII value of *number*. The appendix contains a listing of the Macintosh character set with the ASCII values of each character.

Note that the ASCII character set defines 256 characters, numbered from 0 to 255. You might think, therefore, that sending a number greater than 255 would result in an error message. Not so. Instead, if you use a number greater than 255, numToChar will return the character that is the result of the number mod 256. For example,

```
numToChar(340) = T = numTochar(340 mod 256)
```

The **mod** operator returns the remainder performed by division and is discussed in Chapter 22.

charToNum

charToNum (*string*)

The charToNum function returns the ASCII value of the first character of *string*. If you are including a literal string, it must be surrounded by quotation marks, as in this line:

```
charToNum("a")
```

You can also use chunk expressions inside the parentheses.

Script 21-6 uses the charToNum function to determine whether two text strings are exactly the same.

You call this function with a line such as:

```
put sameText("HyperCard","hypercard")
```

This line will put "false" into the Message box, because the two text strings are not the same—the second one contains no capitalization.

This function works quite simply. It first checks to see if the lengths of the two text strings are the same. If the lengths are not the same, it returns "false." Next it loops through each character of the first string and compares the ASCII value of that character with the character at the same position of the next string using the charToNum function.

```
function sameText text1,text2
  if the number of chars in text1 ≠ ¬
  the number of chars in text2 then
    return false
  end if
  repeat with x = 1 to the number of chars in text1
    if charToNum(char x of text1) ≠ ¬
    charToNum(char x of text2) then
      return false
    end if
  end repeat
  return true
end sameText
```

Script 21-6.   This function determines whether two text containers have *exactly* the same text

Because the ASCII values of, for example, "a" and "A" are not the same, it will return "false" if it encounters even one different character. If the loop executes successfully, then all the characters are the same, and the function returns "true."

You could create a Find button that calls this function to show only text that exactly matches the text for which you are searching.

Constants

HyperCard contains several predefined constants that represent characters that otherwise could not be entered into a string.

Empty

The empty constant contains nothing. This allows you to totally clear the contents of any container with the command

```
put empty into container
```

You can also check any container to see if it does indeed contain text, as shown here:

```
if container is empty
if container is not empty
```

It might seem as though you will not use this constant often, but it is useful when, for example, you need to clear the values of certain variables, such as globals. Putting empty into a variable erases it.

Tab

The tab constant contains a tab character, ASCII character 9. You cannot enter the tab character into a string in the

Message box or in a field because the TAB key is used to select the next field. You also cannot use the TAB key to enter a tab character into text that is in the editor because the TAB key is used there to reformat the scripts. Instead, use the tab constant to put the tab character into text, as shown here:

```
put "abcd" & tab into theText
```

This line puts "abcd" and the tab character into the variable *theText*. You can test to see if some text contains a tab character with the **contains** or **is in** operator:

```
theText contains tab
tab is in theText
```

Here is a function that uses the tab constant and the Offset function to remove all tabs from some text:

```
function stripTabs theText
  repeat while theText contains tab
    delete char offset(tab,theText) of theText
  end repeat
  return theText
end stripTabs
```

Space

It is much easier to insert a space into text that you are typing than to insert a tab character; the SPACEBAR performs no special function on its own. You can include spaces in text by using a statement such as

```
put "abc def" into theText
```

Because the space between the "c" and the "d" is embedded in quotation marks, the space will be part of the text.

Here is an example of a function that transforms all instances in a container of two consecutive spaces into one space. This handler could be useful in cases where you are exporting text to a desktop publishing or word processing program.

```
function strip2Spaces theText
  repeat while theText contains space & space
    delete char offset(space & space,theText) of theText
  end repeat
  return theText
end strip2Spaces
```

Return

As with the tab character, the return character (ASCII character 13) cannot be easily inserted into text, except when you are typing into a field. In the editor, the RETURN key is used to start a new line; in the Message box, the RETURN key sends the message you have typed to HyperCard.

Use the return constant when you need to represent the Return character in a script.

lineFeed

In earlier days of computers, when monitors were patterned after teletype terminals, two characters were needed to correctly signal the end of a line: the return character instructed the typing head of the teletype to move to the left margin, and the linefeed character instructed it to turn the platen so typing could start on a new line. The Macintosh does not need the linefeed character to denote a new line, and few Macintosh programs need it. It is usually displayed as a small box.

Here is a function that uses the lineFeed constant to remove linefeeds from text:

```
function stripLF theText
  repeat while theText contains lineFeed
    delete char offset(lineFeed,theText) of theText
  end repeat
  return theText
end stripLF
```

This function is useful in cases where where you are importing text to HyperCard that has been created on other computers that do need the linefeed to denote a return, such as the IBM PC and its clones. Since the linefeed character is usually represented as a small box on the screen, if you do not remove them, text files imported from the PC will have these small boxes at the end of every line or paragraph.

You might also want to add linefeeds to Macintosh text before it is exported to a PC. Here is a function using line-Feed to add linefeeds after returns in text:

```
function addLF theText
  repeat with x = 1 to the number of chars in theText
   if char x of theText is return then
     put lineFeed after char x of theText
   end if
  end repeat
  return theText
end addLf
```

This function uses a repeat loop to check all the characters in the variable, and thus takes a little longer to execute than the stripLF function.

Quote

The quote constant contains the double quotation mark, which would otherwise be impossible to insert into text because it is used to delimit strings. The quote character is ASCII character 34.

There are a number of uses for the quote constant. If, for example, you want to display a message that includes quotes, you can concatenate quotes to produce the following message:

```
put "Can't open file" && quote & "fileName" & quote¬
into theText
answer theText
```

This script fragment displays an alert in the Answer dialog box, such as the one shown in Figure 21-2.

formFeed

The formFeed constant is used to create a character for which there is no standard equivalent on the Macintosh

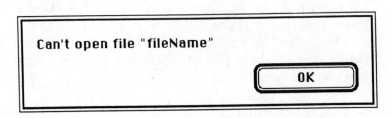

Figure 21-2.   An alert using the Answer dialog box and the quote
                    constant

keyboard—ASCII character 12. It is used by many printers,
including the ImageWriter, to signal that a new page is
beginning.

There are not many uses for this character in Hyper-
Card. You might use it if you are exporting some text to a
file. In Microsoft Word, the formfeed character is used to
insert a new page, and if there are any formfeed characters
in a text file created by HyperCard, Word will treat these as
hard page breaks when it reads the file.

Working with Numbers

Part and parcel of any programming language are the tools it gives you for working with numbers. HyperCard gives you a complete set of built-in functions for handling most number-related operations and provides a syntax for working with numbers (and numbered objects) that is easy to read and understand. While HyperCard is not a program dedicated to working with numbers and thus does not have the power of a program such as a spreadsheet, you can perform many of the same tasks that are often performed with a spreadsheet.

Making Sure Numbers Are Numbers

As discussed in Chapter 21, everything stored in HyperCard is text. This means that you do not have to declare that certain fields or variables can contain only numbers. This gives you a great deal of flexibility when you are creating stacks, but it also causes you some problems.

Virtually all the mathematic operations discussed in this book require that their arguments or parameters be numbers. If one of the parameters is not a number, then the function will give you an error alert of the type shown in Figure 22-1. This error message will display the value on which you are trying to perform an operation, and it will tell you it is not the right type of value for the operation you were performing. In Figure 22-1, the text "test" was placed into a variable, and an attempt was made to multiply the text by 3. To avoid this type of error, you should first check that each container you are working with contains a numeric value. Script 22-1 contains a function that does this for you.

The first thing this function does is put

0123456789.

into the variable *theNums*. This variable contains all the allowed characters. Notice that a period is included to allow for decimal numbers. Then the function loops, or repeats, through each of the characters in the container. If a character in the container is not in *theNums*, then the function returns "false"—the container is not a number. Otherwise, if the loop makes it through all the characters in the container, it returns "true"—the container is a number.

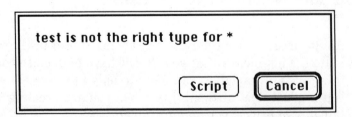

test is not the right type for *

[Script] [Cancel]

Figure 22-1.   This alert appears if you attempt to perform a numeric operation on a container that does not contain a numeric value

```
function isNum theContainer
  put "0123456789." into theNums
  repeat with x = 1 to the number of chars in theContainer
    if char x of theContainer is not in theNums then
      return false
    end if
  end repeat
  return true
end isNum
```

Script 22-1.   This function returns "true" if all the characters in the container are numbers

Script 22-2 is a variation of the isNum function; it tests to see if the container contains a valid numeric expression.

This function works the same way as the previous version. However, it adds more allowable characters:

$()*^/+-"$

These characters allow you to evaluate expressions such as

$4 + 5$

as numbers. Substantial changes would be required to allow

```
function isNum theContainer
  put "0123456789.()*^/+-" into theNums
  repeat with x = 1 to the number of chars in theContainer
    if char x of theContainer is not in theNums then
      return false
    end if
  end repeat
  return true
end isNum
```

Script 22-2.   A revised version of the isNum function allows numeric operators as well as numbers

```
on closeField
  get me
  if isNum(it) is false then
    select text of me
  end if
end closeField
```

Script 22-3. This closeField handler calls the isNum function to
make sure you entered numbers into a field

the function to verify that the container contains an expression that is actually valid.

If you have fields that are designed to hold numbers exclusively, it is best to test the contents of these fields as you enter text into them. In that way, you can be easily prompted to enter correct information and save confusion later on, such as when you are processing the text in fields. This is best taken care of with a closeField handler in the field in question. Script 22-3 shows such a handler.

You can also easily write a function that checks a number to see if it falls within an allowable range, as in Script 22-4. The rangeCheck function returns "false" if the number is less than the low number specified or more than the high number specified.

```
on rangeCheck theNumber,low,high
  if theNumber < low or theNumber > high then
    return false
  else
    return true
  end if
end rangeCheck
```

Script 22-4. This function returns "true" if *theNumber* is a number
that falls in a specified range

```
on closeField
  get me
  if isNum(it) is false then
    select text of me
  else
    if rangeCheck(it,50,100) is false then
      select text of me
    end if
  end if
end closeField
```

Script 22-5.   A modified closeField handler makes sure the field contains a number and then checks to see if it falls in an allowed range

Script 22-5 shows a revised closeField handler that performs two operations. First, it makes sure the value entered into the field is a number. If it is not a number, it selects the text of the field. If it is a number, it checks to see if the number falls within the range of 50 to 100. Second, the function checks to see if that number falls within the allowed range. If the number does not fall within the range, the text of the field is selected; otherwise, nothing happens.

Note: This handler relies on the feature of versions 1.2 and greater that allows you to get the contents of a field with the **Get me** command. "Me" is a special object that normally returns the ID of the object containing the handler. However, if the object containing the handler is a field, then this command returns the text contained in the field. This handler also uses the new (to version 1.2) command **Select text of me**, which selects all the text in the field.

About SANE Functions

Built into the ROM and operating system of the Macintosh is a set of routines for dealing with numbers quickly. This set is called SANE, which stands for Standard Apple Numeric Environment. It contains built-in routines for handling a variety of numeric tasks. It allows a number of functions to be performed by programmers without requiring them to reinvent the wheel. HyperCard uses these SANE functions.

One of the good things about the SANE functions is that, because they are built into the Macintosh, they are implemented in a standard way. This means that if you have an accelerated Macintosh, such as Macintosh II or SE with an accelerator board, and that accelerated Macintosh contains a 68881 numeric coprocessor, then all applications that use SANE can automatically take advantage of that numeric coprocessor. This allows these SANE functions to execute considerably faster on a Mac equipped with the coprocessor than on a standard Macintosh.

The following SANE functions are included in Hyper-Card: Abs, Annuity, Atan, Average, Compound, Cos, Exp, Exp1, Exp2, Ln, Ln1, Max, Min, Round, Sin, Sqrt, Tan, and Trunc. HyperCard also includes a number of mathematical functions that are not part of SANE. All these functions are discussed later in this chapter.

Unusual Numbers and Limits

There are cases where you can perform numeric operations that don't make any sense, such as dividing a number by 0 or attempting to work with numbers that are larger than Hy-perCard (or the Macintosh in general) knows how to work with. Thanks in part to the SANE routines, HyperCard has standard means for dealing with these invalid operations.

Division by 0

If you attempt to divide a number by 0, HyperCard will return "INF," which represents infinity. All other operations you perform on this value will also yield "INF"—subtracting

1 from infinity is still an infinite number. If you are working with a negative infinity, as when you divide −10 by 0, Hyper-Card returns "−INF."

Note: The **div** and **mod** operators, discussed later in this chapter, do not work this way. Instead they summon error alerts.

Large Numbers

HyperCard is able to handle positive numbers as large as 74 digits; negative numbers can be as large as 73 digits because the minus sign counts as a digit. This is an extraordinarily large number, and if you have a need to work with numbers that are larger, you must be figuring something like the square of the national debt. If you try to perform an operation that generates a number larger than 74 digits, Hyper-Card will not return an error message. Instead it will substitute for that number the character "?"; HyperCard returns this character when performing any operations on very large numbers.

Other Invalid Operations

In many other cases, HyperCard returns error messages when invalid operations are performed. In some cases, these operations will generate an error alert, and in some cases special text will be returned. In the following list, "NAN" stands for "Not A Number." Here is a list of some of the values HyperCard returns:

−NAN(001)   Occurs when you attempt to perform an invalid square root, such as the square root of −1

−NAN(002)   Occurs when you attempt to perform an invalid subtraction, such as (10/0)−(10/0)

NAN(004)   Occurs when you attempt an invalid division, such as 0/0

NAN(008)   Occurs when you attempt an invalid multiplication division, such as multiplying 0 by infinity: (10/0) * 0

In all these cases, you can still perform operations on these values, but the values themselves will not change.

The numberFormat Property

Normally, when HyperCard is calculating numbers, it calculates them to six decimal digits and returns that value. However, sometimes you might want to display only two digits to the right of the decimal point; for example, when you are working with dollar figures. The Round and Trunc functions offer some help, but they return integers exclusively and can also introduce errors into the calculation.

At such times, numberFormat is the property to use. The numberFormat property governs only how numbers are *displayed*, not how they are calculated. This means that numbers are calculated to their full precision, but when you display them they are rounded to the degree specified in the "Set numberFormat" line.

Operators

HyperCard's math operators need little explanation: they work in much the same way as we are used to thinking of numbers. One point you should keep in mind about operators, however, is the *precedence*, or the order in which they are evaluated. Operator precedence and grouping are discussed in Chapters 14 and 16.

Standard Arithmetic Operators: + − * /

number1 + *number2*

The + operator evaluates to the sum of *number1* and *number2*, as shown here:

```
3 + 4 -- 7
75 + 1025 -- 1100
```

number1 − *number2*

The − operator evaluates to the value of *number1* less the value of *number2*, as shown here:

```
10 - 3 -- 7
4 - 10 -- -6
```

number1 * *number2*

The * operator evalutates to the value of *number1* multiplied by *number2*, as shown here:

```
2 * 3 -- 6
37 * 54 -- 1998
```

number1 / *number2*

The / operator evaluates to the value of *number1* divided by *number2*. (Also see the **div** and **mod** operators described later in this chapter.)

```
6 / 3 -- 2
5 / 2 -- 2.5
10 / 11 -- 0.909091
10 / 0 -- INF
```

The Exponent Operator: ^

number1 ^ *number2*

Raises *number1* to the power of *number2*. That is, it multiplies *number1* by itself *number2* times. Here are some examples:

```
4 ^ 2 -- 4 squared is 16
2 ^ 16 -- 2 to the 16th is 65536
10 ^ 0 -- 1
10 ^ -1 -- 0.1
10 ^ .5 -- 3.162278
```

The div Operator

number1 **div** *number2*

The **div** operator (**div** stands for "dividend") returns the integer portion of the result of *number1* divided by *number2*, as shown here:

```
4 div 2 -- 2
5 div 2 -- 2
10 div 3 -- 3
```

If you attempt to use the **div** operator where *number2* is 0, you will get an error alert warning you that you cannot perform a div by 0, and execution of your script will halt.

The mod Operator

number1 **mod** *number2*

The **mod** operator (**mod** stands for "modulus") returns the remainder when *number1* is divided by *number2*. That is, it returns the portion left over when the **div** operator, discussed earlier, is performed, as shown here:

```
5 mod 2 -- 1
10 mod 3 -- 1
```

When using the **mod** operator, if *number2* is 0, then an alert will appear, warning you that you cannot perform this operation with 0, and execution of your script will halt.

Functions

You will remember from the discussion of functions in Chapter 14 that functions stand in for numbers when the line is being evaluated, and HyperCard evaluates the line just as if you had specified the number in the line. So it is with math functions.

You will also remember that there are often two forms for functions: a long form and a short form. Again, this is true of math functions. However, some of the math functions do not have a short form. These are functions such as Average, Max, and Min, which can take several arguments.

Trigonometric Functions, Angles, and Radians

The trigonometric functions Atan, Cos, and Sin return numbers that are expressed in *radians*, not degrees. A radian is the measure of the angle created by an arc of the circle that is equal to the radius of the circle. In other words, when you trace an arc around the circle that is equal to the radius of the circle, the length of that arc is one radian. Figure 22-2 illustrates this relationship.

Since the circumference of a circle is equal to 2 * pi * the radius, and a circle equals 360, then 2 * pi radians = 360; therefore

1 radian = 180/pi = 57.29578°

To convert radians to degrees, then, you multiply the radians by 180/pi, or 57.29578. To convert degrees to radians, you multiply the number of degrees by pi/180, or 0.017453. Script 22-6 shows two functions that translate from degrees to radians and from radians to degrees.

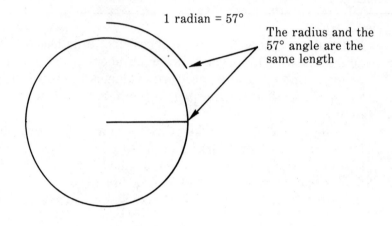

Figure 22-2. A radian is an arc on the circle that is of the same length as the radius of the circle

The arguments that the trigonometric functions take are expressed as degrees, while the numbers they return are in radians.

```
on degsToRads theDegs
  return theDegs * (pi / 180)
end degsToRads

on radsToDegs theRads
  return theRads * (180 / pi)
end radsToDegs
```

Script 22-6. These two functions convert degrees to radians and radians to degrees

Abs

the abs of *number*

abs(*number*)

The Abs function returns the absolute value of *number*, regardless of its sign. For example, both Abs(−7) and Abs(7) return 7.

Annuity

annuity(*interestRate, periods*)

The Annuity function determines the present value of an investment in an ordinary annuity, with an interest rate of *interestRate* and a total number of periods of *periods*. The interest rate should be expressed as the monthly interest rate, and the number of periods is the total number of payments during the life of the annuity. For example, if the yearly interest rate is 12%, you divide that by 12 to get the value 1, which is passed to the annuity function. If the annuity is paid 12 times a year for 30 years, then the number of periods is 360. To calculate the actual value of a monthly payment, multiply that payment by the result of the annuity function.

If you were writing the annuity function in HyperTalk, it would read like this:

```
function annuity rate,periods
  return (1 - (1 + rate) ^ (-periods)) / rate
end annuity
```

Atan

the atan of *number*

atan(*number*)

This function returns the arc tangent of *number* expressed in radians.

Average

average(*itemList*)

The Average function returns the average of the items expressed in *itemList*:

```
put average(1,2,3) -- 2
put average(1,100) -- 50.5
```

Note: The *itemList* value must be numbers separated by commas. If there is more than one line in *itemList*, the average function will evaluate only the first line.

Compound

compound(*interestRate, periods*)

This function returns the value of a compound-interest-bearing account with an interest rate of *interestRate* over a period specified by *periods*.

   If you were to write this function in HyperTalk, it would be

```
function compound interestRate,periods
   return (1 + interestRate) ^ periods
end compound
```

Cos

the cos of *number*

cos(*number*)

The Cos function returns the cosine of *number* in radians.

Exp

the exp of *number*

exp(*number***)**

This function returns the natural exponent of *number*, which is *e* raised to the power of *number*. The mathematical constant *e* has a value of approximately 2.718281828. The exp(3) function performs the same operation as the line "$e \wedge 3$".

Exp1

the exp1 of *number*

exp1(*number***)**

The Exp1 function returns 1 less than the natural exponent of a number, or:

```
(exp1(number) - 1)
```

Exp2

the exp2 of *number*

exp2(*number***)**

This function returns 2 to the power of *number*. It is, therefore, the same as the line "$2 \wedge \textit{number}$". Here are two examples:

```
exp2(2) -- 4
exp2(16) -- 65536
```

Ln

the ln of *number*

ln(*number*)

The Ln function returns the log of *number* to the base of *e:*

```
ln(7) -- 1.94591
```

Ln1

the ln1 of *number*

ln1(*number*)

This function returns the log of (*number* + 1). It first adds 1 to the number and then returns the log of that sum.

Log2

the log2 of *number*

log2(*number*)

The Log 2 function returns the log of the number to the base 2.

Max

max(*itemList*)

This function returns the largest number in the *itemList*, which must be a list of numbers that are organized into items (that is, separated by commas). If *itemList* contains multiple lines, only the first line will be evaluated. Note that there is no long form for this function.

Min

min(*itemList*)

This function returns the smallest number in *itemList*, which is a group of numbers separated by commas. Note that there is no long form for this function.

Random

the random of *number*

random(*number***)**

The Random function returns an integer that is a random number between 0 and *number*.

Round

the round of *number*

round(*number***)**

This function returns *number* rounded to the nearest integer, as shown in here:

```
round(7.1)  -- 7
round(7.5)  -- 8
round(-7.5) -- -8
```

Sin

the sin of *number*

sin(*number***)**

The Sin function returns the sine of *number* expressed in radians.

Sqrt

the sqrt of *number*

sqrt(*number***)**

This function returns the square root of *number*. Here are some examples:

```
sqrt(4) -- 2
sqrt(-1) -- -NAN(001)
sqrt(10) -- 3.162278
```

Tan

the tan of *number*

tan(*number***)**

The Tan function returns the tangent of *number* expressed in radians.

Trunc

the trunc of *number*

trunc(*number***)**

This function returns the integer portion of *number*.

Note: There is a difference between this and the Round function. Although both functions return integers, the Round function returns the integer *closest* to the number, whereas the Trunc function simply returns the integer portion of number, totally disregarding the decimal portion. Here is an illustration of the difference between these functions:

```
put round(5.5) -- 6
put trunc(5.5) -- 5
```

Value

the value of *expression*

value(*expression*)

The Value function returns the value of *expression*, performing any necessary operations that are part of *expression*. Here are some examples:

```
value(10*3) -- 30
value((10/3) * 4) -- 13.333333
```

Commands

HyperCard's math commands perform functions similar to HyperCard operators. These commands operate directly on containers, however, so you do not need to get the value in a container, perform an operation on it, and then put it back.

If you attempt to use any of these commands on a non-numeric container, you will get the alert shown in Figure 22-3, which tells you that the destination container does not contain a number. While it is not possible to directly trap this error message in HyperTalk, it is possible to prevent it by checking the container first to make sure it contains a number, as discussed earlier in this chapter.

The Add Command

Add *number1* to *container*

This command adds the value of *number1* to the number in *container*. It is equivalent to these two commands:

```
get the value of container
put it + number1 into container
```

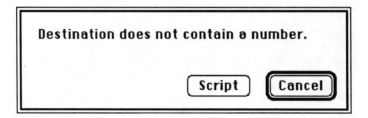

Figure 22-3.   This alert appears if you try to use one of the math commands on a container that does not contain a number

The Subtract Command

Subtract *number1* from *container*

After executing this command, the value in *container* will contain its previous value, minus the value in *number1*.

The Multiply Command

Multiply *container* by *number1*

This command multiplies the value in *container* by *number1*.

Note: The sequence is slightly different for the Multiply command (and the Divide command) than it is for the Add and Subtract commands. The *container* is named first, since that is the value you are changing.

The Divide Command

Divide *container* by *number1*

This command divides the value in *container* by *number1*. As with the Multiply command, the syntax is switched from that of the Add and Subtract commands.

Constants

HyperCard includes several predefined *constants*, which work in much the same way as do variables. However, you do not need to put values into constants—indeed, you cannot— each time you start HyperCard.

Pi

The constant pi contains the value 3.14159265358979323846, an approximation that is considerably better than the value that has served the human race for most of its history.

Pi is used to determine properties of circles. Here is a function that returns the area of a circle, given the radius:

```
function area radius
  return pi * (radius ^2)
end area
```

As shown earlier in this chapter, pi is also used to convert degrees to radians and radians to degrees.

Zero Through Ten

HyperCard also predefines 11 constants referring to each of the first eleven numbers: zero, one, two, three, four, five, six, seven, eight, nine, and ten. The values contained in each of these constants are self-explanatory.

Using these constants, you can construct expressions that might be easier to read:

```
add one to card field "count"
go card two
set hilite of card button one to true
```

First Through Tenth

Just as you can use the constants "Zero" through "Ten" to stand for the actual numbers, you can use the constants

"First" through "Tenth" to stand for the ordinal numbers they represent.

These words are: first, second, third, fourth, fifth, sixth, seventh, eighth, ninth, and tenth. Unlike the number constants, there is no synonym for zero—you can't have a "zeroth" object.

You can use these words in much the same manner as you use the number constants. However, in order to make the statements read more like English, the syntax is reversed: instead of typing **Go card seventh** (as you would type **Go card seven**), you type **Go seventh card**. Here are some examples of how you can use these constants:

```
edit script of seventh background button
send closeField to sixth card field
get sixth line of card field 1
add 5 to first word of theVariable
```

Working with the Date and Time

The Control Panel and 24-Hour Time
Tools for Working with the Date and Time
Date and Time Formats
Calculating with the Date and Time
Some Scripts

HyperCard gives you several interesting and useful tools for working with date and time values. Not only can you retrieve the date and time and place them into containers, you can also convert those values to different formats and perform calculations based on them.

HyperCard's date and time functions use the standard Macintosh routines built into the system. Dates can be calculated correctly for dates between Friday, January 1, 1904, and Monday, February 6, 2040. This is a range of some 4,294,965,600 seconds. If you need to schedule your appointments for mid-March of 2040, you must either write your own routines or find another program.

If you try to work with a date that is outside this range, that is, before January 1, 1904, and after February 6, 2040, HyperCard will work with the seconds *mod* 4294965600. (The Mod function is discussed in Chapter 22.) For example, if you attempt to convert a container holding the value "February 7, 2040" to a short date, it will return "1/1/04." For each day later than February 7, 2040, that you give Hyper-Card, it will add the number of days between the date you give it and 2/6/2040 to 1/1/1904. Dates earlier than January 1, 1904, are handled in the same manner.

Note: Not coincidentally, if you remove the battery from your Macintosh Plus (the SE and the II have unremovable batteries), the internal Macintosh clock is set to January 1, 1904.

The Control Panel and 24-Hour Time

The General portion of the standard Control Panel allows you to specify whether you want to use standard 12-hour time formats or 24-hour (or military) time formats. HyperCard follows your settings from the Control Panel, and displays the time accordingly.

Note: HyperCard does not allow you to set the date on your Macintosh clock. To do this, you should use either the Control Panel or Alarm Clock desk accessory.

Tools for Working with the Date and Time

HyperCard gives you two functions for retrieving the date and time and putting them into containers. You can also work with *ticks*, which are part of the Macintosh's internal time-keeping mechanism.

The Date Function

the <short|long|abbreviated> date

date( )

The Date function returns the current date. If you use the long form of the function, you can include the words "short," "long," or "abbreviated," which govern the form in which the date is returned. If you use the short version of the function, the short version of the date is returned. Date formats are discussed later in this chapter.

The Time Function

the <short | long | abbreviated> time

time( )

This function returns the current time. If you have specified 24-hour time in the Control Panel, it returns the time in that form. If you have specified 12-hour time, it returns the time and also includes an indicator—AM or PM—as the last word, which lets you test for morning or afternoon.

A function that specifies short time returns the same thing as a function that specifies only the time: it defaults to the format of the short time.

Time formats are discussed in more detail later in this chapter.

The Seconds Function

the seconds

seconds( )

This function returns the number of seconds that have passed since midnight, January 1, 1904. This is a very large number, unless you have the clock in your Macintosh set for some time in 1904, and even then it is relatively large.

The Ticks Function

the ticks

ticks( )

The Ticks function returns the number of ticks that have passed since you last turned on the Macintosh. A tick is 1/60 second.

The Convert Command

convert dateContainer **to** *dateFormat*

This Command converts the date contained in *dateContainer* to the form specified in *dateFormat*. This allows you to change the way that containers with dates are displayed, and it also gives you more control over such things as performing mathematical operations on dates.

If the container that you are trying to convert contains an invalid number, such as a negative number of seconds, the conversion will not take place.

One of the interesting features of the Convert command is that it ignores incorrect data. Consider the following example:

```
put "Wednesday, July 1, 1954" into thedate
convert theDate to long date
put theDate -- puts "Thursday, July 1, 1954"
```

Because July 1, 1954, was a Thursday, not a Wednesday, HyperCard has ignored the incorrect day of the week.

Here is another example of the use of Convert:

```
put "7/44/88" into thedate
convert thedate to short date
put thedate -- puts "8/13/88"
```

This command also works for the time:

```
put "25:00" into thetime
convert thetime to short time
put thetime -- puts "1:00 AM"
```

You can also put invalid dates into containers and let HyperCard translate them, as shown here:

```
put "January 300, 1988" into theDate
convert theDate to short date
put thedate -- puts "10/26/88"
```

The result shows that October 26 is the 300th day of 1988.

Date and Time Formats

Dates and times can have several formats, as mentioned in the earlier sections on the Date function and the Time function.

Abbreviated

For containers containing time values, the abbreviated form of the time is the same as the short form. Abbreviated dates simply shorten the words: "Monday" becomes "Mon," "October" becomes "Oct," and so on. "Abbreviated" itself can be abbreviated to "abbr" or "abbrev."

Here is an example of an abbreviated date:

Mon, Nov 10, 1947

Here is the form of abbreviated time:

hr:min am/pm

Short

The short version of the date or time is the same as the information returned by the short form of the functions themselves.

The short form of a date is

mo/day/year

The short form of time is

hr:min am/pm

dateItems

The dateItems format transforms the container into comma-separated integers that represent, in this order, the year, month, day, hour, minute, second, and day of the week.

As discussed later in this chapter, this date format can be used to perform calculations on different parts of the date or time. You can add or subtract values from any of these items:

```
put the date into theDate -- contains "7/20/88"
convert thedate to dateItems
put theDate -- puts "1988,7,20,0,0,0,4"
add 1 to word 1 of theDate
put theDate -- "1989,7.20,0,0,0,4"
```

Long

The long date transforms the date into the form

day, day of month, year

Here is an example of a long date:

Thursday, July 14, 1988

The long time causes the complete time, including seconds, to be put into the container.

Here is an example of long time:

1:54:07 PM

In 24-hour time, this would be

13:54:07

Calculating with the Date and Time

Sometimes you will want to perform calculations using the date and time. You should note, however, that you cannot work directly with date or time values stored in containers unless the format of those values is in seconds. For example, if a container contains the short date, you cannot simply add 1 to the container to transform that container to tomorrow's date. That is because the short date is in the format mo/ day/year and contains the character /, which is not a number, and HyperCard will respond with an alert to that effect.

There are two ways you can perform calculations with dates or times. First, converting any container to seconds format allows you to act on that container, such as adding or subtracting numbers from it. Because there are 86,400 seconds in a day (60*60*24), adding that value to a container or subtracting it from a container that is in the form of seconds adds or subtracts a day.

Second, you can perform operations on the various items that are in a container that is in the dateItems format. For example, to add a year to a container that is in the dateItems format, use this statement

```
add 1 to item 1 of theContainer
```

where *theContainer* is the name of a container — a variable or a field — that is in the dateItems format.

Some Scripts

Here are some useful scripts that use date and time functions.

Days Between Dates

Script 23-1 is a short function that returns the number of days between any two dates.

This function takes two arguments — the starting date and the ending date — and it returns the number of days that have passed between the two dates. It first converts the two

```
function daysBetween startDate,endDate
  convert endDate to seconds
  convert startDate to seconds
  return (endDate - startDate) / 60 / 60 / 24
end daysBetween
```

Script 23-1.   This function returns the number of days between two dates

dates to seconds, which yields very large integers. The difference between these two dates in seconds is then divided by 60 (to get minutes), then again by 60 (to get hours), and by 24 (to get days).

AutoDating Cards

With the newCard handler shown in Script 23-2, you can include a field that shows the date each card in the stack or background was created. Put this handler into a background or stack script, and when you create a new card, it will automatically put the date that card was created into the background field "Date."

```
on newCard
  put the date into bg field "date"
end newCard
```

Script 23-2.   A newCard handler that automatically puts the date into a background field on all new cards

Determining the Speed
of the Computer

You can use the Ticks function to help you determine whether HyperCard is running on a Macintosh with a slow processor (as found in the Mac Plus or SE), or whether a faster processor is being used. Fast processors will be found in such machines as a Macintosh II or an SE that includes an accelerator card. Since it is fair to assume that faster Macintoshes will continue to appear, you cannot assume that your scripts will execute at the same speed on all machines. The checkTiming handler shown in Script 23-3 determines whether the computer is fast or slow.

Once you've run the checkTiming handler, you will have a global variable called *fastCPU* that will contain "true" if the computer is anything faster than a Mac SE. You can then use this variable when performing any operations that might happen too fast on a fast computer, including visual effects

```
on checkTiming
   global fastCPU
   put the ticks into startTicks
   repeat with i = 1 to 50
     put i into tempCounter
   end repeat
   put the ticks into endTicks
   if endTicks - startTicks < 40 then
     put true into fastCPU
   else
     put false into fastCPU
   end if
end checkTiming
```

Script 23-3.   This script determines whether the script is running on a fast or slow Macintosh

and going to different cards quickly for animation. A line such as

```
if fastCpu then wait 10 ticks
```

will halt execution of the script for 1/6 second. Remember to declare the *fastCPU* global in any handlers that use it.

Last Update

Script 23-4 is a function that returns the date of the last update of a stack.

The parameter *stackExpression* contains the name of the stack you want to check. If that variable is empty, the function then places "this stack" into the variable. The next line simply gets item 5 of the version of the stack, which contains the date of the stack's most recent update, converts that to long date, and returns it.

```
function lastUpdate stackExpression
  if stackExpression is empty then
    put "this stack" into stackExpression
  end if
  get item 5 of the version of stackExpression
  convert it to long date
  return it
end lastUpdate
```

Script 23-4.   This function returns the date a stack was last updated

Day of the Week

Script 23-5 is a function that returns the day of week for any date.

You call the function in this manner:

```
put dayofWeek() -- puts the current day
```

Note: If you pass this function with no parameter, it uses the current date. You must also enclose in quotes any date you pass to the function so that the number is not evaluated. For example, if you use the function in this manner

```
put dayofWeek(1/1/90)
```

it will return 0.011111 because HyperCard will evaluate the numbers in parentheses and make its calculation on that value. Enclosing the parameter in quotes, as shown here,

```
put dayofWeek("1/1/90")
```

prevents 1/1/90 from being evaluated and returns "Monday."

```
function dayOfWeek theDate
  if theDate is empty then put the date into theDate
  convert theDate to long date
  return item 1 of theDate
end dayOfWeek
```

Script 23-5.   This function returns the day of the week for any date

Working with Fields

Fields as Buttons
Fields and Messages
Clicking On and Highlighting Words
A HyperText Technique
Pop-Up Fields

Most of this book has dealt with working with buttons as triggers for actions. This chapter will take a look at how you can use fields, or even specific words or lines in fields, as triggers for actions. This means that you can put words or lines in fields and then click the mouse on those words or lines or fields in order to perform certain tasks.

Fields as Buttons

MouseDown and mouseUp messages *are* sent to locked fields, so fields can be used as buttons. There are some good reasons for doing this, along with some negative aspects.

An advantage to using a field as a button is that fields can contain multiple lines. Therefore, you have more flexibility in creating field buttons than regular buttons. For example, you might want to make a three-line button whose functions are integrated, but which performs different functions depending on which line of the field you click on. Because text in a regular button is always on one line, you cannot easily do this. You can with fields.

The major drawback to using a field as a button is the fact that, unlike regular buttons, the only way you can show the name of a field is by actually putting that text into that field. This can prove to be confusing and a nuisance. If the field is a card-level field, this is not much of a problem. However, if the field is a background field, there are several problems. The field must contain the same text on all the cards in the background. This means that you must put the text displayed in the field on every card, which can cause your stack to grow larger than is manageable, especially if you have a large number of cards. It also means that if you are searching for text in a stack, text that is in these fields will be found by the Find command.

Fields and Messages

You will remember from the discussion of messages in Chapter 12 that some messages are not sent to fields when those fields are unlocked. These include the messages that relate to the mouse button — mouseDown, mouseStillDown, and mouseUp. These messages are not sent to unlocked fields, so you can edit text in these fields.

Messages that *are* sent to unlocked fields include the remainder of the mouse messages — mouseEnter, mouseWithin, and mouseLeave. These messages allow you to determine whether you have moved the mouse within a field.

Note that scrolling fields are a special case. MouseUp and mouseDown messages are not sent to a field (whether locked or unlocked) when you click on the scroll bar at the right side of the field; however, other mouse messages *are* sent.

There are some caveats about using certain handlers with fields in which you want to enter text. For example, if you have this mouseWithin handler

```
on mouseWithin
  beep
end mouseWithin
```

the beeping will continue for as long as the mouse cursor is inside the field, even as you attempt to enter text into the field.

A mouseWithin handler on a field can also slow down typing as it executes. If the handler changes anything else on the screen, it can also cause typed characters to be lost, since the insertion point is deselected when anything on the screen changes.

Clicking On and Highlighting Words

Remember that mouseUp and mouseDown messages are sent only to locked fields. Therefore, if you wish to have an action take place when you click on a field, you must make sure the text of the field is locked by checking the Lock Text check box on the Card Info dialog box.

Script 24-1 is a function that selects, or highlights, the word you clicked on and returns the selected word to the line that called it.

First the field is unlocked to allow selection of the text. The repeat loop then double-clicks at the location you clicked the mouse to select a word (just as you double-click on a word

```
function selectedWord
  set the lockText of the target to false
  repeat 2
    click at the clickLoc
  end repeat
  set the locktext of the target to true
  return the selectedText
end selectedWord
```

Script 24-1.   This function selects a word you click on and returns that word to the line that called it

to select it). The field is locked again, and the function returns the selected text to the handler that called it.

A HyperText Technique

One common HyperText technique is to develop links between certain words and other cards in the stack or in other stacks. Script 24-2 shows a handler that clicks on a word and goes to the next card that contains the same word in the same field.

Place this handler in the script of a locked background field. When you click on a word in the field, it first calls the selectedWord function, which highlights the word and returns the selected word to the handler, placing it into the variable *theWord*. The handler puts the name of the field you clicked on into the variable *theField*. Next, it goes to the next card in order to prevent the Find command from finding the selected text on the current card. It then finds the word you selected in the current field and unlocks the screen to display it to you.

```
on mouseUp
  set lockmessages to true
  put selectedWord() into theWord
  put the short name of the target into theField
  lock screen
  go next card
  find whole theWord in field theField
  unlock screen
end mouseUp
```

Script 24-2. This function uses the selectedWord function to find the next occurrence of a word in a stack

You can use this technique to build links to specific cards, using a lookup table to link a word to a card.

Some who have used this technique put an asterisk after the key words that have links to them. Double-clicking on a word will not select an asterisk right after the word; therefore, you must modify the selectedWord handler to verify that the next character is an asterisk, as shown in Script 24-3.

This function uses the selectedChunk function to find out whether or not the character immediately after the selected word is an asterisk. If it is, it returns that word; otherwise, it returns "empty." You can then use this word in a calling function, perhaps to go to a named card.

Selecting Lines

A common feature in the Macintosh user interface is a scrolling field that lists a number of items and allows you to choose from them. Examples include the Font/DA Mover, in which you have a list of fonts and desk accessories that you can

```
function selectedWord2
  set the lockText of the target to false
  repeat 2
    click at the clickLoc
  end repeat
  set the locktext of the target to true
  if char (word 4 of the selectedChunk) + 1 of me is "*" then
    return the selectedText
  else
    return empty
  end if
end selectedWord2
```

Script 24-3.   This modification of Script 24-2 checks to see if the character after a selected word is an asterisk

select by clicking on them. Clicking a button then copies or deletes the font or desk accessory. Unfortunately, HyperCard includes no built-in support for this sort of dialog box, so you need to write it yourself using HyperTalk.

The selectLine function, shown in Script 24-4, selects a line. It is a variation of the selectedWord function presented earlier in this chapter.

This function performs two tasks. First, it selects the entire line. To actually highlight the entire line clicked, you need a different procedure than that used in the selected-Word function discussed earlier. Double-clicking on the word selects only that word. To select the entire line, this handler first clicks on the extreme left edge of the field and then clicks on the next line of the field, also at the extreme left edge, with the SHIFT key. The SHIFT key, remember, allows you to extend the selection.

The one problem with this technique is that it fails on the last line of the field. It would not be too difficult, however, to write a special circumstance for this line.

The second task of this function is to determine exactly which line of the field you clicked on. This task is necessary for two reasons. First, the selectedLine function in Hyper-Card works only with lines that end with returns. While most lines in a list field will end with returns, that might not always be the case. Second, in the case of scrolling fields, some of the lines in the field might have scrolled off the top of the field.

For scrolling fields, the function determines the distance between the place you clicked on and the top of the field and adds the scroll of the field form to that number. This results in a number that indicates the absolute value of the distance from the top of the field to the cursor location, which is then divided by the number of pixels per line in the field (the *text-Height*). The resulting line is then returned to the caller.

```
function selectLine
  -- first select the line
  set locktext of me to false
  click at left of me + 1, the clickV
  click at left of me + 1, the clickV + ¬
  the textHeight of me with shiftKey
  set locktext of me to true
  -- now figure out which line it was
  if the style of me contains "scrolling" then
    return line(trunc(((the clickV - top of me)¬
    + the scroll of me) / the textHeight of me)) of me
  else
    return line(trunc((the clickV - top of me)¬
    / the textHeight of me)) of me
  end if
end selectLine
```

Script 24-4.   This handler selects an entire line of text in a field

If the field is not a scrolling field, the same actions are performed, except the scroll of the field is not taken into account. The two separate routines for scrolling and non-scrolling fields are necessary because HyperTalk gives you an error alert if you attempt to get the scroll of a nonscrolling field.

Now that the line is selected, you need to do something with it. You might, for example, have a button that takes you to the card containing the text you highlighted. This requires a special mouseUp handler in a button that *does not automatically highlight*. The button must not automatically highlight because the act of highlighting a button deselects any selected text. Script 24-5 is a mouseUp handler that first gets the selected text and then highlights the button.

```
on mouseUp
  put the selectedChunk into temp
  if temp is empty then exit mouseUp
  set the hilite of the target to true
  set the hilite of the target to false
  select temp
  -- now do whatever you want
  put the selection
end mouseUp
```

Script 24-5.   This script simulates the autoHilite property of a button

Pop-Up Fields

Another common technique is to include pop-up fields that appear when a button is clicked. These fields can contain such things as help information and annotations for pictures. They are best presented as shadow fields, which makes them seem to float above the card, thus reinforcing their transient nature. There are several ways you can implement these pop-up fields.

Temporary Pop-Ups

Temporary pop-up fields are fields that are only visible as long as you hold down the mouse button. These are good for containing very short explanations. To manage a temporary pop-up field, you must create a button that displays the field and maintains the visibility of that field for as long as the mouse button is down. This is simple to do, as shown in Script 24-6.

Of course, you will need to adjust this script to reflect the name of the field you are showing, as well as whether or not it is a foreground or background field.

```
on mouseUp
   set the visible of card field "note" to true
   wait until the mouse is up
   set the visible of card field "note" to false
end mouseUp
```

Script 24-6.   This mouseUp handler shows and hides a pop-up field

You don't want to hold the button down for too long while reading one of these fields (your mouse finger can get tired), so keep text in these fields short and concise. The buttons that trigger them should be located at the point on the card that the field explains, and you should make sure it is clear which buttons trigger these fields.

More Detailed Pop-Up Fields

If you want to create a pop-up field that contains more detailed information, the technique for temporary pop-up fields is not suitable. Holding down the button to read a large chunk of text is too much work.

If you have longer text, you can include this mouseUp handler in the button that displays the field:

```
on mouseUp
   set the visible of card field "notes" to¬
   not the visible of card field "notes"
end mouseUp
```

If this button is clicked when the field is hidden, it displays the field. If it is clicked when the field is visible, it hides it by setting the visible property of the field to the opposite of its current setting.

You can also click on a field to hide it by including this mouseUp handler in the script of the locked field:

```
on mouseUp
  set the visible of the target to false
end mouseUp
```

Because the field will not receive any messages when it is hidden, you cannot make the field *appear* by clicking on it.

You can use HyperCard's visual effects, along with the Lock Screen and Unlock Screen commands, to make fields appear to zoom open and closed, just as folders do in the Finder.

Script 24-7 shows a modification to the mouseUp handler for a button that displays or hides the field and uses the Zoom Open visual effect. This makes the field appear to open up from the point on the screen where the button is located. When you click the button again, the field zooms closed to the middle of the screen. This technique can be used to reinforce the fact that the field is an annotation field and, therefore, temporary in nature.

```
on mouseUp
  lock screen
  if the visible of card field "notes" is true then
    set the visible of card field "notes" to false
    unlock screen with visual effect zoom close
  else
    set the visible of card field "notes" to true
    unlock screen with visual effect zoom close
  end if
end mouseUp
```

Script 24-7. This handler uses the Zoom Open and Zoom Close visual effects when hiding or showing a pop-up field

Communicating Through Dialog Boxes or the Message Box

Getting Information from Dialog Boxes
Communicating Through the Message Box

Sometimes during the execution of a script you need to either present or receive information. HyperCard gives you three commands for receiving information, and you can use the Message box to present information.

Getting Information from Dialog Boxes

Ask *textExpression* <*with defaultText*>

The Ask command displays the dialog box shown in Figure 25-1, using *textExpression* for the prompt. If you include *defaultText*, this becomes the text proposed for the answer, as shown in the figure. If you do not include any default text, the field is left empty. The following line produced the dialog box shown in the figure:

```
ask "Please enter some text" with "This is some text"
```

The text you enter into this dialog box is placed into the variable "It" when you click the default OK button (or use the

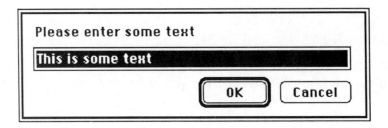

Figure 25-1.   The dialog box produced by the Ask command

ENTER or RETURN key). If you click the OK button without typing new text, the default text will be placed into "It." If you click the Cancel button, "empty" is placed into "It."

Testing to see if "It" is empty is an essential way of allowing cancellation of operations with the Ask dialog boxes and is used in many scripts in this book. No tricks are allowed—an operation should always cancel if the Cancel button is clicked.

The Ask Password Command

Ask Password *<with defaultText>*

The Ask Password command is a variation on the standard Ask command. The difference is that before HyperTalk places the value you entered into the variable "It," that value is first transformed to a numeric value. For example, if you type the word "HyperCard" into this dialog box, the number 1905794429 actually appears.

Note: There is no way to associate or compare a password produced with this command to the password entered into the Protect Stack dialog box. That is a separate password that is not accessible to HyperTalk.

```
on mouseUp
  global thePasswd
  ask password "Please enter the password"
  if it is not thePasswd then
    beep
    answer "Sorry, access denied!"
    set the locktext of the target to true
  else
    set the locktext of the target to false
  end if
end mouseUp

on closeField
  set the locktext of the target to true
end closeField
```

Script 25-1.   These handlers allow you to prevent unauthorized entry of text into a field

The Ask Password command is useful if you want to create a stack that has multiple levels of password protection, instead of the stack-level password protection that HyperCard itself gives you. For example, you might have a field that you want to protect so that only those with the correct password can change the contents of that field. Script 25-1 contains two handlers you can place into the script of a field to take care of this.

For these two handlers to work, the field must first be locked. If you click the mouse on the field to edit the field, you will be greeted with the Ask Password dialog box. If you enter the correct password, which is stored in the global variable *thePasswd*, the script unlocks the field, and you can edit it. If you enter an incorrect password, an Access-Denied alert is presented, and the Macintosh beeps.

Once you have changed the contents of the field and left the field with the TAB key, the closeField handler locks the text of the field.

Passwords used by the Ask Password command are variables. You must store those variables in card fields for use during the next session with HyperCard or they will be lost when you quit HyperCard. Since the values produced by this command are numbers, it is safe to store them—the actual text entered is not visible to others. You can save these passwords in a field that is hidden by setting the visible property of the field to "false," as in this line:

```
set the visible of field "passwords" to false
```

You can use lines such as the following to retrieve the password from the field:

```
global thePasswd
put field "passwords" into thePasswd
```

You also must use the Ask Password command to create passwords to be stored in this field. Additionally, if you have used the Set Password button on HyperCard's Protect Stack dialog box, you have seen how that dialog box asks you for the password twice to make sure that you entered it correctly. Script 25-2 is a function that uses the Ask Password command to do this.

The main part of this function is a repeat loop. The repeat loop first asks for the password. If you click the Cancel button on that dialog box, then the function returns "empty" and stops executing. Otherwise, it places the password into a variable. You are then prompted for a second password, which is also placed into a variable. If the two passwords are the same, then the first password is returned to the line that called the function. Otherwise, the repeat loop executes again and continues to ask you for the password until the two you have typed are identical. Clicking the Cancel button also halts execution of the loop.

You can call this function in the following manner:

```
on mouseUp
  put getPass() into temp
  if temp is empty then exit mouseUp
  put temp into field "password"
end mouseUp
```

```
function getPass
  repeat
    ask password "Please enter the password"
    if it is empty then return empty
    put it into firstPass
    ask password "Enter it again to verify"
    if it  is empty then return empty
    put it into secondPass
    if firstPass = secondPass then
      return firstPass
    end if
  end repeat
end getPass
```

Script 25-2.   This function asks you to type a password twice to ensure you have typed it correctly

This handler first places the value returned by the getPass function into the variable *temp*. If *temp* is empty, that means you have clicked a Cancel button when asked for a password, and the handler stops executing. Otherwise, it puts the encrypted password into a field that stores the password.

Remember, if you make the button that contains this script a visible button, anyone will be able to change the password by clicking it.

One problem with the Ask Password command is that it does not encrypt the password as you type it into the dialog box. Many programs display bullets or asterisks as you type in passwords, to prevent those who might be looking over your shoulder from reading the password. When entering passwords into HyperCard, then, you should be careful so that others do not learn them.

The Answer Command

Answer *textExpression* <with *buttonText* <or *buttonText* <or *buttonText* >>>

The Answer command places on the screen the dialog box shown in Figure 25-2. The dialog box can include one to

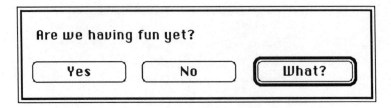

Figure 25-2.   The dialog box produced by the Answer command

three buttons, and the buttons are of a uniform size, no matter how much text you put into them; if the text is too long to
fit in the button, it will be truncated to fit. The last button
you name will be the default button. The command that produced the dialog box in Figure 25-2 is

```
Answer "Are we having fun yet?" with "Yes" or "No" or "What?"
```

When you click one of the buttons, Answer places the text
contained in that button into "It."

Limitations of the Ask and Answer Commands

There are two limitations when working with both the Ask
and Answer commands. The first limitation is the amount of
text that can be placed into the dialog boxes. The boxes are
of fixed size and use the Macintosh's Chicago system font.

There is no easy and reliable way to determine the width of a string of text; therefore, it is not possible to provide exact guidelines for how many characters will fit. A string in the range of 20 to 40 characters is generally used.

A second limitation to the Ask and Answer commands is their location on the screen. The location at which they are shown is fixed at the center of the HyperCard window and cannot be changed. This becomes a problem in such uses as a search-and-replace application of the type presented in Chapter 21; occasionally the text you are highlighting will be obscured by the dialog box. A possible solution to this problem is using the Message box as a kind of dialog box.

Communicating Through the Message Box

You can also use the Message box as a way to communicate. Putting information into the Message box is easy. Just use the Put command to place your text there, as shown here:

```
put "now working....just a moment"
```

This command places the text within the quotation marks into the Message box.

Another technique is to use the Message box as a place to keep you posted on the status of a long operation. For example, if you are doing something with all the cards in a stack, such as getting a value from those cards, the Message box can tell you how far you have gone, as shown in Script 25-3.

The first line of this script places the number of cards you are working with in the variable *numCards*. The next line initializes the display in the Message box. The repeat

```
put the number of cards into numCards
put "Percent done: 0"
repeat with x = 1 to numCards
  go next card
  put trunc(x / numCards * 100) into last word of msg
  -- after this, the commands you want to execute
end repeat
put empty
```

Script 25-3. This script fragment shows how the Message box can be used to keep you updated about the progress of a lengthy operation

loop starts at the current card and moves through the stack one card at a time, performing some operation—not shown—at every card. As it does so, it puts the current percentage completed into the last word of the Message box. When the loop is finished, the line "put empty" clears the Message box. You might want to include the line "hide msg" to hide it.

Communicating with
the World:
Printing and Dialing

Printing
Dialing

This chapter deals with two somewhat disparate topics—printing and dialing. Although they might seem at first glance not to go together, they are both used to help you communicate with others.

Printing with HyperTalk allows you to communicate the contents of your HyperCard stacks to those who might not have HyperCard. With HyperTalk, you can extend some of the functions that you have with the Print Stack and Print Card commands.

Dialing helps with a different kind of communication. With HyperTalk's Dial command you can use HyperCard to help you handle your daily voice communications. Commercial stacks such as Focal Point use HyperCard's Dial command to help you manage cost accounting of your phone work. Used in connection with stacks such as Apple's Address stack, the Dial command makes the task of looking up a phone number and dialing that number as simple as a couple of keystrokes and mouse clicks.

Printing

No programming language would be complete if it couldn't control the means of getting data onto paper. As Chapter 5 showed, HyperCard includes some excellent tools for the user to print cards, stacks, and reports. Unfortunately, you have limited control over how these work with a HyperTalk program.

HyperTalk printing is an extension of standard Hyper-Card printing. Essentially you are able to print specific cards using the current settings of the Print Stack dialog box. First, take a look at the mechanisms you will use for doing this; then you can work with some scripts.

Open Printing

Open printing [*with dialog*]

This command starts the printing process and must be used before you can print from HyperTalk. It displays the dialog box shown here:

```
Now printing page 1...
Type command-period to stop.
```

Once Open Printing is used, you can use the Print Card command to print specific cards. The Close Printing command stops the process.

If the optional *with dialog* parameter is used, the Print Stack dialog box appears, allowing you to specify the manner in which printing will take place—the number of copies, the number of cards per page, and so on. If you click the Cancel button in this dialog box, execution of the script is halted. It effectively sends an Exit to HyperCard command, and all commands after the Open Printing command are ignored. There is no way to trap for this occurrence.

Once printing has been opened, there are several ways to print the cards. Standard HyperCard navigation commands, including Go and Find, can be used to find specific cards. You are not strictly limited to printing one card at a time.

For example, you can type **Print 30 cards** to print a group of cards.

Printing from the Message Window

You can also print selected cards from the message window while browsing. Type **Open printing** into the message window, and the "Now printing" message will appear. You can then use standard card and stack navigation techniques, including clicking buttons and going to other cards and stacks. Each time you want to print a card, type **Print this card** or **Print card**.

If you are printing cards smaller than half size, the printer might not seem to do anything immediately. The ImageWriter will not print at all until you have told Hyper-Card to print enough cards to fill the page horizontally. The LaserWriter will not do anything until you have printed enough cards to fill a page.

When you have found and printed all the cards you want to print, type **Close printing** into the message box. Your pages will be ejected, and the dialog box will clear from the screen.

Some Sample Scripts

As can all aspects of HyperCard, printing can be enhanced by creating specific buttons or scripts. The remainder of the Print discussion gives you some sample scripts that you can use as is, or modify to add additional functions.

Printing Cards with Specific Text

Script 26-1 shows a handler called printCards. This handler takes one argument, which is specific text, and prints all the cards in the stack that contain the text. Script 26-2 shows a mouseUp handler that calls this procedure.

Operation of the printCards handler is pretty straight-forward. The first line of the body of the procedure opens the

```
on printCards whatText
  open printing with dialog
  put empty into cardNumbers
  go first card
  repeat
    find whatText
    put the short id of this card into thisCard
    if cardNumbers contains thisCard then exit repeat
    put return & thisCard after cardNumbers
    print this card
    go next card
  end repeat
  close printing
end printCards
```

Script 26-1.   This handler prints all the cards that contain the text held in the *whatText* variable

printing with the Print Stack dialog box to allow you to select the printing format. The next line puts "empty" into the *cardNumbers* variable used to keep track of the cards that you have printed. The script goes to the first card to make sure the cards are printed in order.

Next an open-ended repeat loop begins that will go on forever if you never exit it. The first thing the repeat loop does is search for the specified text. When the text is found, the handler gets the short ID number of the card and com-

```
on mouseUp
  ask "Print cards with what text?"
  -- the user cancelled
  if it is empty then exit mouseUp
  printCards it
end mouseUp
```

Figure 26-2.   A mouseUp handler that asks the user for text to search for, and then calls the printCards handler, which prints the cards

pares it with the variable *cardNumbers* to see if the card has already been put into that variable. If not, a return and the short ID of the card (held in the variable *thisCard*) are put into that variable, and the card is printed. The script then goes to the next card, and the loop begins again.

Note: If the script did not go to the next card, this handler would keep finding the same text on the first card that it found. It needs to go to the next card to start the search over again.

The variable *cardNumbers* holds the list of found cards, and the current card ID is checked against those in this variable. If this were not done, the Find command would keep looping through the stack, finding the text over and over again, printing forever. Therefore, when the handler has found text in a card that it has already printed, it exits the repeat loop, closes printing, and exits the handler.

The mouseUp handler that calls the printCards handler is also straightforward. This handler could go into a button called Print. It asks you for the text that it should search for and then calls the printCards handler, passing to it the text that you typed. If you click the Cancel button in the Ask dialog box, it will be empty, so the mouseUp handler exits.

Note: When clicking this button, you have three opportunities to stop the process: the Cancel button when asked for the text to find, the Cancel button on the Print Stack dialog box, or pressing COMMAND-PERIOD once the printing process has begun.

Marking Cards to Print

A variation on the printCards handler is one that allows you to mark cards for printing during browsing. At any time, you can click on a "Print selected cards" button. One way to do this is to put on each card a check box button named "Print this card." Since the statuses of check boxes are not stored separately for each card when they are background

```
on mouseUp
  if the hilite of the target is true then
    set the hilite of the target to false
    put false into bkgnd field "print"
  else
    set the hilite of the target to true
    put true into bkgnd field "print"
  end if
end mouseUp
```

Script 26-3.   A handler for a Print check box button that allows the user to specify that a card is or is not to be printed

buttons, you need to store this value in a background field when the user clicks it.

Script 26-3 implements the "Print this card" button. For the button to work correctly, make it a check box, and set the autohighlight of the button to false. Make sure there is a background field called "Print," which allows the script to store whether or not the user wants to print the card. Since you don't need to see the Print field, it can be hidden with the line "set the visible of bkgnd field "print" to false" in the message window or from a script.

The first thing this procedure does is find out if the button containing the script is currently checked or not. If so— if the highlight of the button is true—then it sets the highlight to false and puts "false" into the "Print" field. Otherwise, it does the opposite.

Background buttons retain their value through all the cards on the background. Script 26-4 shows an openCard handler that can be placed into the script of the background that contains this card. This handler sets the value of the Print check box button to the value in the "Print" field. If that field is true, then the highlight of the button is set to true and an x appears in the box. Otherwise, it sets the highlight to false.

```
on openCard
  if bkgnd field "print" is true then
    set the hilite of bkgnd button "print" to true
  else
    set the hilite of bkgnd button "print" to false
  end if
end openCard
```

Script 26-4.   This openCard handler sets the highlight of the Print button for individual cards when they are opened

Script 26-5 goes to the first card in the stack and proceeds through a stack in order. At each card, it checks to see if "true" is in the "Print" field. If so, it prints the card; if not, it goes to the next card. The problem with this approach is that it can take a long time to execute, particularly if there are a lot of cards to be checked and only a few of them are to be printed.

```
on mouseUp
  go first card
  open printing with dialog
  repeat with x = 1 to the number of cards
    if bkgnd field "print" is true then
      print card
    end if
    go next card
  end repeat
  close printing
end mouseUp
```

Script 26-5.   A handler for a button that searches all the cards and prints those that have been checked for printing

```
on mouseUp
   if the hilite of the target is true then
      set the hilite of the target to false
      put false into bkgnd field "print"
      removeCard
   else
      set the hilite of the target to true
      put true into bkgnd field "print"
      addCard
   end if
end mouseUp
```

Script 26-6.   A revised Print button handler that adds the ID of a card to a list to be printed or removes it from the list

A faster approach stores the list of cards to be printed on a separate field of a card called Print. A handler, again for a Print check box button, is shown in Script 26-6. This handler is the same as the one shown in Script 26-3, with the addition of two handlers that perform some of the tasks.

Script 26-7 shows the addCard handler, which adds the ID of the current card to the list of cards to be printed. This list is stored in a field called "Cards to print" on the card Print. The handler simply pushes the current card (to remember where it was), goes to the Print card, and adds the ID of the card to be printed to the end of the list. It then pops the card to go back.

```
on addCard
   push this card
   put the id of this card into thisCard
   go to card "Print"
   get the number of lines in card field "cards to print"
   put thisCard into line it + 1 of ¬
   card field "cards to print"
   pop card
end addCard
```

Script 26-7.   The addCard handler adds the ID of the current card to a list that is contained on a card called Print

```
on removeCard
  push this card
  put the id of this card into thisCard
  go to card "Print"
  repeat with x = 1 to the number of lines in¬
  card field "cards to print"
    if line x of card field "cards to print" is thisCard then
      delete line x of card field "cards to print"
    end if
  end repeat
  pop card
end removeCard
```

Script 26-8.   The removeCard handler removes a card from the list of cards to be printed

The removeCard handler in Script 26-8 removes a card from the list of cards to be printed. Like the addCard handler, it remembers where it came from and goes to the Print card. It repeats the process through the list of cards until it finds the card that is no longer to be printed. It removes that line and then returns.

The last element of this technique for marking cards to print is shown in Script 26-9. This handler is for a button called "Print cards" that is placed on the Print card. This button retrieves the list of the cards to be printed, goes to each card, and prints it in turn.

```
on mouseUp
  put card field "cards to print" into theCards
  open printing with dialog
  repeat with x = 1 to the number of lines in theCards
    go to line x of theCards
    print card
  end repeat
  close printing
end mouseUp
```

Script 26-9.   This handler prints the entire list of cards in the "Cards to print" field

The benefit of this approach is that it prints quickly. It doesn't need to cycle through each card in a stack to find out if it needs to print that card. Instead, it goes directly to each card to be printed and prints it. This is great when you have a large stack and are printing only a couple of cards.

On the other hand, it is a more complicated approach. It requires a separate card to maintain the list of cards to be printed, and when there are many cards to print, adding or removing a card from the list can slow down the process.

These procedures work for a stack, but it would not be hard to use them to build a special printing stack that would allow you to select cards from many different stacks, automatically add cards to the printing list based on specified text, and more. Implementing this approach would involve making sure that the name of the stack, as well as the ID of the card, is stored on each line.

Dialing

When writing applications, you can either use the Dial command itself, or simply use the Phone stack supplied with HyperCard.

The Dial Command

dial source [*with modem [modem parameters]*]

In the Dial command, "source" is any container of numbers that can be dialed. If you are using an actual phone number instead of a variable, remember to put quotes around the numbers so that HyperCard won't try to subtract the last four digits from the first three. You must also do that when you put the phone number into a variable.

If *with modem* is not specified, HyperCard will generate the tones necessary to dial the phone number, and you will be able to hear it being dialed. Usually you can then pick up your phone receiver and hold the mouthpiece next to the speaker of the Macintosh. You can also buy devices that connect the speaker output jack on the Macintosh to the phone, allowing you to dial directly. (Be careful with this device, however. If, for example, the phone rings while you are playing a game, the game sounds may be sent into the phone, and into the ears of both you and the person to whom you are talking.)

If you do specify *with modem*, HyperCard will use your modem to dial. The modem must be connected to the phone or modem connector on the back of the Macintosh. Make sure that the modem is connected. If you have another device, such as an ImageWriter, attached to that port, it will receive garbage characters that it cannot understand.

Modem parameters are commands that you can send to the modem to instruct it to work differently. If no modem parameters are used, the standard command of ATS0=0DT is used. This command sets the modem to use tones to dial. If your phone service does not permit tone dialing, specify ATS0=0DP for pulse dialing. The AT means "attention," and it precedes all modem commands.

All modem commands are sent to the modem *before* the number dialed.

Here are some sample modem commands. These are part of the AT, or Hayes-compatible command set. Each requires AT before it.

S0=0   Tells the modem not to answer the phone. If you specify a number other than 0 after the equal sign, the modem will answer the phone after that many rings

M   Turns the speaker off. Normally, the speaker is on until the modem has connected. This helps you to listen to the modem to make sure it is operating correctly

H   Tells the modem to hang up

+++   Means "Escape." This command gets the modem's attention while it is on line

The following codes can be inserted into a number and will give you more control over how you dial:

Tells the modem to pause. If you need to wait for an outside line when dialing, this comes in handy

@   Tells the modem to wait for silence

W   Tells the modem to wait for a second dial tone

For more information about these codes, consult your modem manual.

Using the Phone Stack

The Phone stack, included by Apple with HyperCard, can be used by any other stack as a universal dialer. This stack, shown in Figure 26-1, allows you to set your own preferences on how to dial—through the speaker, or through the modem with tone or pulse dialing. Since this stack is already written (and every HyperCard user should have it) there is no need to reinvent the wheel.

Using this stack from a script is simple. Script 26-10 shows a sample mouseUp handler that gets a phone number from the user, goes to the Phone stack, and dials, using the preferences in this stack.

This handler uses the Dial command, which is intercepted by the stack script of the Phone stack. The script then takes care of getting the user preferences, adding necessary prefixes, and the like. You can edit the script of the Phone stack to see how it works.

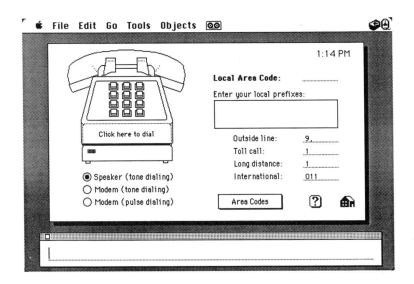

Figure 26-1.   The Phone stack allows the user to record dialing preferences for use by other stacks

```
on mouseUp
  ask "Phone number to dial?"
  if it is empty then exit mouseUp
  push this card
  go to stack "Phone"
  dial it
  pop card
end mouseUp
```

Script 26-10.   A sample handler for interfacing with the Phone stack supplied by Apple

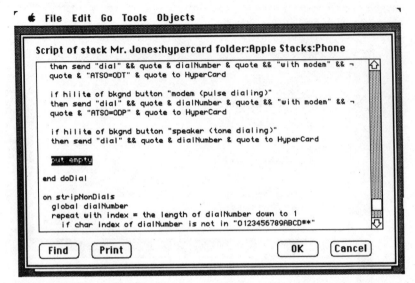

Figure 26-2.   Searching for "put empty" in the script of the Phone
                 stack finds this text

In the first release of this stack, there was a bug that
caused the modem to stay on line after someone answered the
phone at the other end, causing some aching ears as the
modem squealed into them. The bug is fixed in versions of
the stack shipped with HyperCard 1.1 and greater. If you
have an earlier version of the script, here's how to fix it:

1. With the Phone stack open, edit the script of the stack
by choosing Stack Info from the Objects menu.

2. Click the Find button, and search for the text "put
empty". Your screen should look like that shown in Figure 26-2.

```
wait 6 seconds
send "dial" & quote & empty & quote & "with modem" & quote ¬
& "+++ATH" & quote to HyperCard
```

Script 26-11.   A fix for the Phone stack shipped with the first version of HyperCard that tells the modem to hang up when someone answers the phone

3. Click on the line before "put empty", and type the lines shown in Script 26-11. These new lines tell Hyper-Card to dial an empty string with the modem and use the modem command +++ATH. The +++ gets the modem's attention, and ATH tells it to hang up the phone.

Managing Tools
and Menus

Managing Tools
Managing Menus

This chapter discusses selecting and using the different tools from script control. It also discusses using HyperCard's menu items from HyperTalk scripts.

Managing Tools

HyperTalk allows you to choose each of HyperCard's tools from within a script. This can be useful for a number of purposes. As discussed in Chapter 29, among the most commonly chosen are the painting tools, which are used to generate graphics under script control. However, you can also choose the Field and Button tools.

The Field and Button tools allow you to do at least one thing that you cannot otherwise do under script control: delete buttons and fields. There is no direct command for deleting a button or a field; therefore, you must first select the button or field by clicking on it with either the Field or Button tool and then using the Clear command with the doMenu command to delete a button or field.

For example, the mouseUp handler shown in Script 27-1 asks you to point at a button and then deletes that button.

```
on mouseUp
  put "Click on the button you want to delete"
  choose button tool
  wait until the mouseClick
  put the clickLoc into theLoc
  -- first check the card buttons
  repeat with x = the number of card buttons down to 1
    if theLoc is within the rect of card button x then
      click at the loc of card button x
      domenu "clear button"
      choose browse tool
      exit mouseUp
    end if
  end repeat
  -- now check the background buttons
  repeat with x = the number of bg buttons down to 1
    if theLoc is within the rect of bg button x then
      click at the loc of bg button x
      domenu "clear button"
      choose browse tool
      exit mouseUp
    end if
  end repeat
  choose browse tool
end mouseUp
```

Script 27-1.   This handler asks you to point at a button and then deletes that button

The script first chooses the Button tool, which makes all the background and card buttons visible. It then waits for you to click the mouse. When you have clicked the mouse, it saves the location at which you clicked into a variable called *theLoc*. Next, the script checks all the card buttons to see if the location at which you clicked falls within the area of the button.

Note: The loop proceeds through the card buttons in descending order, from the number of buttons down to 1. This is to allow for overlapping buttons. The button with the highest number will be deleted.

If the location at which you clicked falls within the rect of a button, the script selects the button by clicking with the Button tool at the button's location and then performs the Clear Button command with the doMenu command. The script then chooses the Browse tool and exits the mouseUp handler.

The same loop is performed for both card and background buttons. The last line of the script, "choose browse tool," returns you to the Browse tool if you did not click at the rectangle of a button.

You could easily modify this script to handle fields instead of buttons. However, if you are deleting background fields, there is no way to stop the dialog box shown in Figure 27-1 from appearing.

An alternate approach would involve using the Select command to select the button and then performing the Clear Button command.

Figure 27-1.   Deleting a background field summons this dialog box

The Choose Command

choose *<tool>* **tool**

This command makes the specified tool the current tool, just as if you had selected that tool from the Tools menu or palette with the mouse.

The Choose command is used frequently when painting from HyperTalk control; it will be discussed again in Chapter 29, which covers painting.

The Tool Function

the tool

tool( )

The Tool function returns the name of the tool currently in use. Script 27-2 is a short handler that you can place into the script of your Home stack that allows you to switch between the different tools by using the ENTER key:

```
on enterKey
  if the tool is "browse tool" then
    choose button tool
  else
    if the tool is "button tool" then
      choose field tool
    else
      if the tool is "field tool" then
        choose browse tool
      end if
    end if
  end if
end enterKey
```

Script 27-2.   If this handler is placed in the script of your Home stack, it allows you to switch between tools with the ENTER key

The Select Command

Select button|field

You saw in Chapter 21 how the Select command could be used to select chunks of text in fields or in the Message box. The Select command can also be used to select HyperCard buttons and fields. When you use a command such as

```
select card button 7
```

HyperCard switches to the Button tool and selects that button. This one command is equivalent to these two HyperTalk commands:

```
choose button tool
click at the loc of card button 7
```

The Select command can also be used to switch to the Field tool and select fields. If you need to select the text in a field and not the field itself, use this command:

```
select text of card field 1
```

Managing Menus

While HyperCard generally constitutes a complete tool for managing elements of the Macintosh user interface, it does not allow you to create your own pull-down menus. Some external functions and commands, discussed in Chapter 35, take up this slack.

HyperTalk does, however, include the doMenu command, which allows you to execute any command on a pull-down menu, just as if you had physically executed the command with the mouse. This is fortunate because several of those commands have no direct counterparts in HyperTalk.

You can also use the Type command to perform some of the menu commands.

The DoMenu Command

doMenu *menuItem*

The doMenu command performs the action of the pull-down menu command. This allows you to perform several operations for which there are no direct HyperTalk commands, including such things as compacting the stack and quitting HyperCard. Almost any HyperCard menu item can be executed with the doMenu command. The exception is choosing tools, which are on menus but are selected with the Choose command.

Note: If you execute a menu command that causes a dialog box or alert to appear (such as the Open Stack and Page Setup commands), control of the script will be halted the moment the dialog box appears. When you click the OK or Cancel button in any dialog box, control is returned to the script.

This has some profound effects on what you can do with functions you might like to control from within a script. For example, while you can execute the New Stack command from within a stack, you cannot control the name of the stack that is created. You must manually type the name of the stack into the dialog box. You also cannot control the setting of the Copy Current Background check box within that dialog box. The same is true of other menu items that summon dialog boxes or alerts.

If you select a menu item that is not currently available, you will get the error alert shown in Figure 27-2. You will also get this error alert if you incorrectly spell a menu item.

When you specify a menu item, you must give its complete name. Many of the commands on the File menu, as shown in Figure 27-3, include three periods after their names. These periods must be included in the doMenu command for the command to be executed. For example, this command will work:

```
domenu "new stack..."
```

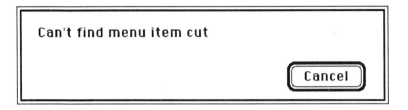

Can't find menu item cut

Cancel

Figure 27-2.   If you attempt to execute a menu command that is
grayed-out, this alert appears

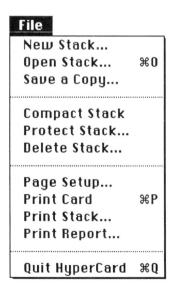

Figure 27-3.   When using the doMenu command, the three periods
that are part of the command name must be included,
as shown in this File menu

The following command will not work:

```
domenu "new stack"
```

Remember that on the Macintosh, the three periods after the command name indicate that the command summons a dialog box. Characters used to indicate the COMMAND-key shortcut for the command are not required.

Note: You can use the doMenu command with menu items that you might not consider to be part of HyperCard. This includes the Apple or Desk Accessory menu items, as well as those that are part of add-on programs, such as Tempo or the MacroMaker program that is included with Apple System's Update 6.0 and greater.

Here is a handler that, when placed into a button, summons the standard calculator from the Control Panel desk accessory:

```
on mouseUp
  domenu "calculator"
end mouseUp
```

Once the calculator appears, control of the Macintosh is passed to that desk accessory. When you close the desk accessory, control is passed to HyperCard.

You might encounter a problem when you have a set of commands in a script *after* a command that summons a desk accessory from a script. For example, if you include this script in a button

```
on mouseUp
  domenu "calculator"
  go card 7
  beep
end mouseUp
```

the last two commands in the script, **Go card 7** and Beep, will be executed *before* the calculator appears. HyperTalk senses that this command will cause control to pass from HyperCard to the desk accessory; therefore, it executes the remaining commands first. This only happens when you choose a menu item that causes a new program to be opened. It works the same way if you use the doMenu command to execute a command from the MacroMaker menu with System 6.0.

The File Menu

Only the PrintCard command on the File menu has a direct counterpart as a HyperTalk command. The functions of each of the other menu items must be performed with the doMenu command.

The Edit Menu

When using commands on the Edit menu, you must be aware that the Cut, Copy, Paste, and Clear commands will change their phrasing depending on what is currently selected or on the Clipboard.

For example, if you have selected text, the Cut and Copy commands will change to Cut Text and Copy Text. The Clear command will change to Clear Text. If you have a button or field selected (with the respective tools), these commands will change to reflect the object you have selected. The same is true of pictures if you are using the Select or Lasso tool.

The Paste item is a little harder to manage because you will not always know what is on the Clipboard. If your script performs a Paste command directly after a Copy or Cut command, the script can count on the Clipboard remaining the same. However, if these operations are performed in different handlers or different buttons, it is possible that the contents of the Clipboard will have been changed.

For example, if a script copies text and then exits, it cannot count on text remaining on the Clipboard. After the script ends, control is returned to you. You could, for example, switch to a paint tool and copy or cut a picture, thus replacing the text on the Clipboard with a picture. If a later script assumes the Clipboard still contains text, it will generate an error alert. You cannot trap this error in Hyper-Talk, nor is there any way to determine the contents of the Clipboard from within a script.

A related problem, not quite as serious, involves the selection. If you are pasting text into a field (or into the Message box), you first must be sure that the selection or insertion point is in the field into which you want to paste the text. If it is not, HyperCard will not perform the action, but will beep once. If the selection is within a field or the Message box and you paste a picture, HyperCard will switch to the Lasso or Select tool and paste the picture onto the card layer.

Note: Although there are separate items on the Edit menu for cutting, copying, deleting, and creating new cards, there is not a separate item for pasting cards. The standard Paste command changes to Paste Card if there is a card currently on the Clipboard.

If you have a card on the Clipboard and hold down the SHIFT key as you pull down the Edit menu, Paste Card changes to Paste Picture, which allows you to paste a small picture of the card on the Clipboard. You cannot use the doMenu command with a keyboard modifier, but you can use the Type command to type the keyboard equivalent of the Paste command, COMMAND-V, and modify it with the SHIFT key, as shown here:

```
type "v" with commandKey,shiftKey
```

The Go Menu

Commands on the Go menu are generally not used with the doMenu command. HyperTalk has equivalents that use the Go command for each item on the Go menu.

The Tools Menu

You cannot use the doMenu command with the Tools menu because the Tools menu does not contain any text items. To select tools, use the Choose command, discussed earlier in this chapter.

The Objects Menu

The commands on the Objects menu can all be performed with the doMenu command.

The first group of menu items—Field Info, Button Info, Card Info, Background Info, and Stack Info—all bring up Info dialog boxes for their respective objects, which are discussed in Chapter 3. Remember that when a dialog box appears, the script that summoned the dialog box stops executing until you click the Cancel or OK button in that dialog box.

Note: The Field Info and Button Info menu items will be grayed-out (disabled) if you are not using the Field or Button tool and if you have not selected a field or button. Before using one of these menu items, you must either choose the correct tool and click at the location of the button or field, or use the Select command, discussed earlier in this chapter.

Bring Closer and Send Farther Commands   Unfortunately there is no way to directly control the number of a field or a button. Instead, you must use the Bring Closer and Send Farther commands to change the ordering of the button or field on a background or card. Before you can use these commands, you must have currently selected a field or button, just as when you are using the Button Info and Field Info commands.

Each time you execute the Bring Closer command, 1 is added to the number of the selected card or field. For example, if you have selected card button 1, the number of that button will be 2 after executing the Bring Closer command.

If you select card button 7 and there are only 7 buttons on the card, the number of the button will not change, and no error will result.

The Send Farther command is the opposite of the Bring Closer command: it decreases button's number.

Button order controls the appearance of buttons on the card. If two buttons overlap, the button with the *larger* number will be on top of the button with the smaller number. If the top button is opaque, it will hide the lower buttons. It will also be the button that first receives button-related messages.

Field order controls the appearance of fields, just as the button order does with buttons. It also controls the order in which the fields are selected with the TAB key. If no field is currently selected, the TAB key selects the first field. Each time you press the TAB key, the next field in order is selected.

New Button Command   The New Button command on the Objects menu behaves differently when you use it with the doMenu command than it does when you use it manually with the mouse.

When you create a new button with the mouse, that button is not named; it will be a transparent button, and the showName and autoHilite properties will be set to "false." However, when you use the doMenu New Button command, the new button will be named New Button. The showName property will be set to "true," the new button will be a rounded rectangle button, and its location will be at the center of the card.

If the editBackground is "true" when you use this command, the button created will be a background button; otherwise it will be a card button.

When using the New Button command from a script, HyperCard implicitly executes the **Choose button tool** command first. After you have executed the New Button command, you should change back to the Browse tool, with the command **Choose browse tool.**

New Field Command   The New Field menu item creates a new five-line transparent field in the center of the card. The field will not be automatically named. If editBackground is in effect when you use this command, the field created will be a background field; otherwise it will be a card field.

The Paint Menus

All items from the Paint menus (with the exception of the Patterns palette) can be chosen in three ways: with the doMenu command, by setting paint properties, or with power keys. Paint menu items and painting from HyperTalk are discussed in Chapter 29.

The Type Command

Another way to perform menu actions is to use the Type command. You can quickly perform many of the HyperCard menu commands from the keyboard using the COMMAND key along with another key. For example, the keyboard equivalent for the Home command under the Go menu is COMMAND-H. You can use this shortcut from a script, as in the command

```
type "h" with commandKey
```

This shortcut is not used often, but as previously mentioned, you can use it to perform a paste operation that you could not otherwise perform.

Script-Related Commands and Functions

The Do Command
Scripts and Objects
The Parameter Functions

The commands and functions discussed in this chapter relate to scripts themselves. The Do command allows you to build and execute commands as a script is executing. The Target function and the "Me" object allow you to determine which object received a message and which object contains the current script. The parameter functions allow a handler or function to determine how many parameters were passed to it.

The Do Command

Do *<task>*

The Do command executes the command that is specified in *task*. The command specified in *task* must be a HyperCard command that is complete on one line.

There are some commands that you cannot use with the Do command. You are limited to the same commands you can enter in the Message box. This means that you cannot use structures that require two or more lines, such as the Repeat structure or If structures because they imply a second line.

Another command you cannot execute with either the Message box or the Do command is the Global command. If you type **Global thisVariable** into the Message box, you will get the error alert shown in Figure 28-1. If you attempt to use the command

```
do "global thisVariable"
```

in a script, you get the same error alert.

A good use of the Do command is in constructing stacks in which you need to execute a number of commands automatically. The stacks can include presentation stacks that use visual effects and sounds to show different cards. You can put all the commands in openStack or openCard handlers, but debugging these handlers is a little difficult, as is stopping them once they have started. While a complete implementation would go on for some time, here is a short example of how you can use the Do command using a card with one field and one button:

1. Create a new card to experiment with.

2. Create a field on that card called "Tasks." Since you might want to execute a large number of tasks, make it

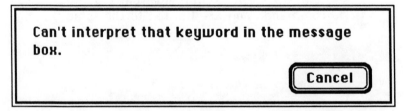

Figure 28-1.   The error alert that appears when you use the Global command in the Message box or with the Do command

a scrolling field by checking the Scrolling check box on the Field Info dialog box.

3. Now create a button to perform the commands you enter into the "Tasks" field. Double-click the button to get the Field Info dialog box, and name the button Do It. Since the button is to work with text selected in the "Tasks" field, make sure the autoHilite check box on the Button Info dialog box is *not* checked.

The "Tasks" field and the Do It button are shown in Figure 28-2.

4. With the Button Info dialog box on the screen, click the Script button to enter the editor. Enter Script 28-1 into the editor.

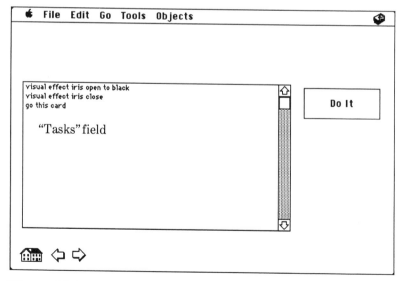

Figure 28-2.   A card illustrating the "Tasks" field, into which you type commands, and the Do It button, used to execute them

```
on mouseUp
  put the selection into theTasks
  if theTasks is empty then
    put card field "tasks" into theTasks
  end if
  repeat with x = 1 to the number of lines in theTasks
    do line x of theTasks
  end repeat
end mouseUp
```

Script 28-1.   Placed in a button, this script executes all the commands you have typed into a card field called "Tasks"

This script is fairly simple. It puts the text selected—which should be in the field "Tasks"—into the variable *theTasks*. If there is no selection, it then puts all the commands in the field "Tasks" into *theTasks*. Next, for each line in *theTasks*, it executes the Do command on that line.

This field/button combination is interesting to work with and allows you to experiment to find what combinations of things you can do with the Do command. You can build up a large list of instructions to be performed and test all of them by simply clicking the button with nothing selected, or you can test only certain lines in the field by selecting those lines and then clicking the button.

Scripts and Objects

HyperTalk includes tools for determining which HyperCard object received the message that the current script is handling. This is useful for a number of purposes; for example, you can more easily write generic handlers.

The Target Function

the target

target( )

The Target function returns a phrase identifying the object that received the message to which the current handler is responding.

Typing **the target** into the Message box always yields the name of the current card because the current card is the first receiver of all messages sent with the Message box.

The Target function allows you to take some shortcuts in HyperTalk programming. You might, for example, have a card containing a number of buttons whose functions are slightly different depending on the name of the button. Instead of putting essentially the same handler in every button script, you can place a mouseUp handler in the script of the card. This script then tests for the name of the target and acts accordingly. This technique is illustrated in Chapter 30, which includes a method for creating a piano keyboard and playing different notes based on the name of the button clicked.

For example, suppose you have a card that contains a map of the world, with a button for each country. Other cards contain more detailed views of each country. These cards would be named after the country they represent. Instead of individually linking each button to the specific card, you merely name the buttons with the name of the country to which they link. You could place the mouseUp handler shown in Script 28-2 into the script of the card containing the world map.

```
on mouseUp
  if "button" is not in the name of the target then
   exit mouseUp
  end if
  get the short name of the target
  go card it
end mouseUp
```

Script 28-2. When placed into a card script, this mouseUp handler goes to a card that has the same name as a button

This handler first tests to make sure you clicked a button and did not click on the card itself. If you did click a button, this handler gets the short name of the target—which represents the button you clicked—and goes to that card.

The Target and Fields

With version 1.2 or greater, you can use the term "target" to refer not to the field itself, but to the *contents* of the field.

When you use the Target function, it refers to the field itself. When you use just "target," it refers to the *contents* of the field. In versions of HyperCard earlier than 1.2, there was no easy way to refer to the contents of a field rather than the field itself.

Here is an example that illustrates the difference:

```
put the target
put target
```

The first line puts the *name* of the field that received the original message into the Message box. The second line puts the *contents* of the field that received the message into the Message box.

Note that "target" works *only* when the target is a field. If the target is a button, card, background, or stack, the script of that object will treat the word "target" as a variable.

The "Me" Object

"Me" is a special object that refers to the object containing the script that is currently executing, unlike the Target function, in which the target is the object that received the message.

In the previous example of the world map, the target is the button that was actually clicked. If you were to put a line such as

```
put the short name of me
```

into the mouseUp handler in the card script, it would put the name of the card, not the button, into the Message box.

"Me" and Fields

In versions of HyperCard prior to 1.2, "Me" always referred to the name or identifier of the container, never to the contents of the container. Just as the target function has changed with version 1.2, so has the function of the "Me" special object.

If the object containing a script is a field, you can then work with the value contained in that field using "Me." With "Me," you can refer to the contents of the field for such things as checking text entry into the field, getting the value of the field, and putting it into a variable. Here are two examples of using "Me" in the script of a field:

```
put the date into me -- puts the date into the field
put me into theVariable -- puts field text into theVariable
```

The Parameter Functions

The parameter functions allow handlers and functions to determine which parameters were passed to them, even if they were not specifically designed to receive parameters. Using these functions gives you more flexibility in writing some scripts.

The Params Function

the params

params( )

This function returns all the elements that were in use when the current handler was called. It returns several items; the exact number depends on the number of parameters that were sent to the handler or function.

The first word that the Params function returns is the name of the handler or script that the Params function is in. The second word will be the first parameter that was passed to the handler. Succeeding parameters are separated by commas, and the parameters are enclosed in quotes.

For example, suppose you use the line

```
testParams 1,2,3
```

where testParams is the name of a handler. You have called this handler and passed to it three parameters. If you include the line

```
put the params
```

in the testParams handler, then it will put the following into the Message box:

```
testParams "1","2","3"
```

The paramCount Function

the paramCount

paramCount( )

The paramCount function returns the number of parameters that were passed to the current handler or function.

The Param Function

the param of *number*

param(*number*)

The Param function allows you to access specific parameters that were passed to the function or handler containing the function. For example, if you want to use the value in the second parameter, you could use either of these lines:

```
the param of 2
param(2)
```

When the function is typed as **the param of 0**, the name of the current handler is returned, allowing you to work with the name of the current handler within that handler.

Using the Parameters Functions

There are several applications for the parameters functions, though their use is fairly rare. You can create functions or handlers that can take a varying number of parameters. Normally, when designing handlers, you specify on the first line of the handler what parameters that handler or function can take and assign variable names to them. However, assigning variable names on this line can be a nuisance, especially if you want the handler or function to be able to take many parameters.

The parameter functions also allow you to discover

whether the proper number of parameters were passed to the handler. Suppose you have written a handler that needs five parameters to operate, and you want the handler to be able to return an error message if more than or fewer than five parameters were passed to the handler. The following script fragment would take care of this:

```
if the paramCount ≠ 5 then
   answer the param of 0 && "needs 5 parameters"
end if
```

This fragment tests to see if the number of parameters was five. If not, it uses the Answer dialog box to tell you what handler was called and that it needs five parameters.

The parameters functions also are useful in debugging. If you have a handler that is not functioning correctly, you can insert a line such as

```
put the params
```

directly after the first line of the handler. This allows you to see exactly what variables were passed to that handler and perhaps get you one step closer to figuring out what went wrong.

If you have a complex script, you could create a global variable called, perhaps, *theHandlers*, which could contain a list of all the handlers that were called during execution of a series of scripts. Declare this global with the following line in each handler in all the scripts that you want to monitor:

```
global theHandlers
```

Directly after this line, you could place the parameters into the variable. Later, you could examine this global variable by putting it into a field, and you could determine exactly which handlers were called, in what order, and which parameters were passed to them. The following line would place the parameters of the current handler after the global *theHandlers:*

```
put the params into line ¬
(the number of lines in theHandlers +1) of theHandlers
```

Unfortunately there is no easy way to have all scripts automatically place their parameters into this global variable. You will have to edit all the scripts you want to monitor and place them there manually.

Painting

Managing Tools
Locking the Screen and Card
Some Scripts

Chapter 27 discussed manipulating the various HyperCard tools from script control. This chapter will go into more detail about using the painting tools from scripts.

Painting from within a script is one of HyperCard's most interesting abilities. The Macintosh, of course, has always been a graphics computer. From the beginning, programs such as MacPaint have used the machine's unique graphic abilities. But if you wanted to do such things as plot functions from within MacPaint, you were out of luck. HyperCard's ability to control painting by HyperTalk scripts gives you the power to plot functions, create customized charting applications, do some limited animation, and more.

Managing Tools

The Click, Drag, and other commands discussed in Chapter 27 can be used to control the painting tools you are using and to move the cursor around the screen in order to paint.

The Choose Tool Command

You can select the tool you want to use with the Choose Tool command.

One annoyance about using the painting tools from within a script is that the mouse pointer will change to the symbol that relates to the tool you are using and will stay visible on the screen while the tool is in use. For example, if you are using the Oval, Rectangle, Rounded Rectangle, or related tool, the mouse pointer will be a cross, and this cross will be visible while these tools are selected. You are permitted to use the Set Cursor command to change the Cursor's appearance while a paint tool is chosen, but it will have no effect on the screen. HyperCard will, in effect, ignore the Set Cursor command.

You should also note that while you are using one of the painting tools, visual effects will not be shown on the screen. If you need to use a visual effect when going to another card or showing the screen, you must first choose the Browse tool.

Drawing

To actually draw on the screen, you must use the Drag or Click commands, which simulate the physical activity of the mouse.

The Drag Command

Drag from *location1* to *location2* <with *keyModifier*>

The Drag command simulates pointing to one location, holding down the mouse button, and dragging the mouse to another location. The variables *location1* and *location2* are sets of two numbers separated by a comma. The first number specifies the number of pixels from the left edge of the screen, and the second specifies the number of pixels from the top of the screen. Both these numbers must be integers; if you attempt to use numbers that have values to the right of the decimal point, HyperTalk will give you a "Can't understand" error alert and abort execution of the script.

The optional *keyModifier* allows you to specify a modifier key to be used with the drag command. Allowable key modifiers are *shiftKey*, *commandKey*, and *optionKey*. You can use several key modifiers by separating them with a comma. For example, *shiftKey* causes the Rectangle tool to constrain its drawings to squares, and *optionKey* causes this tool to draw the line in the current pattern. Therefore, to draw a square with a patterned border, you can use a line such as this:

```
drag from 256,171 to 300,300 with shiftKey,optionKey
```

This would produce a square in the center of the screen with a patterned border.

The speed at which the dragging takes place is governed by the dragSpeed property. The dragSpeed property sets the number of pixels that the tool moves per second. When the dragSpeed property is set at 0 (the default), dragging is almost instantaneous.

There are several painting tools that are not very useful when working with the Drag command. For example, the Lasso, Curve, and Polygon tools will essentially draw straight lines when you use them with the Drag command. The Drag and command can be used only to drag from one location to another, and when the Drag command has finished executing, the mouse button is released. With these tools, however, dragging is continuous to a number of different locations, not just from one point to another.

The Click Command

Click at *location*

The Click command simulates the action of moving the mouse to a specific location and clicking the button. As with the Drag command, *location* is a set of two numbers separated by a comma. Both numbers must be integers or Hyper-Card will abort the script with an error alert.

With most of the painting tools—including the Line, Rectangle, Oval, Rounded Rectangle, and Regular Polygon tools—the Click command will cause a dot to be placed at the location you specify.

When you are using the Lasso tool, a Click command such as

```
click at 256,171 with commandKey
```

will cause any enclosed object that surrounds the specified point to be selected by the Lasso tool.

The userLevel Property

Before you can use any painting tools from script control, you must be sure that the userLevel property is set to at least 3—the Painting level. If you attempt to use a painting tool while the userLevel is set to less than 3, you will get the error alert shown in Figure 29-1.

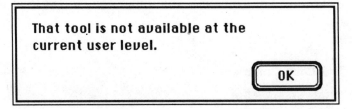

Figure 29-1.   If you attempt to use a painting tool with a user Level that is too low, you get this alert

Here is a script fragment that allows any script to get the value of userLevel and set it to Painting if the user level is set too low:

```
if the userLevel < 3 then
  put the userLevel into saveLevel
  set the userLevel to 3
end if
```

This fragment first tests to discover if the user level is less than 3. If it is, it then saves the value of userLevel into a variable called *saveLevel* and sets userLevel to 3 to allow use of the painting tools. Before the script has finished executing, this line resets the user level:

```
set userLevel to saveLevel
```

Remember, however, if you are going to use the *saveLevel* variable in multiple handlers, you will want to make sure that it is a global variable.

Memory Requirements of Painting Tools

Another potential problem occurs when HyperCard is running in less than its desired 750K of RAM. This can happen if the stack is being run on a 1MB Macintosh without Multi-Finder and if other programs, such as the RAM cache on the Control Panel, are using some of the memory. It can also occur if you have changed the amount of memory allocated to HyperCard in MultiFinder to less than 750K. In either of these cases, it is possible that HyperCard will not have enough memory to use the painting tools, and you will get the error alert shown in Figure 29-2.

Unfortunately, there is no absolutely reliable method for testing to see if there is enough RAM available to HyperCard for the painting tools. While the heapSpace property might seem to be a good candidate for determining if there is enough memory, testing has shown that it is not entirely reliable. Probably the best procedure is to include in the docu-

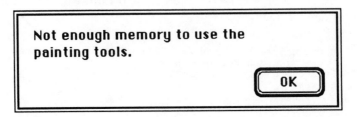

Figure 29-2.   This alert appears if HyperCard does not have enough RAM to use the painting tools

mentation or notes for your stack an indication that it uses the painting tools and thus needs HyperCard's minimum amount of memory to execute.

Locking the Screen and Card

If it is not important to you that you see the process of drawing as it is taking place, you can lock the screen while the drawing is taking place, and then unlock it when the drawing is finished. As discussed in Chapter 20, you can unlock the screen with a visual effect for special purposes.

You can also lock the stack by setting the cantModify property of that stack to "true" when drawing on the card. When this property is "true," you are prohibited from painting on a card or background. However, scripts *can* use the painting tools to draw on the card. All new painting on that card or background will be lost, however, when you go to a different card.

This is actually a benefit to the developer who wants to paint on cards under script control. You can use it when you want to do some drawing on a card and make sure that the card is saved in its original form for later use.

For example, you can use Script 29-1 to draw growing circles in the middle of a card for some special effect, and then make those circles disappear from the card.

The Revert Command

The Revert command discards changes you have made to a card. Since it is a menu command rather than a HyperTalk command, you must use the doMenu command to execute it:

```
doMenu "Revert"
```

The Revert command discards any changes you have made to the card since you last used the Keep command or otherwise saved the changes to the card.

The Keep Command

The Keep command saves the changes you have made to the card. Since Keep is a menu item rather than a HyperTalk

```
on mouseUp
  set cantModify of this stack to true
  choose oval tool
  set drawCentered to true
  repeat 10
    drag from 256,171 to 356,271
  end repeat
  set cantModify of this stack to false
end mouseUp
```

Script 29-1.   This script draws a circle in the middle of the screen, demonstrating the cantModify property of a stack

command, you must use it with the doMenu command like this:

```
domenu "keep"
```

Since the Keep command on the Paint menu has the keyboard shortcut COMMAND-K, you can also execute this command with the Type command:

```
type "k" with commandKey
```

If the cantModify property of the stack is "true," HyperCard will ignore the Keep command.

The Reset Paint Command

The Reset Paint command resets all the painting properties to their default values. Table 29-1 shows the default values for all the painting properties. If you have changed a number of properties and want to restore them, use this command, which will allow either a script or you to know what the properties will be when you use them later.

Some Scripts

There are few limits to what you can do with HyperCard's painting tools. Here are some scripts for handling such things as simple animation and drawing arcs and triangles.

Animation

One of the most interesting uses of HyperCard's painting tools under script control is animation. There are a number of ways you can do animation in HyperCard. For example,

Property	Default Value
Grid	False
Powerkeys	Reverts to setting on User Preferences card in the Home stack
lineSize	1
Brush	8
Pattern	12 (black)
Filled	False
Centered	False
Multiple	False
textAlign	Left
textFont	Geneva
dragSpeed	0

Table 29-1.   Default Values for the Painting Properties

you can create a background that includes the background against which the animation is played, and then create cards that have the individual, moving elements on them. Quickly flipping from card to card can create the illusion of animation.

That process, however, is not as satisfactory as it could be. There is a certain amount of overhead that is required when storing different cards. Also, if you have complex animation sequences, managing the different elements could be difficult.

One solution is to use the Lasso or Select tool to move painted objects around the screen. These tools work well, with some limitations. The Select tool, for example, selects rectangular areas of the picture, so if you are going to animate a part of a picture, you must make sure that it can be easily enclosed within a specified rectangle. The Lasso tool is more useful. If you click inside an enclosed object with the COMMAND key held down, the entire object is selected; simply make sure that the object you want to animate is not connected to other graphics on the card.

With that in mind, here is a simple way you can create a card to experiment with some animation from scripts. It might seem to be a long process, but it's not too difficult, and it should be easy to transport these techniques to other stacks.

1. Create a new card. You can put the new card in a new stack of its own, or in an existing stack.

2. As shown in Figure 29-3, on card 4 of the Art Ideas stack that comes with HyperCard, there is a small picture of a frog. Use the Lasso tool to manually copy this

Figure 29-3.   Card 4 of the Art Ideas stack

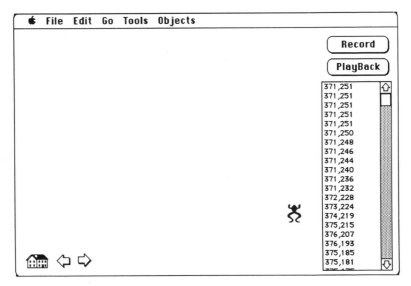

Figure 29-4.   A card for experimenting with frog animation

frog and paste it onto the card you created in the first step.

3. On the new card, create two buttons. Name one Record; it will allow you to record a path for the frog to move around the screen. Name the second Playback; it will actually do the animation. Also create a scrolling field called "Moves." For now you should leave this field visible, but you can hide it later. Figure 29-4 shows this simple card.

4. Type the handler shown in Script 29-2 into the Record button.

5. Type the handler shown in Script 29-3 into the Playback button.

```
on mouseUp
  put empty into theMoves
  put "Click on the item you want to animate..."
  wait until the mouseClick
  put "Hold down the button and drag.  Let go when done"
  wait until the mouse is down
  repeat until the mouse is up
    put return & the mouseLoc after theMoves
  end repeat
  delete first line of theMoves
  put theMoves into card field "moves"
end mouseUp
```

Script 29-2. This is the script for a button called Record

When you click the Record button, the script first asks you to click on the item you want to animate. In this case it is the frog. After you click on the frog, you are then prompted

```
on mouseUp
  set cantModify of this stack to true
  choose lasso tool
  put card field "moves" into theMoves
  click at line 1 of theMoves with commandKey
  put line 1 of theMoves into oldLoc
  repeat with x = 1 to the number of lines in theMoves
    if the mouseClick then exit repeat
    drag from oldLoc to line x of theMoves
    put line x of theMoves into oldLoc
  end repeat
  choose browse tool
  set cantModify of this stack to false
end mouseUp
```

Script 29-3. This script is for the Playback button

to hold down the mouse button and move the mouse around the screen. As you move the mouse, the locations over which you pass are recorded. When you release the mouse button, these locations are stored in the "Moves" field.

To see your animation, click the Playback button. The script first chooses the Lasso tool and clicks at the location of the item you wanted to animate, which is stored as the first line in the "Moves" field. It then drags from one location to the next in turn, and you see the frog move around the screen.

Note: The Playback button first sets the cantModify property of the stack to "true" to ensure that the next time you use the Playback button, the frog will be in the same location it was before. This sort of animation is of limited use for complicated animations (it is virtually impossible to animate several pictures at the same time with this technique).

Drawing Arcs

One of the things you can do from scripts that you cannot easily do by hand is create precise drawings. For example, if you want to draw just a part of an arc of a circle, the only way to do this manually is to draw a circle with the Oval tool by holding down the SHIFT key as you draw, and then erasing the part of the circle that you don't want. However, it is difficult to be precise about this sort of drawing.

With that in mind, here are two handlers that work together to draw arcs. The drawRadius handler, shown in Script 29-4, draws a line of a specified radius from a central point to the edge of a circle at a specified number of degrees. The second draws an arc of specified degrees on the edge of a circle.

The drawRadius handler takes four arguments. The first two are the variables *hCenter* and *vCenter*, which specify the point in the middle of the screen that will be the center of the circle: *hCenter* indicates the number of pixels from

```
on drawRadius hCenter,vCenter,radius,degs
  put (degs * pi / 180) into degs -- convert to radians
  put round(hCenter+ cos(degs) * radius) into theX
  put round(vCenter+ sin(degs) * radius) into theY
  drag from hCenter,vCenterto theX,theY
end drawRadius
```

Script 29-4.   This handler draws a radius at a specified angle

the left edge of the screen, and *vCenter* indicates the number of pixels from the top of the screen. The *radius* variable specifies the radius of the circle. The *degs* variable specifies the point on the circle in degrees at which the radius will be drawn. Before using this handler, any scripts you write should choose the correct tool. Since drawRadius uses the Drag command to draw the radius, you should use the Pencil, Line, or Brush tool.

The first thing the handler does is convert the specified degrees to radians, as discussed in Chapter 22. It does this by multiplying the degrees by pi and dividing the result by 180.

Next, the handler uses the cosine and sine functions to determine the point on the screen to which the line is drawn. The radius is multiplied by the cosine of the degrees, and that is added to *hCenter* to get the horizontal point to which the line will be drawn. The radius is then multiplied by the sine of the degrees and added to *vCenter* to get the vertical point. Next, the Drag command simply drags from the center of the circle to the point defined in the last two calculations.

Figure 29-5 shows a line produced by this handler by using the Line tool. The following was used to draw this line:

```
drawRadius 256,171,100,90
```

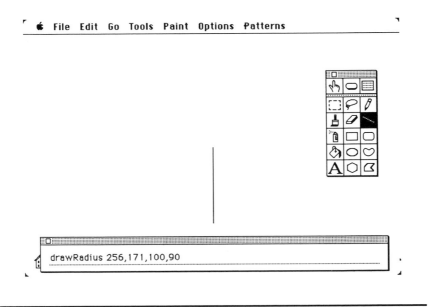

Figure 29-5.   A line produced with the Line tool

The handler drew a line from 256,171 (the center of the Hyp-erCard window), 100 pixels long, at a 90° angle. This indicates that using an angle of 0° would produce a line that is horizontal. To see why this is so, step through the calculations that the handler performs:

1. Converting degrees to radians is handled by the line

   Put (*degs* * pi / 180) into *degs*

   In this case, since the *degs* variable is 90, the line is

   90 * pi / 180

   which yields 1.570796.

2. Calculating the horizontal position is handled by the line

Put round($hCenter$ + cos($degs$) * radius) into $theX$

By substituting the actual values, this line evaluates to

round(256 + cos(1.570796) * 100)

Since the cosine of 1.570796 is 0, and 0 multiplied by 100 is 0, then the horizontal location is still 256.

3. Calculating the vertical position is handled by the next line

Put round($vCenter$ + sin($degs$) * $radius$) into $theY$

Substituting actual values for variable names results in

171 + sin(1.570796) * 100)

The sine of 1.570796 is 1. Multiply 1 by 100, add that to 171, and you get 271—the vertical location.

4. After executing these two lines, the variable $theX$ contains 256, and the variable $theY$ contains 271. The Drag command in the handler then drags from 256,171 (the $hCenter$ and $vCenter$ variables) to 256,271, which draws a straight, horizontal line because the horizontal location does not change.

For an example of how the drawRadius handler can be used, consult the script of the Pie button on the Plots stack that was included with HyperCard.

The drawArc handler in Script 29-5 is similar to the drawRadius handler in several ways. It takes the same parameters as drawRadius, and in addition takes one more: $start$, which specifies the point on the circle at which to start drawing the arc.

The repeat loop at the core of this handler performs the same trigonometric calculations for each point on the arc it is drawing. Instead of drawing a line from the center of the

```
on drawArc xcenter,yCenter,radius,start,degs
  choose brush tool
  set brush to 28
  put empty into oldX
  repeat with x = start to start + degs
    if the mouseClick then exit repeat
    put (x * pi / 180) into theRads
    put round(xcenter + cos(theRads) * radius) into theX
    put round(yCenter + sin(theRads) * radius) into theY
    if oldX is empty then
      put theX into oldX
      put theY into oldY
    end if
    drag from oldX,oldY to theX,theY
    put theX into oldX
    put theY into oldY
  end repeat
end drawArc
```

Script 29-5.   This handler draws an arc

circle, however, it draws lines between points on the arc to one another. The most recent point it calculated is stored in the *oldX* and *oldY* variables, and each time it calculates a new point it draws a line between the old locations and the new ones.

Drawing Triangles

The drawTri handler in Script 29-6 takes five parameters. The first are the variables *xcenter* and *ycenter*, which specify the location of the triangle on the screen. The variable *side1* specifies the length of one side of the triangle, the *angle* variable specifies the angle between two sides of the triangle, and the *side2* variable specifies the length of the second leg of the triangle.

```
on drawTri xcenter,ycenter,side1,angle,side2
  put (angle * pi / 180) into theRads
  drag from xcenter,ycenter to xcenter + side1,yCenter
  put round(xCenter + cos(theRads) * side2) into theX
  put round(yCenter + sin(theRads) * side2) into theY
  drag from xCenter,yCenter to theX,theY
  drag from theX,theY to xCenter + side1, yCenter
end drawTri
```

Script 29-6.   This script draws a triangle based on two sides and their enclosed angle

The handler converts the angle measure to radians and then draws the first side of the triangle. Next, it draws the second side of the triangle, using the same calculations as those used in drawArc to determine where the second side will end. The third side of the triangle is drawn simply by connecting the end of *side1* with *side2*. Experimentation with this handler will allow you to precisely place the triangles on the screen.

Sound and Music

**T
H
I
R
T
Y**

The Macintosh, with its built-in four-voice sound synthesizer, was one of the first microcomputers to feature sound capabilities beyond a small speaker that was clicked at various speeds to make various tones. Early in the history of the machine, programs began to appear that generated specific tones. Some early games were fascinating because of their high-quality digitized sound. It was not until HyperCard, however, that sophisticated sound tools were offered to the average user to include in self-made programs.

Using Sound

There are two uses of sound in HyperCard. The first is as an *alert*, or warning. Beeps are played to warn you of destructive actions or to alert you that a long operation has been completed.

The second use of sound is as the subject of the stack. There are stacks available that are nothing more than collections of sampled sounds. Collections of sampled sounds are available from sources such as groups and on-line services. This use of sound is not discussed in this text.

Perhaps the most important factor in using sound as a warning or alert is restraint. There are probably few things more irritating than using a program that beeps too often. Sound used too often as a warning becomes something like the boy who cried wolf—eventually the user ignores the sound, and the warning is rendered useless. Remember that the Macintosh user can turn off the sound with the Control Panel. When this is done, all the warning sounds issued by the program go unheard and unheeded, although the menu bar flashes.

On standard Macintosh Plus and SE computers, the standard system beep is normally a plain tone—the kind that is sounded when the machine is turned on. On the Macintosh II, this beep can consist of several different kinds of sounds. The System file on the Macintosh II contains several alternate beeps—for example, a monkey chirp or a clang—that the user can set as the standard system beep. Other sounds can be installed into the System file to suit the user's preference. There are several ShareWare and public domain programs available for the Mac Plus and Mac SE that also allow the user to choose the sound of the beep.

What this means for the HyperTalk programmer, and all programmers, is that you should not make any assumptions about the beep. Certain digitized sounds can have unpleasant effects if they are beeped more than once or twice.

Few standards have emerged in the use of beeps on the Macintosh. Some programs rarely, if ever, beep at the user. Some sound one beep to note that an operation is finished. Others sound two beeps when displaying a dialog box that confirms a potentially destructive action.

There are two ways that standard Macintosh applications use beeps:

• **Alerts**   Alert sounds usually accompany a dialog box. They notify the user that some additional information is needed or that the user is about to perform some destructive act, such as deleting some data that is not recoverable. Some programs sound two beeps in this case, emphasizing the importance of the dialog box.

• **Getting Attention** A single beep can get the attention of the user when a lengthy process is finished. One beep is usually sufficient to get the user's attention.

Here are some tips about using sound:

• **Don't go overboard** Remember too many sounds become more irritating than informative. Exercise some restraint about how and when to use alert sounds.

• **Provide a way for the user to turn the sounds off** If your application does use a lot of sounds, provide some way for the user to turn them off. You might have a Preferences card, like the one in the Home stack, that has a check box for sounds. A script could check to see if the user wants sounds in this manner:

```
global doSounds
if the hilite of card button "Use Sounds" is true then
   put true into doSounds
else
   put false into doSounds
end if
```

Now you can include the following lines in any handler that plays sounds:

```
global doSounds
if doSounds is true then beep
```

This gives the user the choice of whether or not sounds are used.

- **Be unobtrusive**   Avoid excessive use of "jingles." The little tune that is appealing the first couple of times can be irritating after thirty times.

- **Provide an alternative warning**   A sound is not enough of a warning for all users. Those who have trouble hearing might not notice the sound. Dialog boxes provide a visual and modal warning, but for certain other things, such as clicking on a button, visual cues such as highlighting the button would be enough.

- **Storage requirements**   Remember that sounds make a lot of demands on disk storage. This will be discussed in greater detail later in the chapter, but it bears reiterating. Consider whether the value added to your application by the sound is worth its space on disk.

All this should not scare you away from using sounds. Remember that sounds can add a great deal to the Macintosh user interface and can help provide a lot of information to the user.

Where Do Sounds Come from?

Sounds are stored in resources, as are many things on the Macintosh, including icons, cursors, and dialog boxes. Hyper-Card stacks (including the Home stack), HyperCard itself, and the Macintosh System file can all include sounds. In HyperCard, sounds that are part of the current stack, the Home stack, and HyperCard can be played by HyperCard. When shipped by Apple, HyperCard includes three sounds: Harpsichord, Boing, and Silence. (The last of these is not a "sound" at all, but it is there, and you can play it anyway. It just doesn't do anything.) Sounds such as these are called sampled, or digitized, sounds.

Sampled Sounds

One of the most useful things a Macintosh can do is record sounds, which are stored on the disk in digital form (similar to the way sounds are stored on a compact disk). There are several devices available that do this. They generally take the form of a small device that connects to one of the serial interface ports on the Macintosh. They usually feature a small microphone and/or jacks, which you can use to connect them to another microphone or a tape record. Software that comes with them "listens" to the sounds from the microphone and records digital versions of these on your disk. Most of these applications will also include tools for editing the sound—erasing parts that you don't want, reversing sounds, changing their tone or pitch, and so on.

Once you have recorded these sounds, you can install them into HyperCard and use the Play command to play them.

The Beep Command

Beep *count*

This command plays the current system beep *count* times. *Count* can be any number or any expression that evaluates to a number. If *count* is not specified, it defaults to a value of 1.

As opposed to sampled sounds that can be installed into HyperCard or stacks, the beep should be used as an alert.

The Play Command

Play *"soundName"* <tempo number> "notes to play"

SoundName is any sound resource that is installed in the current stack, the Home stack, or in HyperCard itself. If a resource by that name is not found, then no sound is played.

SoundName can be a HyperCard expression that evaluates to a sound or the actual name of the sound. If it evaluates to the name of the sound, *soundName*, it must be placed in quotes, as shown, so that HyperCard does not try to evaluate it.

tempo number is a number that indicates how fast the sounds are to be played. Normal, or medium speed, is 100. Numbers higher than 100 cause the notes to be played faster; numbers lower than 100 cause them to be slower. If the number is 1, the notes are played at an extremely slow pace. If the number is 0, they are played at the normal pace. If no tempo is specified, the tempo used the last time Play was called is used, unless this is the first time Play is used, in which case it uses the default value of 100.

Notes to play specifies the notes to be played in the following manner:

"noteName accidental octave duration"

Where the following are true:

• *NoteName* is the note played.

• *Accidental* is # for sharp, b for flat.

• *Octave* specifies the pitch of the scale (4 is the middle octave).

• *Duration* is one of the following:

w	whole note
h	half note
q	quarter note
e	eighth note
s	sixteenth note
t	thirty-second note
x	sixty-fourth note

• Each of these durations can be followed by a period (.) to indicate a dotted note or a 3 to indicate a triplet.

Note: There is another way to express the *noteName*—a numerical method. In this method, for example, 60 is middle C, 72 is C above middle C, and 48 is C below middle C. Since the numbers increment by 1, the accidentals are not necessary. Figure 30-1 shows three octaves on a keyboard with both the notes and their numerical equivalents shown.

When expressing notes, the note and all its arguments are run together, and different notes are separated by spaces. For example, C4q C5 plays a quarter note of middle C, followed by a quarter note of C above middle C. If the octave and duration are not specified, they keep the values from the previous specification. If no notes are specified, the default note of middle C is played.

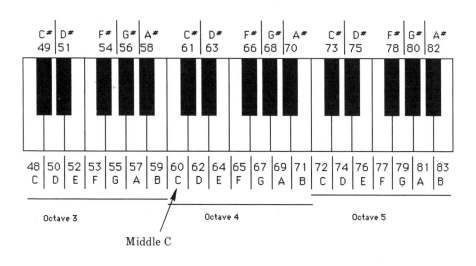

Figure 30-1.   The three middle octaves; for each note, the name of the note as well as its number is shown

When using sampled sounds for tunes, the results might be a little strange. Certain sounds, especially if they are long ones, become quite distorted when played at ranges very deviant from middle C. Longer sounds will usually be cut short. You can stop any sound from playing with the Play Stop command.

The Sound Function

the sound

sound( )

You can use this function to determine whether HyperCard is still playing or has finished. If a sound is currently playing, the Sound function returns the name of the sound. If no sound is playing, "done" is returned.

Once a long sound sequence has started, HyperCard can continue doing things such as going to other cards and performing calculations. Occasionally, however, you may not want it to do so. For example, if a sound is being loaded from a floppy disk, and other work is going on with that disk while the sound is being played, the sound might be crackly or scratchy. In this case, the strain of both playing the sound and accessing the disk is too much for the Mac, and the sound quality is not what it should be. Therefore, you want the Mac to wait while the sound is playing. You can use the Sound function along with the Wait command, as shown here:

```
wait until the sound is "done"
```

You can now do the other things that you need to do. The Wait command will constantly test the sound. While the sound is playing, the Sound function will return the name of the sound. When the sound has finished, it will return "done," the Wait command will stop executing, and further commands can then get to work.

Making a HyperCard Keyboard

It's easy and quick to make a keyboard on a card, and the procedure will illustrate some good techniques for working with HyperCard. You can use this card to test sounds and experiment with some of the sound commands, especially those used to play different notes.

First, take another look at Figure 30-1. This keyboard was drawn in HyperCard using only the button tool. Here's how to do it.

1. Either make a new stack or create a new card in an existing stack.

2. Draw a button where you want the first key to be. This will be the first of the white keys. Double-click the button, and type **48** as its name. Set the type of the button to Rectangle, and make sure that "Show name" and "Auto hilite" are not clicked. Figure 30-2 shows the Button Info dialog box for the button.

3. Copy the button. The best way to do this is to hold down the SHIFT and OPTION keys with the button tool still selected, click the button, and drag it to the right until its left edge just touches the right edge of the previous button. When this is done, you will see only one line. Now double-click this new button, and type **50** as its name.

Because you are using numbers for the button names, you don't need to worry about octave numbers.

4. Repeat this process for all the white keys. If you are making a keyboard like the one shown in Figure 30-1, you need to make 21 white keys. Name them with the numbers shown at the bottom of the keyboard in Figure 30-1.

5. Create the black keys, using essentially the same process you used to create the white keys. The first black key is named with the number 49, as shown in Figure 30-1.

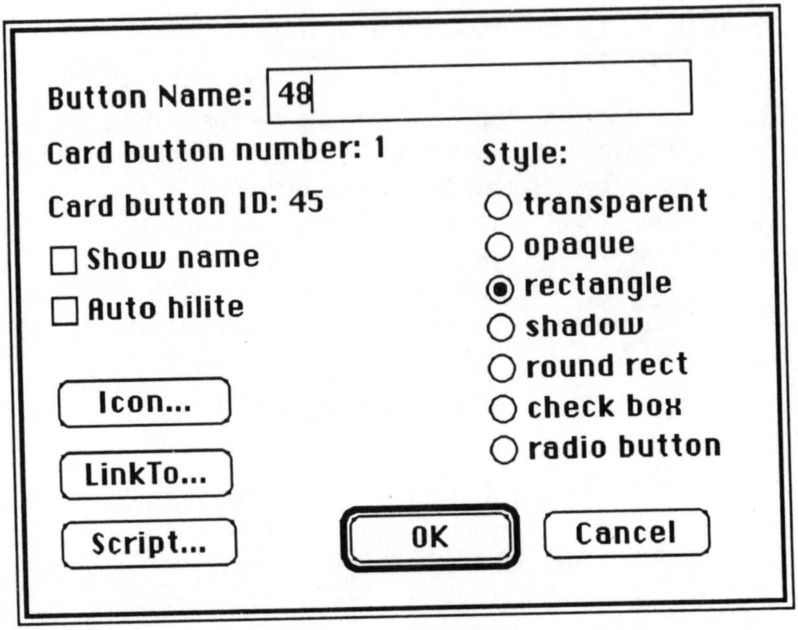

Figure 30-2.   Make the name of the button the same as the number of the note that it will play

Before copying this key to make a keyboard, however, you need to do one thing. Since there is no type for black buttons, use the highlighting property of the buttons to make them black. Select the first button, open the Message window, and type

Set hilite of card button "49" to true

Make sure that you surround 49 with quotes so that HyperCard sees it as the *name* of the button, not its number. The button will blacken.

6. Use the SHIFT-OPTION technique to drag new buttons into the positions of the black keys.

7. Open the script for the card you are on by choosing "Card Info" from the Edit menu, and click the Script button. Into the Edit window, type the handler shown in Script 30-1.

```
on mouseUp
  if "card button" is not in the long name of the target then
    exit mouseUp
  end if
  put the short name of the target into theNote
  put "Play" && quote & "Harpsichord" & quote && theNote
  into theCommand
  do theCommand
  wait until the sound is "done"
end mouseUp
```

Script 30-1.   This script plays the note determined by the name of the button you click

8. When you have typed this, click the OK button to save the script.

You have finished your music card. This application takes advantage of several of HyperCard's features. First, you created a number of new buttons, none of which have scripts in them. This takes advantage of HyperCard's message hierarchy. Because these buttons do not handle the "mouseUp" message, that message is passed to the card the buttons are on, taking with it the names of the targets. Second, you used the do command to build a command that HyperCard executes.

Try your script by clicking on one of the piano keys. Here is what happens: the button cannot handle the "mouseUp" message, so it sends it along to the script, with the name of the object in *the target*. The script then builds a Play command by using the variable *theNote*, which contains the short name of the target — in this case, the number of the key. The Do command then executes the command that was built, and the note is played.

Working with Resources

Utilities for Managing Resources
Where Are Resources?
Icons
Cursors
Sounds
Fonts

One of the definitions of "resource" in Webster's is "a fresh or additional stock or store available at need." Although this definition is not exactly indicative of the purpose served by resources on the Macintosh, its last words do apply. A resource on the Macintosh is a tool or item that is available to meet the needs of a program.

When the Macintosh was being designed, Apple programmers realized that one thing the computer was going to need if it were to succeed would be an easy way to customize programs. For example, when you are writing a program, on some computers all the text of menu items, commands, and the like are created and stored as part of the actual code that composes the program. If you want to change the text of these menus, you need to recompile the entire program. This process can be lengthy and can create many different versions of the program.

The answer that the Macintosh development team came up with was to make this text a part of the *resource fork* of the program, separate from the actual programming code that makes up the program, usually called the program's *data fork.* The resource fork is a separate area of the disk file that makes up the program, and all resources are stored in that fork. Instead of recompiling the program to change the text of a program, it is possible to locate the menu items in the resource fork and replace those menu items with the new text. Changing this text to allow the program to work in different languages is called *localization.*

In addition to allowing programmers to store text items in resources, the Macintosh designers allowed resource forks to include a number of other types of information that programs need. These other types of resources include sounds, icons, pictures, the design of dialog boxes, fonts, desk accessories, and more.

Application programs are not the only Macintosh files that can contain resources. Data files—documents created by applications—also can contain resource forks, which are sometimes used to store information of a kind specific to the kind of file the application creates.

Resources are identified in files and programs with four-letter tags or names called *resource types.* There can be multiple instances of each type of resource in the resource fork of any file. A resource type name usually resembles the English words describing the resource type. Table 31-1 lists some common resource types.

Note: All resource type names consist of four characters. Those resources that do not contain letters in the table have a space, indicated by an underscore, at the end of their names. Resource names are also *case sensitive*—a resource of the type SND_ would be different from one of the type snd_.

Within each type of resource in a resource fork there can be different instances of each type. For example, within the type ICON, there can be several icons. Each particular resource has an ID number as well as an optional name. Each resource's number must be unique to that resource type. For example, there can be only one icon with the number 2002 in any file.

Type	Meaning
ALRT	Alert box design
CNTL	Control design
CODE	Program code
CURS	Cursor design
DITL	Dialog and alert list
DRVR	Desk accessories and others
FOND	Font family
FONT	Font
ICN#	List of icons
ICON	Icon
MENU	Menu
PICT	Picture
STR#	Text strings
STR_	String
WDEF	Window definition
snd_	Sound
XCMD	HyperCard external command
XFCN	HyperCard external function

Table 31-1.   Resource Types Often Used in Macintosh Software

Many of the resource types—such as ICON, PICT, and FONT are common to almost all types of Macintosh programs; therefore, the formats for these types of resources are standard with virtually all Mac applications. As you will see later in this chapter, this is not the case for some types of information stored as resources—in particular, sounds.

Since HyperTalk is not a compiled programming language, you don't need resources to help you with your menus and the like. Why, then, do you need them? The answer is that many of the things you might want to add to your stacks—such as sounds, icons, fonts, and external commands or functions—exist as resources. If you use a sound digitizer to record a sound for use with the HyperTalk Play command, you are creating a resource for that stack. When you choose an icon for a HyperCard button, you are choosing from the icons available to HyperCard.

Utilities for Managing Resources

The bare Macintosh system and HyperCard include no tools for managing resources. There are no means available for you to do such things as copy resources from one file to another. However, there are two tools available—the stand-alone application ResEdit and the HyperCard external command ResCopy—that allow you to examine and copy resources from one file to another.

ResEdit

ResEdit is a stand-alone program from Apple. It is included with most Macintosh development systems that use languages such as C or Pascal, as well as on many on-line services or on disks from user groups. ResEdit is also available from APDA (Apple Programmer's and Developer's Association).

Note: It is important to be aware that this tool can destroy programs or data if misused. When using ResEdit, *always* have a spare copy of the file you are modifying. Changes you make with ResEdit to a program, especially an application program, can cause significant changes in the way that program operates. *Never* erase resources from any file unless you are absolutely sure of what you are doing. Also, you should not run ResEdit when running MultiFinder. Although few problems have been experienced, given the volatile nature of ResEdit, it is best to run the program under the Finder.

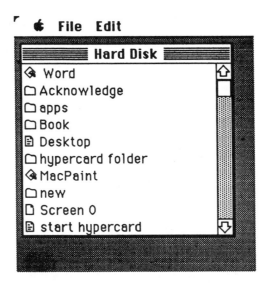

Figure 31-1. The opening screen of ResEdit shows the files and folders on your disk

When you open ResEdit, you are presented with a screen similar to the one shown in Figure 31-1. The scrolling window shows all the files and folders present on your disk. If you have a floppy disk in the machine, the window showing the floppy disk will have a close box in the left corner of the title bar; clicking on this box will close the window and eject the disk. Since you cannot eject a hard disk, there is no Close box on the window representing the hard disk.

You can scroll through the list of files on the disk. Files that do not have a resource fork are shown with an empty icon, while the icons for those that do have resource forks are

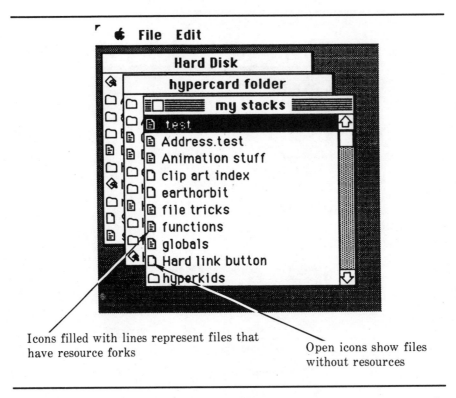

Figure 31-2. Files that do not contain resources are empty in ResEdit, while those that do are filled in

filled in, as shown in Figure 31-2. To open a file, either select the file and chose Open from the File menu, or double-click on the name of the file. If you open a file that does not have a resource fork, you will get the dialog shown in Figure 31-3, which tells you the file has no resource fork and asks if you want to add one.

Once you have opened a file, you get the scrolling window shown in Figure 31-4, which is for the author's Home stack. This scrolling window shows all the types of resources that are present in the file. The resources are sorted alphabetically by resource type. You can open any resource type in the same way you open the file. Once you have opened a resource type, a new scrolling window opens, showing the individual resources of that type. Remember, if you are unsure about

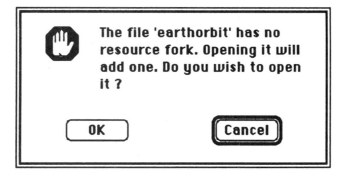

Figure 31-3.   If you open a file that does not contain a resource fork,
ResEdit asks if you want to create one

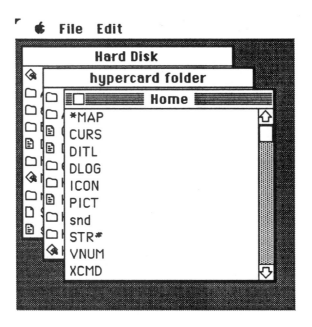

Figure 31-4.   When you open a file with ResEdit, the resources in that
file are shown in a scrolling window

what you are doing, do not modify any resources that you do not completely understand.

At any time, you can click on the Disk window, which is partially hidden by the other windows you have opened. That window comes to the front, and you can open other files in turn.

Copying resources between stacks is easy to do, especially if you are familiar with copying and pasting in general on the Macintosh. To copy a resource from one file to another, simply select a resource in one file, choose the Copy command from the Edit menu, select the window that represents the file to which you want to copy the resource, and choose Paste from the Edit menu.

Note: If you paste into one file a resource that has the same type and number as an existing resource in the destination file, that existing resource will be replaced by the new one. You can change the name and/or number of any resource by clicking on that resource to select it and choosing Get Info from the File menu.

When you close a file that you have changed with ResEdit, you get the dialog box shown in Figure 31-5. This allows you to abandon your changes or save them, and you have one last way to make sure you really want to modify the program.

Later in this chapter you will see how you can create a new ICON resource in ResEdit.

ResCopy

ResCopy, created by Steve Maller of Apple Computer, is a safer and more convenient tool for the HyperCard user than ResEdit. Because ResCopy is a HyperCard external command, it runs within HyperCard, which means you do not have to quit HyperCard to use it. ResCopy includes facilities only for copying or deleting resources, not for altering them; therfore, you are less likely to damage files when using it.

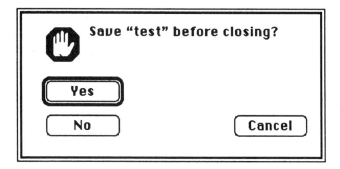

Figure 31-5.   Before you close a file, ResEdit asks if you want to save
the changes you have made to the file

Additionally, it will allow you to copy resources only into
HyperCard stacks, not into applications or files created by
other programs. This, too, increases the safety and thus the
utility of the tool.

Note: ResCopy is copyrighted by Apple Computer, Inc.
Although it is available from many services, you will need a
formal license from Apple to include it with any products
you develop. For more information, contact APDA or Apple
Computer.

The Two Modes of ResCopy

There are two ways of using ResCopy: a manual mode,
which works something like the Macintosh Font/DA Mover,
and a scripting mode, which allows you to automatically copy
resources between files from script control.

Manual Mode   The manual mode of using ResCopy summons the screen shown in Figure 31-6. When you use Res-

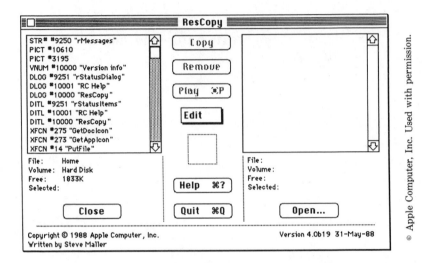

© Apple Computer, Inc. Used with permission.

Figure 31-6. Steve Maller's ResCopy is an excellent utility for moving resources between stacks

Copy in this manner, it allows you to open stacks and other files and see the resources that are part of those files. If the file is a HyperCard stack, you are able to copy resources from other files into the stack. If the file is an application or non-HyperCard document, it is opened in read-only mode, which means you cannot alter that file.

ResCopy includes functions that simplify working with the common types of HyperCard resources. When you are working with resources that have ICON, CURS, or snd＿ types, you can quickly see what these resources contain.

If the resource is a CURS (cursor) resource, clicking on that resource in one of the list boxes changes the mouse cursor to that cursor, until you click the mouse again. Resources may not be named, so it is possible that you will not know what a particular cursor looks like until you see it on the screen.

ResCopy does the same thing for ICON type resources. When you click on an ICON type resource in one of the scrolling list boxes, that resource is displayed in the small box at the middle of the screen. Again, this lets you examine the icons to make sure you have selected the correct icon before copying it.

If you click on a resource of the type snd—, you can then click on the Play button in the middle of the ResCopy window and hear the sound. Sounds will be discussed later in this chapter.

Script Mode   In addition to being able to use ResCopy in its manual mode, you can use ResCopy from within a script to automatically copy resources. This is useful if you have developed a stack and want to provide an automatic installation procedure.

The syntax for using ResCopy from a script is

ResCopy *fromFile, toFile, resType, resID/resName*

The variable *fromFile* defines the name of the file containing the resource you want to copy. If it is the actual name of a stack, it must be enclosed in quotes; it can also be a variable containing the name of a file. The name of the file should include the full pathname of the file, including the name of the disk the file is on, as well as any folders that contain it.

The variable *toFile* defines the name of the file to which you are copying the resource. As with the *fromFile* variable, this should be the complete pathname of the stack. ResCopy cannot add resources to files that are not HyperCard stacks; therefore, if this file name is not a HyperCard stack, ResCopy will beep at you and not perform the copy.

The *resType* variable tells ResCopy what type of resource you are copying. For example, if you are copying an icon, then the value of this variable would be "ICON."

For the last parameter, you can include either the ID number of the resource or its name, if it has one.

ResCopy and the Home Stack

When you use ResCopy to copy resources into HyperCard stacks, those resources are immediately available for use by that stack as soon as it has finished copying. An important exception to this is copying resources into the Home stack using HyperCard version 1.2.

When HyperCard is working with most stacks, it loads into memory from disk new resources as they are needed. If it sees that resources have been added to a stack, it then loads those resources the next time the resources are needed. This means that you can install new externals, icons, sounds, and the like into most stacks and use them as soon as you need them.

However, HyperCard does not do this with the Home stack. Instead, when HyperCard first opens the Home stack (when you start HyperCard), all the resources from Home are loaded into memory, and it does not load them again later. Therefore, when you add resources to Home, you must quit HyperCard and start it over again when you want to use those resources. While this is a minor nuisance when adding resources to the Home stack, it probably increases both the speed and reliability of HyperCard.

Where Are Resources?

As mentioned earlier in this chapter, resources are located in the resource fork of an application or document on the Macintosh. However, much the same hierarchy that works with HyperTalk messages and commands also works with resources.

The Current Stack

Of course, all the resources that are part of the current stack are available within that stack. Sounds that are part of a stack are playable by using the Play command within that stack. Since resources cannot be attached to specific backgrounds or cards, you don't need to worry about that part of the hierarchy.

The Home Stack

All resources that are part of the Home stack are available to the other stacks you run. This has the same advantages that it has when you are writing commonly used handlers or functions. If you use a resource often, you can install it into the Home Stack and use it whenever you like, which saves some disk space and keeps you from having to worry about whether a specific stack has a needed resource.

HyperCard

HyperCard itself contains a number of resources that are available to all the stacks you use. Notably, all the standard icons that are available for buttons are contained within HyperCard, as well as several sounds and the Flash external command.

Note: While you *can* install useful resources into HyperCard itself, it is not good practice to do so. It is possible that adding resources to an application program can adversely effect that program's functions. Also, if you install resources into HyperCard itself, when the next version of HyperCard appears, you will have to repeat the process to install the same resources into that new copy of HyperCard. Save yourself some time and trouble, by leaving HyperCard in the state you received it.

The System File

The System file contains much of the brains of the Macintosh. Buried within the System file are the programs that the Macintosh needs to start up, as well as much of the programming that allows it to work at all. The System file also contains its own resource fork (in fact most of the System file *is* the resource fork), which includes many resources that are used by HyperCard and other programs.

The resources in the System file that you are most concerned about are the icons in that file. The ICON type resources in the System file are used by HyperCard and will appear in the list of icons shown when you click the Icon button on the Button Info dialog box. The standard Macintosh System file includes only a few icons—those for alerts, including the stop sign, the warning sign, and others. However, since desk accessories are generally part of the System file, any icons used by desk accessories will be shown by HyperCard.

Not all the resources used by HyperCard can be installed in the System file, as discussed in the section on sounds later in this chapter. It is a good idea, as with the HyperCard program itself, to *not* install resources into your System file for use with HyperCard.

Icons

Icons are among the most visible of resources. When you choose the Icon button on the Button Info dialog box, you see a list of all the ICON type resources that are available to that stack. The ICON resources included in this dialog box are drawn from the hierarchy discussed in the previous section.

Creating an Icon with ResEdit

The best way to understand icons and other resources is through an example. The procedure discussed here is not guaranteed to make a nice-looking icon—that's up to you.

But it will show you how to create icons and install them into your stacks.

1. Create a new HyperCard stack using the New Stack command on the File menu. For now you don't need to put any buttons, fields, or pictures on this stack. This will be the stack into which you place the new icon, so if you want to put the icon into an existing stack, be sure to use the Save a Copy command on the File menu so you will have a backup copy of the stack.

2. Make sure you are not running in MultiFinder. To start without MultiFinder, use the Set Startup item on the Finder's Special menu and click the Finder radio button. Then use the Restart command on the same Special menu to restart the Macintosh.

3. Locate ResEdit and open it by double-clicking on its icon. Once it is open, you will see a scrolling window showing the files and folders on your disk. Locate the stack to which you want to add the icon and open it.

When you open the stack, it will probably not have a resource fork, and you will get the dialog box shown earlier in Figure 31-3. Click the OK button on this dialog box to add a resource to the file. When you have done so, an empty window representing the resource fork of the stack will appear.

4. The next step is to actually add the ICON type resource to the file. With the file window at the front of all the windows, choose New from the File menu. The dialog box shown in Figure 31-7 will appear. This dialog box allows you to tell ResEdit what type of resource you want to create. Scroll through these resource types until you come to the one called ICON and click on it, as shown in the figure. Once you have selected this type of resource, click the OK button.

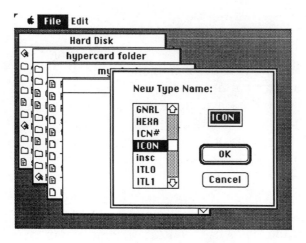

Figure 31-7. This ResEdit dialog box allows you to add a new resource type to a file

5. Once again, choose the New command from the File menu. When you clicked on it in step 4, a resource type was created for your file. Using the New command in this step causes a particular instance of the resource to be created. Notice that a square appears in the Icon window, and a new window appears in which you can draw with the mouse, as shown in Figure 31-8. This is the window in which you create your icons.

6. The best way to disover the size limits of the icons is to draw one with the mouse. Drawing an icon works the same way that using the pencil in Fat Bits works in HyperCard. If you click the mouse on a white pixel, it turns black; if you click it on a black pixel, it turns white. Holding the mouse button down and moving it draws lines.

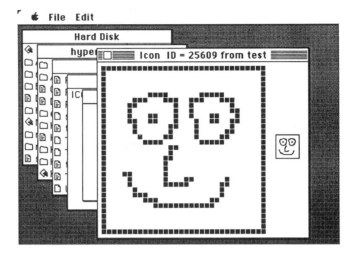

Figure 31-8.   The window that allows you to draw a new icon

The largest an icon can be is 32×32 pixels, and if you have used the Macintosh for a long time, you have seen that experienced artists can create a wide variety of designs within that limitation. Of course, icons do not have to take up the full 32 pixels in either direction and can in fact be much smaller.

7. When you have finished drawing your icon, click on the Close box in the left corner of the Icon window's title bar to close the icon.

8. Give your icon a name. First, click on the icon to make sure it is selected. Then choose the Get Info command on the File menu, and you will see a window like the one in figure 31-9. In the field labeled "Name," type something like **MyIcon**. When you have typed the name, close this window.

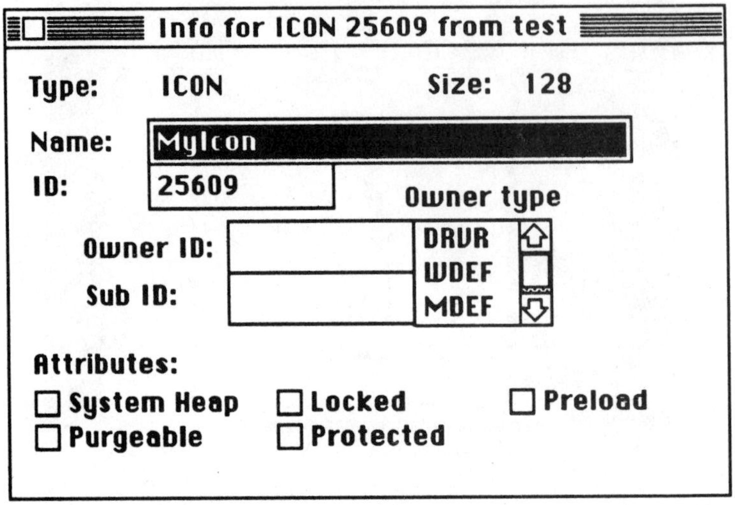

Figure 31-9. ResEdit's Info window allows you to assign a number and name to the icon

9. Close the window that lists all the resources in your stack. When you close it, you will get a dialog box similar to the one shown in Figure 31-5, which asks if you want to save the changes to the file. Click the OK button.

10. Start HyperCard and open the stack you have just modified. To display the icon with a button, create a new button and choose Button Info from the Objects menu. Click the Icon button on the dialog box that appears.

If you have created your icon successfully, it should appear in the scrolling list of icons. The point at which it appears will depend on the number that ResEdit assigned to the icon. When you find it, click on it and then on the OK button at the bottom of the dialog box. The button you just created will have your icon on it.

The creation of icons with ResEdit is not difficult, and there are some adaptations to the process that give you more flexibility.

First, ResEdit supports the Clipboard. If you are skilled at using the drawing tools in HyperCard you can create the icon in HyperCard (keeping it within the 32×32-pixel icon size limit), copy it, open ResEdit, and paste the drawing into the Icon window.

Second, there are some other tools available for creating icons. Other shareware or public domain icon utilitites are available from on-line services or user groups. Nevertheless, you can do quite a bit with ResEdit by itself.

Icons and Buttons

Icons are always associated with buttons. To assign an icon to a button, use the Icon button on the Button Info dialog box. A list will appear that shows all the buttons available in the button hierarchy.

When you copy a button and paste it into a new stack, the icon associated with that button travels with the button, and that icon becomes installed in the new stack.

Cursors

Cursor designs, like icons, are stored in the resource forks of Macintosh applications and documents. Cursors, again like icons, are available through the hierarchy that travels from the current stack through the System file.

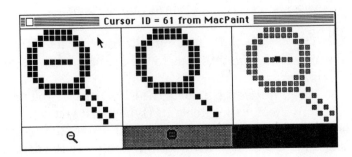

Figure 31-10. ResEdit's window for editing the cursor

Creating and installing a cursor by using ResEdit is slightly different from designing an icon. Cursors are smaller than icons and are limited to a size of 16×16 pixels.

The ResEdit window for editing a cursor is shown in Figure 31-10. This window has three panes for modifying the cursor: the first pane shows the cursor as it appears against a white background, the second as it appears against a gray background, and the third as it appears against a black background. Experimentation with these three panes and use of the cursors in HyperCard will teach you how these work together.

To use a cursor in HyperCard, you use the global property Cursor, with the Set command. With HyperCard versions 1.2 and later, you can refer to the cursor either by its ID number or by its name:

```
set cursor to 10768
set cursor to "myCursor"
```

Sounds

One of HyperCard's most exciting features is its ability to play digitized sounds with the Play command and to play those sounds at different pitches. Using several commercial devices, such as the MacRecorder discussed in Chapter 35, it is possible to record virtually any sound you want and to create your own synthesized sounds. Stacks comprising sampled sounds are also available from many sources, both commercially and through shareware or public domain sources.

Sounds, like icons and cursors, are contained in resource forks of applications and documents. Unlike icons and cursors, however, which were part of the Macintosh design from the very beginning, sounds are a relatively new component of the Macintosh's software toolbox, which leads to some problems. The major problem is that until recently there was no standard method for storing digitized sounds on the Macintosh, which means that not all programs that produce sounds could be played on HyperCard. The various sound formats and tools that allow you to convert between them are discussed in the next section of this chapter.

Another problem is that sounds that are part of the System file are not available to HyperCard, unlike icons and cursors that are contained in the System file. This is due to the larger memory requirements of sounds.

Sounds are digitized or recorded by circuitry in the digitizing device, which tests the sound at evenly spaced intervals, and records the numeric value of the sound at the time it tests it. This is called *sampling*. Sounds are continuously varying wave forms, and computers can sample sounds only at certain speeds, which in turn affects the quality of the sound when it is being played back and the amount of space the sound will require on disk and in memory.

The standard sound sampling rates on the Macintosh are 22,000, 11,000, and 7300 samples per second. The HyperTalk Play command is capable of playing sounds recorded at each of these sampling rates. Additionally, some digitizers, such as the MacRecorder, can compress sounds considerably. At the present time, however, HyperCard cannot play these compressed sounds.

There is a one-to-one ratio of the sampling rate to the amount of disk space taken by the sound. For each sample of sound, one byte must be stored on disk. That means that if you are recording at 22,000 samples per second, you will use approximately 22K of disk space per second recorded. Clearly, at this rate you will use up a great deal of space very quickly.

When you sample a sound at the lower sampling rates, you lose some of the sound quality. When sampling at a lower rate (called *down sampling*), you generally lose some of the higher frequencies. The lower rates, such as 7300 samples per second, might be fine for speech, but if you want to include quality music in your stack, you will have to sacrifice the disk space.

Sounds also require a great deal of memory while Hyper-Card is playing them. The entire sound must be loaded into memory before it is played. If you want to use long or complex sounds, you should use your sound editing software to separate the sounds into small, manageable portions.

If you are only using sounds in your stacks that have been recorded by others, the preceding discussion should be a help to you. If you want to record your own sounds, the issues become more complex, and you should consult the documentation that was included with the digitizing hardware you use. The manual for the MacRecorder is particularly good at providing details about the problems and tradeoffs involved when you use sounds in stacks. Another source is an excellent two-part article by Tim Oren of Apple Computer: "Interactive Sound in HyperCard," *Hyperage*, Volume 1, Issues 1 and 2. The same articles are reprinted in their entirety in Danny Goodman's *HyperCard Developer's Guide* (New York: Bantam Books, 1988).

Different Sound Formats
and Converting Them

As mentioned earlier in this chapter, in the early days of sounds on the Macintosh, there was no standard format for storing sounds as resources or as files. Predictably, this has led to some chaos and confusion about manipulating sounds.

The first successful sound digitizing system for the Macintosh was the hardware and software combination known as "MacNifty SoundCap." The format used by the SoundCap software (now available as SoundWave, from Impulse, Inc.) consequently became something of a *de facto* standard for sound files. Instead of storing sounds as resources in SoundCap format, sounds are stored as numeric values in the data forks of the files containing those sounds. This makes it hard to transfer the sounds from a SoundCap file to a HyperCard stack—but not impossible. Among the first external commands available for HyperCard was one called SoundCapToRes, which extracts the data from a SoundCap file and converts it to an snd__ resource that is installed in a stack. This external command is available from user groups or on-line services. The stack is called Sound Convert 1.0. If you happen to have a number of sounds recorded in the SoundCap format, you should locate this stack.

The SoundEdit software included with MacRecorder is also a good tool for converting these sounds. SoundEdit opens SoundCap files and allows you to edit them. You can then save those sounds as resources in a HyperCard stack; Sound-Edit automatically saves them in the correct format.

Another sound format that you might encounter is the one used by MacroMind's VideoWorks program. VideoWorks is the most successful Macintosh animation program, and because sound is an integral part of realistic animation, the program includes support for sounds. VideoWorks stores its sounds as resources of the type CSND, either in a Video-Works file or in a special file called Sounds. As with the SoundCap format, SoundEdit can open VideoWorks sound files, and it allows you to save them into HyperCard snd__ format.

Fonts

Fonts are resources that are installed primarily in the System file of your Macintosh. However, it is possible to install fonts directly into a stack if you need to distribute your stack to others and want to make sure they have the same font you are using.

Fonts are installed into the System file by using the Font/DA Mover program, shown in Figure 31-11. In its default mode, the Font/DA Mover will open only the System file or a "suitcase" file that contains only a font. However, it is possible to open other Macintosh files by holding down the OPTION key as you click the Open button in the Font/DA Mover. This will show you all the files on your disk, including HyperCard stacks. If you install a font into a stack, it will be available for use in that stack; if you install it into the Home stack, it will be available to all your stacks.

Generally, installing fonts into stacks should be done with care, and there are several issues you should consider beforehand.

One of the most important issues to consider is violation of the copyright of the owner of the font. You will have a specific license to use a font on your computer or printer, particularly if you use a LaserWriter or PostScript-compatible printer, and have purchased downloadable fonts from Adobe or other sources. Distributing that font could put you in violation of copyright law and leave you legally liable.

Another consideration is the disk space taken up by the font and whether the benefits from using the font are worth the sacrifice of the disk space. You might find that they are not.

You should also remember that if you are using a font in paint text—text placed on the screen with the painting tools—you do not need to worry about including the font on the stack or violating a copyright because paint text becomes part of the array of pixels that make up the graphics portion

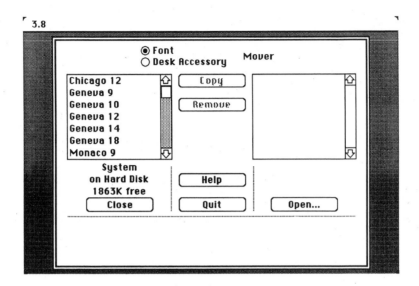

Figure 31-11. The Font/DA Mover

of the card or background. Only text contained in fields requires that HyperCard have that font resource available to it. If you have a very fancy font that you want to use in your designs, consider using paint text instead of field text.

External Commands
and Functions

About External Commands and Functions
Sources of External Commands and Functions
Some Useful Externals
To Use or Not to Use
The Ethics of Using Externals

Chapter 31 discussed the resource fork of Macintosh applications and files and how the resource fork of a HyperCard stack can contain such things as icons, sounds, and fonts. This chapter discusses the use of external commands and functions, which are also placed in the resource fork of stacks and of HyperCard itself.

About External Commands and Functions

One of the most brilliant concepts built into HyperCard is its extensibility, which allows programmers who are working with languages such as C, Pascal, or Assembler to create new commands and functions that work in the HyperCard environment. When added to a stack, these commands and functions, called *externals*, behave in exactly the same manner as HyperCard's built-in facilities. They are available to the entire hierarchy of commands—if you have a command or function in your Home stack, it is available to all the other stacks you use.

External commands, or XCMDs, work in the same manner as HyperTalk commands or handlers that you create. To use one you simply make sure that the XCMD is available to the hierarchy of messages, which means that it is installed in the resource fork of either the current stack or the Home stack (or of HyperCard itself, but that is not a good idea—see Chapter 31.)

External functions, or XFCNs, work in the same manner as HyperTalk functions. You pass the function a parameter, and it in turn sends some information back to the line that called it.

Installing Externals

Install externals into your stack in the same manner you install other resources, such as icons or sounds. The stacks authors use to distribute their externals often include buttons that will automate the installation process. Otherwise, you can use a tool such as ResCopy or ResEdit.

When you install certain externals, make sure that all the resources that are part of the external are installed. Some popular external commands and functions are not entirely self-contained in one resource. Some, such as the doList XFCN discussed later in this chapter, will place their own dialog boxes on the screen, and in order to do so, will need to have their DITL and DLOG resources installed along with the XFCN resource. Always consult the documentation for the external to make sure you are installing it correctly.

Sources of External Commands and Functions

Where do you get them? Many external commands and functions are available as part of commercial stacks that you buy. You can usually copy externals from these stacks using tools such as ResCopy or ResEdit.

A number of developers have placed their external commands and functions in the public domain. Many of these are available from sources such as CompuServe or BMUG (Berkeley Macintosh Users' Group). They often include buttons that make it easier for you to install them into your own stacks.

The Developer Stack

A good source of externals is Steve Drazga's Developer Stack. This stack, available on CompuServe, on a BMUG disk, and from other sources, constitutes a library of many useful external commands and functions. Each external in the stack contains a button which installs that external into your own stack. It also includes documentation for each of the externals in the stack. Keep a copy of this stack on your hard disk, and use it as a library of external commands and functions. When you acquire new externals, it is very easy to add them, along with their documentation, into the Developer Stack. This will help you maintain records of where you got externals and information such as licensing, usage instructions, and so on. The Developer Stack is shown in Figure 32-1.

XCMD Register Stack

Another useful source of information is the XCMD Register stack, also available from many user groups and on-line services. The XCMD Register stack was developed by Brian Mennell of Pisces Publishing, and a sample screen is shown in Figure 32-2. Unlike the Developer Stack, the XCMD Register stack does not actually *contain* the commands it documents. Instead, it includes descriptions for a large number of externals, as well as the names and addresses of the companies or individuals who actually created the externals. It also includes information about acquiring an external and lists its location and file name on the Genie and CompuServe on-line services. This is a good stack to have if you are using exter-

Figure 32-1. The Developer Stack is a useful library of external commands and functions, as well as handy buttons and scripts

The XCMD Register

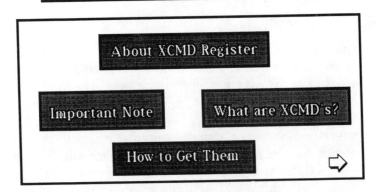

Figure 32-2. The XCMD Register stack contains information about a number of externals

nals and need to make sure you have the right commands to distribute them.

Some Useful Externals

New XCMDs and XFCNs appear regularly on disks from BMUG and on CompuServe. The Developer Stack contains over 40 of them. Out of this list, here are some XCMDs and XFCNs that every serious HyperCard developer should have. Since there are so many externals available, and new ones are appearing all the time, the following can do little more than indicate the wide variety of things that external commands and functions can do.

ResCopy

ResCopy, created by Steve Maller of Apple Computer, was discussed in Chapter 31. ResCopy is an XCMD that gives you the ability to copy resources between stacks. It allows you to install resources into HyperCard stacks, and it can open other programs or files for copying resources from those files.

FileName

The fileName XFCN also was written by Steve Maller at Apple Computer. It gives HyperTalk scripts the ability to present you with a standard Open File dialog box (called an SFGetFile dialog box in Macintosh jargon). When this dialog box is presented, you can use standard Macintosh techniques for navigating through folders and between disks. When you choose a file and click the OK button, it returns a complete pathname, describing the location of the file selected, to the script that called the function. When calling this function, the script can request that only files created by a specific application or of a certain type be listed.

The complete pathname returned by fileName is in this form:

hard disk:folder:folder:fileName

The first words in the pathname constitute the name of the disk the file name is on. After the first colon, the name or names of the folders in which the file is contained are separated by colons. After the final colon is the name of the file.

For example, suppose you use the fileName XFCN and choose a file called Text located in the Data folder of a disk named Hard Disk. The function would return this pathname to the line that called it:

hard disk:data:text

Script 32-1 is a short function that extracts only the name of the file from this string of text. It is good for display purposes only. If you are displaying the name of the file you are working on, you probably don't want to display the entire pathname of the file. Remember that when you refer to a file in a HyperTalk command that works with files (such as Open, Read, Write, or Close), you must include the entire pathname of the file or HyperCard will assume the file is in the current folder.

NewFileName

The newFileName function, written by Andrew Gilmartin of Brown University (a prolific author of externals), performs the flipside of the fileName function. Instead of asking you to locate an existing file on disk, this function allows you to explicitly locate where a new file is to be created on disk. If you type in the name of a file that already exists, it asks you whether or not the file is to be replaced.

Like the fileName function, newFileName returns the complete path of the file whose name you have typed in, including the name of the disk and any folders that the file is in.

```
function shortName pathName
  repeat while pathName contains ":"
    delete char 1 to offset(":",pathName) of pathName
  end repeat
  return pathName
end shortName
```

Script 32-1. This function extracts the name of a file from the full pathname

SortItems

The sortItems function, written by Marvin G. Nelson, has a container as its parameter. It returns the container with the items sorted in a specified manner. One of the drawbacks of HyperTalk is that it does not include a function to sort a container by lines or items; HyperTalk can only sort stacks. Sorting routines written in HyperTalk are generally slow.

Other externals are available that sort containers by lines or words.

DoList

The doList external function places a dialog box in the middle of the screen, as shown in Figure 32-3. It was written by James L. Paul. This dialog box includes a scrolling list of items, as well as two buttons. Click on one or more of the lines in the scrolling list and then click the OK button, and the doList function returns the number of the line on which you clicked. If you click the Cancel button, the function returns 0.

This is a very handy feature that would be nice to have included in HyperCard, allowing you to create dialog boxes of a type that would be difficult to create with HyperTalk. One problem with the doList function, however, is that if you

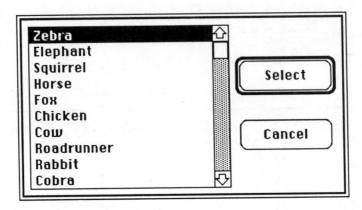

Figure 32-3. The doList XFCN provides a dialog box that includes a scrolling list

are using a long list of choices that will appear in the scrolling field, it can take the external a fairly long time to make the dialog box appear.

PopUpMenu

A recent and welcome addition to the Macintosh user interface in general is the pop-up menu. Pop-up menus can be triggered by clicking buttons or fields. When you hold the mouse button down on such a button, a longer list of items pops up. You move the mouse vertically through the items, and release it on the one you want. More and more software manufacturers are adopting these pop-ups to save space on the screen—one pop-up can take the place of a set of radio buttons. Programs such as PageMaker 3.0, Microsoft Word 4.0, dBASE Mac, and Acknowledge use pop-ups extensively.

Essentially, the PopUpMenu external function works in the same way as pop-ups do in other programs: you pass parameters to the function that includes the list of items you want to have pop up, and it returns a number that tells you which of those items will pop up. The PopUpMenu external function was written by Andrew Gilmartin of Brown University.

Others

Besides the few externals already mentioned in this chapter, there is a wealth of externals available. Harry Chesley of Apple Computer, for example, has written a set of external commands and functions that allow HyperTalk to control the serial interface at the back of the Macintosh. This means that scripts can be written to communicate with other devices, including modems, videodisk players, and data acquisition devices. These externals are available from APDA (290 Southwest 43rd St., Renton, WA 98055).

To Use or Not to Use

One question you will need to answer early when developing an application is whether you are going to use external commands and functions. There are good arguments on each side.

On the side of using externals, the plain truth is that there are things that standard HyperTalk simply does not provide. For example, with the standard Open File or Save File dialog box, there is no way to provide a list box showing files on a disk and automatically ask the user whether he wants to replace a file when creating a new one. Other externals are available for such things as sorting items or lines in a container, providing your applications with pull-down menus, and the like. If you need these features, the answer is clear: you should use externals.

On the other hand, using external commands and functions sometimes seems to be a non-HyperCard procedure. Since external commands and functions are distributed in compiled form, this violates the open-code nature of HyperCard.

Externals also make your stack somewhat more fragile than it would be using plain HyperTalk. It is virtually impossible to create situations with HyperTalk that cause the Macintosh to bomb or operate unpredictably. Scripts can always be halted with the COMMAND-PERIOD key combination, while externals cannot. Since externals are, by their very nature, working closer to the machine and behind your back, you are taking a chance on corrupted or lost data or work. Before you use an external command or function, make sure that you have tested it thoroughly and that it is safe.

Generally the rule should be that if you can accomplish something with HyperTalk, do it. If you *really* need a feature that is not provided with HyperTalk, or if you have an external that performs *much* better than a HyperTalk command or function, then you should consider using an external.

The Ethics of Using Externals

One of the difficulties of using external commands and functions, especially in stacks you hope to distribute to others, is making sure you have a right to distribute and use the external.

Externals are usually distributed as compiled code, so it is possible that you have stacks containing externals, and you might not even be aware of the name of the person who created it. Always keep a copy of the stack from which you got the external—it will usually include documentation about how to use it, as well as information about the licensing and distribution of the external command.

Communication with Other Programs

Importing and Exporting Text
Working with Structured Text Files
Working with Unstructured Text
Importing and Exporting Graphics

Any program that manages data will frequently need to share that data with other programs. There are few things more frustrating than entering a lot of data into a program, and then finding that you need to re-enter that data when you change programs. The Macintosh, in general, provides a certain amount of data interchangeability with its standard Clipboard. Virtually anything on the screen that can be selected can be copied and pasted into other programs. Most word processors, for example, allow you to paste graphics into them within the text.

If you have more than a small amount of data to transfer, however, the Clipboard is not adequate. It works fine for small text selections and graphics, but for larger groups of data, more work is involved. HyperCard gives you several tools for transferring data. For pictures, the Import Paint and Export Paint commands read and write MacPaint type graphics files. The Read and Write commands are used for text.

Importing and Exporting Text

Aside from the Clipboard, the means you have to import and export text is the standard text file. A *text file* is a file that contains only the common ASCII set of text characters, along with the extensions to the ASCII set that are used by the Macintosh. Text files can be opened or read by virtually any word processor, as well as most database and spreadsheet programs. These programs are also able to write ASCII text files. HyperTalk gives us four commands for working with text files: Open File, Close File, Read, and Write.

The Open File Command

Open file *fileName*

Before you can use any text file, you must prepare that file for writing by using the Open File command. If a file by the same name exists on disk, you will be able to read from that file. If you write to an existing open file, the text you write will replace the text in the file already on disk. If the file does not exist, it will be created for you.

The *fileName* must include the entire pathname of the file. The pathname includes the name of the disk on which the file resides, as well as any folders that it is in. The disk name and each folder name must end with a colon (:). Here is a pathname for a file named Text that is located in a Data folder on a hard disk named Hard Disk:

"Hard Disk:Data:Text"

Spaces are significant in pathnames. If you put a space anywhere in the name of the disk, the folder, or the file, those spaces will b counted. For example, " file" is not the same as "file". Precision is important. If only a file name is given, the HyperCard will assume that the file is in the same folder as HyperCard itself.

You may use a variable that contains the path for the file instead of an actual file name. If you use an actual file name, it must be enclosed in quotes (including the full path), so that HyperTalk does not try to interpret it as a variable.

Chapter 32 recommends the use of the fileName and newFileName XFCNs. These functions allow you to use standard Macintosh Save and Open dialog boxes in your scripts, simplifying the process of opening a file. With them, you can use standard Macintosh techniques for navigating through disks and folders to find a file. These functions return the full pathname of the file, which is often difficult to remember.

If you attempt to open a file that is already open, you will be presented with the alert "Got error -49 while trying to open file *fileName*," shown in Figure 33-1. Here instead of *"fileName,"* the name of the file will be shown. It is not possible to trap this error with HyperTalk.

The Close File Command

Close file *fileName*

This command tells HyperCard that you are finished with the file. It is important that all opened files be closed when you are finished with them. If you attempt to open a file that

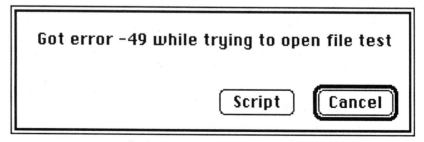

Figure 33-1.   The alert that appears when attempting to open a file that is already opened

has not been closed, the error message "Got error -49 while trying to open file *fileName*" will appear. Since you cannot trap for this error from within a script, execution of the script will be stopped.

Closing files is also important when using the Macintosh RAM cache from the Control Panel. All text written to a file will not necessarily be written to that file until it is closed; some may remain in the RAM cache. Closing the file writes the text from the cache to disk.

If a script has halted without closing a file—for example, if you have pressed COMMAND-PERIOD to stop the script, then the file will be left open. It is possible to close open files by typing **Close file** and the file name into the Message box. An error alert, "No open file named *fileName*," shown in Figure 33-2, will appear, but the file will be closed anyway.

The Read Command

read from file *fileName* **until character**

read from file *fileName* **for** *number of bytes*

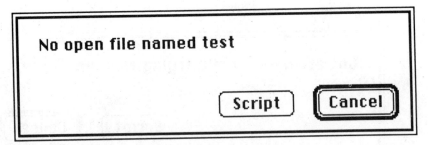

Figure 33-2.   Attempting to read or write to a file that has not been opened brings up this alert

This command reads text from the file *fileName* which must be an open file, and places the text that is read into the local variable *it*.

The first form of the Read command allows you to specify a character to which HyperCard will read. It reads all the text up to and including this character. Common forms of the command are

```
read from file filename until tab -- reads until next tab
read from file filename until return
read from file filename until empty -- reads the entire file
```

The second form of the command allows you to specify a certain number of characters to read. This can allow you to buffer text, reading it all at one time and processing it later. The number of bytes can be any number smaller than 16,384. If you specify a larger number, HyperCard will only read 16,384 characters. You will find it is more practical to read far smaller pieces of text at one time, because Hyper-Talk bogs down when dealing with large blocks of text. There is little performance difference in reading and working with one large block of text as opposed to many small blocks.

When this command has executed, further Read commands will start at the first character not read by the last read command. For example, if you execute the command

```
read from file "test" for 1000
```

then the next read you do from that file will begin with character 1001. Don't worry about reading more characters than are in a file: if you ask to read more characters, the Read command will read to the end of the file and then stop. Script 33-1 uses this version of the Read command to determine the length of the file.

```
function fileLeng fileName
   -- initialize the variables
   put empty into fileLength
   open file fileName
   repeat
      -- read 16K from the file
      read from file fileName for 16384
      -- no more text in the file
      if it is empty then exit repeat
      -- add the number of characters we read to the variable
      add the number of characters in it to fileLength
   end repeat
   -- send back the number of characters
   close file fileName
   return fileLength
end fileLeng
```

Script 33-1. This function, fileLeng, reads a file and returns the length of the file in characters

If you attempt to read from a file that has not been opened, the error alert "No open file named *fileName*" will appear.

The Write Command

write *source* to file *fileName*

This command writes the contents of *source* to the file *fileName*. The variable *source* can be any HyperCard data, including the following:

Source	Command
Fields	write field ID 17 to file *fileName*
Variables	write *theText* to file *fileName*
Functions	write average (1,2,3,4) to file *fileName*
Chunk expressions	write line 17 of field "test" to file *fileName*

The Write command puts the text into the file starting at the place the file was last written to or read from.

If you attempt to write to a file that has not been opened, the error alert "No open file named *fileName*" will appear. There is no way to trap for this error in HyperTalk.

The Write command starts reading at the character after the last character read or written. For example, if your last file-related command was to read 1000 characters from a file, your next Write command will start writing at character 1001. If your last Write command wrote 100 characters to the file, the next character you write will be 101.

Mixed Reading and Writing

Sometimes you might need to change some specific information in a file while leaving the rest intact. There are a couple of ways to do this.

The first method is to read the entire file and place it into some HyperCard data structure, such as a field. You can then use standard HyperCard commands to change specific information in the field, and then write the entire field out again. For example, you might read an entire file into a specific field, and then use this command:

```
put newText into line 17 of field "old text"
```

Now you can reopen the file and write this field to the file. This approach has its pluses and minuses. On the plus side, you use standard HyperCard expressions to change the text. On the minus side, you lose something in performance. Reading the entire file takes some time, and HyperCard's expressions for finding text in a field are relatively slow, especially if you are working with large chunks of text. You need to keep this limitation in mind because HyperCard text fields can be no larger than 30,000 characters.

It is possible to both read and write to a file during the same "open." That is, you can open a file, read some information from it, write some new information to it, and close it, thus appending the new information to the file. There are a couple of things to keep in mind when you are doing this, however. When working with text files, it is useful to imagine that the disk's read/write head is moving along through the text file, reading and writing to the file at the place it is currently located. You can think of the read/write head as a pointer to a specific spot in a file. This pointer always points to the location in the file that is immediately after the character you have just read or written. The next read or write will start at that location.

When reading from a file, you have no problems. Suppose you want to read 100 characters from the file, close it, and be done with it. No problem. On the other hand, suppose you need to open a file, write 100 characters to it, and close it. No problem, but only if you want to totally replace the file with those 100 characters. When you close a file after writing to it, the end of the file is set at the character following the one you just wrote. That means that any text that was in the file starting at character 101 will be lost.

How can you change the first 100 characters of the file and leave the rest intact? It turns out to be easy. Write the 100 characters and, instead of closing the file, read from the file until its end, and then close it. The read/write head, or pointer, will be moved to the end of the file, and the file will be closed. No problem.

Script 33-2 illustrates this principle of reading and writing to files, and the way it works is noted in the comments embedded in the script.

Some Tips for Working with Files

One of the things you want to do when opening files for writing is make sure that the user has a chance to avoid writing over, and thus destroying, a file that already exists. This is taken care of if you are using the newFileName XFCN (discussed in Chapter 32), but plain HyperTalk doesn't give you any help. Scripts 33-1 and 33-3 show some handlers that work together to give you a file name.

```
on mouseUp
  open file "test"
  write "abcdefghijklmnopqrstuvwxyz" to file "test"
  close file "test"
  -- the file "test" now contains the alphabet in lower case
  open file "test"
  write "12345678" to file "test"
  -- the pointer is now at the ninth character in the file
  -- (the letter "i").  If we were to close the file now,
  -- characters 9 through 26 (i through z) would be lost.
  -- Instead, we read from the file, to move the pointer
  -- to the end of the file.
  read from file "test" until empty
  close file "test"
  -- now let's read the entire file,
  -- and put it into the message
  -- box to illustrate the change we have made
  open file "test"
  read from file "test" until empty
  put it
  -- the Message Window will now show
"12345678ijklmnopqrstuvwxyz"
  close file "test"
end mouseUp
```

Script 33-2.   This handler illustrates how the read/write head is positioned in a file and shows how to change specific information in a text file

The purpose of the newFileName function is to ask the user for a file name, and return the name of that file to the handler that called it. It uses the Ask command to do this, and the dialog box that it creates is shown in Figure 33-3. The "repeat" line is used to allow the function to keep asking the user for a file name until it gets a name that does not already exist. This function could be called with a line such as "put newFileName() into theFile."

After getting the name of the file from the user, new-FileName calls the fileLeng function shown in Script 33-1.

```
function newFileName
  repeat
    ask "Enter name of file to write."
    --the user canceled
    if it is empty then return empty
    put it into fileName
    -- did the file have characters in it?
    if fileLeng(fileName) is > 0 then
      answer "Replace existing" && fileName & "?"¬
      with "Yes" or "No"
      if it is "No" then
        next repeat
      else
        return fileName
      end if
    else
      return fileName
    end if
  end repeat
end newFileName
```

Script 33-3.   NewFileName gets a file name from the user. If the file exists, it asks if the user wants to replace it

Figure 33-3.   The newFileName function shown in Script 33-3 uses the standard Ask command to create this dialog box

This function opens the file and reads text from it. The file-Leng function does nothing but read all the characters in the file and count them, returning the number of characters to the handler that called it.

If fileLeng returns a value other than 0 to newFile-Name, then the file already exists, and a dialog box asks if the user wants to replace the file on disk. This dialog box uses the Answer command and is shown in Figure 33-4. If a length of 0 is returned, the file did not already exist or was empty, and the file name is returned to the handler that called the newFileName function. FileLeng, by the way, is a useful function. Because it reads the text in fairly large chunks, it can quickly determine the size of even a large file.

Good programmers always check this sort of thing for the user. Especially when typing in pathnames, it is easy for the user to type the name of an already existing file. Programs should always attempt to catch as many errors as possible, particularly when data could be destroyed as a result.

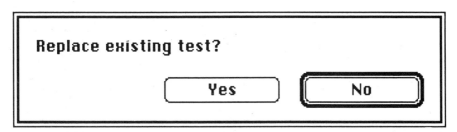

Figure 33-4.   If the file exists, newFileName asks the user if the file is to be overwritten

Working with Structured Text Files

Structured text files contain a stream of text, in which certain elements of the files are separated from one another by common elements, so that you can determine where one part of a file begins and another ends. In a fairly common application, you may have a file or database that consists of items of inventory. For each item you have in stock, you keep the following information: part number, description, price, and quantity on hand. Each of these items is called a *field* in a database program. In this case, the meaning of the word "field" is the same as it is in HyperCard. In a database program, all the information that relates to one part is called a *record.* This is analogous to a card in HyperCard. Clearly, there is a connection between the two worlds: fields are fields, a database record is a card, and a database file is a stack.

It is not unreasonable to want to transfer information from database programs to HyperCard, and the other way around. Perhaps you were using an older filing program to store your Rolodex of names and addresses, and now want to move that information into HyperCard. Or perhaps you now have data in HyperCard that you want to transfer to another, more powerful program.

HyperCard, however, is not able to read the native files created by other programs. HyperCard cannot, for example, read directly a native file created by the Double Helix or 4th Dimension databases; it can only read and write text files which are composed of standard ASCII text characters. Text files act as intermediary files between HyperCard and the other program. This is only natural; when programmers create a program such as Double Helix or 4th Dimension, they structure data in special ways so that they can access that data quickly and easily.

The first step in transferring data from another program is to create a file that is composed of ASCII text only. Most database programs make this fairly easy to do with an Export or Transfer command.

Delimiters

For two programs to communicate data, they must agree on how the data is going to be structured. They need to agree on what in the text file constitutes a field and what constitutes a record. Programs do this most commonly by agreeing on certain characters that separate fields and records from one another. These characters are called *delimiters*. The most common method of doing this on the Macintosh is to use the tab character (ASCII character 9) to delimit the fields and the return character (ASCII character 13) to delimit the record. That is, text followed by a tab denotes one field, and fields followed by a return denote one record. This is commonly called the *tab-delimited format*, and most Macintosh database programs support this format.

Another common delimiter is the comma (ASCII character 44). The comma is not as useful to use as the tab, though, because the text itself can contain a comma, as in the case of "John Brown, Jr." Fields that contain commas are usually surrounded by quotes. HyperCard can be made to read text in this format, but it is difficult to do so. As with tab-delimited files, comma-delimited files end the record with a return character.

Starting with HyperCardVersion 1.1, Apple has provided buttons (in the Button Ideas stack) that perform some data importing and exporting. These buttons are not as flexible or powerful as scripts that you create yourself, but they provide a good starting point for custom buttons. They allow you to use different delimiters, import text as paragraphs or as data, and export text.

Reading Delimited Text

To read a delimited text file, you need to know a couple of things about the text file. You must first know how the file is structured: What are the delimiters that separate the various elements of the file from one another? Which delimiters are used to separate fields and which to separate records?

You also need to know what you are going to do with the text once you read it: Into which fields in the HyperCard stack are you going to place the various fields from the text file?

Figure 33-4 shows a handler, readFile, that reads the contents of a text file and places the text from different fields in this text file into different background fields in the stack. To make things easy, first assume a one-to-one relation exists between the text file and the stack; that is, text that is in the first field in the file will be placed into the first field in the stack. Second, work with a tab-delimited file. As mentioned earlier, tab-delimited files are about as standard as anything on the Macintosh.

One thing you need to know is how many fields there are in the text file. The handler in Script 33-4, readFile, takes two arguments. The first is the name of the file that you are to read (including, of course, the full pathname to the file), and the number of fields that are in the record. The handler assumes that the text will be imported into the current stack and that the fields for this stack have already been created. This handler is included in a button in the mouseUp handler, shown in Script 33-5. This button, called Import, would be placed on the first card of the stack.

Note that this readFile handler is no more than a starting point for an Import button. There are many things that could be done to it to give more flexibility. Those that need that flexibility can modify this button, use the buttons from the Button Ideas stack or turn to some other commercial stacks that do much the same thing.

Writing Delimited Text

Writing delimited text is, not surprisingly, a lot easier than reading it. In writing, the script has full control over what goes in the text file and doesn't need to worry about something that another program has put there.

When writing a file, there are a couple of things you need to understand from the outset. You need to know which fields you are going to write: Will you write all the background fields or only some of them? Will you write the card

```
on readFile fileName,numFields
  open file fileName
  put "dummy"into it
  repeat until it is empty
    repeat with x = 1 to numFields
      read from file fileName until tab
      -- empty?
      if it is empty then exit repeat
      -- remove the tab
      delete last char of it
      put it into bkgnd field x
    end repeat
    if it is empty then exit repeat
    -- now read last field, which ends with a return
    read from file fileName until return
    -- delete the return
    delete last char of it
    put it into file numFields
    domenu "New Card"
  end repeat
  close file fileName
end readFile
```

Script 33-4.   A simple script that reads a tab-delimited text file and places the contents of the file into fields in a stack

```
on mouseUp
  -- this script goes into a button
  -- along with the "readFile",
  -- handler and the "fileLeng" function.  It reads a tab
  -- delimited file from disk, and puts the data into a stack
  put newfilename() into fileName
  if fileName is empty then exit mouseUp
  ask "How many fields are there?"
  -- the user cancelled
  if it is empty then exit mouseUp
  put it into numFields
  readFile fileName, numFields
  beep
  answer "Done!" with "OK"
end mouseUp
```

Script 33-5.   A mouseUp handler that calls the readFile handler to read a file

fields? What delimiters are you going to use? Which cards will you write? You also need to know about some anomalous characters that might be in the fields you are writing.

Script 33-6 shows writeFile, the handler that illustrates the process. This handler includes a couple of parameters that allow you to write a more generalized handler that can work in numerous cases. Note that we are passing several parameters to this handler. Here is the function of each parameter:

- **theFile** Holds the name of the file you are writing

- **startCard** Holds the number of the first card you are to write

- **numCards** Holds the number of cards to write

By using these three parameters, you can start writing with a certain card number and write a specific number of cards after that. This allows you to sort a stack on a certain field. You can find out which is the first card that contains the data you want and count the number of cards that follow it. This might be good for a mail-merge operation you might use to send letters to only a specific group of people.

- **fDelim**   Holds the character that ends the field
- **rDelim**   Holds the character that ends the record

Using these variables allows you to change the delimiters easily. Though the tab-delimited format is the most common, in some instances a comma-delimited format might be useful.

The first thing this handler does, after it has opened the file, is determine the number of background fields. It puts this number into the variable *numFields* for later use. It then puts the short ID of the current background into the variable *bkgndID*. This is necessary because many stacks will have more than one background. For example, if the script tried to get the value of background field 10 when there were only

```
on writeFile theFile, startCard, numCards, fDelim, rDelim
  -- this handler writes "numCards" cards
  -- starting with card "startCard",
  -- to the file theFile, using the field delimiter
  -- "fDelim" and the record deliminator "rDelim"
  set cursor to 4
  open file theFile
  put the number of background fields into numFields
  put the short id of this background into bkgndID
  go card startCard
  repeat with x = startCard to startCard + numCards
    go next card
    if the short id of this background is not bkgndID then
      next repeat
    end if
    repeat with y = 1 to numFields -1
    get bkgnd field y
    write cleanText(it) & fDelim to file theFile
    end repeat
    get bkgnd field numFields
    write cleanText(it) & rDelim to file theFile
  end repeat
  close file theFile
  answer "Done!" with "OK"
end writeFile
```

Script 33-6.   WriteFile writes all the background fields on a specified number of cards to a text file

9 background fields on a particular background, HyperTalk
would send an error to the user and halt the script. The line
"if the short id" tests to make sure that the current card is of
the same background. If it is not, execution of the script
returns to the top of the repeat loop, and the card is not
written.

After setting up these initial variables, the script begins
the actual writing process. The repeat loop executes from the
value of *startCard* (the first card you are writing) to the
value of *startCard* + *numCards* (the number of cards to
write). The first thing the script does is go to the card to
write.

There are several ways you could have written the instructions in this loop that take us to the specific card. The line "go card x" instead of the line "go next card" would have worked. However, when HyperCard goes to a card based on its number, it needs to look at the beginning of the stack and then count forward that many cards. This process is fast enough that you really don't notice it, but when working with large stacks you need every bit of performance boost you can get.

When the script gets to the card, another loop is started. This one executes from 1 to the number of fields minus 1. You do not write all the fields because you want to place a different delimiter at the end of the last field. It gets the contents of this field, and then calls the function cleanText, which is shown in Script 33-7.

The purpose of cleanText is indicated by its name—it removes characters from the text that you don't want to include in the file. HyperCard fields can have returns in them. If you are writing this text to a file, however, you do not want to include those returns; they would confuse whatever program is reading the text, causing it to see ends of records where they do not exist, and the data would be scrambled when retrieved into a database. (The special case of the standard HyperCard Address stack and how to work with it is discussed later in this chapter.) In the place of returns, insert linefeeds (ASCII character 10), which most programs can understand.

It is rare that HyperCard fields can contain tabs, but since they could also confuse another program, they should be removed.

The cleanText function executes two repeat loops. While the text it is working with contains a tab, it deletes the first tab character it finds by using HyperTalk's Offset function. After removing the tabs, it replaces the returns with linefeeds, again using the Offset function. When this is all finished, it returns the altered text to writeFile, which writes it and the field delimiter to the file.

After processing all these fields, you need to do the same with the last field, which is contained in *numFields*. This

```
function cleanText theText
   repeat while theText contains tab
      delete char(offset(tab,theText)) of theText
   end repeat
   repeat while theText contains return
      put lineFeed into char(offset(return,theText)) of theText
   end repeat
   return theText
end cleanText
```

Script 33-7.   This function removes tabs from text and replaces any returns with linefeeds

time add the record delimiter, *rdelim*, to the file. The repeat loop ends, and execution moves to the next record.

After writing the specified number of cards, writeFile closes the file (an important step), tells the user it is finished, and ends.

WriteFile will not work on its own. It needs a "front end," something that can pass the information it needs to it. Script 33-8 shows a mouseUp handler that gets the needed information from the user, checks to see if the file already exists, and then calls writeFile.

This mouseUp handler is similar to the one in Script 33-5. It also uses a repeat loop to get the name of the file. This time, when *fileName* is called, check to see if the file contains text. If it does, the user is asked if the file should be replaced. This is merely good programming practice, giving the user a chance to reconsider a potentially destructive act, and it is mandated by Apple's *Human Interface Guidelines.*

Next, ask for the delimiters. ASCII values are requested because you cannot get certain characters from the keyboard, including the TAB, RETURN, and ENTER keys, among others—the very ones you might need. Use the numToChar function to convert these ASCII values into characters so they will be easier to send to writeFile. You could have such a handler take care of the conversion, but it would need to do so many times and thus slow the process down.

```
on mouseUp
  -- this script goes into a button,
  -- along with the "readFile",
  -- handler and the "fileLeng" function.  It reads a tab
  -- delimited file from disk, and puts the data into a stack
  repeat
    ask "Enter name of file to write."
    --the user canceled
    if it is empty then exit mouseUp
    put it into fileName
    -- does the file exist?
    if fileLeng(fileName) > 0 then
      answer "Replace " && quote & fileName & quote & "?"¬
      with "Yes" or "No"
      if it is "No" then
        next repeat
      else
        exit repeat
      end if
  end repeat
  -- get the delimiters
  answer "Use standard TAB & RETURN delimiters?"¬
  with "No" or "Yes"
    if it is "No" then
        ask "Please type the ASCII value for fld delimiter."
        put numToChar(it) into fDelim
        ask "Please type the ASCII value for rec delimiter."
        put numToChar(it) into rDelim
    else
        put tab into fDelim
        put return into rDelim
    end if
  ask "Please enter the card number to start" with "1"
  put it into startCard
  ask "Please enter number of cards to write" ¬
  with the number of cards
  put it into numCards
  writeFile fileName, startCard, numCards, fDelim, rDelim
end mouseUp
```

Script 33-8.   A mouseUp handler for a button that uses the new-FileName and writeFile handlers to write a specified number of cards to a stack

After getting the delimiters, find out which card to start with and how many cards to write. Assign these numbers to variables, and then call writeFile. Note that in the mouseUp handler, you referred to the file with the variable *fileName*, but in the writeFile handler, you call it *theFile*. This was not included to confuse you, but to illustrate that these variables are local variables, and that the same information can be called by different names in different places. Normally, you want to be consistent with this—not for HyperCard's sake, but for your own when you later modify the script and need to understand it.

Note: Neither the Read nor the Write file buttons discussed here are necessarily complete implementations of these functions. They work within their limits, but there is plenty of room to add a more efficient user interface to these functions and ways to enhance their performance. However, they do illustrate the basic problems of reading and writing files and go a long way towards getting the hard work done.

Merging with Word Processors

One of the things you need to do with your data is merge it with files created in your word processor. You have undoubtedly received mail that has your name merged into a letter, making the letter appear to be written to you personally. You may have even perpetrated this kind of letter. Since one of the things you do with HyperCard is store information such as names and addresses, it makes sense for that you should want to create data documents from HyperCard. In the discussion that follows, it is assumed that you are working with Microsoft Word. Some notes are included about WordPerfect, but you should consult your word processor manual for details about its data document format requirements.

Not coincidentally, Word is able to work with tab-delimited files. It can read documents that have the fields delimited by tabs and the records deliminated by returns. Microsoft Word is also able to read files in which the fields are delimited by commas. This ability requires you to work in a special way with fields that contain commas as part of the text (even when you are working with tab-delimited files). For those fields, you must include quotes around the fields. Script 33-9 shows a function that adds these quotes. If the parameter *theText* contains a comma, this function adds quotes at the beginning and ending of the text, and then returns the text.

Another requirement of Word is that the first record in the file contain a Data header. This header is actually a separate record, formatted in the same way as the remainder of the data. Instead of the data, however, it contains the names of all the fields that are in the file. This allows the main document, which contains the text into which the data document will be merged, to refer to the fields by name. Script 33-10 shows a handler, writeHeader, that writes this header. It assumes that tabs are to be used as delimiters and that all the background fields are to be written to the stack.

```
function addQuotes theText
    if theText contains "," then
        put quote before theText
        put quote after theText
    end if
    return theText
end addQuotes
```

Script 33-9. This function puts quotes before and after fields that contain commas

```
on writeHeader theFile
   open file theFile
   put the number of background fields into numFields
   repeat with x = 1 to numFields -1
      get the short name of background field x
      write addQuotes(it) & tab to file theFile
   end repeat
   get the short name of background field numFields
   write addQuotes(it) & return to file theFile
   close file theFile
end writeHeader
```

Script 33-10.   This handler writes the names of the background fields in a stack to a tab-delimited file

For more information on merging with Microsoft Word, consult Microsoft's manual. A good discussion of this can also be found in *Microsoft Word for the Macintosh: The Complete Reference* by Michael Fischer (Berkeley, Calif: Osborne/McGraw-Hill, 1988).

Creating merge files for other word processors is a similar process but other word processors might want different delimiters. Both Mac and PC WordPerfect, for example, use the Control-E character (ASCII character 5) followed by a return as the field delimiter, and Control-R (ASCII character 18) followed by a return, as the record delimiter. To change Script 33-9 so that it uses these characters, replace "tab" with "numToChar(5)" and replace "return" with "numToChar(18)". Fields with embedded commas do not need quotes in WordPerfect, so the addQuotes handler is not necessary, nor is the header record.

The Address Stack

The Address stack provided with HyperCard presents a different case than do many stacks. In most stacks, and in virtually all database and filing programs, different items of information are assigned to different fields. In the case of a name and address file, the name will usually be one field, the address another, and the city, state, and ZIP code would all have their own fields. However, in the HyperCard Address stack there are only two fields: "Name and Address," and "Phone Number." If you were to use standard techniques for writing this stack to a delimited file, you would get into some trouble. A merge document would see all of "Name and Address" as one field, and you would lose control over what information is included in the letter and how it is formatted.

Instead, treat every line in the "Name and Address" field as a separate field, and delimit the lines accordingly. (For this example, you will not use the "Phone Number" field, but it should be easy to modify the handler to deal with this field.) Script 33-11 shows a mouseUp handler that can be placed into a button on this stack for exporting the stack to Microsoft Word. Note that this handler uses the addQuotes, fileLeng, and newFileName functions discussed earlier. They must be in the script of the button (or in a script that is in the hierarchy) for this button to work.

After getting the name of the file, this handler first writes the Data header to the file. To make things easy, name the fields in the text file after the line they are on in the "Name and Address" field. The stack, as shipped by Apple, has seven lines in it; if you have modified this field, you need to change the script. The first six fields are written with a tab for the delimiter, and the last one with a return for the delimiter.

The handler now writes all the cards to the file. The repeat loop with the x counter handles the individual cards. The inner repeat loop with the y counter handles the individual lines in the field. Note that when we get each line in the field, that line usually contains the return that separates it from the next line. If there is one, we remove it.

Next, the addQuotes function is called, and the result is written to the file, with a tab at the end of it. The same thing

```
on mouseUp
  -- this writes the entire address stack to
  -- a Microsoft Word Merge document
  put newFileName() into theFile
  open file theFile
  -- first, we'll write the data header
  -- the standard address stack has 7 lines
  repeat with x = 1 to 6
    write "Line" && x & tab to file theFile
  end repeat
  -- the last field
  write "Line 7" & return to file theFile
  -- Now, cycle through the cards, writing them all
  put the number of cards into numCards
  go first card
  repeat with x = 1 to numCards
    -- allow the user to halt
    if the mouse is down then exit repeat
    repeat with y = 1 to 6
      get line y of field "Name and Address"
      if last char of it is return then
        delete last char of it -- removes the return
      end if
      write addQuotes(it) & tab to file theFile
    end repeat
    get line 7 of field "Name and Address"
    if last char of it is return then
      delete last char of it
    end if
    write addQuotes(it) & return to file theFile
    go next card
  end repeat
  close file theFile
  answer "Done!" with "OK"
end mouseUp
```

Script 33-11.   A mouseUp handler that writes the HyperCard Address stack to a Microsoft Word data file for merging

is done for the final line in the field, except return is used as the delimiter. The script goes to the next card, and the process repeats.

At the beginning of the x loop, the line "if the mouse is down then exit repeat" is included. This allows the user to halt the process without resorting to COMMAND-PERIOD. Since HyperTalk cannot trap for COMMAND-PERIOD, we need to allow for a clean exit, which makes sure the file is closed. Using the mouse button for this is simple to accomplish. A more advanced version of the script might ask the user if the process should actually be stopped and act accordingly.

This script does not deal with cases where the user might only want to write certain cards to the file. That would definitely add utility to the button, but is beyond the scope of this book.

Working with Unstructured Text

At times you may want to retrieve text in an unstructured manner. For example, you might have a stack that you use for gathering and managing notes. Occasionally you use an editor other than HyperCard—such as Microsoft Word, MacWrite, or a desk accessory—to create those notes. When this is the case, you will need to import your files into Hyper-Card in a very different manner.

Remember that structured text contains records made up of fields. Records normally end with a return character. In text editors, however, the return character delimits a paragraph, and you might want to include many paragraphs in one field. Again, as part of the Button Ideas stack that is included with HyperCard version 1.1 and greater, the Import button allows text to be brought into HyperCard as text—meaning unstructured text—or data—meaning structured text.

This button imports text in chunks of 16,384 characters (16K), and then puts that text into a field. It creates a new card, reads another 16K of text, puts it into the same field on a new card, and so on until it has read the entire stack.

One factor that makes this hard to do is that this kind of text is not regular. Using this button will bring all the text in, but it might require some tweaking once the text is in HyperCard. However, HyperCard's excellent Find command is useful for working with text like this. There are several specialized stacks available on services such as CompuServe that are designed to work in special instances. Some of these stacks are discussed in Chapter 32.

Importing and Exporting Graphics

The tools that HyperCard uses to import and export graphics are not as flexible, from a scripting point of view, as the tools that are used for text. You cannot, for example, select a graphic and save it to a file with no intervention or help from the user.

Import Paint

The Import Paint command on HyperCard's File menu, as shown in Figure 33-5, is used to import bit maps from Mac-Paint and similar applications. This command is only available when a Paint tool is in use. It brings up a standard Open File dialog box and only shows files that have a file type of PNTG. This file type denotes a MacPaint-compatible file. Programs such as SuperPaint, FullPaint, DeskPaint, and others can create this kind of file.

Since HyperCard can deal with only as much graphics as fit in a standard Macintosh window and most Paint-type programs can work with much larger canvases, this command imports only the top-left corner of the file. The Hyper-Card (and standard Macintosh) window, recall, is 512 pixels wide and 342 pixels tall. Anything outside those boundaries is ignored by this command.

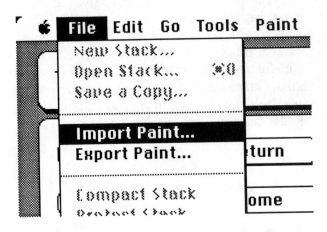

Figure 33-5. The Import Paint command from the File menu is only available when a Paint Tool is selected

Therefore, you might need to do some work on your graphic before you bring it in to HyperCard. Different Paint programs work in different ways, but they all have a way to move the graphic around on the page.

You can use this command from within a script, but it is not possible to control which file is opened from within a script. Since the command always opens a standard Get File dialog box, the user must find the file from which to import manually.

Like all menu commands, Import Paint can be called with HyperTalk's doMenu command:

```
doMenu "Import Paint..."
```

Remember that since the three dots appear on the menu item, they must be used in the text of the menu item to be executed.

Export Paint

The Export Paint command, shown in Figure 33-6, works in the same way as the Import Paint command. It is only available when a Paint Tool is in use and always opens a standard Put File dialog box. Again, there is no way for a script to insert a file name into this dialog box. HyperCard will create a file on disk that has the file type PNTG and the creator MPNT; it is a MacPaint document, but can be opened by other painting or desktop publishing programs. The 512×342-pixel HyperCard screen will occupy the top-left corner of the document.

As with Import Paint, Export Paint can be executed from within a script with the doMenu command.

Using the Clipboard

The Clipboard can also be used from within a script to copy or paste graphics. Again, it works with the doMenu com-

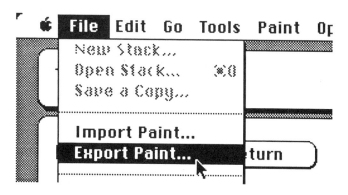

Figure 33-6.   The Export Paint command on the File menu

Figure 33-7.   Attempting to paste a picture from within a script causes this alert if there is no picture on the Clipboard

mand. With a graphic selected, the command doMenu Copy Picture will place a copy of that graphic on the Clipboard. Cut Picture will cut the picture from the card or background.

To Paste a graphic, use the command doMenu Paste Picture. You must be certain, however, that the Clipboard does indeed contain a graphic. The Paste item on the File menu changes depending on what the Clipboard contains—text, picture, button, field, or some other graphic. If you attempt to use this command when there is no picture on the Clipboard, the error alert shown in Figure 33-7 will appear. There is no way to trap for this error from HyperTalk.

See Chapter 29 for more details on working with the Painting tools from within HyperTalk.

HyperCard with CD-ROM and Networks

HyperCard and CD-ROM
HyperCard and Networks
Read-Only Stacks in General

This chapter discusses the special considerations involved in creating HyperCard applications or stacks for use on CD-ROM drives and for shared use on a network. These special cases have some problems in common, but each case also presents problems unique to itself.

HyperCard and CD-ROM

The CD-ROM industry has been nascent for the past three or four years, with industry leaders promising each year the arrival of a new generation of applications that would make CD-ROM as ubiquitous as hard-disk drives. At the time of writing, this has not happened, and it is debatable whether it ever will. Nevertheless, HyperCard is a program uniquely suited to the capabilities of CD-ROM.

CD-ROM: a Primer

What is CD-ROM, and why is it so interesting? If you've walked into a consumer electronics or music store anytime in the last few years, you doubtless have noticed the rapid growth of compact disk (CD) music. *Compact disk* is the generic term for the technology and the physical disk. *CD-ROM* stands for "compact disk—read-only memory." It defines the use of the disk as a read-only device for a computer.

CD music has done well for a number of reasons. First, compact disks are a *digital* as opposed to an *analog* medium. An analog medium is one that represents the data it contains as a constantly changing wave form. On a record, a physical wave exists that vibrates the stylus as it passes through the record's groove. This vibration is amplified by the record player and played through the speaker. With digital music, the music is sampled 44,000 times a second, and a number is produced that describes the music—its amplitude, tone, and so on—at the time it is sampled. That number is encoded onto a CD. When the music is played back, the circuitry inside the player reads the number from the disk and uses it as an instruction on how to vibrate the speaker. This digitizing of music means that the hissing noise heard on a recording that is copied in an analog medium is eliminated. CD music is, therefore, crisper and sharper than are records or cassette tapes.

Another reason for the success of CD music is physical. On a CD, the actual recording surface is encased in clear plastic, so it is more difficult to damage the quality of the music on the disk by scratching it. Compact disks are also easier to store and catalog than are vinyl records (which are too large) or cassette tapes (which are too small).

The widespread rapid acceptance of CD music will affect the anticipated growth of CD-ROM in the computer world. First, although it is a new *computer* technology, it is not a new technology to consumers. Many Macintosh users have acquired libraries of CD music and so are comfortable with these disks. Second, because many manufacturers are now making CD players, it should not take long for CD-ROM drives to arrive at prices that are close to (or only slightly higher than) CD music drives. A CD-ROM drive will eventually cost less than a 20MB hard disk. Third, there are a number of factories capable of pressing CD-ROM disks: the technology is the same for CD-ROM as it is for CD music. Finally, because of their economy of scale, it is possible to press CD-ROM disks for well under five dollars each.

The most important characterisic of CD-ROM is the large amount of room it gives you. CD-ROMs can hold as much as 600MB of information—about 14 40MB hard disks or 700 800KB floppy disks. That sort of room gives developers the ability to store large amounts of information on disk and distribute it at a relatively low cost. The computer industry has never had this capability before. It is also no coincidence that one of HyperCard's limits is its maximum stack size of 550MB; Bill Atkinson has said that the potential of CD-ROM was an important factor in his planning and creation of HyperCard.

Now for the bad news about CD-ROM. Perhaps their most limiting characteristic is that they are read-only. Information is stored on CDs by a laser beam that burns a small pit into the disk (another laser in the CD player shines on the disk and determines where the pits are). Once a pit has been burned into a disk by a laser device, there is no way to "unburn" that pit to erase the information. There are no devices for home recording of CD music. Instead, CD-ROM is a *publishing* medium: one not for you to store your own information on, but one that allows publishers to distribute information (including text, pictures, and sound) so you can browse through that information as you would a book.

Second, CD-ROM drives do not offer the speed that hard disks offer. Most modern hard disks can access any place on a hard disk in less than 20 milliseconds. However, CD-ROMs have an average access time of well over 100 milliseconds, and they are often slower than a floppy disk.

Clearly there is a trade-off. While there are problems with CD-ROMs—including the difficulty of creating large applications because of hard-disk capacity and the slow speeds of the drive—there are clear benefits to its ability to store nearly half a gigabyte of data on one inexpensive disk.

Using Stacks on CD-ROM

Using a HyperCard stack on a CD-ROM disk is not very different from using a HyperCard stack on a hard disk. The CD-ROM disk appears to you on the Finder desktop and from within HyperCard as if it were just another hard disk. If the stack has been developed correctly, the developer has taken CD-ROM limits and performance into consideration and has created the stack to allow you quick and easy access to all the information on the disk. There are, however, a couple of facts about CD-ROM you should remember.

You cannot modify the stack. CD-ROMs are locked devices, which means that you cannot open up a script and alter it to make it work in different ways.

However, you *can* copy information from a stack located on a CD-ROM to your own hard disk. This means the stack should support all the levels of copying and pasting that HyperCard itself supports. You should be able to copy and paste text into your word-processed documents, pictures, HyperCard, or your graphics program. You should also be able to copy cards or ranges of cards onto your hard disk to allow you to modify them. If your hard disk has enough room on it, you should also be able to copy entire stacks to your hard disk—either with HyperCard's Save a Copy command or from the Finder. Once the stack is on your own hard disk, you should be able to modify it as much as you like, provided it is not password protected.

Aside from the slow speed of most CD-ROM drives and your not being able to modify stacks, working with stacks on a CD-ROM is only slightly different than working with stacks on your hard disk.

Scripting and Design Issues

Programming for CD-ROM brings up several issues that are present when developing stacks for floppy disk distribution, but become more accented when you are distributing on CD-ROM.

Programming for CD-ROM can be broken into three general phases: development, testing, and mastering.

Development in CD-ROM taxes the resources of most programmers because it can hold far more than the average hard disk. Generally, you should start working on the stack on a very large hard disk. A hard disk of at least 100MB is preferable, although you can develop on smaller disks. If you are using a hard disk that cannot contain at one time all the information you will eventually include on the CD-ROM, you will have to work with separate hard disks and merge all the information only when you send it to the presser for mastering.

Testing, for CD-ROM applications, is perhaps even more important than for other applications. You cannot easily and cheaply distribute updated disks. It is important, therefore, that you make sure your application is as bug-free as possible so you can avoid the expense of creating a new master to fix one or two bugs.

Mastering is the process by which the disk manufacturer creates a master from which all your CD-ROMs will be produced. The manufacturer actually puts together—either on a large hard disk or on something like a nine-track tape unit—all the data that will eventually go on the CD-ROM.

The mastering process is much more expensive than actually pressing the disk. Once you have a master disk, it is fairly inexpensive to produce the CD-ROMs themselves.

One thing you need to remember about CD-ROM is that just because it *can* contain as much as 550MB, it does not *have* to contain that much information. If you want to distribute only 80MB, CD-ROM is still the way to go.

Speed

An important factor to consider when developing for CD-ROM is that the speed of access on the CD-ROM drive will almost certainly be slower than it is on the hard disk on which you develop the application. Take this into account, and plan as much as possible for the slower medium.

Hard-Code Links

You will remember from Chapter 18 that links made to different cards by their ID numbers are quicker than links made by card number or name. Whenever possible, therefore, you should hard code those links so that they are by card number. The script presented in that chapter for creating hard-code links could be changed to work automatically with a wide variety of buttons and stacks. After you have done the initial developmental work, change the links from the slower links to the faster ones.

Finding Text

HyperCard's Find command is optimized to work quickly on information that is subject to frequent change. Because a CD-ROM is a read-only device, the text on that disk will *never* change once you have mastered it. Therefore, using HyperCard's Find command might not be the best method for locating text. There are several alternative methods, however, that use both native HyperCard capabilities and add-on products.

You might consider building into your stack an index that lists all the possible words you might want to look up in your stacks. Include with the index a listing of all the cards in which each word occurs, using the ID numbers of those cards. When you want to find a word, use the "lookup table" you have created to go directly to the correct card, rather than using the HyperCard Find command.

Several software manufacturers, such as KnowledgeSet, have created software packages for HyperCard that build their own indexes of all the words contained in a HyperCard stack. This software technology is known as a *retrieval engine*, because its purpose is to retrieve information from the CD-ROM. Using the XFCN that is part of that software, you can quickly determine which card contains the desired text. Retrieval engines offer greatly improved performance over HyperCard's Find command; the one produced by KnowledgeSet is approximately 200 times faster. There is a price to pay for that performance: the index for the stack is likely to be as large as 60% of the original stack size. Nevertheless, if you have an application that includes a large amount of text, and you want to provide very fast random access to any word in the stack, you should consider this option. Remember, however, that on a CD-ROM you will have the room to include extensive indexes, which will benefit anyone using your stack.

Preloading

A useful technique for speeding up many operations is *preloading*. HyperCard maintains a cache of the cards you have looked at recently and consequently goes to those cards more quickly. Thus you can force cards into this cache by first going to them.

For example, suppose that you have ten cards that you will be using for animation. The animation is achieved by showing slightly different cards in quick succession. The first time those cards are shown they will not move as quickly as they will in subsequent showings. If you preload those cards before doing the animation, you make it appear much smoother. Script 34-1 is a handler that preloads a specified number of cards.

This handler first locks the screen, so you do not see the cards going by. It then sets lockMessages to "true" to speed up preloading, and it remembers at which card it started.

```
on preLoad numCards
  lock screen
  set lockmessges to true
  push this card
  put "Just a moment..."
  repeat with x = 1 to numCards
    go next card
    set cursor to busy
  end repeat
  pop card
  set lockMessages to false
  hide msg
  unlock screen
end preLoad
```

Script 34-1.   This handler preloads several cards to speed up their later showing

The text "Just a moment..." is placed into the Message box to let you know that something is happening. The repeat loop then executes as many times as specified on the line that called the handler, each time going to the next card. When the loop has finished executing, the line "pop card" returns you to the card you started at. The handler then sets lock-Messages to "false," hides the Message box, and stops.

To call this handler, you can use a line such as "preLoad 10" to preload ten cards. Preloading cards in this manner can greatly speed up accessing a stack, especially when you are card flipping to display various cards. You should limit the number of cards you specify to preload, because when you preload a large number of cards, you lose the benefits of the process.

User Interface Considerations

Creating a flexible user interface is important when you are working with the large amount of data you can fit on a CD-ROM. Organizing a stack in a linear, card-to-card manner might work well on a small stack, but this can cause problems when working on a large stack or a collection of stacks. In these cases you should consider increasing the number of links between cards, which allows more lateral links for movement between related cards or stacks and obviates the need to return to a menu or main card before going to another stack.

Preferences

It is important to remember when creating stacks for use on a read-only disk that sophisticated users will *not* be able to alter your stacks to make them work in ways they prefer. To accommodate the different ways people like to use Hyper-Card, you should include a preferences card that gives them some control over how the stack operates.

Small Stacks Versus Large Stacks

The large amount of room on CD-ROMs creates the problem of how to structure your stacks. HyperCard is able to work with stacks as large as the capacity of a CD-ROM, so you might be tempted to create a stack that uses up all or most of this room. However, you should plan your stacks carefully.

First, the HyperCard Find command will work much faster (as will most commands that go to different cards) in a smaller stack than it will in a larger stack. If your application will be searching only on specified parts of the information, try to structure the series of stacks so that information that belongs together, or should be searched together, is in the same stack.

Second, many users will want to copy your stacks to their own hard disks so they can modify those stacks. That will be easier if you have implemented your application as a series of small stacks rather than as one large stack. Of course, making large stacks is a good method of copy-protecting your work; few users will want to copy a multi-megabyte stack to their hard or floppy disks to give to others.

HyperCard and Networks

In many cases, creating stacks for use on a network is much the same as creating stacks to be used on other locked disks, such as CD-ROMs.

Network Background

A *network* is a set of two or more computers physically connected to one another. It has four components: cabling, software, a server, and a client or workstation.

The *cabling* is the *physical* element that connects several computers to one another. The cabling that Apple provides for connecting Macintoshes to Macintoshes (or to LaserWriters) is called LocalTalk; it is easy to install. In addition to LocalTalk, there are other ways to connect the computers. Farallon Computing manufactures a set of cables called PhoneNet that is compatible with LocalTalk but uses standard phone wires to connect the machines.

Once two computers are connected with one another, *network software* is used; this allows one machine to use devices connected to another machine. The devices that are most commonly shared in networks of Macintoshes are hard disks; therefore, *file-sharing software*, which allows computers to share their hard disks, is the most common type of network software. Examples are Apple's AppleShare software and TOPS.

Another common type of network software is electronic mail. Using electronic mail software on a network allows one user to send messages to another user who is also connected to the network.

A *server* is a computer on the network that has made its hard disk available to other computers on the network.

A *client* or *workstation* is a computer that is using a hard disk made available to it by another computer.

Note: Connections made between two computers by a network are different from connections made by modem or direct serial interface connection. Network connections are generally faster than modem connections and more transparent; that is, if your machine is a client machine, using a hard disk that is connected to a server machine is not very different from using a hard disk directly connected to your own machine.

Floppy or hard disks connected directly to your computer are called *local disks*, while those you are using from a network server are called *networked* or *server volumes*.

Using HyperCard on a Network

Once you have mounted or connected a server volume to your machine, there are a few more issues you need to consider before running HyperCard or stacks located on a server.

Running HyperCard on a Server

When the server volume is mounted on your computer, you can use it just as you use a local disk, so it might seem to be a good idea to run HyperCard itself from the server volume. This is your only choice if you do not have a hard disk connected directly to your Macintosh. However, there are three considerations you need to remember when doing this.

Speed   The entire HyperCard program is not loaded into your computer's memory when you run the program. Instead, certain parts of the program are kept on disk until they are needed. For example, the part of the program that includes the painting tools is only loaded when those tools are needed. This means that shifting to different tools will be much slower when you are running HyperCard from a server than when you are running HyperCard from a local hard disk since server access is much slower.

Multiple Access   Many Macintosh programs are *multi-launch programs*, which means that if the application program is on a server, several people who are using the server can open that application at the same time. HyperCard is not a multilaunch program: if one person on the network is running a copy of HyperCard on a server, no others will be able to run that same program.

The Home Stack   Since HyperCard also needs frequent access to the Home stack, your performance will be much better if you run HyperCard and Home from a local disk (either hard disk or floppy) rather than from a server volume.

Using Stacks on a Network Server

Using a stack that resides on a server is similar to using a stack that resides on your own hard disk. The primary thing you need to remember about using such stacks is that you may not be able to *change* the stack that resides on the server.

In network terms, you will be able to use stacks on a server when these two conditions are met:

- You must *mount* or *attach* the server volume from the server. This means that you must use your networking software to make the volume available to your machine. The mechanisms for doing this will vary depending on the network software you are using, but once you have mounted the volume, virtually all Macintosh networking software allows you to access that volume from within HyperCard (or any other application) as if it were on a hard disk connected directly to your machine.

• You must have *read access* to the volume or folder that contains the stack, which means that the networking software permits you to open a file. If you are using TOPS, you automatically have read access to any file on a volume you mount. If you are using AppleShare or compatible software, you may not be able to open some folders on volumes that you mount.

Once you have made a server volume available to your computer and located the stack you want to use, you can use it just as if you were using it on a local disk.

When working with a stack on a server volume, you may not be able to change a stack, depending on the following factors:

• You must have *read/write access* to the volume or folder containing the stack, which means that not only can you look at a stack or other document on the server volume, but you can also change the stack or document. For security reasons, most networking schemes allow volumes and files to be protected so that only authorized people can change the stack. When you are using a network, you will need to enter the password before attempting to mount the networked disk or volume.

• If others are not currently using the stack when you open it, you will be able to modify the stack. If others *are* using the stack when you open it, it will be opened as a *read-only* stack, and the lock icon will appear on the menu bar.

Scripting and Design Issues

There are some special issues you should consider when developing HyperCard stacks for use on networks, just as there were with CD-ROMs.

First, you cannot assume that other users will have read/write access to the stack. You should include tests so that your scripts are aware of the mode in which the stack is running. This issue is discussed in more detail in the next section of this chapter.

The second issue is speed. The LocalTalk network hardware that Apple supports transfers information at the rate of 230,000 bits per second. Although this transfer rate is much faster than the fastest of modems, it is not nearly as fast as information transfer direct from hard disk. Additionally, if the network has many users on it and there is a lot of network traffic, performance will be even slower. You should keep this in mind when using or developing stacks on a network server. As discussed earlier for use with CD-ROMs, preloading is a good technique, but this temporarily increases the amount of data that is moving across the network cables. While preloading might help an individual user accessing a stack, it might slow down others on the network.

Network Helpers

As of this writing, APDA is in the process of preparing a set of tools called HyperAppleTalk. Several other developers also have created some tools that allow stacks to communicate with one another on a network.

Generally, these tools allow stacks to communicate with each other by sending messages. For example, if a user at one computer on the network draws something on the screen, the HyperCard stack can send a message to another stack, telling it how and where to draw the circle.

Read-Only Stacks in General

One thing that stacks designed for use on either CD-ROMs or networks have in common is that they will probably be used in a locked mode. When a stack is locked, of course, you cannot change the contents of the stack.

There are, however, some exceptions to this rule that allow scripts in read-only stacks to make some changes to the stacks. These exceptions give scripts some abilities that you can take advantage of when creating read-only stacks.

The cantModify Property

The cantModify property, as discussed in Chapter 13, is set to "true" for any stack that is on a locked volume or is otherwise locked.

One use for this property is to allow a script to determine if it is in a stack that is locked. If the property is "true," the stack is almost certainly locked from the Finder or is on a locked disk.

Another thing to remember about the cantModify property is that while *you* may not directly modify a card in a stack for which this property is "true," *scripts* can modify that card. As discussed in Chapter 29, this is useful when you want a script to paint onto a card but you want to save that card in its unchanged form for the next time it is opened. You can use any of HyperCard's tools from within scripts to modify a card.

The userModify Property

The userModify property is a global property that allows you to make changes to a card on a locked stack. All changes that are made to that card either by you or by a script are lost when you go to a different card, but before they are lost, those changes can be saved into variables for later use. With this capability you can create query-by-example cards for large stacks, which would allow you to type information into a blank card. A script could then extract the information you typed in before it is lost and search through the cards in the stack, comparing each card to see if it meets the criteria you typed.

Some Useful HyperCard Add-ons and Resources

Tools to Help You Script
Other Useful Tools
Increasing the Power of HyperCard

The HyperCard market is blossoming; products to help you make the most out of HyperCard and products created using HyperCard are appearing regularly. This chapter takes a look at some of the most useful auxiliary programs that were available at the time of writing. Doubtless, by the time you read this book there will be more.

Tools to Help You Script

Some of the first tools that appeared for HyperCard were, perhaps predictably, tools that made up for some of the deficiencies of HyperCard itself. These include tools to help you document or gather scripts from other stacks and tools to help you build scripts.

Script Report

Script Report was created by Eric Alderman and is available from Heizer Software. It is a HyperCard application that extracts all the scripts from a stack and places them into a hierarchy that makes it easy to find variables, handlers, functions, and the like. If you use an outlining program such as Acta or More, Script Report can save the scripts to a text file in a format that allows these programs to read the report in a structured manner.

ScriptExpert

ScriptExpert, shown in Figure 35-1, is a program developed by Dan Shafer, author of one of the first books on HyperTalk as well as several other books related to programming the Macintosh. ScriptExpert is published by HyperPress.

If you are new to scripting and have a fear of entering HyperTalk scripts into the Message box, then you should take a look at ScriptExpert. The program features several screens that display all the HyperTalk commands. You build scripts one line at a time by clicking on the buttons that have the name of the command or function you wish to execute. If the command or function requires parameters, ScriptExpert is smart enough to ask you for the correct parameters. It also includes tools for copying the scripts you have created into your own stacks.

ScriptExpert also allows you to build visual effects. You are given lists of visual effects, which you can put together into sequences and play back over and over again until you have found the combination that suits you.

ScriptExpert is primarily for those who fall between the novice and experienced user—those who have learned enough to know they want to script and know something about the commands but who are not comfortable entering scripts themselves.

Toolboxes

Because HyperCard has been called a "software erector set," it is not surpising that several manufacturers have developed toolboxes, or parts kits, for HyperCard. These include backgrounds, cards, buttons, fields, icons, and sounds, which

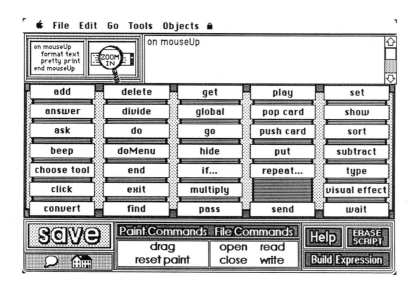

Figure 35-1.   The main screen from Dan Shafer's ScriptExpert

you can include in your own stacks. There are several of these toolboxes on the market, and more are appearing all the time. The following is a discussion of some of the more useful toolboxes available at the time of writing.

The Developer Stack

Produced by Steve Drazga, the Developer Stack is a useful compendium of buttons, functions, scripts, XFCNs, and XCMDs. The Developer Stack includes information about how to use each item in the stack, including fairly complete documentation for the function or button. Also, for each item in the stack, the Developer Stack includes a button that makes it easy for you to install that item into your own stack. If you are doing a lot of scripting, this is a useful stack to keep on your hard disk (see also Chapter 32).

101 Scripts and Buttons for HyperCard

Produced by MacroPac International, 101 Scripts and Buttons for HyperCard is also a compendium of useful buttons, scripts, and externals. Unlike the Developer Stack, which is a collection of public domain or shareware tools, 101 Scripts and Buttons for HyperCard seems to have been created entirely by MacroPac International. Like the Developer Stack, this stack contains a wide variety of useful commands and functions.

Perhaps most interesting is a series of related XFCNs and standard Macintosh dragging properties. DragRect provides a shimmering outline of an object, such as a window, as it is moved from one location to another on the screen. Drag-Grow provides an effect similar to what you see when you resize a window. DragSelect provides the ability to define a region on the screen and is usually used to select multiple objects, such as when you want to copy or delete multiple files in the Finder. Finally, IntersectRect allows you to determine whether one rectangle intersects another, which is useful for identifying objects selected with DragSelect.

The ZoomRect XCMD provides the same ability to create a zooming effect as the command visual effect Zoom Open, although the XCMD provides much more flexibility than the built-in command. You can zoom from and to any two rectangles on the screen, and you can control the look of the effect by modifying the number of intermediate rectangles to be drawn, the amount by which they can overlap, and the speed at which they appear. This provides some impressive zooming effects.

PaintView is a useful XCMD that allows you to choose any paint file from disk and view it in a show-page mode. You then can position a rectangle representing the size of a card anywhere on the image and import that selection.

APDA

The Apple Programmer's and Developer's Association is Apple's semiofficial means of distributing development tools to the public. APDA is a membership organization, and to buy products through APDA, you must become a member at a cost of $25 a year. Most of APDA's products are reasonably priced—the toolkits for use with HyperCard are priced at $10.

One of the most useful of APDA's documents is *Stack Design Guidelines*, a 120-page book that discusses many of the crucial issues you must consider before and during the process of designing stacks.

Other utilities available from APDA include the Hyper-Card AppleTalk toolkit, which allows a stack on one Macintosh to send messages to a stack on another Macintosh via Apple's LocalTalk cabling. The HyperCard Serial Toolkit allows HyperCard stacks to communicate with devices connected to one of the serial interface ports on the Macintosh.

You can write to APDA at 290 SW 43rd St., Renton, WA 98055.

On-line Services

Since the introduction of HyperCard, the on-line services have been a great source of information about the program. *On-line services* are services that you can connect to with your Macintosh and a modem. They are good sources of such things as shareware or public domain HyperCard stacks, button ideas, and external commands. Additionally, many knowledgeable HyperCard users frequent these services, allowing you to get quick help on HyperCard points with which you are having trouble.

Heizer Software

Heizer Software, located in Pleasant Hill, California, is a useful resource for HyperCard developers—both as a source of useful utilities and as a potential publisher of your Hyper-Card products. Heizer Software's growing library includes a number of useful HyperCard tutorials and utilities, including Script Report and this author's own stack, Port Authority.

Heizer Software is located at 1941 Oak Park Blvd, P.O. Box 232019, Pleasant Hill, CA 94523.

Other Useful Tools

Some other tools available for HyperCard allow you to create or import sound or icon resources from other sources.

MacRecorder

MacRecorder, from Farallon Computing in Berkeley, California, is a sound digitizer. Its hardware consists of a small box that connects to the modem port on the back of your Macintosh. On the box is a microphone, a volume dial, and two jacks for connecting audio cables.

MacRecorder also includes two applications for digitizing its sounds. SoundEdit is a sophisticated sound digitizing program that also includes a number of tools for doing such things as reversing the sound, adding an echo, or synthesizing sounds. Sounds recorded or created with this program can be saved into HyperCard to be played with the Play command.

MacRecorder also includes a HyperCard stack called HyperSound, shown in Figure 35-2, that allows you to record sounds with the MacRecorder from within HyperCard. While this stack includes virtually none of the sound editing tools of SoundEdit, its user interface is easier to use, and the stack is a lot of fun.

Scanners

A scanner is a device that reads or translates an image from paper into a form that can be used by the Macintosh. Typically, scanners are used to digitize photographs or drawings from paper and bring them onto the Macintosh screen or

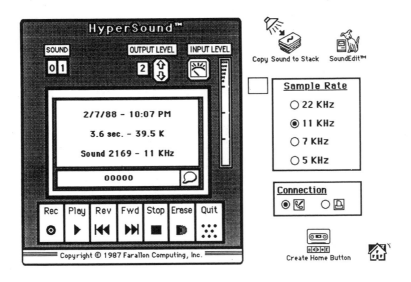

Figure 35-2.   HyperSound allows you to record sounds with the
MacRecorder and HyperCard

disk for use in such applications as desktop publishing. In
this way such things as logos or photographs can be integrated into desktop-published documents.

As far as HyperCard goes, you can use scanners to digitize images that can be used in your stacks. The Clip Art
stack that comes with HyperCard contains several such
images.

For HyperCard users, one of the most interesting scanning tools available is the Apple Scanner, announced in
August 1987. The Apple Scanner, like the MacRecorder,
comes with a stand-alone application as well as a stack.
While the stand-alone application will be of more interest to
desktop publishers, the HyperScan stack was designed by
Bill Atkinson to bring images into HyperCard. HyperScan is
a HyperCard stack that includes a set of external commands

that allow you to adjust the brightness and contrast of the image you are scanning to make it look good in HyperCard. HyperScan also allows you to preview a page to be scanned and select the portion of the page that is imported into HyperCard.

Increasing the Power of HyperCard

Several third-party products have appeared that provide HyperCard with capabilities that are not part of the package that is shipped by Apple.

Reports!

The Reports! software package, from Mediagenics, includes several tools that allow you to create more sophisticated report printouts than you can with HyperCard. You should consider using Reports! if you are using HyperCard for a database application to do such things as record sales and monitor inventory.

One part of Reports! is a stand-alone application, shown in Figure 35-3, that you use to actually create the printed report you want to use. You place background fields on the page, and you can also include pictures from the cards and summary (total) fields. An editor in the Reports! program allows you to insert HyperTalk handlers, just as you do in HyperCard, to perform tasks that are not built into the program.

The second part of Reports! is the Report card—a card that is installed in all stacks that use the Reports! package. This card includes the buttons that execute the external functions which actually print the report. All printing is done from within HyperCard.

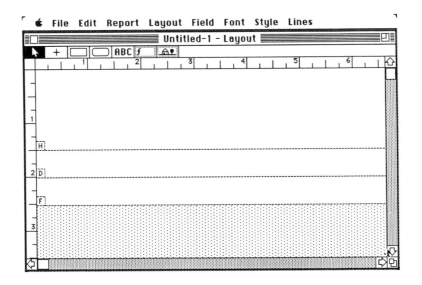

Figure 35-3.   Reports! for HyperCard allows you to design reports
based on information stored in HyperCard stacks

VideoWorks HyperCard Driver

VideoWorks, produced by MacroMind, was one of the first
animation tools available for the Macintosh. Since its initial
release several years ago, the program has matured considerably, with new versions offering new power. VideoWorks
has been used by companies such as Ashton-Tate, Apple, and
Microsoft to produce the "Guided Tours" of their products.

The VideoWorks HyperCard driver consists of a driver
file that must be placed in the same folder as HyperCard
itself (or the system folder or the same folder the current
stack is in), as well as a HyperCard external command that
allows you or a script to run the movie.

VideoWorks movies exist as files on disk that are played by the driver in HyperCard. Animations played by this driver seem to float over the top of the card, sometimes going over card and background buttons, sometimes going underneath them, between the button and the card. You can choose to clear the card display, playing the animation on a blank screen. On a screen larger than the original Macintosh screen, the entire screen is available to play the movies—a benefit to those who are creating presentations with Hyper-Card, but want to use the entire screen. For an experienced HyperCard scripter familiar with VideoWorks, it only takes an hour or two with the driver to learn how to use it.

While you can do animation within HyperCard, large projects are difficult to manage. The VideoWorks Hyper-Card driver solves this problem—you can edit or create the animation in VideoWorks and play it back from HyperCard. The driver also adds one capability not present in Hyper-Card: displaying color animation on the Mac II.

If you need animation, this is the tool to consider. MacroMind also supports VideoWorks with disks full of all types of clip animation.

HyperDA

HyperDA, from Symmetry Software, is a desk accessory that allows you to open and browse through many HyperCard stacks. HyperDA can run on a Macintosh with only 512K of RAM (HyperCard itself requires at least 750K of RAM, so it needs at least a 1MB Macintosh), opening up some of the power of HyperCard to users of these machines. HyperDA also allows Macintosh users with only 1MB to take advantage of HyperCard features and another program in Multi-Finder at the same time. HyperDA can also be used to open a second HyperCard stack when you are already using one stack. HyperCard itself does not allow you to have two stacks open at the same time. HyperDA does not support the complete set of HyperCard functions or all the capabilities of HyperTalk. This is not surprising: if it did, it would be as powerful as HyperCard itself.

Essentially, HyperDA allows you to do many of the things you can do while in Browsing mode. This means you can go to different cards or find text. You can copy text to paste it into other programs. However, you cannot use tools other than the Browse tool, which means you cannot create, copy, or delete buttons, nor can you create or paste graphics.

Following is a list of the HyperTalk commands, functions, and messages that HyperDA supports.

beep	mouseDown
closeBackground	mouseStillDown
closeCard	mouseUp
closeStack	openBackground
dial	openCard
doMenu	openStack
enterKey	pop
find	push
go [to]	returnKey
hide	show
idle	tabKey

In addition to making HyperDA, Symmetry Software is also licensing a set of functions to developers. These functions permit other applications programs to open HyperCard stacks in the same manner that HyperDA opens them. This will allow developers of other applications to create their Help files as HyperCard stacks and link those stacks to their applications.

Indexing Utilities

As useful as HyperCard's Find command is, it does have its limitations. It works well on small stacks without a great deal of text, but for large stacks with a great deal of text in them, the Find command can become quite slow.

Several manufacturers, typically those with experience in the CD-ROM industry, have addressed this problem with add-on software programs. These are applications or external commands that index all the words in a stack and include in those indexes the locations of each word. External functions then query the index and report back to you the card ID number and the exact location of the text on the card. Such programs are available from KnowledgeSet, Xyphias, and Discovery Systems.

There are some negative aspects to these indexing programs. First, the index files are separate from HyperCard and thus add a level of complexity to installing onto disk a stack that uses them. Second, the index files can become quite large—from 60% to 150% of the size of the stack being indexed. Third, if you are creating applications for sale to others, the licensing fees asked for by developers can have a substantial effect on the price you will need to charge for the stacks.

All of the indexing utilities tried at the time of this writing provide better performance than that provided by the HyperTalk Find command.

You encounter another limitation of HyperCard when you attempt to store large text files. Fields, you will remember, can contain a maximum of 30,000 bytes. If you want to index large files, you will need to break the files up into 30K chunks, which might be difficult.

One way around this limitation is provided by the stack called Texas, which is available on on-line services or through user groups. Written by Mark Zimmerman, the Texas stack indexes, from within HyperCard, text-only files on your hard disk and allows you to view those files.

Texas creates an index for the text file and then uses that index to locate particular words in the text. The indexing process creates two text files on disk, which are used to locate words in the original file. For example, a file containing a large portion of this book was 976,000 bytes on disk for 178,000 words. Indexing this file took about 20 minutes. The two index files created by Texas totalled 847K on the disk, so you should make sure you have plenty of room on your hard disk before indexing a file. Some lines from the text of this book as they appear in Texas are shown in Figure 35-4.

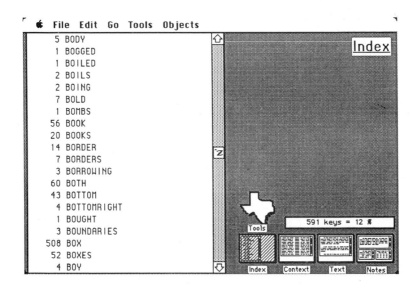

Figure 35-4.   Texas allows you to view selected words in context

Once a file has been indexed, Texas presents you with a scrolling field that lists all the words in your file alphabetically and shows how many times the word occurs in the file. Clicking on one of the words shows you the lines in the file that contain that word, and clicking on one of those lines takes you to a field showing the complete file. From there, you can scroll through the file or quickly jump to another word in the file. No matter how large the file, once it has been indexed, you will be able to find particular text in the file quickly and easily.

One advantage of Texas is its complete openness. You can send a formatted disk, along with a self-addressed, stamped envelope, to the author, and he will send you a complete, commented listing of the C code of the XFCNs and XCMDs that actually do the hard work of indexing and locating text. The file structure for the index files is also documented, so modifying the commands to suit your own purposes is not impossible.

Obviously Texas is not for everyone, nor will it work well for all applications. Since it keeps the text it works with in separate text files, it will not help those who want to speed the finding of text stored in HyperCard fields. Other indexing tools have appeared and will be appearing that address those concerns. For the time being, however, Texas is a good program for those who can take advantage of its unique features.

ASCII Table

Fonts
Control Characters
Special HyperCard Characters
Special Characters
A Script to Print All Characters

Every programming book needs an ASCII table.

ASCII represents the American Standard Code for Information Interchange. It defines the standard set of characters produced by computers, terminals, teletype machines, and so on. It defines characters up to and including the value of 127, which encompasses most alphanumeric characters. However, the characters represented by ASCII values 128 through 255 may be different from manufacturer to manufacturer. Different computer manufacturers, as well as different font manufacturers, have adopted different coding schemes for these characters. As Table A-1 shows, there is some divergence in the way certain characters are encoded for some fonts, even on the Macintosh.

Fonts

The chart is shown in two typefaces. The Geneva typeface is a bit-mapped font for the Macintosh screen and ImageWriter printer. Helvetica is a LaserWriter font for PostScript printers. The two fonts are different for ASCII characters 217 through 255. Most other Macintosh bit map fonts will have

ASCII Value	Geneva	Helvetica	Character Name/Key
0			
1			CONTROL-A
2			CONTROL-B
3			CONTROL-C
4			CONTROL-D
5			CONTROL-E
6	\	\	CONTROL-F
7			CONTROL-G
8			CONTROL-H
9			**TAB***
10			**LINEFEED***
11			CONTROL-K
12			**FORMFEED***
13	¶	¶	**RETURN***, CONTROL-M
14			CONTROL-N
15			CONTROL-O
16			CONTROL-P
17			CONTROL-Q
18			CONTROL-R
19			CONTROL-S
20			CONTROL-T
21			CONTROL-U
22			CONTROL-V
23			CONTROL-W
24			CONTROL-X
25			CONTROL-Y
26			CONTROL-Z
27			
28			
29			
30	–	-	
31			
32			SPACEBAR*

Table A-1.   The Macintosh ASCII Table

ASCII Value	Geneva	Helvetica	Character Name/Key
33	!	!	
34	"	"	
35	#	#	
36	$	$	
37	%	%	
38	&	&	
39	'	'	
40	(	(	
41	)	)	
42	*	*	
43	+	+	
44	,	,	
45	–	-	
46	.	.	
47	/	/	
48	0	0	
49	1	1	
50	2	2	
51	3	3	
52	4	4	
53	5	5	
54	6	6	
55	7	7	
56	8	8	
57	9	9	
58	:	:	
59	;	;	
60	<	<	
61	=	=	
62	>	>	
63	?	?	
64	@	@	
65	A	A	

Table A-1.   The Macintosh ASCII Table (*continued*)

ASCII Value	Geneva	Helvetica	Character Name/Key
66	B	B	
67	C	C	
68	D	D	
69	E	E	
70	F	F	
71	G	G	
72	H	H	
73	I	I	
74	J	J	
75	K	K	
76	L	L	
77	M	M	
78	N	N	
79	O	O	
80	P	P	
81	Q	Q	
82	R	R	
83	S	S	
84	T	T	
85	U	U	
86	V	V	
87	W	W	
88	X	X	
89	Y	Y	
90	Z	Z	
91	[	[	
92	\	\	
93	]	]	
94	^	^	
95	—	—	
96	`	`	
97	a	a	
98	b	b	

Table A-1.   The Macintosh ASCII Table (*continued*)

ASCII Value	Geneva	Helvetica	Character Name/Key
99	c	c	
100	d	d	
101	e	e	
102	f	f	
103	g	g	
104	h	h	
105	i	i	
106	j	j	
107	k	k	
108	l	l	
109	m	m	
110	n	n	
111	o	o	
112	p	p	
113	q	q	
114	r	r	
115	s	s	
116	t	t	
117	u	u	
118	v	v	
119	w	w	
120	x	x	
121	y	y	
122	z	z	
123	{	{	
124	|	|	
125	}	}	
126	~	~	
127			
128	Ä	Ä	OPTION-u,A
129	Å	Å	OPTION-SHIFT-A
130	Ç	Ç	OPTION-SHIFT-C
131	É	É	OPTION-e,E

Table A-1.   The Macintosh ASCII Table (*continued*)

ASCII Value	Geneva	Helvetica	Character Name/Key
132	Ñ	Ñ	OPTION-n,N
133	Ö	Ö	OPTION-u,O
134	Ü	Ü	OPTION-u,U
135	á	á	OPTION-e,a
136	à	à	OPTION-`,a
137	â	â	OPTION-i,a
138	ä	ä	OPTION-u,a
139	ã	ã	OPTION-n,n
140	å	å	OPTION-a,a
141	ç	ç	OPTION-c,c
142	é	é	OPTION-e,e
143	è	è	OPTION-`,e
144	ê	ê	OPTION-i,e
145	ë	ë	OPTION-u,e
146	í	í	OPTION-e,i
147	ì	ì	OPTION-`,i
148	î	î	OPTION-i,i
149	ï	ï	OPTION-u,i
150	ñ	ñ	OPTION-n,n
151	ó	ó	OPTION-e,o
152	ò	ò	OPTION-`,o
153	ô	ô	OPTION-i,o
154	ö	ö	OPTION-u,o
155	õ	õ	OPTION-n,o
156	ú	ú	OPTION-e,u
157	ù	ù	OPTION-`,u
158	û	û	OPTION-i,u
159	ü	ü	OPTION-u,o
160	'	†	OPTION-t
161	°	°	OPTION-SHIFT-8
162	¢	¢	OPTION-4
163	£	£	OPTION-3
164	§	§	OPTION-6

Table A-1.   The Macintosh ASCII Table (*continued*)

ASCII Value	Geneva	Helvetica	Character Name/Key
165	●	•	OPTION-8
166	¶	¶	OPTION-7
167	ß	ß	OPTION-s
168	®	®	OPTION-r
169	©	©	OPTION-g
170	™	™	OPTION-2
171	´	´	OPTION-e,SPACEBAR
172	¨	¨	OPTION-u,SPACEBAR
173	≠	≠	OPTION-EQUAL
174	Æ	Æ	OPTION-SHIFT-'
175	Ø	Ø	SHIFT-OPTION-o
176	∞	∞	OPTION-5
177	±	±	SHIFT-OPTION-EQUAL
178	≤	≤	OPTION-,
179	≥	≥	OPTION-.
180	¥	¥	OPTION-y
181	µ	µ	OPTION-m
182	∂	∂	OPTION-d
183	Σ	Σ	OPTION-w
184	∏	∏	OPTION-P
185	π	π	OPTION-p
186	∫	∫	OPTION-f
187	ª	ª	OPTION-9
188	º	º	OPTION-0
189	Ω	Ω	OPTION-z
190	æ	æ	OPTION-q
191	ø	ø	OPTION-o
192	¿	¿	OPTION-?
193	¡	¡	OPTION-1
194	¬	¬	OPTION-l
195	√	√	OPTION-v
196	ƒ	ƒ	OPTION-f
197	≈	≈	OPTION-x

Table A-1.   The Macintosh ASCII Table (*continued*)

ASCII Value	Geneva	Helvetica	Character Name/Key
198	Δ	Δ ·	OPTION-j
199	«	«	OPTION-\
200	»	»	OPTION-SHIFT-\
201	…	…	LEADERS, OPTION-;
202			
203	À	À	OPTION-`,A
204	Ã	Ã	OPTION-n,A
205	Õ	Õ	OPTION-n,O
206	Œ	Œ	OPTION-SHIFT-q
207	œ	œ	OPTION-q
208	–	–	
209	—	—	OPTION-SHIFT-_
210	"	"	OPTION-[
211	"	"	OPTION-SHIFT-[
212	'	'	OPTION-]
213	'	'	OPTION-SHIFT-]
214	÷	÷	OPTION-/
215	◇	◊	OPTION-SHIFT-V
216	ÿ	ÿ	OPTION-u,y
217	✿	Ÿ	OPTION-SHIFT-`
218		⁄	OPTION-SHIFT-1
219		¤	OPTION-SHIFT-2
220		‹	OPTION-SHIFT-3
221		›	OPTION-SHIFT-4
222		fi	OPTION-SHIFT-5
223		fl	OPTION-SHIFT-6
224		‡	OPTION-SHIFT-7
225		·	OPTION-SHIFT-9
226		‚	OPTION-SHIFT-0
227		„	OPTION-SHIFT-w
228		‰	OPTION-SHIFT-e
229		Â	OPTION-SHIFT-r
230		Ê	OPTION-SHIFT-t

Table A-1.   The Macintosh ASCII Table (*continued*)

ASCII Value	Geneva	Helvetica	Character Name/Key
231		Á	OPTION-SHIFT-y
232		Ë	OPTION-SHIFT-u
233		È	OPTION-SHIFT-i
234		Í	
235		Î	
236		Ï	
237		Ì	
238		Ó	
239		Ô	
240			
241		Ò	
242		Ú	
243		Û	
244		Ù	
245		ı	
246		ˆ	
247		˜	
248		¯	
249		˘	
250		˙	
251		˚	
252		¸	
253		˝	
254		˛	
255		ˇ	

Table A-1.   The Macintosh ASCII Table (*continued*)

the same basic character set as Geneva, and most Adobe-created PostScript fonts will have the same character set as Helvetica. If you are printing to a LaserWriter and have Font Substitution checked in the Page Setup dialog box, Helvetica will be printed instead of Geneva.

Control Characters

For characters 1 through 26, you will find that the right column shows the CONTROL key equivalent. As discussed in Chapter 21, if you have a Mac SE or II keyboard, you can use the controlKey message to test for these characters. For example, to test for CONTROL-a, you would use the following handler, which should be placed in a card, background, or stack script:

```
on controlKey num
   if num is 1 then
   -- commands to perform actions
end controlKey
```

Only certain control characters actually display something on the screen. Generally, a small box is inserted into the text if there is no defined character for an ASCII value. With ImageWriters, these boxes will be printed, but Laser-Writers will simply skip the characters.

Special HyperCard Characters

Certain characters are represented by constants in Hyper-Card, as discussed in Chapter 21. In Table A-1, those constants are shown in the right column in boldface.

In HyperCard scripts, the ¬ character is generated by pressing OPTION-RETURN. In other programs, or to enter this character into a HyperCard field, use OPTION-L.

Special Characters

The Macintosh includes many characters that are used in languages other than English. These characters—such as é and ç—are often formed by first pressing the OPTION key along with another key and then releasing the OPTION key and pressing a third key. These key combinations are shown in the table.

For example, to display the character é , you first hold down the OPTION key and then type **e**. Nothing appears on the screen until you release the OPTION key and type **e** again.

If you are in doubt about that keys produce any of these characters, you can use the Key Caps desk accessory that is included with the standard Macintosh System software. This desk accessory shows a keyboard and the characters produced by each key. It is very handy—you can type characters into it, copy them, and then paste them into HyperCard (or any other application).

A Script to Print All Characters

Script A-1 shows a mouseUp handler that you can place into a button to generate an ASCII table something like the one shown in Table A-1. It places the number of the character, followed by the character itself, on each line of a field called "Characters." This field should be a scrolling card field.

```
on mouseUp
  repeat with x = 0 to 255
    put x && numToChar(x) into line x¬
    of card field "characters"
  end repeat
end mouseUp
```

Script A-1.   Place this handler in a button and it will put the entire range of ASCII characters into a field

Acknowledge™	SuperMac Technologies
Adobe™	Adobe Systems, Inc.
Adobe Illustrator™	Adobe Systems, Inc.
APDA™	A.P.P.L.E. Co-op
Apple®	Apple Computer, Inc.
Apple Scanner™	Apple Computer, Inc.
AppleShare®	Apple Computer, Inc.
AppleTalk®	Apple Computer, Inc.
Ashton-Tate®	Ashton-Tate
CompuServe®	CompuServe, Inc.
Cricket Draw™	Cricket Software
Dataframe XP40™	SuperMac Technologies
dBASE III®	Ashton-Tate
DeskPaint™	Zedcor, Inc.
Developer Stack™	Steve Drazga
DiskFit™	SuperMac Technologies
Double Helix®	Odesta Corporation
Excel™	Microsoft Corporation
FileMaker®	Nashoba Systems, Inc.
Finder™	Apple Computer, Inc.
Focal Point™	MediaGenics
4th Dimension®	Acius-ALI
FreeHand™	Aldus Corporation
FullPaint®	Ashton-Tate
GEnie™	Genie Computer Corporation
Glue™	Solutions International
Helvetica®	Linotype Co.
HyperCard®	Apple Computer, Inc.
HyperDA™	Symmetry Software
HyperScan™	Apple Computer, Inc.
HyperSound™	Farallon Computing
HyperTalk™	Apple Computer, Inc.
ImageWriter®	Apple Computer, Inc.
ImageWriter LQ™	Apple Computer, Inc.
LaserWriter®	Apple Computer, Inc.
LocalTalk™	Apple Computer, Inc.
Mac® Plus	Apple Computer, Inc.
MacDraw®	Apple Computer, Inc.
Macintosh®	Apple Computer, Inc.
Macintosh Plus®	Apple Computer, Inc.

TRADEMARKS

Macintosh SE®	Apple Computer, Inc.
Macintosh II®	Apple Computer, Inc.
MacPaint®	Apple Computer, Inc.
MacRecorder™	Farallon Computing
MacWrite®	Apple Computer, Inc.
McSink™	Signature Software
Microsoft®	Microsoft Corporation
MultiFinder™	Apple Computer, Inc.
Omnis™	Blyth Software
PageMaker®	Aldus Corporation
PhoneNet™	Farallon Computing
PostScript®	Adobe Systems, Inc.
QuickDraw™	Apple Computer, Inc.
QuicKeys™	CE Software
Reports!™	Nine To Five Software, Inc.
Rolodex®	Rolodex Corporation
SANE®	Apple Computer, Inc.
ScriptExpert™	HyperPress Publishing Co.
SmallTalk™	Xerox Corporation
SoundCap™	Fractal Software
SoundEdit™	Farallon Software
Stackware™	Apple Computer, Inc.
SoundWave™	Impulse, Inc.
Suitcase™	Software Supply
SuperPaint™	Silicon Beach Software
Tempo™	Affinity Microsystems
TOPS®	Sun Microsystems, Inc.
VideoWorks™	MacroMind, Inc.
WordPerfect®	WordPerfect Corporation

The manuscript for this book was prepared and submitted
to Osborne/McGraw-Hill in electronic form. The acquisitions
editor for this project was Jeffrey Pepper, the technical
reviewers were Michael Fischer and John and Patricia Hedtke,
and the project editor was Dusty Bernard.
Text design by Judy Wohlfrom, using Century Expanded
for text body and Eras Demi for display.
Cover art by Bay Graphics Design Associates. Color separation
by Phoenix Color Corporation. Screens produced with InSet
from Inset Systems, Inc. Book printed and bound by
R.R. Donnelley & Sons Company, Crawfordsville, Indiana.